COLLINS
COMPLETE GUIDE TO
BRITISH
COASTAL WILDLIFE

T0382104

Paul Sterry and Andrew Cleave

Collins

HarperCollins Publishers
1 London Bridge Street
London SE1 9GF

www.harpercollins.co.uk

HarperCollins Publishers
Macken House, 39/40 Mayor Street Upper
Dublin 1, D01 C9W8, Ireland

Collins is a registered trademark of
HarperCollins Publishers Ltd.

First published in 2012

25 24
10

A catalogue record for this book is available from the British Library.

ISBN 978 0 00 741385 0

Acknowledgements
Almost all of the photographs were specially taken for this book, and
this would not have been possible without the help and assistance of
many individuals and organisations. These include John Chamberlain of
Dunmanus Seafoods, Andy Clements, Anthony Dobson, Steve Downey
of Chef Direct – Bristol, Michael Foord, Andy Horton, Ren Hathway and
family, Lee Morgan, Pat and Sue O'Reilly of First Nature, Joe Pender, Rob
Read, Paul Semmens, Stella Turk and Ian Wrigley.
    Special thanks are due to the following: Mark and Susie Groves of
Island Sea Safaris, St Mary's, Isles of Scilly; Andy and Christine Carr, Isle
of Berneray, Outer Hebrides; Chris Brown, Derek Scales and the staff at
the Display Development Department, Weymouth Sealife Centre (Merlin
Entertainments); and the staff of the Calshot Activities Centre Field Studies
Department, Hampshire.
    The authors would also like to thank those involved in the creation of
the book: Shane O'Dwyer, the designer; the editor, Susi Bailey; David and
Namrita Price-Goodfellow of D & N Publishing; and Myles Archibald and
Julia Koppitz of HarperCollins.

Edited and designed by D & N Publishing, Baydon, Wiltshire

Colour reproduction by Nature Photographers Ltd
Printed and bound in Bosnia and Herzegovina by GPS Group

CONTENTS

HOW TO USE THIS BOOK

With a few exceptions, the main identification section (the species descriptions) of *Complete British Coastal Wildlife* has been designed so that the text and main photographs for each species face each other on the left and right pages, respectively; special features, relevant to identification, have sometimes been added as insets in the text pages; some species are depicted entirely as cut-out photographs. The main photographs are labelled so that the identity of the species is clear. The text has been written to complement the information conveyed by the photographs. By and large, the order in which the species appear in the main section of the book roughly follows standard classification.

THE CHOICE OF SPECIES

Coastal wildlife is such a huge subject that selecting an appropriate array of species was always going to be hard. And *Complete British Coastal Wildlife* is not just a book about sea-shore life: it caters for readers with a whole range of interests. While selecting the species and planning the book's content we had in the back of our minds an imaginary family spending a couple of weeks' holiday on the coast. They might spend one day rock-pooling, the next visiting a seabird colony; at other times they might spend hours watching waders on an estuary, studying coastal flowers or just beachcombing. The choice of species in part reflects the diversity of life on the coast but also the many alternative delights it has to offer the visitor.

SPECIES DESCRIPTIONS

At the start of each species description the most commonly used and current English name is given. This is followed by the scientific name of the species in question, which comprises the species' genus name first, followed by its specific name. In a few instances, reference is made, either in the species heading or the main body of the text, to a further subdivision – subspecies – where this is pertinent.

The text has been written in as concise a manner as possible. Each description begins with a summary of the species in question. For some groups, such as birds, the species descriptions are necessarily complicated because the subjects themselves are complex. In these instances, to avoid potential ambiguities, subheadings break up the rest of each species' description. Different subheadings are used for different divisions within the natural world. For example, in the section covering birds, typical subheadings would be **ADULT MALE**, **ADULT FEMALE**, **JUVENILE**, **VOICE** and **STATUS**; for the section on invertebrates, typical subheadings might include **ADULT**, **LARVA** and **STATUS**; and for the section covering wildflowers, typical subheadings might include **FLOWERS**, **FRUITS**, **LEAVES** and **STATUS**. With seashore plants and animals, the zone at which they are found is described using the following terms: splash zone, upper shore, middle shore, lower shore and shallow sub-littoral (just below the lowest spring tide).

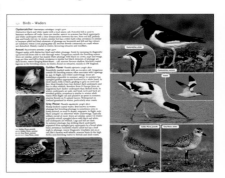

INTRODUCTORY SPREADS

Throughout the book, each significant division within the natural world has a dedicated introductory section; in the majority of cases, two pages are allocated to this. These sections are lavishly illustrated and the straightforward text helps the reader understand the group's natural history and its significance to coastal ecology.

PHOTOGRAPHS

Great care has gone into the selection of photographs for this book and in many cases the images have been taken specifically for this project. Preference was given to photographs that serve both to illustrate key identification features of a given species, and to emphasise its beauty. In many instances, smaller inset photographs illustrate features useful for identification that are not shown clearly by the main image.

EXPLORING THE COAST

The coast is a wonderful place for study, exploration and relaxation, but it is not without its challenges. There are inherent dangers associated with some areas of shoreline, and the sheer power of the sea and tides should always be respected and never underestimated.

SAFETY FIRST

When exploring the coast, the need for common sense and reasonable caution cannot be stressed too highly. The terrain and the sea are unforgiving, and a tiny mistake, which inland would be without consequence, can have dire repercussions in the coastal environment. Remember also that it is not just you who will be affected if you get into difficulties: somebody will have to come to your rescue, putting themselves, and potentially the lives of others, at risk.

When it comes to cliffs and precipitous coastal slopes, most people have the good sense to keep well away from edges and drops. But remember that invariably the grass or clifftop vegetation will be more slippery, and the soil often more friable, than you expect: a small slip could potentially result in a slide into oblivion. That may sound melodramatic, but caution is the watchword when walking on cliffs and steep coastal slopes.

The biggest threat to safety comes from the sea itself, in the form of the rising and falling tides. These days there is no excuse for not knowing the state of the tide at any given location, at any given time of day: tide tables can be bought in book form, information is available on the Internet, and applications are even available for modern-generation mobile phones.

Exploring and studying the seashore is best done on a falling tide. Although it is usually obvious when the tide has turned, be sure to make a note of the timing of low tide before you start your exploration. Once the tide has turned, you should assemble your belongings and retreat up the beach. The speed at which the tide comes in often catches people unawares – it is most rapid mid-way between high and low tides. Location also has a bearing on matters. On a rocky shore, the main danger is being cut off on a promontory that becomes surrounded by the sea, while on an estuary or sand flat, there is a real danger that the incoming tide can outpace the speed at which you can walk.

When it comes to rough, stormy days, avoid exploring the seashore altogether, or at least confine your activities to sheltered spots. Despite their name, freak waves are not uncommon and can easily sweep you off your feet; once you lose your footing, it is hard to regain it.

A network of channels and saltmarsh, such as here on the north Norfolk coast, should be explored with great caution.

RESPECT FOR THE ENVIRONMENT

Many coastal habitats are fragile and easily damaged by trampling, so consider your own physical impact on the environment and respect any advice and warnings offered about how to minimise it. Sand dunes are a case in point here.

You should also be aware of the potential for disturbing wildlife. Exercise common sense when visiting a seabird colony – it is usually obvious when you are causing disturbance – and view feeding and roosting birds from a distance to ensure they are not bothered by your presence. If you must take a dog with you, keep it on a lead at all times.

CLOTHING AND FOOTWEAR

Clothing is obviously a matter of personal choice and common sense, but as any seasoned coastal explorer will tell you, the seashore can be a deceptively chilly place. To combat changes in temperature, wear several layers of clothing that can easily be removed or replaced. Remember also to take a waterproof layer with you.

Stout walking boots, whose soles have a good grip, are the most sensible footwear in most coastal situations. However, if you are going rock-pooling on a rocky shore, consider wearing neoprene diving boots. Not only does it not matter if you get these and your feet wet, but the boots keep your feet amazingly warm and the material protects your feet and ankles from scrapes and bruises caused by sharp-edged, slippery rocks.

INTRODUCING COASTAL WILDLIFE

The extent of *Complete British Coastal Wildlife* embraces not only the seashore proper and inshore coastal waters, but also the terrestrial strip of land broadly covered by the phrase 'within sight of the sea'.

OUR GLORIOUS COASTAL WILDLIFE

With the exception of species that have extremely precise habitat requirements, or whose range geographically isolates them from the maritime environment, the majority of British terrestrial plant and animal species can be found near the sea somewhere in the region. Clearly, to include all these species in a book of this size would be impossible and ultimately pointless: it would simply overload the book with unnecessary species.

Terrestrial species that thrive near the coast, perhaps because of the milder climate for example, are included in the book, along with plants and animals whose range is exclusively coastal. But the bulk of the book is devoted to the seashore proper.

The seashore comprises such a rich set of habitats for wildlife that a book of this size cannot hope to include every species that occurs there. However, *Complete British Coastal Wildlife* does attempt to illustrate and describe every commonly encountered plant and animal on the seashore's littoral zone: those habitats found between the ranges of highest high tide and lowest low tide. In addition, many species that occur in shallow sub-littoral waters (just below the lowest low-tide mark) are also included. These can sometimes be found while snorkelling or, out of their usual range, in large rock pools. Inshore seas are also extremely productive and provide endless scope for those interested in seabirds, cetaceans and seals. The content of this book reflects both the productivity of this environment and its interest and significance to naturalists.

ABOVE: Wembury, in south Devon, is a haven for marine life and a wonderful destination for the seashore enthusiast.

LEFT: The rocky shore is not only a diverse place for wildlife, but it can be a colourful one too; here, Snakelocks Anemones and coralline seaweeds catch the eye.

THE LURE OF THE COAST

The British coast has always been important for people. In the past, its greatest significance was perhaps that it provided a source of food and a means of earning a living, and of course this continues to this day. But it also acts like a magnet to visitors from inland, such that there can be few British people who don't visit the coast at least once a year. Some are attracted by the intrinsic beauty of our rocky coastlines or the sheer scale and lonely isolation of many estuaries and northern beaches. A sense (sadly misplaced these days) that these landscapes and habitats are untamed and unaffected by man is part of the attraction. But wherever you go on the coast it is impossible to ignore the wildlife, and indeed the plants and animals are the most important drawcard for many of us. It is for such natural historians and budding marine biologists that *Complete British Coastal Wildlife* is designed.

The seas around Lundy, which lies off the north Devon coast, are protected to a degree by Marine Nature Reserve status, the first of its kind in Britain.

COASTAL WILDLIFE AND CONSERVATION

Of course, it is not just naturalists who are drawn to the coast – visitors with a whole range of other interests and pursuits are also catered for. These include general holidaymakers who enjoy the ambience of the seaside without necessarily knowing precisely why they like it. Ramblers and hikers are lured to the coast for its scenic beauty and, sometimes, its demanding terrain, and for sailors, anglers and watersports enthusiasts the attraction is obvious. But because Britain is so densely populated, this puts coastal habitats and the marine environment generally under enormous pressure. The result is that for many sensitive species of wildlife the space available to them diminishes year on year, and they themselves become marginalised.

It is important that all of us who visit the coast and enjoy the wildlife delights it has to offer remember that, large or small, we all make an impact. Shooting and bait-digging have obvious and significant impacts on wildlife. Out-of-control dogs or windsurfers can cause untold damage to ground-nesting seabird colonies or roosting waders, for example. But even our very presence can cause disturbance and damage, if we fail to consider the consequences of our actions.

It is important that people continue to visit the coast to explore, observe and marvel at its wildlife spectacles, because it is only with their enthusiasm that the wholesale exploitation and disturbance of these precious habitats can be averted. Although individuals can always make a difference, generally a more powerful way of putting forward the conservation message comes from belonging to a society that campaigns for wildlife on behalf of its members. Organisations that fulfil this role include the Royal Society for the Protection of Birds (RSPB), The Wildlife Trusts and the Marine Conservation Society (*see* p. 376 for contact details).

STUDYING COASTAL LIFE

Many people are happy enough to wander along the coast and encounter what they see by chance on their travels. But a few techniques and some straightforward equipment can greatly increase the range of species you discover, and the ease with which they can be observed.

BIRDWATCHING

Birds are among the easiest coastal animals to observe and it is little wonder that they attract a disproportionate amount of interest from coastal visitors. Visit the right places at the right times and you will be treated to wildlife spectacles on a grand scale.

Binoculars and telescopes are essential parts of the modern-day birdwatcher's armoury. Lightweight, waterproof binoculars come in a range of prices and specifications, but 8×40 models (8× magnification, 40mm objective lens diameter) are probably the best all-round specifications for coastal birdwatching.

Visit a seabird colony during the breeding season and you may find that your optical equipment is slightly redundant. In locations where the birds are protected from disturbance – from people and ground predators – many species are indifferent to human observers to the point of being tame.

Estuary birdwatching requires different tactics. Feeding waders are probably easiest to observe on a rising tide, but the best observations generally come when the tide finally pushes the birds off their feeding grounds and they fly to a high-tide roost. Local knowledge is invaluable when it comes to locating the best spots for observation without causing disturbance.

A hardy and dedicated band of birdwatchers devote their time to watching migrating seabirds (mostly in autumn), a pursuit known as 'seawatching'. Onshore gales offer the best opportunities for observing the birds at close range, and headlands in the west of Britain are most rewarding.

Thousands of Knots take to the air on the Wash, in one of Britain's greatest wildlife spectacles.

SEASHORE ETIQUETTE

When studying life on the rocky shore, many amazing discoveries are made simply by turning over stones and boulders. It is vital to replace these as you found them; by doing so, you restore the shaded, sheltered niches that the inhabitants beneath the stones rely on and without which they would die.

STUDYING MARINE LIFE

Searching for and studying marine creatures on the shore is a pursuit beloved of children but one that most naturalists take with them into maturity. Rocky shores are probably the most rewarding habitats, and budding marine biologists soon learn the best places to look: under rock overhangs, beneath boulders, under seaweed and, above all, in rock pools.

A variety of nets is always useful for catching active animals, and remember also to take with you a range of trays or shallow buckets for your prize specimens. Transfer anything you catch as quickly as possible because many marine creatures soon die out of water.

It is always worth leaving seaweeds and seashore debris in a tray to settle for a while. Many marine creatures become inactive, hide or contract into unrecognisable shapes when disturbed, and can take several minutes to return to normal.

Studying marine life will take you to some wonderful places, such as Land's End, Cornwall.

STORMS AND STRANDLINES

Storms and the crashing waves they produce are always impressive and leave a lasting impression on those who witness them. Understandably, they also have a profound effect upon marine life, sweeping many creatures from the relative safety of their realm and throwing them up onto the shore. Immediately after a gale it is therefore always worth searching along the strandline. All sorts of deep-water creatures can appear, but the trick is to get there before the gulls have discovered this bountiful supply of food.

The strandline offers rich pickings for the seashore enthusiast and is most productive after winter storms.

TIDES, ZONATION AND EXPOSURE

Toxic to most terrestrial plants and animals, sea water is the stuff of life for intertidal and marine creatures. Its chemistry is important, of course, but so too are the physical aspects of tide and current, which shape our coastline and affect the lives of marine creatures on a daily basis.

TIDES

Manifesting itself on coasts as tides, the rise and fall of sea-level on a regular basis results from the gravitational effect of the Moon. The tidal influence on British shores is profound: every six hours or so, all intertidal seashore plants and animals are exposed to air, then covered by sea water. The extent of the tides (tidal range) is dictated in the main by the phases of the Moon and changes on a daily basis throughout a 28-day period; atmospheric pressure also affects tidal range.

Tidal range is most extreme during full and new phases of the Moon; these periods are referred to as 'spring' tides. The tidal range is least extreme when the Moon is half waxing and half waning; these periods are referred to as 'neap' tides. The proximity of the Moon to the Earth influences its gravitational pull and hence the range of the tides. The most extreme tides occur when the Moon is closest to the Earth, during the spring and autumn equinoxes, in March and September, respectively.

High tide is never at the same point on any given beach on consecutive days. Tidal range also varies around Britain, affected by the geography of the coast. For example, the funnelling effect of the Bristol Channel means that the tidal range here is 10m or more in places; elsewhere in the region, tidal range can be as little as 1m, although 3–5m is typical of most stretches of shore.

Rocky shore at high tide.

Rocky shore at low tide.

ZONATION

The intertidal zone's plant and animal inhabitants have evolved to cope with different degrees of exposure to air and sea-water inundation. Consequently, they are usually found at precise zones on the shore; these are most obvious on rocky coasts. The growth of different lichen and seaweed species provides the most immediate evidence of zonation, appearing as bands of different colours. The effect is most noticeable on the west coast of Britain, where the tidal range is large and where rocky shores are often steep rather than shelving.

WAVES AND EXPOSURE

Clearly, waves have a battering effect upon seashore plants and animals, and the degree to which any given stretch of shoreline is exposed to waves has a strong bearing on what lives there. Some plants and animals have adapted to these seemingly hostile conditions while others thrive only where they are sheltered from the full force of the elements, such as by a headland.

Waves are caused by wind – the faster the wind and the further it has travelled over the sea, the larger and more powerful the waves. The prevailing wind in Britain comes from the west, and our most severe gales come from that direction too. Consequently, our most exposed shores are found in western Britain, and it is here that the differences in shoreline

ABOVE: **Colourful and distinctive zonation on a rocky shore.**

RIGHT: **Rough seas battering the Isle of Portland.**

inhabitants are most profound when comparisons are made between exposed and sheltered locations on the same stretch of coast.

SALINITY

Although traces of every element can be found in sea water, it is the presence of salt – sodium chloride – that is by far the most significant for marine life. Fresh water has a salinity of 0.05%, while true sea-water salinity is 3–3.5% (salinity measures the weight of salt, in grams, per kilogram of water).

In most circumstances, sea-water salinity is a constant to which true marine creatures are adapted and on which they depend. Estuaries are an exception to the rule and present a challenge for the plants and animals found there. With each tide the salinity changes from virtually fresh when the tide is out, to fully marine when the tide is in. These changes in salinity would be enough to kill most species adapted to either fresh water or truly marine conditions. So estuary inhabitants are special indeed, adapted to cope with the daily osmotic challenges their environment throws at them.

INTRODUCING COASTAL HABITATS

In habitat terms, the coastline is Britain's crowning glory. Although development has marred considerable stretches of our shoreline, particularly in southern England, those that remain unspoilt there, and elsewhere in Britain and Ireland, are truly wonderful and harbour some of our most charismatic wildlife. The rich intertidal zone, bathed twice daily by an advancing and retreating tide, and the offshore waters are fundamental to the diversity and abundance of life around our coasts. In all its varied forms, our coastline is a paradise for the natural historian.

Dramatic cliffs on the Lleyn Peninsula in north Wales are typical of many parts of western Britain.

COASTLINE LENGTH

Assessing the length of the British coastline is one of those puzzles that is a bit like asking the question 'How long is a piece of string?'. It all depends on how you measure it, and obviously if the route takes into account coastal footpaths then it will be considerably shorter than if you were to walk at the sea's edge, taking in every nook and cranny. A basic guide to the length of the coastline of Great Britain (England, Wales and Scotland) comes from the Ordnance Survey: the main land mass is 17,820km long when measured at mean high-water mark using 1:10,000 maps; but when all offshore islands are also taken into account, it is a staggering 31,368km in length. Scotland and its islands make up the lion's share of this figure, with 18,588km of coastline.

Nowhere in Britain is more than 113km from the sea. Even if the route to the coast involves hideously congested roads, this means than nobody in Britain is more than three hours' drive from the sea; the vast majority of us live within an hour or so of the coast.

OUR VARIED COASTLINE

As well as being extremely long relative to the land area, our coastline is also incredibly varied. The most striking and fundamental differences lie in the geology and composition of the coast at any given point, and this has a profound influence on its topography and appearance, and the habitats and wildlife that it supports. As a result, we have everything from cliffs and headlands to rocky shorelines, sandy beaches and dunes, shingle beaches, estuaries, mudflats and saltmarshes; the contrast ranges from some of the most rugged terrain imaginable, to some of the flattest landscapes on the planet. Very few countries can boast such variety in such a small space.

The sea is a constantly eroding influence on the coast and has shaped our image of the coast, literally and figuratively. Hard rocks such as granite resist this erosion better than soft rocks like chalk, limestone and sandstone. So it is just as well that granite is very much a feature of western Britain, the region battered by our worst weather and most elemental seas.

The erosion caused by the sea acts in a variety of ways. Physical pounding by waves is a powerful factor, exploiting weaknesses and cracks in the rock. Pockets of air trapped in the rocks are compressed by wave action, adding to the shattering effects of the sea. And

ABOVE: **Chalk and limestone cliffs** are a feature of the Dorset coast, with dramatic formations found at Swyre Head.

Marked only by ripples in the sand, the flat appearance of a sandy beach belies the abundance of life that lies buried beneath.

LEFT: **Bishop Rock**, nearly 7km off the Isles of Scilly, is the most southwesterly point in the British Isles. At just 46m by 16m, it is also the smallest land mass in the world to have a building on it.

RIGHT: **Muckle Flugga** is the northernmost part of Unst in the Shetland Isles, and the most northerly accessible site in Britain.

abrasion by pebbles, rocks and sand adds to the attrition of rocks that defiantly stand and face the elemental forces of the sea.

Sand and shingle beaches are a testament to the constructive abilities of the sea, the materials from which they are made being deposited by a process called longshore drift. In reality, sand and shingle formations are constantly changing, with continual erosion as well as deposition occurring. The process and the balance can change, or be upset: currents can change, sometimes unwittingly influenced by man, resulting in shingle and sand being removed faster than it is deposited.

OUR CHANGING COASTLINE

Anyone who knows the sea accepts that change is a fact of coastal life. From the state of the tides to the erosion of cliffs, few things on the seashore remain constant for long. But in many parts of Britain, change has stepped up a pace, the main cause being rising sea-levels. Climate change is clearly an important factor here, as it is globally. In Britain, however, the land is still rebounding from the weight of the ice mass that covered us during the last Ice Age; consequently, the south of England is sinking by about 0.5cm a year while the north of Scotland is rising. Although a valiant effort is made in some parts of Britain to thwart the effects of coastal erosion, most authorities accept its inevitability. Today, 'strategic withdrawal' is the buzz phrase among coastal ecologists.

Coastal defences have long included the building of groynes and barriers to slow or halt erosion, or to promote the deposition of sediment by longshore drift. However, although often effective at the local level, they can have a negative knock-on effect elsewhere on the coast and can actually increase erosion.

ROCKY SHORES

Battered by waves and scoured by tides, Britain's rocky shores are dramatic and impressive destinations for any budding marine biologist. The intertidal zone offers a wealth of opportunities for exploration and supports a greater diversity of marine creatures than any other coastal habitat. At low tide, rock pools and gulleys positively teem with life, and scores of crabs, molluscs and small fish await discovery.

Sheltered rocky shores, such as here in Old Town Bay on St Mary's in the Isles of Scilly, support abundant and diverse communities of seaweeds.

SEAWEEDS GALORE

For the keen student of seaweeds, the rocky shore is the place to visit, because the vast majority of British species are found in this habitat. That is not to say that you will find every species on all rocky shores. Quite the opposite is true: while a few species are almost universal in occurrence, most have evolved to cope with different degrees of exposure to air and to wave action, and many have restricted geographical ranges, favouring either warmer southern seas or cooler northern ones. And rocky substrates are not uniformly suited to supporting seaweeds. For example, although granite is a hard rock, some forms are so easily eroded by wave action that larger seaweed species, as well as barnacles and mussels, cannot attach themselves.

A HARSH ENVIRONMENT

The battering effect of waves and tide are obviously a challenge for animals living on rocky shores. Limpets and barnacles overcome this partly by protecting themselves with a hard shell; limpets clamp themselves down using their muscular foot, while barnacles essentially glue their shells to rock. In sheltered gullies and rock pools, sea anemones are conspicuous, as are blennies, prawns and Shore Crabs. A careful search under stones may reveal other species of crabs, including retiring hermit crabs living in the empty shells of periwinkles and Dog Whelks. Many animals of rocky shores are year-round residents, but during the summer months more unusual species visit from deeper waters.

INVERTEBRATES OF ROCKY SHORES

Crustaceans are well represented on rocky shores, crabs probably being the most familiar and common examples of the group. Among their numbers, the Edible Crab is the most distinctive, with its reddish shell and piecrust margin. Crabs are mainly opportunistic feeders, often scavenging dead organic matter and other tasty morsels.

BIRDLIFE OF ROCKY SHORES

While marine invertebrates can be found in abundance on rocky shores, birdlife is rather restricted. Many of the marine creatures here either attach themselves firmly to the substrate or hide in crevices or under stones at low tide. Consequently, opportunities for feeding birds are comparatively limited and it takes a specialist to make a living here. Turnstones and Oystercatchers are regularly seen, while the Purple Sandpiper is seldom found anywhere apart from rocky shores during its winter residence in Britain.

ABOVE: A Purple Sandpiper foraging for food on a rocky shore. This hardy species, which breeds in the Arctic and winters on our shores, is seldom found out of sight of the sea. Indifferent to breaking waves, birds use their long bills to seek out tiny periwinkles and crustaceans from rock crevices and empty barnacle shells.

A good rock pool will harbour a wide range of plants and animals, including some sub-littoral species. These organisms survive because the pool ensures permanent inundation by sea water.

SANDY SHORES AND SHINGLE

Razorshells on a Norfolk beach,
washed up after a winter storm.

Beloved of holidaymakers, sandy shores also have much to offer the visiting naturalist. Beneath the surface of the sand lives an abundance of marine worms and molluscs, whose presence would go largely undetected were it not for the feeding activities of birds and the profusion of dead shells found along the strandline.

MARINE LIFE OF SANDY SHORES
Although the shells of marine bivalve molluscs are commonly washed up on the shore, in life they are much harder to find. Typically, they live buried in the sand and open their shells to reveal their feeding siphons only when covered by water and undisturbed. At low tide you would never know they were present, let alone in such numbers, although keen-eyed observers can sometimes spot a slight depression in the sand below which lies a mollusc.

In addition to the molluscs that live largely buried on the sandy shore, a range of other invertebrates also make a living here. Prawns are often abundant, as are Shore Crabs, both of which rely on camouflage and partial burial in sand to avoid detection by predators. Burrowing starfish and sea urchin species also live here and flatfish are usually common.

BIRDLIFE OF SANDY SHORES
Outside the breeding season, look for Sanderlings as they follow the line of breaking waves in search of small invertebrates. Black-headed Gulls are always in evidence along the shoreline. Offshore, fish and crustaceans provide a rich supply of food for those bird species that are sufficiently well adapted to catch them. During the summer months, terns can be seen plunge-diving here, while in winter grebes, Red-throated Divers and seaducks may exploit this resource.

SAND DUNES
On the landward side of a sandy beach, colonising plants – notably Marram, the classic dune grass species – establish stable dune systems. Subsequently, these are colonised by maritime plants such as Sea Spurge, as well as grassland species such as Viper's-bugloss and Common Bird's-foot Trefoil. Stable dune systems offer potential for birds such as Ringed Plovers and terns to nest. Sadly, however, human disturbance effectively excludes these species from almost all suitable areas in southern England.

Sea Spurge is a distinctive and characteristic
member of the sand-dune community of plants.

SHINGLE

Shingle is a challenging environment for any plant or animal, as by its very nature it is unstable, incredibly free-draining and lacking anything that resembles conventional soil. Despite this, a few plant species are hardy enough to survive here. Indeed, specialists such as Sea-holly, Yellow Horned-poppy and Sea-kale are seldom found anywhere else.

Contrary to all expectations, a surprising number of invertebrates manage to live among the pebbles that comprise a shingle beach. Many feed on the small amount of detritus that accumulates in the interstices close to the high-tide mark.

Shingle beaches also offer opportunities for nesting birds, including waders, terns and gulls. Inevitably, however, human disturbance excludes them from most sites in the south, except where the birds are afforded special protection. Nesting colonies are generally more successful in more remote, northern locations.

The Scaly Cricket *Pseudomogoplistes vicentae* is confined to a handful of coastal shingle beaches in Britain and the Channel Islands; it lives in the interstices and feeds on detritus.

Hutchinsia *Hornungia petraea* is very locally common on south-facing dunes along the south Wales coast. It is a member of the cabbage family and an early flowerer, often in bloom in late February.

Sea-holly growing on a shingle beach on the Hampshire coast.

MUDFLATS, ESTUARIES AND SALTMARSHES

To the unenlightened eye, estuaries and mudflats may seem like featureless expanses of mud and little else. However, the vast numbers of birds that feed on these habitats during the winter months testify to their unseen productivity and the extraordinary diversity of invertebrate life they support.

BENEATH THE SURFACE

Evidence for the wealth of marine life found in mudflats and estuaries is not always easy to detect, although worms casts and the carpet of small marine molluscs on the surface hint at the productivity in the mud itself. In fact, incredible numbers of invertebrates do thrive in the oozing substrates that make up our estuaries and mudflats, their numbers supported by the organic matter deposited when river meets sea. Lugworm and ragworm species are typical representatives of their kind, while marine molluscs include various species of cockles, clams and other bivalves, as well as minute but abundant Laver Spire Shells.

Lugworm casts at Budle Bay, Northumberland. Home to internationally important concentrations of waders and wildfowl in winter, Britain's estuaries and mudflats are among the finest in the world. Vast numbers of invertebrates live buried beneath the surface in the treacherous sediment.

ESTUARY BIRDLIFE

It is between autumn and spring that estuaries and mudflats come into their own in terms of birdlife. During the summer months, many of the species so familiar on our estuaries in winter are nesting elsewhere, many in the Arctic. But once breeding is complete, they return to our estuaries in autumn.

Outside the breeding season, waders are the most characteristic group of estuary birds. Each species has a bill length and feeding strategy adapted to suit a particular food source and this helps reduce feeding competition. Wildfowl are also present in good numbers: Shelduck filter minute animals from the mud with their bills, while Brent Geese and Wigeon favour plant material.

Curlews use their long, curved bills to probe the soft mud for invertebrate prey, particularly juicy Lugworms.

A colourful saltmarsh community on the north Norfolk coast in July, with abundant Common Sea-lavender.

SALTMARSHES

During the winter months, most estuaries are positively dreary in botanical terms, studded with a mosaic of bedraggled-looking vegetation and very little else. But come the summer months, the upper reaches of the mudflats – those areas least affected by the tides – come to life. Specialist salt-tolerant plants colonise and stabilise the oozing mud, creating saltmarsh. Able to cope with twice-daily inundation by sea water, these colonisers include species of glasswort and sea-lavender, as well as Sea Purslane and Annual Sea-blite.

CLIFFS

For breathtaking scenery and a sense of untamed nature, coastal cliffs offer unrivalled opportunities for the visiting naturalist. Man has had minimal impact on these areas, and during the spring and summer months a few select locations where the substrate is suitable are crowded with breeding seabirds and carpeted with colourful flowers.

SEABIRD COLONIES

Great Britain has some of the finest seabird cliffs in Europe, with populations of birds such as Razorbill and Gannet that are of global importance. The best time to visit a colony is between April and July, when the sight, sound and smell of the birds will be at its height.

Many seabird populations are under threat. Locations, such as Fair Isle, once harboured thriving populations but now have dwindling numbers of many species. Exploitation of fish stocks, and plundering of the sea generally, are at the heart of the problem.

Located in the Firth of Forth, Bass Rock supports the largest Gannet colony in the world, with more than 80,000 nest sites.

A stunning display of Thrift on the west coast of the island of Lundy, off the north Devon coast.

BELOW: In Britain, the Fiery Clearwing moth *Pyropteron chrysidiformis* is entirely restricted to stretches of grassy undercliff on the south coast of Kent.

Because each species has unique nesting requirements, not every seabird will be found on every cliff. Where stable ledges occur, Guillemots and Kittiwakes can be abundant, while Puffins favour grassy slopes in which they can excavate burrows. Some seabirds are solitary nesters but many, such as Cormorants and gulls, form loose colonies, their concentration due as much to the limited availability of nesting sites as to anything else. A fundamental requirement for any seabird colony is the close proximity of good feeding grounds.

CLIFFTOP FLOWERS

Without doubt, the displays of flowering Thrift that carpet long stretches of cliffs in western Britain are the most glorious botanical highlights our coasts have to offer. By any standards, these are world-class floral spectacles. Pretty in pink, Thrift is the undeniable star of the show, although a supporting cast of Sea Carrot, Sea Campion and various species of sea-spurrey adds botanical diversity and a colourful counterpoint to the scene.

UNDERCLIFFS

The appearance of maritime cliffs is influenced by factors such as the rock type and the degree of exposure to which a particular stretch of coast is subjected. Broadly speaking, however, they can be categorised as either hard or soft cliffs. Hard cliffs, where the rocks resist erosion, tend to be steep or sheer. By contrast, soft cliffs are gently sloping, easily eroded, and prone to slumping and landslips. This interesting landscape supports a richer diversity of species than hard cliffs, and is home to a number of extremely habitat-specific plants and invertebrates.

COASTAL TERRESTRIAL HABITATS

Inland of the seashore proper, and not subject to the daily rhythms of the tides, are a number of interesting terrestrial habitats. Although they have their counterparts inland, subtle maritime influences mean they have a distinct character of their own.

COASTAL GRASSLAND

Grassland can be found throughout the British Isles and is by no means unique to the coast, but where it is found within sight of the sea it often has distinct qualities. In ecological terms, grassland is typically thought of as a man-made or man-influenced habitat, created by selective management (grazing or cutting) once tree and scrub cover has been removed from the landscape. But on exposed, west-facing cliffs, for example, it is likely that many patches of grassland represent the climax vegetation for that spot, the effects of wind and salt spray ensuring that more substantial plants cannot survive. Elsewhere, grassland often grows on distinctly saline soil, ensuring that interesting salt-tolerant species predominate.

ABOVE: **Elmley Marshes RSPB reserve in north Kent, coastal grazing marsh at its finest.**

BELOW: **The Maid of Kent beetle *Emus hirtus* is confined to Elmley Marshes, where it spends much of its life inside fresh cowpats; both adults and larvae feed on other insects.**

Sheltered parts of Britain, and areas of southeast England in particular, are home to some extensive stretches of coastal grazing marsh. Such places that remain relatively untouched are typically protected, to a degree, by nature reserve status. Unique plants and animals are found here, and the habitat is especially important for breeding waders and other wetland birds.

MACHAIR

Machair grassland is unique to northwest Scotland and western Ireland. The relatively short turf has developed on windblown shell sand that lends a calcareous influence to the free-draining soil. Often cut for hay and sometimes grazed in winter, machair is a floral delight in May and June. It is adversely affected by changes in agricultural use (it is entirely destroyed by ploughing, for example) and is the subject of considerable conservation interest.

Maritime heath on the Pembrokeshire coast, with Western Gorse and Heather predominating.

MARITIME HEATH

Heathland communities of plants develop on acid, free-draining soils, and include species of heather (hence the habitat's name) and gorse as their most characteristic members. Heathland is found locally across southern Britain and is a feature of many stretches of coast in western Britain, especially where the underlying rock is granite. Heather, Bell Heather, Gorse and Western Gorse are the dominant species in coastal heathland, and the habitat is at its most colourful in floral terms from midsummer to early autumn.

Maritime heath vegetation is typically no more than knee-high, the plants 'pruned' by the wind and inhibited by salt spray. In particularly exposed locations, the vegetation is known as 'waved heath', the habitat having a rippled appearance that echoes waves on the sea. These botanical 'waves' are mostly a feature of Heather and Bell Heather, and are caused when the side of a plant facing the prevailing wind and salt spray (typically facing west) is killed off, while growth continues on the sheltered (typically east-facing) side.

GLOSSARY

Abdomen Hind section on an invertebrate's body.

Acute Sharply pointed.

Alien Introduced by Man from another part of the world.

Annelid A segmented worm, phylum Annelida.

Antennae Slender, paired sensory organs on the head of an invertebrate.

Barbel Fleshy filament growing from the head or mouth of a fish.

Brackish Mixed fresh and sea water.

Bryozoan Belonging to the phylum Bryozoa.

Calcareous Chalky, composed of calcium carbonate.

Carapace Hard upper surface of a crustacean's shell.

Cardinal teeth Projections from the middle of a bivalve mollusc's shell hinge.

Carpus Crustacean leg segment basal to the propodus.

Caudal Relating to the tail.

Cephalothorax Fused head and thorax found in some invertebrates.

Cerata Dorsal projections in some sea slugs, containing branches of the digestive tract; they are often armed with stinging cells.

Chaeta (plural Chaetae) Chitinous bristle.

Chela Crustacean appendage whose terminal segment is movable against an immovable one on the propodus (hence, chelate).

Cirri Hair-like filaments used during feeding (e.g. in barnacles).

Colonial Organisms that remain together, having been produced asexually.

Compound eye Eye structure comprising numerous cells and lenses, not a single lens.

Coralline Calcareous and coral-like (as in certain seaweeds).

Coxa Ventral projections from thoracic segments in amphipod crustaceans.

Crenulate With a finely notched edge.

Dactylus Movable finger of decapod crustacean claws.

Dentate Toothed.

Dorsal Upper surface.

Epibiotic Growing on the surface of another organism.

Epiphytic Growing on the surface of a living plant.

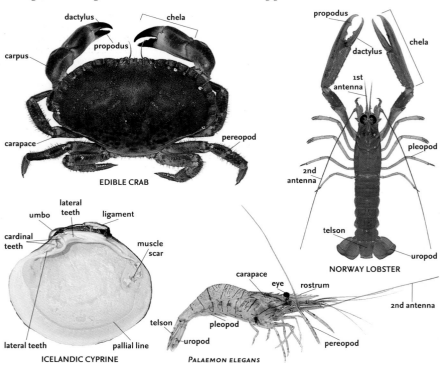

EDIBLE CRAB

NORWAY LOBSTER

ICELANDIC CYPRINE

PALAEMON ELEGANS

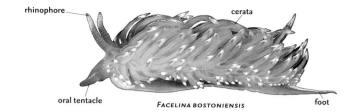

rhinophore — cerata

oral tentacle — *FACELINA BOSTONIENSIS* — foot

Gnathopod Leg-like crustacean appendage, modified to serve as a jaw.

Holdfast Root-like structure that anchors seaweeds to rocks.

Hydranth Feeding polyp of a hydroid colony, with stinging tentacles and a mouth.

Hydroid General term embracing members of the cnidarian class Hydrozoa.

Intertidal Zone between highest and lowest tides.

Invertebrate An animal without a backbone.

Juvenile Stage in the life cycle between larva and adult, typically unable to reproduce.

Lamella Thin plate.

Larva Pre-adult growing stage in the life cycle of certain species, differing in morphology from juveniles and adults.

Lateral teeth Projections from the shell hinge of bivalve molluscs, both in front of and behind cardinal teeth.

Littoral zone Shore zone exposed to influences of tides and waves, and with alternating exposure to air and sea water, including spray.

Lower shore Shore zone around low-tide level.

Moult Process seen in birds during which old feathers are lost and replaced by new ones; also applies to certain invertebrates that shed their skins.

Ocelli Eye-like markings.

Operculum Plate found in some invertebrates (e.g. some tubeworms and molluscs) used to seal off entrance to shell.

Opposite Arising in opposite pairs on a stem.

Pallial line Line inside a bivalve mollusc's shell marking the extent of attachment of mantle.

Papillae Tiny nipple-like protuberances.

Parapodia Leg-like lateral appendages on segments in annelids, each parapodium comprising a dorsal notopodium and ventral neuropodium.

Parasite Organism that obtains food and shelter in or on another living organism, the host, which does not benefit.

Pedunculate Borne on a stalk.

Pelagic Favouring the open sea.

Pereopod Forked limb of Malacostraca crustacean, used for walking and feeding.

Pinnate Branched like a feather.

Plankton Organisms that drift in the water column.

Pleopod Abdominal limb in crustaceans.

Propodus Decapod crustacean leg segment immediately below claw.

Reticulate With a netted pattern.

Rhinophores Paired sensory tentacles seen in sea slugs, posterior to oral tentacles of opisthobranch molluscs.

Salinity Measure of dissolved salt concentration in sea water.

Sedentary Attached to a substrate but capable of movement.

Sessile Permanently attached to a substrate.

Spicule Tiny spine, present in the body and skin of sponges and echinoderms.

Sub-littoral zone Shore zone below the low-tide mark.

Telson Tail-like last segment in a crustacean's body; often flattened and used in movement.

Thorax Middle section of the body of some invertebrates.

Tubercle Small rounded projection.

Umbo Strongly curved dorsal section of bivalve mollusc shells.

Uropod Abdominal appendage in certain crustaceans; in decapods, uropods are paired and adjacent to the telson, forming the 'tail fan'.

Ventral Relating to the belly or lower surface of an animal.

Wingspan The distance from one wingtip to the other in birds.

INTRODUCING SEAWEEDS

Seaweeds are the most important plants on the seashore, and on sheltered coasts with suitable substrates they come to dominate the scene. Each species is adapted to rather precise degrees of exposure to waves and air, and to tidal influence, the result being a huge diversity around the British coast as a whole.

WHAT ARE SEAWEEDS?

Many seaweed species reach a considerable size and complexity of form, giving them more than a passing resemblance to flowering plants. However, despite these superficial similarities, seaweeds are algae – simple and relatively primitive plants in an evolutionary context, which have more in common with the minute planktonic algae that colour the water column than higher plants.

Apart from the fact that they do not reproduce by flowering, seaweeds differ from higher plants in the simplicity of their internal structure: the complex vascular system of flowering plants is absent, and what appear to be 'roots' (the holdfasts with which many seaweeds attach themselves to rocks) merely serve to anchor the plants; they do not take up nutrients and water.

Seaweeds do have one thing in common with other plants, flowering ones included – they produce their own food by photosynthesis. This complex internal process involves the use of sunlight energy, trapped by a pigment called chlorophyll, to convert carbon dioxide and water to glucose, with oxygen given off as a by-product. Chlorophyll is green, and indeed many seaweed species are greenish in overall appearance. But others are brown or red, the green pigment being masked by others of a different hue.

Serrated Wrack growing on Dorset's Jurassic coast.

Seaweed reproduction is surprisingly complex for such relatively simple organisms, and the detail is beyond the scope of a book of this nature. However, in simple terms there are two stages in the life cycle, which involves a process called alternation of generations. In many species, one stage is minute (in some cases microscopic) and what we recognise as 'seaweeds' are in fact the second, spore-producing stage in the life cycle.

SEAWEED CLASSIFICATION

The modern view of seaweed classification holds that the three main groups – all easily recognised as seaweeds of some kind or another – are not closely related. Colour is a useful guide for separating the groups in the field: the Chlorophyta, or green seaweeds, are considered to be true plants and their chlorophyll is not masked by other pigmentation; the Rhodophyta, or red seaweeds, are also regarded as true plants (some species are chalky and coralline in appearance), their green chlorophyll being masked by red phycoerythrin pigment,

Seaweeds growing on the lower shore in north Devon.

and sometimes bluish phycocyanin pigments too; but the Phaeophyceae, or brown seaweeds, are not considered to be plants in the strict sense, and their green chlorophyll is masked by brown fucoxanthin pigment.

SEAWEED STRUCTURE

The structure and form of British seaweeds varies tremendously between species, each one having evolved to cope with factors affecting them on a daily basis: exposure to air, depth and length of immersion in sea water, and damaging wave action, for example. Recognising the distinct structural differences can also be useful in identification.

Seaweeds attach themselves to a substrate (usually rock, but sometimes shells or buried stones) using a holdfast; this can range from simple in appearance to branching complexity, depending on the species. The rest of the seaweed is called the 'frond' (usually linked to the holdfast by a stem-like 'stipe'), of which three basic forms can be recognised: a slender filament; a network of slender branches; or a broad, flat 'lamina'. In terms of the way any given seaweed species divides, the branches may be simple and aligned in opposite pairs; they may alternate along the stipe; they may be arranged in whorls; or the stipe and frond may divide dichotomously (equally) throughout.

ZONATION

The influence of tides on British shores, caused by the gravitational pull of the Moon, is profound. For many seashore creatures this means that every six hours or so they will either be exposed to air or covered by sea water. All seashore life is affected by these daily changes, but on rocky shores in particular, seaweeds demonstrate the effect better than any other group. Each species has evolved to cope with differing degrees of exposure to air or inundation by the tide, and to differing degrees of exposure to waves. As a result, the position on any given shoreline where a particular species can grow is limited; typically, this leads to the creation of obvious zones that are identified by the colour of the seaweed in question. The effect is most noticeable on the west coast of Britain, where the tidal range is large and where rocky shores are often rather steep.

ABOVE: **Sea Lettuce**; BELOW: **Gutweed**

Sea Lettuce *Ulva lactuca* Length to 40cm
Membranous green seaweed. Grows attached
to rocks on protected shores; often in rock
pools on upper and middle shores. **FRONDS**
are irregular in outline;
often tattered,
so exact shape
can be difficult
to determine.
STATUS
Widespread
and locally
common.

Sea
Lettuce

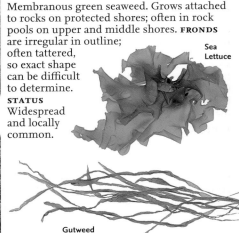

Gutweed

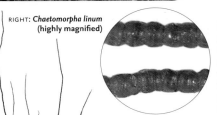

RIGHT: *Chaetomorpha linum*
(highly magnified)

Gutweed *Ulva intestinalis* Length to 75cm
Aptly named green seaweed of sheltered
estuaries, brackish lagoons and upper
shore rock pools. **FRONDS** comprise
variably constricted membranous tubes
that inflate with oxygen in sunshine.
STATUS Widespread and locally
common.

Chaetomorpha linum Length to 10cm
Delicate, filamentous green seaweed. Grows in tangled tufts
in sheltered sandy bays and in rock pools where sand collects.
FRONDS consist of chains of single cells, arranged like a string
of beads. **STATUS** Widespread and locally common.

Velvet Horn *Codium tomentosum* Length to 20cm
Distinctive green seaweed. Grows attached to rocks on
mid- to lower shore. **FRONDS** are dark greenish and branch
dichotomously, ending in rounded tips. Texture is rather felt-
like. **STATUS** Widespread and locally common.

*Chaetomorpha
linum*

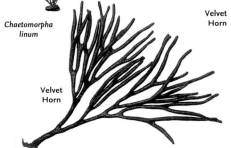

Velvet
Horn

Velvet
Horn

Cladophora *Cladophora rupestris* Length to 20cm

Delicate green seaweed that looks matted when out of water. Grows on rocks and in pools on middle shore. **FRONDS** comprise much-branched tufts of fine strands. **STATUS** Widespread and locally common. **SIMILAR SPECIES Hen Pen** *Bryopsis plumosa* (length to 10cm) is green and feathery or fern-like. Grows on sheltered rocky shores and on stones in pools, from mid- to low-tide mark. Widespread but scarce.

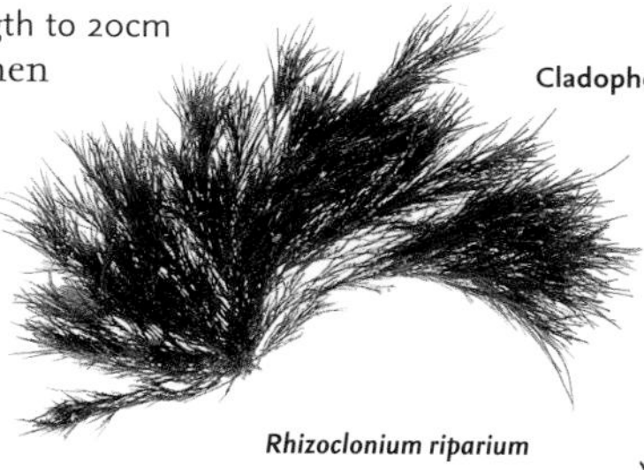

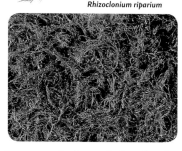

Cladophora

Rhizoclonium riparium

Rhizoclonium riparium Length to 25cm

Thread-like seaweed that forms dense mats (like tangled wool) that 'spring back' when squeezed. Found on mid-shore on sheltered coasts, often in areas of freshwater run-off, and brackish areas of estuaries. **FRONDS** are slender, green and undivided. Root basally. **STATUS** Widespread and locally common.

Mermaid's Tresses

Chorda filum Length to 7m

Long, rope-like yellowish-brown seaweed. Grows attached to rocks by a basal disc on sheltered shores, at or below low-tide mark. **FROND** is slender and unbranched. **STATUS** Widespread and locally common.

Dictyota dichotoma Length to 25cm

Rather delicate, flat yellowish-brown seaweed. Grows on rocks and in pools on the mid- to lower shore. **FRONDS** are rather ribbon-like and divide dichotomously; tips are indented. **STATUS** Widespread and locally common.

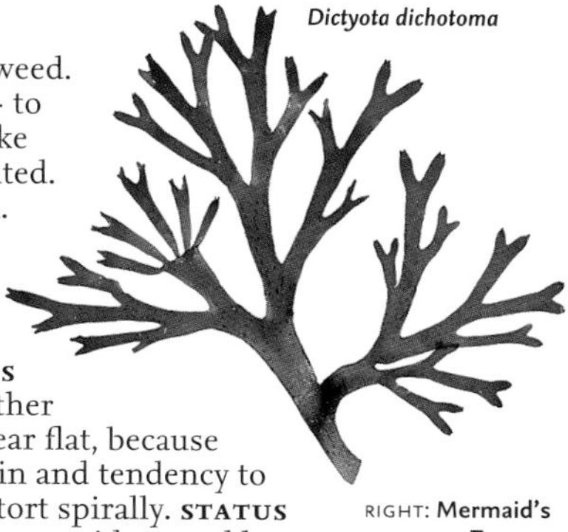

Dictyota dichotoma

Petalonia fascia Length to 30cm

Distinctive yellowish-brown seaweed. Grows attached to stones and rocks; lower shore and sub-littoral zone. **FRONDS** are elongate and rather thin; seldom appear flat, because of ruffled margin and tendency to twist and contort spirally. **STATUS** Introduced; now widespread but only locally common.

RIGHT: **Mermaid's Tresses**

Peacock's Tail

Padina pavonica
Width to 10cm

Distinctive seaweed, typically with a slightly 'chalky' and hairy appearance. Found in shallow pools on sheltered rocky shores. **FRONDS** comprise fan-shaped lobes with concentric bands. **STATUS** Very local, mainly on S coasts from Devon to Hampshire.

Petalonia fascia

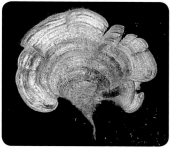

Peacock's Tail

Kelp

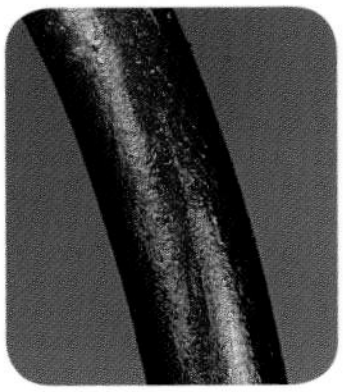

Kelp stem

Kelp or Oarweed *Laminaria digitata*
Length to 1.5m
Robust olive-brown seaweed. Often forms
dense beds, with only floating fronds, not
stipes, visible at most low tides. **FROND** comprises
a tough, smooth and flexible stipe and broad blade,
divided into strap-like segments; attached to rocks
by branched holdfast. **STATUS** Widespread and
locally common. **SIMILAR SPECIES Golden Kelp** *L.
ochroleuca* (length to 2m) has a distinct yellowish
colour. Grows in sheltered sites, attached to rocks on lower shore.
Stipe is inflexible (snaps) and broad blade is divided into strap-like
segments. **STATUS** Restricted to SW England and very locally common.

Cuvie stem

Cuvie *Laminaria hyperborea* Length to 3m
Impressive brown seaweed. Grows on rocky shores; mainly sub-littoral
but sometimes just exposed at extreme low tide. **FROND** comprises a
textured, inflexible stipe (snaps) and broad blade divided into strap-
like segments; holdfast is branched. **STATUS** Commonest in W and N
Britain; absent from the SE.

Sea Belt or Sugar Kelp *Saccharina latissima*
Length to 1.5m
Distinctive brown seaweed of sheltered rocky
shores. Grows on lower shore. **FROND** comprises
a stout but slender stipe and strap-shaped
blade with a crinkly margin.
Holdfast is relatively small.
STATUS Widespread
but commonest in
the N and W.

Cuvie

Sea Belt

Furbelows
holdfast

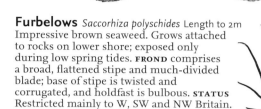

Furbelows *Saccorhiza polyschides* Length to 2m
Impressive brown seaweed. Grows attached
to rocks on lower shore; exposed only
during low spring tides. **FROND** comprises
a broad, flattened stipe and much-divided
blade; base of stipe is twisted and
corrugated, and holdfast is bulbous. **STATUS**
Restricted mainly to W, SW and NW Britain.

Dabberlocks *Alaria esculenta* Length to 1.5m
Distinctive yellowish-brown seaweed. Grows
on exposed rocks at extreme low water. **FROND**
comprises a slender stipe and midrib with a delicate
blade; usually looks tattered by late summer. **STATUS**
Restricted to W and N Britain; absent from the SE.

Thongweed *Himanthalia elongata* Length to 1m
Slender yellowish-brown seaweed. Grows attached to
rocks on the lower shore, on rather sheltered coasts.
FROND is strap-like and rather narrow (less than 1cm
across); grows from centre of tough
button-like structure attached to rock.
STATUS Widespread and locally common
in W and N Britain; absent from most of
the SE.

Furbelows

Thongweed

Thongweed

Dabberlocks

BELOW: Thongweed
'button'

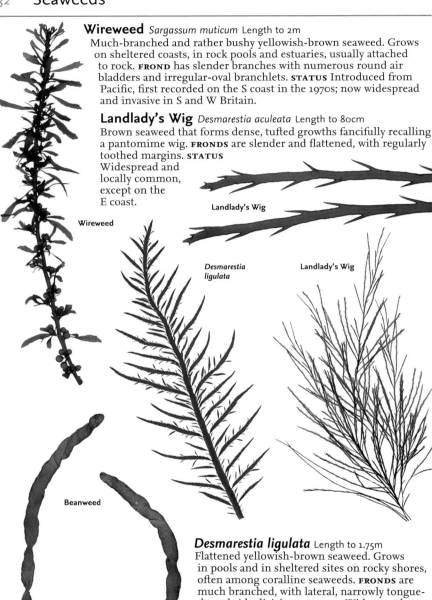

Wireweed *Sargassum muticum* Length to 2m
Much-branched and rather bushy yellowish-brown seaweed. Grows
on sheltered coasts, in rock pools and estuaries, usually attached
to rock. **FROND** has slender branches with numerous round air
bladders and irregular-oval branchlets. **STATUS** Introduced from
Pacific, first recorded on the S coast in the 1970s; now widespread
and invasive in S and W Britain.

Landlady's Wig *Desmarestia aculeata* Length to 80cm
Brown seaweed that forms dense, tufted growths fancifully recalling
a pantomime wig. **FRONDS** are slender and flattened, with regularly
toothed margins. **STATUS**
Widespread and
locally common,
except on the
E coast.

Landlady's Wig

Wireweed

*Desmarestia
ligulata*

Landlady's Wig

Beanweed

Desmarestia ligulata Length to 1.75m
Flattened yellowish-brown seaweed. Grows
in pools and in sheltered sites on rocky shores,
often among coralline seaweeds. **FRONDS** are
much branched, with lateral, narrowly tongue-
shaped side divisions. **STATUS** Widespread,
commonest in the SW.

Beanweed *Scytosiphon lomentaria* Length to 20cm
Delicate but distinctive yellowish-brown seaweed.
Grows in pools and in sub-littoral waters on
sheltered shores. **FRONDS** are slender and tubular, constricted
at intervals and resembling strings of beans. **STATUS** Widespread
and locally common.

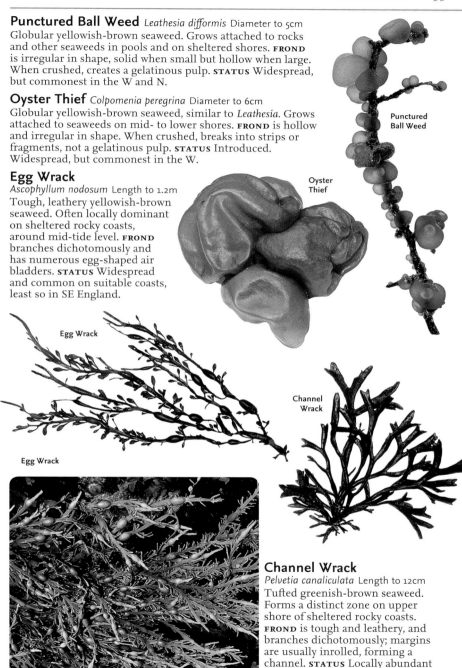

Punctured Ball Weed *Leathesia difformis* Diameter to 5cm
Globular yellowish-brown seaweed. Grows attached to rocks
and other seaweeds in pools and on sheltered shores. **FROND**
is irregular in shape, solid when small but hollow when large.
When crushed, creates a gelatinous pulp. **STATUS** Widespread,
but commonest in the W and N.

Oyster Thief *Colpomenia peregrina* Diameter to 6cm
Globular yellowish-brown seaweed, similar to *Leathesia*. Grows
attached to seaweeds on mid- to lower shores. **FROND** is hollow
and irregular in shape. When crushed, breaks into strips or
fragments, not a gelatinous pulp. **STATUS** Introduced.
Widespread, but commonest in the W.

Punctured
Ball Weed

Oyster
Thief

Egg Wrack
Ascophyllum nodosum Length to 1.2m
Tough, leathery yellowish-brown
seaweed. Often locally dominant
on sheltered rocky coasts,
around mid-tide level. **FROND**
branches dichotomously and
has numerous egg-shaped air
bladders. **STATUS** Widespread
and common on suitable coasts,
least so in SE England.

Egg Wrack

Egg Wrack

Channel
Wrack

Channel Wrack
Pelvetia canaliculata Length to 12cm
Tufted greenish-brown seaweed.
Forms a distinct zone on upper
shore of sheltered rocky coasts.
FROND is tough and leathery, and
branches dichotomously; margins
are usually inrolled, forming a
channel. **STATUS** Locally abundant
on suitable coasts, mainly in W
Britain; virtually absent from the SE.

Serrated Wrack

Fucus serratus Length to 65cm
Familiar and easily identified
greenish-brown seaweed. Often
dominant on lower shore on
moderately exposed rocky coasts.
FROND is flattened, with a distinct
midrib and serrated margins.
Swollen reproductive structures
develop at frond tips in winter.
STATUS Widespread and locally
common except in the SE.

Serrated Wrack

Serrated
Wrack

Spiral Wrack

Spiral
Wrack

Spiral Wrack

Fucus spiralis Length to 20cm
Aptly named greenish-brown
seaweed. Grows on upper shore,
below *Pelvetia* zone, on sheltered
rocky coasts. Also found,
unattached, in very sheltered sea lochs. FROND divides dichotomously and twists spirally
along its length. Swollen reproductive structures form at frond tips. STATUS Widespread
and locally common.

Bladder Wrack *Fucus vesiculosus* Length to 80cm
Distinctive greenish-brown seaweed. Found in a
range of habitats but commonest on moderately
sheltered rocky shores. FROND is broad and
flattened, and divides dichotomously. Typically,
has paired air bladders along its length; bladders
can be absent in exposed situations. STATUS
Widespread and locally common.

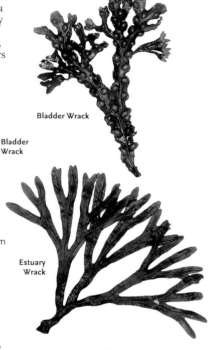

Bladder Wrack

Bladder
Wrack

Estuary Wrack *Fucus ceranoides* Length to 40cm
Much-branched greenish-brown seaweed.
Grows attached to stones in sheltered habitats
where salt and fresh water mix, notably in
estuaries. FROND divides dichotomously and is
flattened, with a midrib and pointed frond tips.
STATUS Locally common. SIMILAR SPECIES
Two-headed Wrack *F. distichus* (length to 10cm)
is a greenish-brown seaweed of exposed rocky
shores in the N, mainly Shetland. Fronds divide
dichotomously and lack air bladders.

Estuary
Wrack

Moss Wrack

Moss Wrack,
growing
amongst Thrift

Sea Oak

Moss Wrack *Fucus cottonii* Length to 3cm
Tiny tufted brown species, barely recognisable as a
Fucus seaweed. Grows as dense patches on mud, in
sheltered spots on upper reaches of saltmarshes in NW
Scotland. FROND is branched and moss-like. STATUS Very local.

Sea Oak *Halidrys siliquosa* Length to 1m
Much-branched greenish-brown seaweed. Grows on rocky
shores in moderately exposed sites; sometimes found in pools.
FROND divides alternately into narrow blades. Reproductive
structures and air bladders are pod-like and stalked. STATUS
Widespread and locally common, least so in the SE.

Cystoseira baccata
Length to 1m
Bushy, much-branched
greenish-brown seaweed.
Grows on rocks; mostly
sub-littoral but
sometimes in pools.
FROND branches
alternately into narrow
sections; has striking air
bladders at base of side
branches; tips are spiky.
STATUS Locally common in SW Britain.
SIMILAR SPECIES **Rainbow Wrack** C. *tamariscifolia*
is bushy and iridescent blue-green underwater.
Locally common in SW.

Rainbow Wrack

Cytoseira
baccata

Furcellaria lumbricalis
Length to 25cm
Tufted, much-branched reddish-
brown seaweed. Grows attached
to rocks with a small holdfast,
on lower shore. FROND has stiff,
cylindrical stems; these taper
towards tips, which often are
bifurcate. STATUS Locally
common except in SE.

Furcellaria
lumbricalis

Irish Moss Chondrus crispus Length to 20cm
Much-branched, slightly slippery-feeling
seaweed. Usually reddish or purplish brown,
but sometimes partly bleached greenish yellow.
Grows on rocks on lower shore and in pools. FROND
branches dichotomously towards tip, into broad, flat
blades with rounded margins. STATUS Widespread
and locally common.

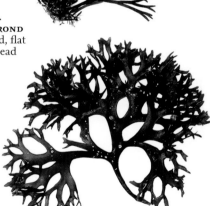

Grape Pip Weed

Grape Pip Weed,
close up

Irish Moss

Grape Pip Weed
Mastocarpus stellatus Length to 10cm
Tough, broadly branched reddish-brown
seaweed. Grows attached to rocks on
lower shore. FROND has slightly curled or
channelled blades, with pip-like projections
produced towards margins in female plants.
STATUS Locally common, least so in the SE.

Calliblepharis ciliata Length to 30cm
Colourful, distinctive red seaweed. Grows on rocks; sub-littoral zone and lower shore. FROND is flattened and elongate, with frilly marginal outgrowths; fronds branch from basal holdfast. STATUS Widespread and locally common, mainly in the S and W. SIMILAR SPECIES *Gelidium spinosum* (length to 20cm) is a tough, branched red seaweed. Grows on rocks on lower shore and on kelp stems. Frond is flattened, with smaller, oval side branches and branchlets. Locally common, mainly in the W and SW.

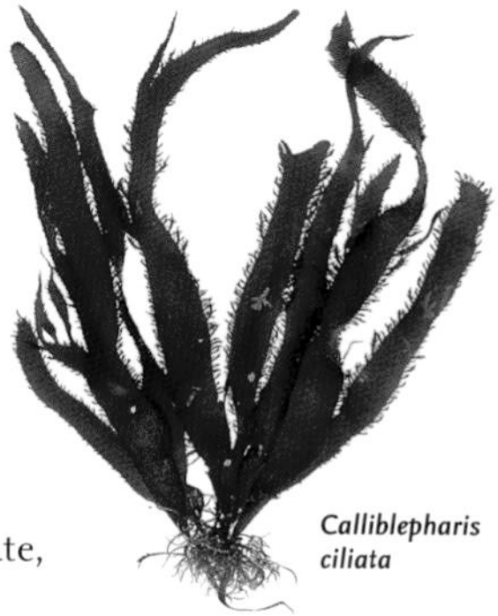

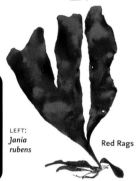

Calliblepharis
ciliata

Red Rags Dilsea carnosa Length to 45cm
Distinctive, bright red seaweed. Grows on rocks on lower shore and among kelps. FROND is broad, flattened and elongate, sometimes dividing or tearing towards tip. STATUS Locally common except in the SE.

Coral Weed Corallina officinalis Length to 10cm
Calcified red seaweed with a pink chalky appearance. Grows on rocks, on lower shore and in pools, in moderately sheltered locations. FROND appears jointed and divides pinnately; overall shape is fan- or fern-like. STATUS Widespread and locally common except in E England. SIMILAR SPECIES *Jania rubens* (length to 20cm) is pink and coralline; forms branched, tufted mats attached to larger seaweeds and rocks. Locally common in the SW only.

LEFT:
*Jania
rubens*

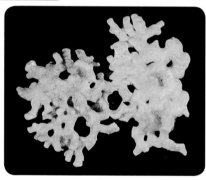

Red Rags

ABOVE: **Coral Weed**; RIGHT: *Lithothamnion* sp.

Maerl Lithothamnion sp.
and *Phymatolithon* sp.

Phymatolithon sp.

Maerl is a term applied to several coralline seaweed species that grow unattached on sheltered offshore seabeds, forming gravel-like layers where undisturbed. Bleached maerl is washed up after gales. *Lithothamnion* sp. grow as branched, twiggy and coral-like structures; *Phymatolithon* sp. form more lumpy, nodular structures. STATUS Both genera are widespread, particularly in the W and N, but scarce or absent from the SE.

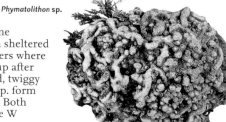

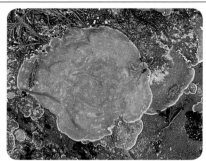

ABOVE: *Lithophyllum incrustans*
BELOW: **Pink Plate Weed**

Lithophyllum incrustans Diameter to 10cm
Rock-encrusting pink seaweed that looks more like rock or coral than a plant. One of several similar (and hard to identify) species, many of which have different growths depending on where they grow. FROND is flattened, adpressed to rock on which it grows, and hard. STATUS Widespread and locally common in suitable habitats.

Pink Plate Weed *Mesophyllum lichenoides*
Diameter to 15cm
Distinctive calcified seaweed that forms pink plates, recalling a terrestrial bracket fungus. Grows attached to *Corallina* on lower shores. FROND is lobed and fan-shaped, with a pale margin and darker concentric bands. Usually pink, sometimes bleached yellow. STATUS Locally common in the SW.

Bead-weed

Dumontia contorta

Bead-weed *Lomentaria articulata* Length to 10cm
Distinctive red seaweed whose form vaguely recalls structure of the saltmarsh plant Common Glasswort (p. 62). Grows attached to rocks and larger seaweeds on lower shore. FROND is much divided and constricted along its length into oval bead-like segments. STATUS Commonest in the W and N; absent from much of the SE.

Dumontia contorta Length to 20cm
Long-stranded reddish-brown seaweed, attached to rocks on lower shore. FRONDS are solid when young, tubular to flattened-cylindrical when older and often twisted. STATUS Widespread and locally common. SIMILAR SPECIES Sea Noodle *Nemalion helminthoides* (length to 20cm) is gelatinous, tubular and reddish brown, resembling overcooked noodles. Locally common only in the S and W.

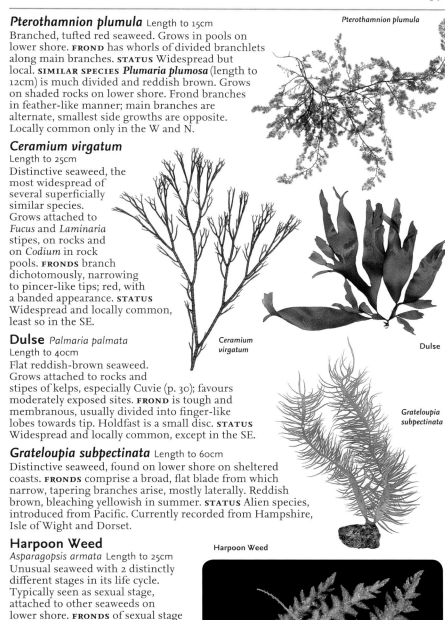

Pterothamnion plumula Length to 15cm

Branched, tufted red seaweed. Grows in pools on lower shore. **FROND** has whorls of divided branchlets along main branches. **STATUS** Widespread but local. **SIMILAR SPECIES** *Plumaria plumosa* (length to 12cm) is much divided and reddish brown. Grows on shaded rocks on lower shore. Frond branches in feather-like manner; main branches are alternate, smallest side growths are opposite. Locally common only in the W and N.

Pterothamnion plumula

Ceramium virgatum

Length to 25cm
Distinctive seaweed, the most widespread of several superficially similar species. Grows attached to *Fucus* and *Laminaria* stipes, on rocks and on *Codium* in rock pools. **FRONDS** branch dichotomously, narrowing to pincer-like tips; red, with a banded appearance. **STATUS** Widespread and locally common, least so in the SE.

Ceramium virgatum

Dulse *Palmaria palmata*

Length to 40cm
Flat reddish-brown seaweed. Grows attached to rocks and stipes of kelps, especially Cuvie (p. 30); favours moderately exposed sites. **FROND** is tough and membranous, usually divided into finger-like lobes towards tip. Holdfast is a small disc. **STATUS** Widespread and locally common, except in the SE.

Dulse

Grateloupia subpectinata Length to 60cm

Distinctive seaweed, found on lower shore on sheltered coasts. **FRONDS** comprise a broad, flat blade from which narrow, tapering branches arise, mostly laterally. Reddish brown, bleaching yellowish in summer. **STATUS** Alien species, introduced from Pacific. Currently recorded from Hampshire, Isle of Wight and Dorset.

Grateloupia subpectinata

Harpoon Weed

Asparagopsis armata Length to 25cm
Unusual seaweed with 2 distinctly different stages in its life cycle. Typically seen as sexual stage, attached to other seaweeds on lower shore. **FRONDS** of sexual stage comprise whorls of finely divided 'frothy'-looking segments, and barbed, bare 'harpoons'. Asexual stage resembles a red woolly ball and is sub-littoral. **STATUS** Introduced, now widespread in the SW and NW.

Harpoon Weed

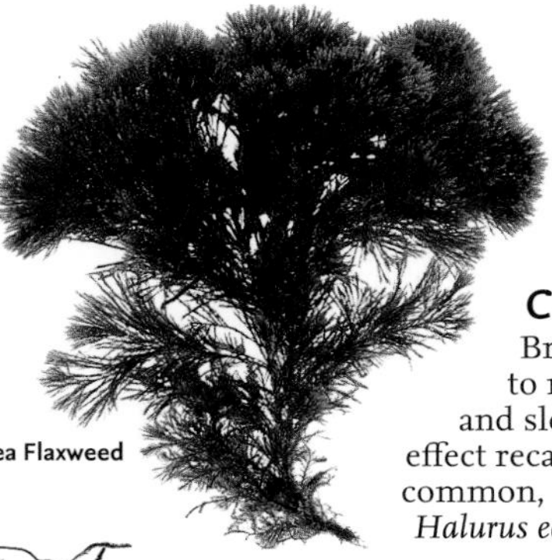

Sea Flaxweed

Stypocaulon scoparium Length to 15cm

Much-branched brown seaweed. Grows attached to rocks in pools and on lower shore, often where sand collects. **FRONDS** comprise tufted bunches of hair-like growths. **STATUS** Locally common, mainly in the SW.

Cladostephus spongiosus Length to 15cm

Branched reddish-brown seaweed. Grows attached to rocks in pools on mid-shore. **FROND** is branched and slender, the branches with whorls of branchlets; the effect recalls a pipe cleaner. **STATUS** Widespread and locally common, except in the E. **SIMILAR SPECIES Sea Mare's-tail** *Halurus equisetifolius* (length to 15cm) is red and branched, with whorls of incurved branchlets. Overall effect recalls freshwater plant Mare's-tail *Hippurus vulgaris*. Locally common only in the SW. **H. flosculosus** (length to 20cm) is tufted and grows in pools on sheltered rocky shores. Fronds comprise stiff hairs, attached to substrate by fibrous base. Locally common in the W.

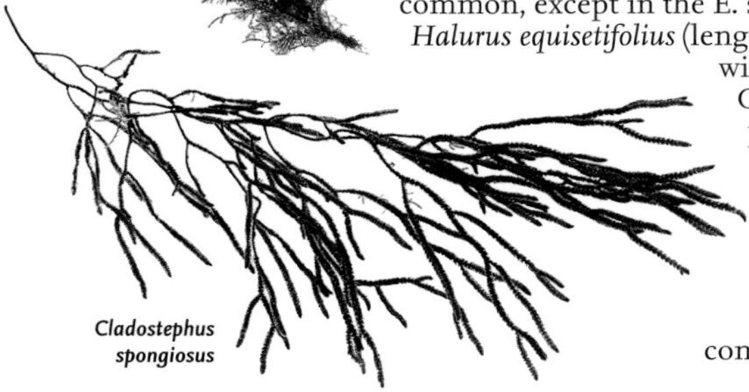

Sea Flaxweed

Cladostephus
spongiosus

Bifurcaria bifurcata Length to 40cm

Tough yellowish-brown seaweed. Grows in rock pools and sheltered spots on lower shore. **FROND** divides evenly, the fork curved in a distinctive manner. **STATUS** Confined to SW Britain.

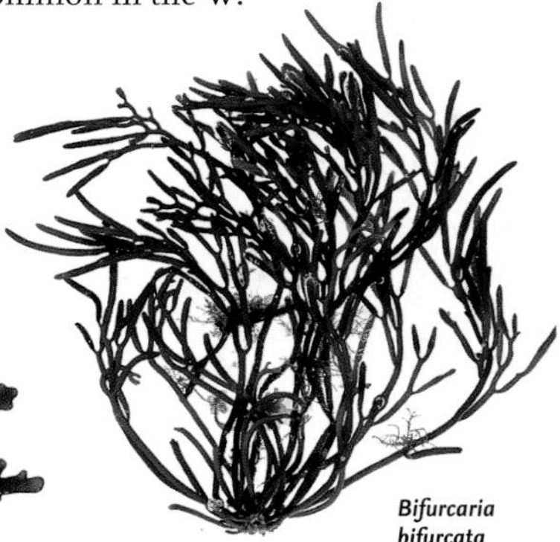

Pepper
Dulse

Bifurcaria
bifurcata

Pepper Dulse

Osmundea pinnatifida
Length to 20cm

Tough, rather cartilaginous reddish-brown seaweed. Grows, often in lush abundance, on rocks on mid- to lower shore. Tolerates moderately exposed sites. **FROND** is flattened and branched, the effect like a fern, notably a filmy-fern. **STATUS** Widespread and locally common except in SE England.

Phycodrys
rubens

Phycodrys rubens Length to 25cm

Distinctive red seaweed. Grows sub-littorally, attached to rocks; sometimes washed up. **FROND** comprises a tough stem with membranous red blades; these recall oak leaves. **STATUS** Locally common only in W and N Britain.

Polysiphonia lanosa Length to 10cm

One of several confusingly similar reddish seaweeds. Grows epiphytically on Egg Wrack (p. 33); other species grow on rocks. **FROND** comprises branched, segmented stems, appearing as tufts; these collapse out of water. **STATUS** Locally common. **SIMILAR SPECIES** Several confusingly similar filamentous *Polysiphonia* species are also widespread, growing attached to rocks in pools and on lower shore.

Polysiphonia lanosa

Polysiphonia sp.

BELOW: Sea Beech

Sea Beech

Sea Beech
Delesseria sanguinea
Length to 20cm
Distinctive red seaweed. Grows attached to rocks; usually sub-littoral but sometimes in pools on lower shore. **FROND** comprises a tough midrib and lateral veins, and membranous blades; overall effect recalls a Beech leaf. **STATUS** Locally common only in W Britain.

Laver

Laver *Porphyra* sp. Length to 50cm
Represented by 5 superficially similar species. Most grow attached to rock, but some are epiphytic on larger seaweeds. **FRONDS** All are thin and membranous, ranging from red or purple to yellowish green. **STATUS** Widespread and locally common. **SIMILAR SPECIES** *Nitophyllum punctatum* (length to 45cm) is membranous, pink and fan-shaped; variably divided towards tip. Female plants are dotted with dark reproductive structures. Locally common only in W and NW Britain.

Laver

INTRODUCING TERRESTRIAL NON-FLOWERING PLANTS

Terrestrial non-flowering plants range from single-celled algae, through mosses, liverworts and horsetails, to complex ferns, plants with roots and a vascular system that transports food and water. Seaweeds are algae but are covered separately on pp. 26–41. Terrestrial non-flowering plants photosynthesise, trapping sunlight energy using pigments (including chlorophyll) and creating food. But their reproduction is primitive: they do not produce flowers or seeds, but instead produce spores as part of their life cycles.

Sandhill Screw-moss *Syntrichia ruralis* ssp. *ruraliformis* Height to 5cm
Forms dense, extensive patches in sand dunes. **LEAVES** are yellowish green, recurved and tapering, and end in a thin point. Spore capsule is reddish, cylindrical and upright, the mouth lined with teeth when mature. **STATUS** Locally common.

Whitish Feather-moss *Brachythecium albicans* Spreading
Forms an open carpet on bare, sandy soil in dunes. Stems are branched and spreading, with numerous upright branches. **LEAVES** are yellowish green, oval and pointed-tipped; stems are densely cloaked. Spore capsules are rarely produced. **STATUS** Locally common.

Haircap mosses *Polytrichum* sp. Height to 10cm
Several *Polytrichum* species are widespread, some forming carpets in damp dune-slacks. **LEAVES** are narrow and spreading in all species; plants themselves resembling miniature conifer shoots. **STATUS** Locally common.

Field Horsetail *Equisetum arvense* Height to 75cm
Herbaceous perennial that forms spreading patches in damp coastal grassland. **STEMS** include sterile shoots with ridged stems that carry whorls of unbranched branches, and fertile shoots that appear in early spring and ripen in May. **STATUS** Widespread and common.

Bracken *Pteridium aquilinum* Frond to 2m
Our commonest fern. Often carpets coastal slopes and cliffs with dry, acid soils. **FRONDS** are compact with curled tips at first. Mature fronds are green and are repeatedly divided 3 times. Spore cases are borne around frond margins. **STATUS** Widespread and locally abundant.

Hay-scented Buckler-fern
Dryopteris aemula Frond to 50cm
Fresh green fronds smell of hay when crushed and remain green through winter. **FRONDS** are repeatedly divided 3 times and have pale brown scales on stalk. **STATUS** Locally common only in SW England, W Scotland and W Ireland. Favours W-facing slopes.

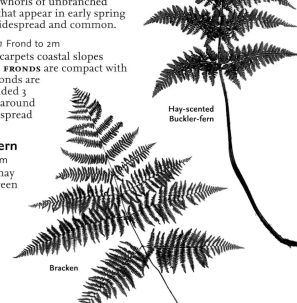

Hay-scented Buckler-fern

Bracken

Sandhill Screw-moss

Whitish Feather-moss

Haircap mosses

Field Horsetail

Bracken

Hay-scented Buckler-fern

Sea Spleenwort
Asplenium marinum Frond to 30cm

Classic maritime fern. **FRONDS** are leathery, shiny and bright green; they taper at both ends and have broad, oblong lobes and a green midrib. **STATUS** Confined to coastal caves and crevices in the W that are subject to sea spray.

Lanceolate Spleenwort
Asplenium obovatum Frond to 30cm

Maritime fern. **FRONDS** are fresh green; they do not taper towards base and pinnae are often folded down. **STATUS** Confined to walls and rocky banks in the W, usually within sight of the sea.

Polypody
Polypodium vulgare Frond to 50cm

Typical of damp, wooded valleys but also common in stable, damp dune-slacks. **FRONDS** are dark green, leathery, divided simply and borne on slender stalks. They appear in May and persist overwinter. **STATUS** Widespread and locally common.

Adder's-tongue
Ophioglossum vulgatum Frond to 10cm

Unusual fern of damp dune-slacks. **FROND** is bright green, oval and borne upright on a short stalk. Spores are borne on a tall fertile spike. **STATUS** Widespread but only locally common.

Small Adder's-tongue
Ophioglossum azoricum Height to 4cm

Similar to Adder's-tongue (above) but much smaller and often with paired leaves. **FROND** is bright green, oval and borne on a short stalk. Spores are borne on a short fertile spike. **STATUS** Very locally common in short coastal grassland in W Britain.

Maidenhair Fern
Adiantum capillus-veneris Frond to 35cm

Delicate-looking clump-forming fern with pendulous fronds that grows in rock crevices. **FRONDS** comprise bright green fan-shaped pinnae borne on a dark, wiry, divided stem. **STATUS** Restricted to damp, shady gullies and cliffs, usually on calcareous rocks, in SW Britain.

Royal Fern
Osmunda regalis Frond to 3m

Large and impressive fern of damp, shady places, mostly on acid soils. **FRONDS** are triangular overall, repeatedly divided 2 times into oblong lobes. Separate central fertile fronds, covered in golden spores, appear Jun–Aug. **STATUS** Widespread and locally common on shady sea cliffs.

Lanceolate Spleenwort

Sea Spleenwort

Polypody

Sea Spleenwort

Lanceolate Spleenwort

Adder's-tongue

Polypody

Small Adder's-tongue

Royal Fern

Maidenhair Fern

INTRODUCING ALGAE, LICHENS AND FUNGI

Neither plants nor animals, fungi are classified in their own kingdom. They digest their food externally and absorb the nutrients to enable growth. Many species form complex relationships with other organisms. One such group are the lichens; here, a partnership involves a fungal body that harbours a photosynthesising partner, usually an alga.

Trentopohlia sp. Encrusting
Colourful algae. Similar to an encrusting lichen and one of the commonest symbionts in lichen partnerships. Usually found on shady, damp rocks. **STATUS** Commonest in the W.

Cladonia sp. Spreading
Several *Cladonia* lichens are common in dunes and maritime heaths. Some form intricate networks of densely packed blue-grey or whitish wirewool-like strands. Others resemble miniature stag's antlers and a few comprise scaly stalks topped with red spore-producing bodies. **STATUS** Locally common.

LEFT AND RIGHT:
Cladonia sp. lichens

Sea Ivory *Ramalina siliquosa* Length 3cm
Branched, tufted lichen of coastal rocks and stone walls. Grows well above the high-tide mark but tolerates salt spray. Branches are flattened and grey, with disc-like spore-producing bodies. **STATUS** Locally common. Abundant on W coasts.

Dogtooth Lichen *Peltigera canina* Spreading
Forms dense mats on the ground, typically favouring sandy soils on dunes. Lichen body is attached to the ground by root-like structures on lower surface. Tooth-like reproductive structures appear on upper surface. **STATUS** Locally common.

Black Lichen *Lichina pygmaea* Encrusting
Patch-forming lichen comprising densely packed, branched and flattened tufts that are dark brown. Grows on middle shore, attached to rocks and often in crevices. **STATUS** Common on suitable substrates.

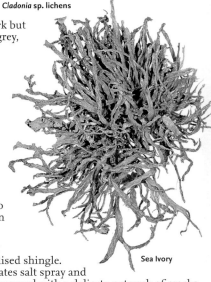

Sea Ivory

Black Tar Lichen *Verrucaria maura* Encrusting
Patch-forming lichen of coastal rocks and stabilised shingle. Often found just above barnacle zone, and tolerates salt spray and periodic immersion. Surface is sooty black and covered with a delicate network of cracks. Sometimes mistaken for oil. **STATUS** Common on suitable substrates.

Trentopohlia sp.

Cladonia sp.

Sea Ivory

Dogtooth Lichen

Black Lichen

Black Tar Lichen

Caloplaca marina Encrusting
Bright orange lichen forming irregular patches up to 5cm across on rocks around the high-water mark. Tolerant of salt spray and brief immersion in sea water. **STATUS** Widespread around coasts of Britain and Ireland; commonest in the W.

Yellow Scales *Xanthoria parientina* Spreading
One of our most familiar and colourful lichens; grows inland but most spectacular on coasts. Forms bright orange-yellow patches on rocks and walls. Surface comprises leafy, narrow scales that are rather wrinkled. **STATUS** Widespread and common.

Map Lichen *Rhizocarpon geographicum* Spreading
Aptly named rock-encrusting lichen. Surface is yellowish and etched with black spore-producing bodies. When 2 neighbouring colonies meet, boundaries are defined by black margins, creating a map-like appearance. **STATUS** Locally common on coasts.

Golden Hair Lichen *Teloschistes flavicans* Width to 7cm
Distinctive lichen, entirely restricted to coastal heaths and short cliff-side vegetation. Comprises a network of bright orange interweaving strands that form a wirewool-like mass. **STATUS** Local in suitable habitats in W Britain.

Crab's-eye Lichen *Ochrolechia parella* Spreading
Encrusting, patch-forming lichen found on walls and rocks. Surface is greyish with a pale margin. Clusters of raised, rounded and flat-topped spore-producing structures give rise to its common English name. **STATUS** Common on coasts of W Britain.

Black Shields *Tephromela atra* Encrusting
Patch-forming lichen. Grows on rocks, at and just above the high-tide mark; tolerates salt spray. Grows inland but commonest on coasts. Surface is knobbly and grey, while spore-producing structures are rounded and black with pale grey margins. **STATUS** Common on suitable substrates.

Anaptychia runcinata Width to 10cm
Cushion-forming lichen comprising numerous overlapping, flattish olive-brown lobes that are slightly leathery. Grows on rocks and stone walls, usually within sight of the sea. **STATUS** Common on suitable substrates.

In western Britain, lichens typically grow in profusion on coastal rocks. Several species often grow in close proximity to one another, showing zonation according to their tolerance of sea spray.

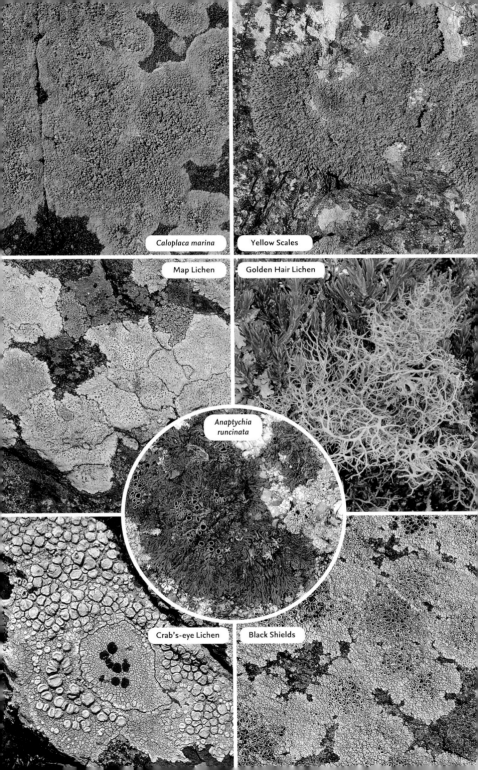

Caloplaca marina

Yellow Scales

Map Lichen

Golden Hair Lichen

Anaptychia runcinata

Crab's-eye Lichen

Black Shields

Field Mushroom

Agaricus devoniensis Width to 7cm
Dune-living relative of the Cultivated Mushroom; grows mostly buried in sand. **FRUIT BODY** comprises an off-white cap, usually covered with sand. Gills are pink at first, maturing brown. White stem is always buried and hidden. **STATUS** Locally common. **SIMILAR SPECIES Field Mushroom** *A. campestris* (Width to 8cm) is the classic 'mushroom' of short grassland and common near the coast. Its off-white cap and stem stand clear of the ground; gills are pink, maturing dark brown.

Egghead Mottlegill
Panaeolus semiovatus Height to 15cm
Distinctive toadstool. Found in coastal grassland on weathered dung of cattle and horses. **FRUIT BODY** comprises domed, wrinkled and creamy-white cap. Gills mature blackish and stem is slender and white. **STATUS** Locally common.

Parasol *Macrolepiota procera* Height to 30cm
Impressive grassland mushroom. **FRUIT BODY** comprises a whitish cap with brown scales, measuring 20cm or more diameter. Gills are whitish and stem is slender and covered with dark scales. **STATUS** Common in dunes and short coastal turf.

Dune Waxcap *Hygrocybe conicoides* Height to 8cm
Colourful mushroom of dunes and coastal grassland. **FRUIT BODY** comprises a conical yellow or orange cap, gills and slender stem. Whole fruit body often blackens with age, sometimes becoming entirely black. **STATUS** Locally common.

Tiny Earthstar *Geastrum minimum* Width to 3cm
Miniature earthstar. **FRUIT BODY** has 6–10 ray segments that curl back with maturity; often encrusted with sand beneath. Spore sac is up to 1cm across, borne on a short stalk and with a fibrous opening. **STATUS** Rare, restricted to N Norfolk dunes.

Dwarf Earthstar *Geastrum schmidelii* Width to 3cm
Small buffish earthstar. **FRUIT BODY** has 5–8 ray segments that curl back with maturity. Spore sac is up to 1cm across, borne on a short stalk and with a pleated opening. **STATUS** Scarce and local, in dunes in England and Wales, mainly in the W and N.

Winter Stalkball *Tulostoma brumale* Height to 3cm
Distinctive stalked puffball. **FRUIT BODY** comprises a spherical spore sac with an apical opening, borne on a stalk whose length increases as winter progresses. **STATUS** Locally common in sandy dune soils; abundant in a few sites on the N Norfolk coast.

Grey Puffball *Bovista plumbea* Width to 2.5cm
Familiar dune puffball. **FRUIT BODY** is white and smooth at first. In maturity, outer layer is shed, revealing a grey spore sac with apical pore; fruit body becomes detached and blows around in the wind. **STATUS** Widespread and common.

Dune Stinkhorn *Phallus hadriani* Height to 15cm
Unmistakable. First appears as a pinkish-lilac 'egg'. **FRUIT BODY** emerges as a white stem carrying a honeycombed head covered in the smelly brown spore mass; flies eat this and disperse spores. **STATUS** Local; restricted to dunes and associated with Marram.

Geoglossum cookeianum Height to 7cm
A so-called 'earthtongue'. **FRUIT BODY** is blackish with a broad, flattened and furrowed head tapering into a short stem. **STATUS** Widespread and common in dunes.

Agaricus devoniensis

Parasol

Tiny Earthstar

Dwarf Earthstar

Egghead
Mottlegill

Dune Waxcap

Grey Puffball

Winter
Stalkball

Dune Stinkhorn

Geoglossum
cookeianum

INTRODUCING FLOWERING PLANTS

Common Sea-lavender in a north Norfolk saltmarsh.

Sand dunes and Marram.

Flowering plants are very much a feature of our coast. There are the generalist plants that, although locally abundant on the coast, are also found inland – Bramble and Common Nettle are examples. But then there are the coastal specialities, found nowhere else. Plants growing on the coast must tolerate harsh environmental conditions: in many locations, salt spray is a constant factor, while some species even thrive with occasional or regular immersion in sea water.

SALTMARSH PLANTS

Mudflats often form where currents slow as rivers empty into the sea. Deposited with the sediment is a rich soup of organic matter, and it is little wonder that a range of specialist plants have evolved to exploit this resource. They must, however, be able to tolerate both freshwater run-off and daily immersion in sea water from the tide. Their roots bind the muddy substrate, leading to the formation of saltmarshes. Community members include glassworts, Sea Purslane, species of sea-lavender and Common Cord-grass.

SANDY COASTS

Our beaches, so beloved of holidaymakers, are formed of shifting sand, which without some binding influence would remain constantly on the move. The restraint is provided by plants, or rather their roots. Along the strandline the process of colonisation is started by Sea Sandwort, but the real star of the show is Marram grass; were it not for this species, sand dunes would never become stable. The dunes themselves are forever growing from the constant deposition of sand by the sea. Inland from the beach, grassland communities develop, with shrubs and even trees colonising the oldest parts of the dune system.

ABOVE: **Sea-holly growing on shingle.**

RIGHT: **Thrift carpeting a coastal slope on Lundy.**

SHINGLE FLORA

In a temperate environment, the shingle beach must surely be one of the most challenging habitats for a plant. The pebbles themselves are abrasive, the substrate is incredibly free-draining, and what little debris collects (soil is too grand a word for it) is likely to be salt-laden. But a group of hardy specialists do thrive here, including Sea-holly, Yellow Horned-poppy and Sea-kale.

SEA CLIFFS

For breathtaking scenery and a sense of untamed nature, coastal cliffs are hard to beat. Part of their charm, in spring at least, comes from the colourful plants that flower on their tops and ledges. Unrivalled in its impact, Thrift forms colourful pink carpets and in many western areas is the dominant cliff species. A pleasing contrast is provided by the presence of Sea Carrot, Sea Campion and various species of sea-spurrey.

Sea Buckthorn

French Tamarisk

Sea Buckthorn *Hippophae rhamnoides* Height to 10m
Dense, thorny, branched shrub. Native of coastal sand dunes but planted inland. FLOWERS are tiny and greenish, male and female flowers on separate plants (Mar–Apr). FRUITS are bright orange berries (on female plants only). LEAVES are narrow and greyish green. STATUS Native to E coast but planted elsewhere. NOTE Bracket fungus *Phellinus hippophaeicola* is found only on Sea Buckthorn trunks.

French Tamarisk *Tamarix gallica* Height to 8m
Straggly, windswept tree. FLOWERS are minute, pink and 5-petalled; in long sprays (May–Jun). FRUITS are wind-dispersed. LEAVES are greenish blue and scale-like. STATUS Introduced as a windbreak and sometimes naturalised.

Wild Privet *Ligustrum vulgare* Height to 10m
Branched semi-evergreen shrub of calcareous dunes and scrub. FLOWERS are 4–5mm across, creamy white, fragrant and 4-petalled; in terminal spikes (May–Jun). FRUITS are shiny, globular and poisonous, ripening black in autumn; borne in clusters. LEAVES are shiny, untoothed, oval and opposite. STATUS Widespread and locally common, mainly in the S.

Elder *Sambucus nigra* Height to 10m
Deciduous shrub or small tree with spreading, outcurved main branches and corky bark. Grows in coastal scrub, doing best on calcareous and nitrogen-enriched soils. FLOWERS are 5mm across and creamy white; in flat-topped clusters, 10–20cm across (Jun–Jul). FRUITS are clusters of blackish-purple berries. LEAVES are unpleasant-smelling and divided into 5–7 leaflets. STATUS Widespread and common.

Elder

Blackthorn *Prunus spinosa* Height to 6m
Densely branched shrub with spiny twigs and blackish-brown bark. Dominates coastal scrub in many parts. FLOWERS are white, 5-petalled, to 17mm across; produced prolifically (Feb–Mar). FRUITS are sloes: to 2cm long, ovoid and blue-black. LEAVES are ovate, toothed, to 4.5cm long. STATUS Widespread and common.

Grey Willow *Salix cinerea* Height to 6m   **Blackthorn**
Large shrub or small tree with downy grey twigs. A typical scrub species. FLOWERS are ovoid catkins, with males and females on separate trees (Mar–Apr). Female catkins are yellower than males and produce plumed seeds. LEAVES are oblong, pointed and short-stalked. Upper surface is matt; lower surface is downy and grey in spring, acquiring rusty hairs by autumn in some forms. STATUS Widespread and common.

Grey Willow

Creeping Willow

Creeping Willow *Salix repens* Height to 1.5m
Low-growing, creeping shrub with downy twigs. Grows in coastal dune-slacks. FLOWERS are ovoid catkins (Apr–May). LEAVES are ovate, usually untoothed, to 4cm long; hairless above, silkily hairy below. STATUS Widespread and locally common.

Ivy *Hedera helix* Height to 20m
Evergreen climber that also carpets the ground. Found in coastal woods and scrub. FLOWERS are yellowish green and 4-parted; in globular heads (Sep–Nov). FRUITS are berries that ripen purplish black. LEAVES are glossy, dark green, and 3- or 5-lobed with paler veins. STATUS Widespread and common.

Ivy

Sea Buckthorn

Phellinus hippophaeicola

Elder, fruits

French Tamarisk

Elder

Wild Privet

Blackthorn

Wild Privet, fruits

Blackthorn, fruits

Ivy, fruits

Grey Willow

Creeping Willow

Ivy

Common Nettle *Urtica dioica* Height to 1m
Familiar stinging nettle. Favours disturbed, nitrogen-enriched soils. **FLOWERS** are pendulous catkins, borne on separate-sex plants (Jun–Oct). **FRUITS** resemble flowers. **LEAVES** are oval and toothed, to 8cm long. **STATUS** Widespread and common.

Small Nettle *Urtica urens* Height to 50cm
Similar to Common Nettle (above) but smaller and annual. Grows on disturbed ground. **FLOWERS** are pendulous catkins, males and females on same plant (Jun–Sep). **FRUITS** are similar to female flowers. **LEAVES** are oval, pointed-tipped and toothed; to 4cm long. **STATUS** Widespread and locally common.

Pellitory-of-the-wall *Parietaria judaica* Height to 7cm
Spreading, downy perennial with reddish stems. Colonises walls and rocky ground. **FLOWERS** appear in clusters at leaf bases (Jun–Oct). **FRUITS** are clustered at leaf bases. **LEAVES** are oval, up to 5cm long and stalked. **STATUS** Widespread in England, Wales and Ireland; commonest on W coasts.

Common Nettle

Knotgrass *Polygonum aviculare* Height to 1m (often prostrate)
Branched annual of bare coastal ground. **FLOWERS** are pink and arise in leaf axils (Jun–Oct). **FRUITS** are nut-like, enclosed by withering flower. **LEAVES** are oval and leathery, with a silvery basal sheath. **STATUS** Widespread and common.

Ray's Knotgrass
Polygonum oxyspermum Prostrate
Mat-forming annual of coastal sand and shingle beaches. **FLOWERS** are pinkish white and arise in leaf axils (Aug–Sep). **FRUITS** are nut-like and protrude beyond withering flower. **LEAVES** are oval, leathery and alternate, sometimes with slightly inrolled margins. **STATUS** Local; commonest in the W.

Sheep's Sorrel   Common Sorrel

Sea Knotgrass *Polygonum maritimum* Prostrate
Similar to Ray's Knotgrass (above) but perennial and woody at base. Grows on sand and shingle beaches. **FLOWERS** are pinkish and arise in leaf axils (Jul–Sep). **FRUITS** are nut-like and protrude well beyond withering flower. **LEAVES** are grey-green and rolled under at margins. **STATUS** Rare; SW Britain only.

Common Sorrel *Rumex acetosa* Height to 60cm
Usually upright perennial of coastal grassland. Often turns red when mature. **FLOWERS** are reddish; in slender spikes (May–Jul). **FRUITS** are nut-like. **LEAVES** are green, arrow-shaped and narrow; taste mildly of vinegar. **STATUS** Widespread and common.

Sheep's Sorrel *Rumex acetosella* Height to 25cm
Upright perennial of bare, acid soils. **FLOWERS** are greenish and borne in slender spikes (May–Aug). **FRUITS** are nut-like. **LEAVES** are arrow-shaped with basal lobes pointing forwards; upper leaves clasp stem. **STATUS** Widespread and common.

Common Nettle

Small Nettle

Pellitory-of the-wall

Knotgrass

Ray's Knotgrass

Sea Knotgrass

Common Sorrel

Sheep's Sorrel

Curled Dock *Rumex crispus* Height to 1m

Upright perennial of coastal grassland and disturbed soils. FLOWERS are flattened and oval; borne in dense, upright, leafless spikes (Jun–Oct). FRUITS are oval and untoothed, usually with a single tubercle. LEAVES are narrow, up to 25cm long with wavy edges. STATUS Widespread and common.

Broad-leaved Dock *Rumex obtusifolius* Height to 1m

Familiar upright perennial of coastal grassland and disturbed ground. FLOWERS are borne in loose spikes that are leafy at base (Jun–Aug). FRUITS have prominent teeth and 1 tubercle. LEAVES are broadly oval, heart-shaped at base and up to 25cm long. STATUS Widespread and very common.

Clustered Dock

Rumex conglomeratus Height to 1m

Upright perennial with a zigzag stem and spreading branches. Found in coastal grassland and undercliffs, often on damp soil. FLOWERS are borne in leafy spikes (Jun–Aug). FRUITS are small and untoothed, with 3 elongated tubercles.

Curled Dock   Broad-leaved Dock

Clustered Dock, flowers

LEAVES are oval; lower leaves are heart-shaped at base and often waisted. STATUS Mostly common except in Scotland.

Shore Dock *Rumex rupestris* Height to 1m

Spreading perennial, similar to Clustered Dock (above). Restricted to freshwater seepages on rocky shores and at cliff bases. FLOWERS are borne in spikes, leafy only at base (Jun–Jul). FRUITS have large, inflated tubercles. LEAVES are greyish and blunt. STATUS Rare; restricted mainly to S Cornwall and Isles of Scilly.

ABOVE: **Shore Dock, fruit**
LEFT: **Shore Dock, flowers**

Fiddle Dock *Rumex pulcher* Height to 30cm

Perennial whose branches spread at right angles. Favours well-drained soils, often in coastal areas. FLOWERS are borne in spikes in widely separated whorls (Jun–Aug). FRUITS are toothed with 3 tubercles. LEAVES are up to 10cm long, waisted and violin-shaped. STATUS Local; restricted to S England and S Wales.

Springbeauty

Claytonia perfoliata Height to 30cm

Annual, introduced from N America but now widely naturalised on dry, sandy soil. FLOWERS are white, 5-petalled and 5mm across; in loose spikes (Apr–Jul). FRUITS are capsules. LEAVES are oval and stalked at base; flowering stems bear fused pairs of perfoliate leaves. STATUS Widespread and locally abundant.

Fiddle Dock, flowers

ABOVE: **Fiddle Dock, fruit**
RIGHT: **Fiddle Dock**

Hottentot-fig *Carpobrotus edulis* Creeping

Exotic-looking fleshy perennial, introduced from S Africa. Forms carpets on coastal cliffs and banks. FLOWERS are usually yellow (sometimes fading pinkish), 7–10cm across and many-petalled (May–Aug). FRUITS are swollen and succulent. LEAVES are dark green, succulent, 3-sided, 6–7cm long and narrow. STATUS Naturalised in SW Britain.

Curled Dock

Curled Dock

Broad-leaved Dock

Curled Dock

Broad-leaved Dock

Clustered Dock

Shore Dock

Fiddle Dock

Springbeauty

Hottentot-fig

Babington's Orache *Atriplex glabriuscula* Prostrate

Spreading, mealy annual of shingle and bare coastal ground. Stems are usually reddish and whole plant often turns red in autumn. **FLOWERS** are borne in leafy spikes (Jul–Sep). **FRUITS** are diamond-shaped, maturing silvery white. **LEAVES** are triangular or diamond-shaped. **STATUS** Locally common.

Frosted Orache *Atriplex laciniata* Usually prostrate

Distinctive silvery-grey plant, characteristic of sandy beaches. Stems are usually flushed pink. **FLOWERS** are whitish; borne in clusters (Jul–Sep). **FRUITS** are diamond-shaped and toothed. **LEAVES** are fleshy, mealy, toothed and diamond-shaped. **STATUS** Widespread, locally common and exclusively coastal.

Grass-leaved Orache

Grass-leaved Orache *Atriplex littoralis* Height to 1m

Upright annual of bare coastal ground. **FLOWERS** are small and greenish; borne in spikes with small leaves (Jul–Sep). **FRUITS** are greenish, toothed and warty. **LEAVES** are long and narrow, sometimes with shallow teeth. **STATUS** Locally common.

Red Goosefoot *Chenopodium rubrum* Height to 60cm

Variable upright annual, favouring nitrogen-enriched soils. Stems often turn red in old or parched specimens. Coastal plants are sometimes prostrate. **FLOWERS** are small; borne in upright, leafy spikes (Jul–Oct). **FRUITS** are rounded and almost enclosed by sepals. **LEAVES** are shiny, diamond-shaped and toothed. **STATUS** Widespread and common, mainly in the S.

Red Goosefoot

Saltmarsh Goosefoot

Chenopodium chenopodioides Height to 30cm

Recalls Red Goosefoot (above) but mature leaves are always red below and whole plant is often red-tinged. Grows in drying mud of lagoons on coastal grazing marshes. **FLOWERS** are reddish green; borne in clusters (Jul–Sep). **FRUITS** are enclosed by sepals. **LEAVES** are diamond-shaped and untoothed. **STATUS** Restricted mostly to Thames Estuary; N Kent is its stronghold.

Saltmarsh Goosefoot

Stinking Goosefoot *Chenopodium vulvaria* Height to 30cm, often prostrate

Spreading, mealy plant of slightly disturbed, often nitrogen-enriched soils, mainly near coasts. **FLOWERS** are green, mealy and borne in clusters (Jul–Sep). **FRUITS** are similar to flowers. **LEAVES** are green, mealy and smell strongly of rotting fish. **STATUS** Rare and very local, mainly in S England.

Stinking Goosefoot

Sea Beet

Sea Beet *Beta vulgaris* ssp. *maritima* Height to 1m

Sprawling, clump-forming perennial of cliffs, shingle beaches and other coastal habitats. **FLOWERS** are green and borne in dense, leafy spikes (Jul–Sep). **FRUITS** are spiky, often sticking together in a clump. **LEAVES** are dark green, glossy and leathery, with reddish stems; shape varies from oval to triangular. **STATUS** Widespread and locally common.

Sea Beet, flowers

Babington's Orache

Frosted Orache

Red Goosefoot

Grass-leaved Orache

Stinking Goosefoot

Saltmarsh Goosefoot

Sea Beet

Sea Purslane *Halimione portulacoides* Height to 1m
Spreading, mealy perennial that sometimes forms rounded clumps.
Restricted to drier reaches of saltmarshes. **FLOWERS** are yellowish; borne
in spikes (Jul–Oct). **FRUITS** are lobed. **LEAVES** are grey-green; basal
leaves are oval, stem leaves are narrow. **STATUS** Widespread and
locally common.

Common Glasswort *Salicornia europaea* Height to 30cm
Fleshy yellowish-green annual that fancifully recalls a
miniature cactus. Often appears segmented. Entirely coastal.
A classic saltmarsh plant that tolerates tidal immersion in sea
water. **FLOWERS** are tiny; appear at stem junctions, of equal size
and in 3s (Aug–Sep). **FRUITS** are minute seeds. **LEAVES** are small,
paired and fleshy. **STATUS** Locally abundant.

Common
Glasswort

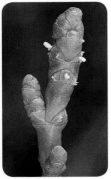

Perennial Glasswort *Sarcocornia perennis*
Height to 30cm
Branched, patch-forming succulent
perennial with woody lower stems that turn
orange with age. Coastal; restricted to drier
reaches of saltmarshes; **FLOWERS** are small and
yellow (Aug–Oct). **FRUITS** are minute; appear at stem
junctions, in 3s, the central fruit largest. **LEAVES** are small, paired
and fleshy. **STATUS** Local in S and E England, and in S Wales.

Perennial Glasswort, flowers

Annual Sea-blite *Suaeda maritima* Height to 50cm
Much-branched annual of saltmarshes. Forms small clumps that
vary from yellowish green to reddish. **FLOWERS** are tiny and green;
1–3 appear in axils of upper leaves (Aug–Oct). **FRUITS** produce
dark, flattish seeds. **LEAVES** are succulent, cylindrical and pointed.
STATUS Widespread and locally common.

Shrubby Sea-blite *Suaeda vera* Height to 1m
Evergreen perennial with woody stems. Restricted to coastal shingle and upper
saltmarshes. **FLOWERS** are tiny and yellowish; 1–3 appear in leaf axils (Jun–Oct). **FRUITS**
produce black seeds. **LEAVES** are succulent, bluish green and semicircular in cross
section. **STATUS** Locally common in SE England.

Sand Dart *Agrotis ripae*, a moth
whose larvae feed on a range
of sand-dune plants, notably
Prickly Saltwort and
Sea Rocket.

Prickly Saltwort, flowers

Prickly Saltwort
Salsola kali Height to 50cm
Prickly annual of sandy beaches,
usually growing near the strandline.
FLOWERS are tiny and yellowish,
appearing at leaf bases (Jul–Oct).
FRUITS are similar to flowers. **LEAVES**
are swollen, flattened-cylindrical
and spiny-tipped. **STATUS** Locally
common.

Sea Sandwort
Honckenya peploides Prostrate
Mat-forming perennial that is
familiar on stabilised coastal shingle
and sandy beaches. **FLOWERS** are
greenish white and 6–8mm across (May–Aug). Petals are
slightly shorter than sepals. **FRUITS** are yellowish green and
pea-like. **LEAVES** are oval and fleshy; borne as opposite pairs
on creeping stems. **STATUS** Locally common on most suitable
coasts.

Coast Dart *Euxoa cursoria*, a moth
whose larvae feed on a range of
plants of sandy shores, notably
Sea Sandwort.

Sea Purslane

Common Glasswort

Common Glasswort, flowers

Perennial Glasswort

Annual Sea-blite

Shrubby Sea-blite

Prickly Saltwort

Sea Sandwort

Sea Mouse-ear *Cerastium diffusum* Height to 20cm
Low annual that is sometimes prostrate. Covered in sticky hairs and found on sandy ground, mainly near the sea. FLOWERS are white and 3–6mm across, with notched petals (Apr–Jul). FRUITS are capsules. LEAVES are ovate and dark green; bracts do not have transparent margins. STATUS Locally common.

Sea Pearlwort *Sagina maritima* Height to 8cm
Wiry but fleshy annual. Found on bare, dry ground, mainly near the sea. FLOWERS have minute greenish petals and 4 longer purplish sepals that do not spread in fruit (May–Sep). FRUITS are capsules. LEAVES are fleshy and blunt. STATUS Widespread but local.

Procumbent Pearlwort *Sagina procumbens* Prostrate
Creeping perennial of damp, bare ground. Forms mats comprising a central rosette with radiating shoots that root at intervals, giving rise to erect flowering stems. FLOWERS are green, petal-less and borne on side shoots (May–Sep). FRUITS are capsules. LEAVES are narrow; bristle-tipped but not hairy. STATUS Widespread and common on coasts.

Lesser Sea-spurrey *Spergularia marina* Prostrate
Straggly, often stickily hairy annual. Found on drier, grassy upper margins of saltmarshes. FLOWERS are deep pink and 6–8mm across; 5 petals are shorter than sepals (May–Aug). FRUITS are capsules. LEAVES are narrow, fleshy and pointed; in opposite pairs on trailing stems. STATUS Widespread and locally common.

Greater Sea-spurrey *Spergularia media* Height to 10cm
Robust, fleshy perennial associated with drier upper reaches of saltmarshes. FLOWERS are pinkish white and 7–12mm across; 5 petals are longer than sepals (Jun–Sep). FRUITS are capsules. LEAVES are fleshy, bristle-tipped and semicircular in cross section. STATUS Widespread and common around coasts.

Rock Sea-spurrey
Spergularia rupicola Height to 20cm
Stickily hairy perennial, often with purplish stems. Found on cliffs and rocky places near the sea. Sometimes forms clumps with woody bases. FLOWERS are pink, 5-petalled (petals and sepals equal) and 8–10mm across (Jun–Sep). FRUITS are capsules. LEAVES are narrow, flattened and fleshy; borne in whorls. STATUS Locally common in the W.

LEFT: Rock Sea-spurrey, flowers
RIGHT: **Crescent Dart** *Agrotis trux lunigera* (Length 16mm) is a speciality of coastal cliffs in southwest Britain. The moth flies in July and August and its larvae feed mainly on Rock Sea-spurrey and Thrift.

Red Campion *Silene dioica* Height to 1m
Hairy biennial or perennial of hedgerows, grassy banks and cliffs. FLOWERS are reddish pink and 2–3cm across; male flowers are smaller than females and on separate plants (Mar–Oct). FRUITS reveal 10 reflexed teeth when ripe. LEAVES are hairy; borne in opposite pairs. STATUS Widespread and common.

Sea Mouse-ear

Sea Pearlwort

Procumbent Pearlwort

Lesser Sea-spurrey

Greater Sea-spurrey

Rock Sea-spurrey

Red Campion

ABOVE: **Nottingham Catchfly**, in day time

RIGHT: **Yellow Horned-poppy**, flower

Yellow Horned-poppy, fruit

Sea Campion *Silene uniflora* Height to 20cm
Cushion-forming perennial of cliffs and shingle beaches. **FLOWERS** are white and 20–25mm across; on upright stems (Jun–Aug). **FRUITS** are capsules. **LEAVES** are grey-green, waxy and fleshy. **STATUS** Widespread and locally common.

Nottingham Catchfly *Silene nutans* Height to 50cm
Downy, sticky perennial of chalk grassland and shingle beaches. **FLOWERS** are nodding, 17mm across and pollinated by moths; pinkish-white petals are inrolled by day but roll back at dusk (May–Jul). **FRUITS** are capsules. **LEAVES** are oval; lower leaves are stalked, stem leaves are unstalked. **STATUS** Local.

Sand Catchfly *Silene conica* Height to 35cm
Stickily hairy annual of sandy coastal soils. **FLOWERS** are 4–5mm across with 5 notched and pinkish petals (May–Jul). **FRUITS** form within inflated, flagon-shaped capsules. **LEAVES** are narrow and downy. **STATUS** Scarce; mainly coastal SE England.

Yellow Horned-poppy
Glaucium flavum Height to 50cm
Blue-grey clump-forming perennial of shingle beaches. **FLOWERS** are 6–9cm across with yellow petals (Jun–Sep). **FRUITS** are elongated, curved capsules up to 30cm long. **LEAVES** are pinnately divided; clasping upper leaves have shallow, toothed lobes. **STATUS** Locally common but absent from the far N.

Danish Scurvygrass *Cochlearia danica* Height to 20cm
Compact, often prostrate annual of sand, shingle and walls, mainly on coasts. **FLOWERS** are 4–6mm across with 4 white petals (Jan–Aug). **FRUITS** are ovoid and 6mm long. **LEAVES** comprise long-stalked heart-shaped basal leaves and stalked ivy-shaped stem leaves. **STATUS** Widespread and common around most coasts.

English Scurvygrass *Cochlearia anglica* Height to 35cm
Biennial or perennial of estuaries and mudflats. **FLOWERS** are 10–14mm across with 4 white petals (Apr–Jul). **FRUITS** are elliptical and 10–15mm long. **LEAVES** are long-stalked and narrow; stem leaves clasp stem. **STATUS** Locally common.

Common Scurvygrass *Cochlearia officinalis* Height to 50cm
Biennial or perennial of saltmarshes, coastal walls and cliffs. **FLOWERS** are 8–10mm across with 4 white petals (Apr–Oct). **FRUITS** are rounded to ovoid, 4–7mm long and longer than stalk. **LEAVES** are kidney-shaped at base, arrow-shaped on stem. **STATUS** Widespread and locally common.

Common Whitlowgrass
Erophila verna Height to 20cm
Variable hairy annual of dry, bare places. **FLOWERS** are 3–6mm across with 4 deeply notched whitish petals (Mar–May). **FRUITS** are stalked elliptical pods. **LEAVES** are narrow and toothed; form a basal rosette. **STATUS** Widespread and common.

Common Whitlowgrass

Sea Campion

Nottingham Catchfly, at night

Sand Catchfly

Yellow Horned-poppy

Danish Scurvygrass

English Scurvygrass

Common Scurvygrass

Common Whitlowgrass

Yellow Whitlowgrass *Draba aizoides* Height to 12cm
Compact, tufted perennial of limestone cliffs and walls. **FLOWERS** are 8–9mm across, with 4 yellow petals; in dense, terminal clusters (Mar–May). **FRUITS** are elliptical and 8–12mm long. **LEAVES** are narrow, with marginal and terminal bristles; appear as a basal rosette. **STATUS** Rare; Gower Peninsula only.

Shepherd's-cress *Teesdalia nudicaulis* Height to 25cm
Tufted, often hairless annual of bare, sandy ground and shingle. **FLOWERS** are 2mm across with 4 white petals, 2 of which are shorter than others (Apr–Jun). **FRUITS** are heart-shaped and notched. **LEAVES** are pinnately lobed and form a basal rosette. **STATUS** Locally common in the S; rare elsewhere. (*See also* Hutchinsia, p. 17.)

Wild Cabbage *Brassica oleracea* Height to 1.25m
Tough perennial of chalk cliffs and seabird colonies. **FLOWERS** are 25–35mm across; borne in elongated heads (Apr–Aug). **FRUITS** are cylindrical and 8cm long. **LEAVES** are grey-green; lower leaves are fleshy and often eaten by larvae of the Large White butterfly (p. 184). **STATUS** Local; mainly SW England and W Wales.

Wild Cabbage

Lundy Cabbage
Coincya wrightii Height to 90cm
Impressive perennial. **FLOWERS** are 8–12mm across with 4 yellow petals; borne in showy heads (May–Jun). **FRUITS** are elongated pods. **LEAVES** are grey-green and cabbage-like. **STATUS** Restricted to Lundy Island in the Bristol Channel, where it is very locally common. NOTE Sole foodplant for 2 beetles endemic to Lundy: Bronze Lundy Cabbage Leaf Beetle *Psylliodes luridipennis* and Lundy Cabbage Weevil *Ceutorhynchus contractus* ssp. *pallipes*.

Lundy Cabbage

ABOVE: Bronze Lundy Cabbage Leaf Beetle
RIGHT: Lundy Cabbage Weevil

Perennial Wall-rocket
Perennial Wall-rocket

Diplotaxis tenuifolia Height to 80cm
Branched perennial with a strong smell of culinary Rocket when crushed; waste ground, usually near the sea. **FLOWERS** are 15–30mm across with 4 petals (May–Sep). **FRUITS** are cylindrical with 2 rows of seeds. **LEAVES** are pinnately lobed. **STATUS** Commonest near coasts in S England, particularly the Thames Estuary.

Hoary Stock *Matthiola incana* Height to 80cm
Downy greyish annual or perennial with a woody base to stem. Grows on sea cliffs. **FLOWERS** are fragrant and 25–50mm across, with 4 white to purple petals (Apr–Jul). **FRUITS** are cylindrical pods up to 13cm long. **LEAVES** are narrow and untoothed. **STATUS** Scarce and doubtfully native, although possibly so in S England and S Wales.

Sea Stock *Matthiola sinuata* Height to 80cm
Downy grey-green perennial with a non-woody base. Grows on coastal dunes and cliffs. **FLOWERS** are fragrant and 25–50mm across, with 4 pinkish petals (Jun–Aug). **FRUITS** are narrow, elongated pods. **LEAVES** are narrow with toothed or lobed margins. **STATUS** Rare; SW Britain and Channel Islands only.

Yellow Whitlowgrass

Shepherd's-cress

Wild Cabbage

Lundy Cabbage

Perennial Wall-rocket

Hoary Stock

Sea Stock

Black Mustard *Brassica nigra* Height to 2m
Robust greyish annual of sea cliffs and waste ground. **FLOWERS** are 12–15mm across with 4 yellow petals (May–Aug). **FRUITS** are flattened and pressed close to stem. **LEAVES** are stalked, the lower ones pinnately lobed and bristly. **STATUS** Locally common in England and Wales; rather scarce elsewhere.

Sea Radish *Raphanus raphanistrum* ssp. *maritimus* Height to 60cm
Robust, roughly hairy annual. Found on stabilised shingle, sand dunes and coastal grassland. **FLOWERS** are yellow (May–Jul). **FRUITS** are pods with up to 5 beaded segments. **LEAVES** comprise pinnate lower leaves and narrow, entire upper leaves. **STATUS** Locally common in the S and SW only.

Black
Mustard

Sea
Radish

Sea Radish,
fruit

Sea Rocket *Cakile maritima* Height to 25cm
Straggling, fleshy, hairless annual of sandy and shingle beaches. **FLOWERS** are 6–12mm across, pink or pale lilac; borne in terminal clusters (Jun–Sep). **FRUITS** are waisted pods, the upper half largest. **LEAVES** are shiny and pinnately lobed. **STATUS** Widespread and locally common.

Sea
Rocket

Sea-kale
Crambe maritima Height to 50cm
Robust perennial. Forms expansive domed clumps on shingle and sandy beaches. **FLOWERS** are 6–12mm across with 4 whitish petals; in flat-topped clusters (Jun–Aug). **FRUITS** are oval pods. **LEAVES** are fleshy with wavy margins; lower leaves are 25cm long and long-stalked. **STATUS** Very locally common around coasts of England, Wales and Ireland.

Sea
Kale

Sea Kale, leaves

English Stonecrop
Sedum anglicum Height to 5cm
Mat-forming perennial with wiry stems. Found on rocky ground, shingle and old walls. **FLOWERS** are star-shaped and 12mm across, with 5 white petals that are pink below (Jun–Sep). **FRUITS** are dry and red. **LEAVES** are 3–5mm long, fleshy and often tinged red. **STATUS** Widespread and locally common, especially in the W.

Biting Stonecrop *Sedum acre* Height to 10cm
Mat-forming perennial of well-drained ground such as sand dunes and old walls. **FLOWERS** are star-shaped and 10–12mm across, with 5 bright yellow petals (May–Jul). **FRUITS** are dry and splitting. **LEAVES** are fleshy, crowded and pressed close to stem; they taste hot. **STATUS** Widespread and locally common.

Burnet Rose, fruit

Burnet Rose *Rosa pimpinellifolia* Height to 50cm
Clump-forming shrub whose suckers and stems bear numerous straight thorns and stiff bristles. Associated mainly with sand dunes and calcareous grassland. **FLOWERS** are 3–5cm across with 5 creamy-white petals; usually solitary (May–Jul). **FRUITS** are spherical, 5–6mm across and purplish black when ripe. **LEAVES** comprise 7–11 oval leaflets. **STATUS** Widespread, but only locally common.

Burnet
Rose

Black Mustard

Sea Radish

Sea Rocket

Sea Kale

English Stonecrop

Biting Stonecrop

Burnet Rose

Bramble *Rubus fruticosus* Height to 3m
Scrambling shrub with arching,
rooting stems, armed with variably
shaped prickles. Major component
of coastal scrub. **FLOWERS** are 2–3cm
across and white or pink
(May–Aug). **FRUITS** are
familiar blackberries.
LEAVES have 3–5
toothed leaflets. **STATUS**
Widespread and common.

Bramble,
fruits

Bramble, flowers

Silverweed
Potentilla anserina Creeping
Low-growing perennial with long, creeping stems.
Found in damp grassy places and on bare ground. **FLOWERS** are 15–20mm across with
5 yellow petals (May–Aug). **FRUITS** are dry and papery. **LEAVES** are divided into up to 12
pairs of leaflets covered in silvery silky hairs. **STATUS** Widespread and common.

Gorse *Ulex europaeus* Height to 2m
Evergreen shrub with straight, grooved spines, 15–25mm long.
Favours coastal slopes, mainly on acid soils. **FLOWERS** are 2cm
long, yellow and coconut-scented, with 4–5mm-long basal bracts
(Jan–Dec, but mainly Feb–May). **FRUITS** are hairy pods. **LEAVES**
are trifoliate when young. **STATUS** Widespread and common.

Western Gorse *Ulex gallii* Height to 1.5m
Dense evergreen shrub with spines that are almost smooth
and 25mm long. Found on acid soils, often near coasts. **FLOWERS**
are 10–15mm long and yellow, with 0.5mm-long basal bracts
(Jul–Sep). **FRUITS** are hairy pods. **LEAVES** are trifoliate when young.
STATUS Restricted mainly to W Britain and Ireland; common on
coastal cliffs in the W.

Silverweed

Broom
Cytisus scoparius Height to 2m
Branched, spineless deciduous
shrub with ridged, 5-angled green
twigs. Favours acid soils. **FLOWERS**
are 2cm long, bright yellow; solitary
or in pairs (Apr–Jun). **FRUITS** are
oblong blackening pods that explode
on dry, sunny days. **LEAVES** are usually
trifoliate. **STATUS** Widespread and
common on coasts.

Hairy Greenweed
Genista pilosa Height to 1m, but often prostrate
Low-growing shrub of maritime heaths
and sea cliffs. **FLOWERS** are yellow and
borne in terminal heads (May–Jun). **LEAVES**
are silvery-downy below. **STATUS** Very locally
common, on the N Cornish coast and in W Wales.

Broom, flowers

Sea Pea *Lathyrus japonicus* Height to 12cm
Spreading grey-green perennial with stems up to 1m long. Entirely restricted to coastal
shingle and sand. **FLOWERS** are 2cm long and purple, fading to blue; in heads of 2–15
flowers (Jun–Aug). **FRUITS** are swollen pods, 5cm long. **LEAVES** comprise 2–5 pairs of
oval leaflets and angular stipules. **STATUS** Local; mainly in S and E England.

Bramble

Silverweed

Gorse

Western Gorse

Broom

Hairy Greenweed

Sea Pea

Wood Vetch *Vicia sylvatica* Height to 1.5m
Elegant straggling perennial of coastal slopes. **FLOWERS** are 12–20mm long, white and purple-veined; in spikes of up to 20 flowers (Jun–Aug). **FRUITS** are hairless black pods. **LEAVES** comprise 6–12 pairs of oblong leaflets and end in a branched tendril. **STATUS** Widespread, local and commonest in the W.

Spring Vetch *Vicia lathyroides* Height to 20cm
Delicate annual of coastal grassland on sandy soils. **FLOWERS** are 5–8mm long, reddish purple and solitary (Apr–Jun). **FRUITS** are black pods. **LEAVES** comprise 2–4 pairs of bristle-tipped leaflets and unbranched tendrils. **STATUS** Widespread but local.

Wood
Vetch

Tufted Vetch *Vicia cracca* Height to 2m
Scrambling scrub and grassland perennial. **FLOWERS** are 8–12mm long and bluish purple; in 1-sided spikes up to 8cm tall (Jun–Aug). **FRUITS** are hairless pods. **LEAVES** comprise up to 12 pairs of leaflets and a branched tendril. **STATUS** Widespread and common.

Common Restharrow *Ononis repens* Height to 70cm
Creeping, woody perennial with spineless stems. Found on calcareous soils. **FLOWERS** are 10–15mm long and pink, and wings and keel are of similar length; in clusters (Jul–Sep). **FRUITS** are pods that are shorter than calyx. **LEAVES** are stickily hairy and trifoliate, with oval leaflets. **STATUS** Locally common.

Tufted
Vetch

Spiny Restharrow *Ononis spinosa* Height to 70cm
Similar to Common Restharrow (above) but upright, with spiny stems. Favours grassland on heavy soils. **FLOWERS** are 10–15mm long and deep pink, with wings shorter than keel (Jul–Sep). **FRUITS** are pods that are longer than calyx. **LEAVES** are trifoliate with narrow, oval leaflets. **STATUS** Local, mainly in England.

Common
Bird's-foot
Trefoil

Kidney Vetch *Anthyllis vulneraria* Height to 30cm
Silky perennial of calcareous grassland and coastal slopes. **FLOWERS** are yellow, orange or red; in paired kidney-shaped heads, 3cm across (May–Sep). **FRUITS** are short pods. **LEAVES** comprise pairs of narrow leaflets, the terminal one being the largest. **STATUS** Widespread and locally common.

Common Bird's-foot Trefoil
Lotus corniculatus Height to 10cm
Sprawling grassland perennial. **FLOWERS** are red in bud, and yellow and 15mm long when open; in heads on stalks to 8cm long (May–Sep). **FRUITS** are slender pods; splayed like a bird's foot when ripe. **LEAVES** have 5 leaflets. **STATUS** Widespread and common.

Black
Medick

Black Medick
Medicago lupulina Height to 20cm
Downy annual of short grassland. **FLOWERS** are small and yellow; in dense spherical heads (8–9mm across) of 10–50 flowers (Apr–Oct). **FRUITS** are spirally coiled, spineless and ripen black. **LEAVES** are trifoliate. **STATUS** Widespread and common.

Black Medick,
fruits

Wood Vetch

Spring Vetch

Tufted Vetch

Common Restharrow

Spiny Restharrow

Kidney Vetch

Common Bird's-foot Trefoil

Black Medick

Orange Bird's-foot, fruits

Bird's-foot
Ornithopus perpusillus Height to 30cm
Low-growing, often trailing downy annual of dry, sandy places. **FLOWERS** are 3–5mm long, creamy and red-veined; in heads of 3–8 flowers (May–Aug). **FRUITS** are constricted pods, arranged like a bird's foot when ripe. **LEAVES** comprise 5–13 pairs of leaflets. **STATUS** Locally common on English and Welsh coasts.

Orange Bird's-foot
Ornithopus pinnatus Height to 20cm
Straggly annual of maritime heaths. **FLOWERS** are orange-yellow and usually paired (Apr–Sep). **FRUITS** are constricted pods, arranged like a bird's foot when ripe. **LEAVES** comprise usually 3 pairs of leaflets plus a terminal one. **STATUS** Local on Isles of Scilly (especially Tresco) and Channel Islands.

Hare's-foot Clover
Trifolium arvense Height to 25cm
Spreading annual, covered in soft hairs. Grows in dry, grassy areas, on sandy or gravelly soils. **FLOWERS** are pale pink and shorter than filament-like calyx teeth; in dense egg-shaped to cylindrical heads that are 2–3cm long (Jun–Sep). **FRUITS** are concealed by calyx. **LEAVES** are trifoliate and comprise narrow leaflets. **STATUS** Widespread and locally common in England and Wales; absent from N Scotland and mainly coastal in Ireland.

Rough Clover *Trifolium scabrum* Height to 15cm
Downy annual of bare grassland, often on gravel. **FLOWERS** are white; in unstalked heads that are 10mm long (May–Jul). **FRUITS** are concealed by calyx. **LEAVES** are trifoliate with oval leaflets, hairy on both sides, and with lateral veins. **STATUS** Locally common on coasts of S England and S Wales.

Knotted Clover *Trifolium striatum* Height to 20cm
Hairy annual of dry, grassy places, usually near coasts. **FLOWERS** are pink; in unstalked egg-shaped heads that are 15mm long (May–Jul). **FRUITS** are concealed by calyx. **LEAVES** are trifoliate with spoon-shaped leaflets, hairy on both sides and without obvious lateral veins. **STATUS** Locally common in the S.

Subterranean Clover *Trifolium subterraneum* Prostrate
Low-growing hairy annual, found in short grassland on sand and gravel, usually near coasts. **FLOWERS** are 8–12mm long and creamy white; in clusters of 2–6 in leaf axils (May–Jun). **FRUITS** are pods that 'burrow' into the soil, pushed by elongating stalks. **LEAVES** are trifoliate, with broadly oval, notched leaflets. **STATUS** Local, mainly in the S.

Subterranean
Clover

Suffocated Clover *Trifolium suffocatum* Prostrate
Low-growing annual of coastal sand and gravel. Easily overlooked because it soon withers and dries. **FLOWERS** are small and whitish; in clusters surrounded by leaves (Apr–May). **FRUITS** are pods. **LEAVES** are trifoliate and long-stalked. **STATUS** Local, mainly on S coast of England.

Orange Bird's-foot

Hare's-foot Clover

Rough Clover

Subterranean Clover

Bird's-foot

Knotted Clover

Suffocated Clover

Strawberry Clover *Trifolium fragiferum* Height to 15cm
Perennial with creeping stems that root at nodes. Found in grassy places, mostly on clay near the sea. **FLOWERS** are pink; borne in globular heads, 10–15mm across (Jul–Sep). **FRUITS** are inflated pinkish heads that resemble pale berries. **LEAVES** are trifoliate, with unmarked oval leaflets. **STATUS** Local in the S.

Bird's-foot Clover *Trifolium ornithopodioides* Prostrate
Low-growing, hairless annual of bare coastal grassland. **FLOWERS** are 5–8mm long, white or pale pink; in heads of 1–5 flowers (May–Oct). **FRUITS** are small pods. **LEAVES** are trifoliate, with toothed oval leaflets. **STATUS** Very local in S England, S Wales and S Ireland.

Long-headed Clover *Trifolium incarnatum* ssp. *molinerii* Height to 30cm
Robust, downy annual of coastal cliffs. **FLOWERS** are pale pink; in cylindrical heads, 3–4cm long (May–Jun). **FRUITS** are inflated heads with spreading calyx teeth. **LEAVES** are trifoliate with oval leaflets. **STATUS** Very locally common on the Lizard Peninsula and Jersey.

Sea Clover *Trifolium squamosum* Height to 30cm
Downy annual of coastal grassland and sea walls. **FLOWERS** are pinkish; borne in rounded to egg-shaped heads, 1cm long (Jun–Jul). **FRUITS** resemble miniature teasel heads. **LEAVES** are trifoliate. **STATUS** Local in S England; Thames and Severn estuaries are strongholds.

White Clover

Red Clover

Red Clover
Trifolium pratense Height to 40cm
Downy grassland perennial. **FLOWERS** are pinkish red; in dense, unstalked heads, 2–3cm across (May–Oct). **FRUITS** are concealed by calyx. **LEAVES** are trifoliate, with oval leaflets marked with a white crescent; stipules are triangular and bristle-tipped. **STATUS** Widespread and often very common.

White Clover
Trifolium repens Height to 40cm
Creeping, hairless perennial that roots at nodes. Found in grassy places. **FLOWERS** are creamy white, becoming brown with age; in long-stalked rounded heads, 2cm across (May–Oct). **FRUITS** are concealed by calyx. **LEAVES** are trifoliate; rounded leaflets have a white mark and translucent lateral veins. **STATUS** Widespread and often very common.

Western Clover *Trifolium occidentale* Prostrate
Low-growing perennial of bare coastal ground. Recalls White Clover (above). **FLOWERS** are mostly creamy white but reddish towards centre of flower heads, which are 2cm across (Apr–Jul). **FRUITS** are concealed by calyx. **LEAVES** are trifoliate, with unmarked leaflets. **STATUS** Locally common in Cornwall and the Channel Islands.

Strawberry Clover

Bird's-foot Clover

Sea Clover

Long-headed Clover

Red Clover

White Clover

Western Clover

Sea Stork's-bill, flower

Sea Stork's-bill *Erodium maritimum* Usually prostrate
Stickily hairy annual of bare coastal ground. FLOWERS are 3–5mm across; petals are tiny, whitish, often absent and usually fall by 9am (May–Jul). FRUITS are long and beak-like. LEAVES are oval, lobed and stalked. STATUS Local, commonest in the SW.

Musk Stork's-bill *Erodium moschatum* Height to 25cm
Stickily hairy annual of maritime sandy soils and bare coastal ground; smells of musk. FLOWERS are 25–30mm across with pink petals that are easily lost; in dense heads (May–Jul). FRUITS are long and beak-like. LEAVES are pinnate, with toothed oval lobes and broad stipules. STATUS Local, mainly in the SW.

Common Stork's-bill *Erodium cicutarium* Height to 30cm
Stickily hairy annual of bare grassy places near the sea. FLOWERS are 8–14mm across with pink petals that are easily lost; in loose heads (May–Aug). FRUITS are long and beak-like. LEAVES are finely divided and feathery; stipules are narrow. STATUS Widespread and locally common, especially on the S coast of England.

Common Stork's-bill

Herb-Robert

Herb-Robert
Geranium robertianum Height to 30cm
Hairy annual of hedgerows and banks; also grows on shingle. FLOWERS are 12–15mm across with pink petals and orange pollen; in loose clusters (Apr–Oct). FRUITS are hairy with a long 'beak'. LEAVES are hairy and deeply cut into 3 or 5 pinnately divided lobes; often tinged red. STATUS Widespread and common.

BELOW: Sea Heath, flowers

Little Robin *Geranium purpureum* Height to 30cm
Similar to Herb-Robert (above) but more slender and often tinged red. Restricted to coastal banks and shingle. FLOWERS are 7–14mm across with pink petals and yellow pollen (Apr–Sep). FRUITS are distinctly wrinkled. LEAVES are hairy and deeply cut into 3 or 5 pinnately divided lobes. STATUS Local in S Britain.

Sea-heath *Frankenia laevis* Prostrate
Branched, mat-forming woody perennial. Grows on upper reaches of saltmarshes. FLOWERS are 5mm across with 5 crinkly pink petals (Jun–Aug). FRUITS are capsules. LEAVES are small and narrow with inrolled margins; densely packed and opposite. STATUS Local, mainly in S and SE England.

Dune Pansy *Viola tricolor* ssp. *curtisii* Height to 12cm
Perennial of dry coastal grassland. FLOWERS are 15–25mm long and yellow (Apr–Aug). FRUITS are egg-shaped. LEAVES are narrow with leaf-like stipules. STATUS Local on coasts of W Britain.

Dwarf Pansy *Viola kitaibeliana* Height to 10cm
Low-growing annual of bare dune grassland. FLOWERS are 5mm long, whitish with a yellow centre and purple veins (Apr–May). FRUITS are egg-shaped. LEAVES are rounded and stalked. STATUS Found on Bryher in the Isles of Scilly, and on the Channel Islands.

Sea Stork's-bill

Musk Stork's-bill

Common Stork's-bill

Herb-Robert

Little Robin

Sea-heath

Dune Pansy

Dwarf Pansy

Sea Spurge *Euphorbia paralias* Height to 60cm
Upright perennial of sandy beaches and dunes. **FLOWERS** are yellowish with petal-like bracts and horned lobes (petals and sepals are absent); in umbel-like heads (Jun–Oct). **FRUITS** are smooth. **LEAVES** are grey-green, fleshy and closely packed up stems. **STATUS** Widespread and locally common on coasts of S and W England, Wales and Ireland.

Portland Spurge *Euphorbia portlandica* Height to 40cm
Hairless greyish perennial; branches at base. Found in coastal grassland and on sea cliffs. **FLOWERS** have lobes with long, crescent-shaped horns (petals and sepals are absent); in umbel-like clusters (Apr–Sep). **FRUITS** are rough. **LEAVES** are spoon-shaped with a prominent midrib. **STATUS** Locally common on coasts of SW and W Britain.

Common Mallow

Marsh-mallow

Common Mallow *Malva sylvestris* Height to 1.5m
Perennial of disturbed coastal ground. **FLOWERS** are 25–40mm across with 5 purple-veined pink petals, much longer than sepals; in clusters from leaf axils (Jun–Oct). **FRUITS** are round, flat capsules. **LEAVES** are rounded at base of plant, 5-lobed on stem. **STATUS** Widespread and common only in the S.

Tree Mallow *Lavatera arborea*
Height to 3m
Imposing woody biennial, covered in starry hairs. Favours rocky coasts, often near seabird colonies. **FLOWERS** are 3–5cm across, with dark-veined pinkish-purple petals; borne in terminal clusters (Jun–Sep). **FRUITS** are round, flat capsules. **LEAVES** are 5–7-lobed. **STATUS** Locally common on W coasts of Britain and S and W Ireland.

Marsh-mallow *Althaea officinalis* Height to 2m
Attractive downy perennial with starry hairs; very soft to the touch. Found in coastal wetlands and upper reaches of saltmarshes. **FLOWERS** are 35–40mm across and pale pink (Aug–Sep). **FRUITS** are flat, rounded capsules. **LEAVES** are triangular with shallow lobes. **STATUS** Locally common on S coasts of Britain and Ireland.

Common Evening-primrose
Oenothera biennis Height to 1.5m
Downy biennial of waste ground and dunes. **FLOWERS** are 4–5cm across, yellow, and open only on dull days or evenings (Jun–Sep). **FRUITS** are capsules. **LEAVES** are lanceolate with red veins. **STATUS** Locally common naturalised alien.

Marsh Pennywort *Hydrocotyle vulgaris* Creeping
Low-growing perennial and an atypical umbellifer. Found in damp grassy vegetation, often in dune-slacks. **FLOWERS** are tiny, pinkish and hidden by the leaves; borne in small umbels (Jun–Aug). **FRUITS** are rounded and ridged. **LEAVES** are round and dimpled, with broad, blunt teeth. **STATUS** Widespread, but commonest in the W.

Marsh Pennywort, flowers

Sea Spurge

Portland Spurge

Common Mallow

Tree Mallow

Marsh-mallow

Common Evening-primrose

Marsh Pennywort

Slender Hare's-ear *Bupleurum tenuissimum* Height to 50cm
Slender, easily overlooked annual. Restricted to coastal
grassland. FLOWERS are yellow and borne in tiny umbels,
3–4mm across, surrounded by bracts and arising from leaf
axils (Jul–Sep). FRUITS are globular. LEAVES are narrow and
pointed. STATUS Local; coastal S and E England only.

Sea-holly *Eryngium maritimum*
Height to 60cm
Distinctive hairless perennial
of coastal shingle and sand.
FLOWERS are blue; borne in
globular umbels, up to 4cm long
(Jul–Sep). FRUITS are bristly.
LEAVES are waxy, blue-green
and Holly-like, with spiny white
margins and white veins. STATUS
Widespread only on the coasts of
England, Wales and Ireland.

Slender Hare's-ear

Sea-holly

Alexanders *Smyrnium olusatrum* Height to 1.25m
Stout and sometimes clump-forming, hairless biennial.
Favours disturbed coastal ground, hedgerows and tracksides,
mainly on calcareous soils. FLOWERS are yellowish; borne in umbels, 4–6cm across, with
7–15 rays (Mar–Jun). FRUITS are globular, ridged and black when ripe. LEAVES are dark
green, shiny and 3 times trifoliate. STATUS Introduced and alarmingly invasive, mainly
on S and SE coasts of England and Ireland.

Scot's Lovage *Ligusticum scoticum* Height to 80cm
Robust hairless perennial, often forming sizeable clumps. Stems are ribbed and purplish,
and hollow towards base. Found on cliffs and stabilised coastal grassland. FLOWERS are
white; borne in flat-topped umbels, 4–6cm across, on long reddish stalks
(Jun–Aug). FRUITS are oval and flattened, with 4 wings. LEAVES are bright
green, shiny and 2 times trifoliate, with oval leaflets and inflated, sheathing
stalks. STATUS Locally common on Scottish and N Irish coasts.

Rock-samphire *Crithmum maritimum* Height to 40cm
Spreading, branched, hairless perennial of maritime rocky habitats and
stabilised coastal shingle. FLOWERS are greenish yellow; borne in umbels,
3–6cm across, with 8–30 rays and numerous bracts (Jun–Sep). FRUITS are
egg-shaped, ridged and corky. LEAVES are divided into narrow, fleshy
lobes, triangular in cross section. STATUS Widespread and common
around coasts of S and W Britain and Ireland.

Corky-fruited Water-dropwort *Oenanthe pimpinelloides* Height to 1m
Upright, hairless perennial with solid, ridged stems. Favours damp grassy
places near coasts, particularly on clay soils. FLOWERS are white; borne in flat-
topped terminal umbels, 2–6cm across, with 6–15 rays (May–Aug). FRUITS are
cylindrical, with swollen
corky bases. LEAVES are
1- or 2-pinnate with
narrowly oval to wedge-
shaped leaflets. STATUS
Scarce and only locally
common, in S England.

Corky-fruited
Water-dropwort

Corky-fruited
Water-dropwort,
fruit

Corky-fruited Water-dropwort,
flower

Slender Hare's-ear

Sea-holly

Alexanders

Scot's Lovage

Corky-fruited Water-dropwort

Rock-samphire

Wild Celery *Apium graveolens* Height to 1m
Upright, hairless biennial with a strong smell of celery. Stems are solid and grooved. Favours rough coastal grassland. FLOWERS are white; borne in short-stalked or unstalked umbels, 3–6cm across (Jun–Aug). FRUITS are globular. LEAVES are shiny and pinnate; basal leaves are 1- or 2-pinnate with toothed diamond-shaped lobes; stem leaves appear trifoliate. STATUS Commonest in coastal S England.

Sea Carrot *Daucus carota* ssp. *gummifer* Height to 75cm
Hairy perennial with solid, ridged stems. Found in rough coastal grassland and on cliffs. FLOWERS are white (pinkish in bud); in stalked, flattish umbels, up to 7cm across, with a red central flower and divided bracts beneath (Jun–Sep). FRUITS are oval, with spiny ridges; fruiting umbels are flat. LEAVES are 2- or 3-pinnate with narrow, slightly fleshy leaflets. STATUS Widespread and locally common in SW Britain only. NOTE Subspecies *D. c. carota* (known as Wild Carrot) is widespread inland, less so near coasts; it has less fleshy leaves and concave umbels in fruit.

Hog's Fennel

Honewort *Trinia glauca* Height to 15cm
Hairless grey-green waxy perennial of short grassland on limestone soils. FLOWERS are white, borne on separate-sex plants; male umbels are 1cm across, females 3cm across (May–Jun). FRUITS are egg-shaped and ridged. LEAVES are 2- or 3-pinnate with narrow lobes. STATUS Rare; S Devon and N Somerset only.

Hog's Fennel *Peucedanum officinale* Height to 1.5m
Hairless, dark green perennial with solid stems. Restricted to coastal grassland on clay soils. FLOWERS are deep yellow and borne in open umbels, 15–20cm across (Jul–Sep). FRUITS are narrowly ovate. LEAVES are 4- to 6-trifoliate with flattened, narrow segments. STATUS Restricted to a few sites on the Thames Estuary. Locally abundant beside Faversham Creek, Kent.

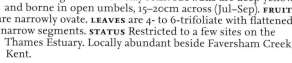

Sea-milkwort *Glaux maritima* Height to 10cm
Low-growing and usually creeping, hairless perennial of upper reaches of saltmarshes and sea walls. FLOWERS are 5–6mm across and comprise 5 pink petal-like sepals; borne on upright shoots (May–Sep). FRUITS are dark brown capsules. LEAVES are ovate, succulent and borne in opposite pairs on trailing stems. STATUS Widespread and locally common throughout.

Fisher's Estuarine Moth *Gortyna borelii*, a moth whose larvae feed exclusively inside the stems and roots of Hog's Fennel.

Brookweed *Samolus valerandi* Height to 12cm
Hairless, pale green perennial of damp saline or calcareous soils. FLOWERS are 2–3mm across with 5 white petals, joined to halfway; in terminal clusters (Jun–Aug). FRUITS are spherical capsules. LEAVES are spoon-shaped; they appear mainly as a basal rosette. STATUS Widespread but local and mainly coastal.

Bog Pimpernel *Anagallis tenella* Creeping
Delicate, hairless perennial with trailing stems. Grows on damp coastal ground, including dune slacks, mainly on acid soils. FLOWERS are pink and funnel-shaped with 5 lobes, to 1cm long; on slender, upright stalks (Jun–Aug). FRUITS are capsules. LEAVES are rounded, short-stalked and paired. STATUS Widespread and locally common only in W.

Brookweed, flowers

Wild Celery

Sea Carrot

Honewort

Hog's Fennel

Sea-milkwort

Brookweed

Bog Pimpernel

Cornish Heath, flowers

Heather *Calluna vulgaris* Height to 50cm

Dense evergreen undershrub of acids soils on coastal heaths. FLOWERS are 4–5mm long, bell-shaped, and usually pink but sometimes white; borne in spikes (Aug–Sep). FRUITS are capsules. LEAVES are short, narrow and borne in 4 rows along stem. STATUS Widespread and locally common on suitable soils.

Bell Heather *Erica cinerea* Height to 50cm

Hairless evergreen undershrub of acid soils; favours drier locations than Heather (above). FLOWERS are 5–6mm long, bell-shaped and purplish red; in spike-like heads (Jun–Sep). FRUITS are capsules. LEAVES are narrow, dark green and borne in whorls of 3 up the wiry stems. STATUS Widespread and locally common, on N and W coasts.

Cornish Heath *Erica vagans* Height to 90cm

Low shrubs that cover extensive areas on suitable soils, mainly on the Lizard Peninsula, Cornwall. FLOWERS are small and pale pink; in tall, dense spikes (Aug–Sep). FRUITS are capsules. LEAVES are narrow and arranged in 4s or 5s. STATUS Locally dominant in a few locations on the Lizard Peninsula, notably Kynance Cove.

Common Centaury, flowers

Common Centaury

Centaurium erythraea Height to 25cm
Variable hairless annual, found in coastal grassland and on sand dunes. FLOWERS are 10–15mm across, unstalked, pink and with 5 petal-like lobes, opening fully only in sunshine; in terminal clusters and on side shoots (Jun–Sep). FRUITS are capsules. LEAVES are grey-green and oval, those on stem narrower than basal leaves (10–20mm across), which form a rosette. STATUS Widespread and common, except in Scotland.

Seaside Centaury

Centaurium littorale Height to 15cm
Similar to Common Centaury (above) but more compact, with subtle differences in the leaves and flowers. Associated with sandy coastal ground, mainly in the N. FLOWERS are 10–16mm across, unstalked and pink, with 5 petal-like lobes; in dense, flat-topped clusters (Jun–Aug). FRUITS are capsules. LEAVES are grey-green; basal leaves form a rosette and are 4–5mm wide, while stem leaves are narrower still and parallel-sided. STATUS Locally common on coasts of N and NW Britain.

Lesser Centaury *Centaurium pulchellum* Height to 15cm

Slender annual that usually branches from near the base. Recalls Common Centaury (above) but lacks a basal rosette of leaves. FLOWERS are 5–8mm across, short-stalked and dark pink; in open clusters (Jun–Sep). FRUITS are capsules. LEAVES are narrowly ovate and appear only on stems. STATUS Widespread but local in England and Wales only; mainly coastal and commonest in the S.

Round-leaved Wintergreen *Pyrola rotundifolia* Height to 20cm

Elegant plant of damp, calcareous soil in wet dune slacks. FLOWERS are 8–12mm across, white and bell-shaped; S-shaped style protrudes beyond petals (May–Aug). FRUITS are capsules. LEAVES are rounded and form a basal rosette. STATUS Widespread but very local.

Round-leaved Wintergreen, flowers

Heather

Bell Heather

Cornish Heath

Common Centaury

Seaside Centaury

Lesser Centaury

Round-leaved
Wintergreen

Agdistis bennetii, a plume moth whose larvae feed only on Common Sea-lavender.

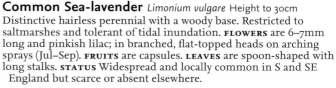

Common Sea-lavender *Limonium vulgare* Height to 30cm
Distinctive hairless perennial with a woody base. Restricted to saltmarshes and tolerant of tidal inundation. FLOWERS are 6–7mm long and pinkish lilac; in branched, flat-topped heads on arching sprays (Jul–Sep). FRUITS are capsules. LEAVES are spoon-shaped with long stalks. STATUS Widespread and locally common in S and SE England but scarce or absent elsewhere.

Lax-flowered Sea-lavender *Limonium humile* Height to 25cm
Similar to Common Sea-lavender (above) but with subtle differences in the appearance of the flower heads and leaves. Restricted to saltmarshes. FLOWERS are 6–7mm long and pinkish lilac; in open, lax clusters with well-spaced flowers; sprays branch below the middle (Jul–Sep). FRUITS are capsules. LEAVES are narrow and long-stalked. STATUS Local in England, Wales and S Scotland; widespread and fairly common on Irish coasts.

Matted Sea-lavender
Limonium bellidifolium Height to 25cm
Recalls Common Sea-lavender (above) but with subtle differences in the appearance of flower heads and leaves; plant branches from near base. Restricted to saltmarshes. FLOWERS are 5–6mm long and pale pinkish lilac; in arching sprays with many non-flowering shoots below. FRUITS are capsules. LEAVES are spoon-shaped and mainly basal; wither before flowering shoots appear. STATUS Locally common on N Norfolk coast only.

Rock Sea-lavender *Limonium binervosum* Height to 30cm
Hairless perennial of coastal cliffs and rocks; occasionally on stabilised shingle beaches. FLOWERS are 6–7mm long and pinkish lilac; in small, well-spaced clusters on sprays that branch from below the middle (Jul–Sep). FRUITS are capsules. LEAVES are narrow and spoon-shaped with winged stalks. STATUS Locally common on suitable coasts.

Portland Sea-lavender *Limonium recurvum* ssp. *portlandicum*
Height to 30cm
Compact perennial that is entirely restricted to coastal limestone cliffs and crags. FLOWERS are 6–7mm long and pinkish lilac; in dense, curved sprays (Jul–Aug). FRUITS are capsules. LEAVES are spoon-shaped and mainly basal. STATUS Entirely restricted to the Isle of Portland, Dorset. NOTE Other *L. recurvum* subspecies occur on nearby calcareous cliffs.

Common
Sea-lavender

Lax-flowered
Sea-lavender

Thrift *Armeria maritima* Height to 20cm
Attractive cushion-forming perennial that often carpets suitable coastal cliffs. Sometimes also grows in saltmarshes. FLOWERS are pink and borne in dense globular heads, 15–25mm across; carried on slender stalks (Apr–Jul). FRUITS are capsules. LEAVES are dark green, long and narrow. STATUS Widespread and locally abundant on suitable coasts. NOTE The sole foodplant for larvae of the **Thrift Clearwing** (p. 188) and **Black-banded** (right) moths.

Black-banded *Polymixis xanthomista*, a moth whose larvae feed almost exclusively on Thrift.

Lax-flowered Sea-lavender

Common Sea-lavender

Matted Sea-lavender

Rock Sea-lavender

Portland Sea-lavender

Thrift

Sea Bindweed *Calystegia soldanella* Creeping
Prostrate perennial of sand dunes; sometimes also on stabilised shingle. **FLOWERS** are 3–5cm across, funnel-shaped, and pink with 5 white stripes; on slender stalks (Jun–Aug). **FRUITS** are capsules. **LEAVES** are kidney-shaped, fleshy, up to 4cm long and long-stalked. **STATUS** Widespread but locally common only in the S.

Oysterplant *Mertensia maritima* Creeping
Spreading plant of stony beaches, often growing around the high-tide mark. **FLOWERS** are bell-shaped, pinkish in bud but soon turning blue (Jun–Aug). **FRUITS** are capsules. **LEAVES** are narrowly oval, fleshy and blue-green. **STATUS** A N species; Orkney and Shetland are its best locations.

Wood Sage

Viper's-bugloss *Echium vulgare* Height to 80cm
Upright biennial covered in reddish bristles. Grows in dry grassland, mainly on sandy and calcareous soils, and is common on coasts. **FLOWERS** are 15–20mm long, funnel-shaped, and bright blue with protruding purplish stamens; borne in tall spikes (May–Sep). **FRUITS** are rough nutlets. **LEAVES** are narrow and pointed; basal leaves are stalked. **STATUS** Widespread and common in England and Wales; scarce elsewhere.

Wood Sage

Wood Sage
Teucrium scorodonia
Height to 40cm
Downy perennial, found on coastal cliffs with acid soils. **FLOWERS** are 5–6mm long, yellowish and lack an upper lip; borne in leafless spikes (Jun–Sep). **FRUITS** are nutlets. **LEAVES** are oval, heart-shaped at base, and wrinkled. **STATUS** Widespread and locally common.

Wild Thyme *Thymus polytrichus* Height to 5cm
Creeping, mat-forming perennial with slender woody runners. Plant is faintly aromatic, smelling of culinary thyme. Grows in dry coastal grassland and on cliffs and dunes. **FLOWERS** are 3–4mm long and pinkish purple; in dense terminal heads with dark purplish calyx tubes, on 4-angled stems that are hairy on 2 opposite sides (Jun–Sep). **FRUITS** are nutlets. **LEAVES** are ovate, short-stalked and borne in opposite pairs. **STATUS** Widespread and common throughout.

Bittersweet *Solanum dulcamara* Height to 1.5m
Downy, scrambling perennial that is woody at base. Grows in scrub, and often on stabilised shingle beaches. **FLOWERS** are 10–15mm across with 5 purple petal-like corolla lobes and projecting yellow anthers; in hanging clusters of purple stems (May–Sep). **FRUITS** are poisonous egg-shaped red berries, up to 1cm long. **LEAVES** are oval and pointed. **STATUS** Widespread and common throughout, except in the N and in Ireland.

Wild Thyme

Sea Bindweed

Oysterplant

Wood Sage

Bittersweet

Viper's-bugloss

Wild Thyme

Foxglove, rosette

Foxglove *Digitalis purpurea* Height to 1.5m
Downy greyish biennial or short-lived perennial
of coasts and sea cliffs with acid soils. FLOWERS
are 4–5cm long, the pinkish-purple (occasionally
white) corolla with darker spots in throat; in
tall, elegant spikes (Jun–Sep). FRUITS are green
capsules. LEAVES are 20–30cm long, downy, oval
and wrinkled; form a rosette in 1st year, from
which flowering spike appears in 2nd. STATUS
Widespread and common on suitable soils.

Common Toadflax
Linaria vulgaris Height to 75cm
Hairless greyish-green perennial; upright but
often much-branched. Grows in dry grassland,
and on undercliffs and dunes. FLOWERS are 15–25mm long and yellow, with orange
centres and long spurs; in tall, cylindrical spikes (Jun–Oct). FRUITS are capsules. LEAVES
are narrow, linear and borne on stems. STATUS Widespread and locally common; scarce
in Ireland.

Yellow-rattle *Rhinanthus minor* Height to 45cm
Upright annual, semi-parasitic of roots of other plants. Stems are stiff and 4-angled.
Grows in coastal grassland and on stabilised dunes. FLOWERS are 10–20mm long, the
corolla yellow, 2-lipped and somewhat tubular and straight; in spikes with triangular,
leaf-like green bracts (May–Sep). FRUITS are inflated capsules inside which ripe seeds do,
indeed, rattle. LEAVES are oblong with rounded teeth. STATUS Widespread and common.

Yellow Bartsia *Parentucellia viscosa* Height to 40cm
Stickily hairy, unbranched annual, semi-parasitic on roots of other plants. Grows in
damp coastal grassland, often in dune-slacks. FLOWERS are 15–35mm long, with a bright
yellow corolla; in leafy spikes (Jun–Sep). FRUITS are capsules. LEAVES are lanceolate and
unstalked. STATUS Very locally common in S and SW England and W Ireland.

Common Broomrape *Orobanche minor* Height to 40cm
Upright purplish-tinged annual that lacks chlorophyll and parasitises roots of pea family
members, notably clovers. Found in grassy places, often in sand dunes. FLOWERS are
10–18mm long, the tubular pinkish-yellow corolla having purple veins; in open, upright
spikes (Jun–Sep). FRUITS are capsules, concealed by dead flowers. LEAVES are scale-like.
STATUS Locally common in S England, Wales and S Ireland.

Red Valerian *Centranthus ruber* Height to 75cm
Branched greyish-green perennial of broken rocky ground, chalk
cliffs and old walls. FLOWERS are 8–10mm long, with a reddish or
pink (sometimes white)
corolla; in dense terminal
heads (May–Sep). FRUITS
have a feathery pappus.
LEAVES are ovate and
untoothed; in opposite
pairs. STATUS Introduced
and widely naturalised
around coasts.

RIGHT: **Common Broomrape, ssp.**
maritima, an exclusively coastal
subspecies that parasitises Sea-holly
FAR RIGHT: Red Valerian, white form

Foxglove

Common Toadflax

Yellow-rattle

Yellow Bartsia

Common Broomrape

Red Valerian

Buck's-horn Plantain Plantago coronopus Height to 15cm
Downy greyish perennial of disturbed coastal ground and cliffs. **FLOWERS**
are 2mm across with a brown corolla and yellow stamens; in slender spikes,
2–4cm long (May–Jul). **FRUITS** are capsules. **LEAVES** are 20cm long, 1-veined
and divided; in basal rosettes. **STATUS** Widespread and common.

Sea Plantain Plantago maritima Height to 15cm
Coastal perennial of cliffs and saltmarshes; tolerates salt spray. **FLOWERS**
are 3mm across with a brown corolla and yellow stamens; in slender
spikes, 2–6cm long (Jun–Aug). **FRUITS** are capsules. **LEAVES** are strap-like
and untoothed, with 3–5 faint veins; in basal rosettes. **STATUS** Widespread
and common.

Ribwort Plantain Plantago lanceolata Height to 15cm
Perennial of disturbed ground and tracks. **FLOWERS** are 4mm across
with a brown corolla and white stamens; in dense heads, 2cm long,
on stalks up to 40cm long (Apr–Oct). **FRUITS** are capsules. **LEAVES**
are narrow, to 20cm long, with 3–5 distinct veins; in basal rosettes.
STATUS Widespread and common.

Buck's-horn
Plantain

Ribwort
Plantain

Sea Arrowgrass
Triglochin maritima Height to 50cm
Plantain-like saltmarsh perennial.
FLOWERS are 3–4mm across, 3-petalled
and green, edged with purple; in slender,
long-stalked spikes (May–Sep). **FRUITS** are
egg-shaped. **LEAVES** are slender. **STATUS**
Widespread and locally common.

Sea Aster Aster tripolium Height to 75cm
Salt-tolerant plant of saltmarshes and
sea cliffs. **FLOWERS** comprise umbel-like
clusters of flower heads, each 1–2cm
across with yellow disc florets and
bluish-lilac ray florets (Jul–Sep). **FRUITS**
are achenes. **LEAVES** are fleshy and
narrow. **STATUS** Locally common.

Sea
Aster

Goldilocks Aster
Aster linosyris Height to 60cm
Attractive upright perennial of limestone
sea cliffs. **FLOWERS** comprise numerous
heads of yellow flowers, each 1cm across
(Jul–Sep). **FRUITS** are achenes. **LEAVES** are
slender. **STATUS** Rare, restricted to cliffs
in Somerset and S Devon.

Sea Arrowgrass

LEFT: Star-wort Cucullia asteris is a
mainly coastal moth whose larvae feed
on Sea Aster and Sea Wormwood.

Golden-samphire
Inula crithmoides Height to 75cm
Attractive plant of saltmarshes, coastal
shingle and sea cliffs. **FLOWERS** are borne in heads, 15–30mm across,
with yellow ray florets and orange-yellow disc florets (Jul–Sep). **FRUITS**
are achenes. **LEAVES** are narrow and fleshy. **STATUS** Locally common
only around the coasts of SW Britain and Ireland.

Jersey Cudweed Gnaphalium luteoalbum Height to 30cm
Creeping, woolly annual of damp sandy ground. **FLOWERS** are
yellowish; borne in ovoid heads, 3–5mm long (Jun–Oct). **FRUITS** are
achenes. **LEAVES** are oblong. **STATUS** Rare, on coasts of N Norfolk
(Holkham), Dorset and the Channel Islands.

Buck's-horn Plantain

Sea Plantain

Ribwort Plantain

Sea Arrowgrass

Sea Aster

Goldilocks Aster

Golden-samphire

Jersey Cudweed

Blue Fleabane *Erigeron acer* Height to 30cm
Roughly hairy plant of grassland, shingle and dunes.
FLOWERS are borne in heads, each 12–18mm across, with
bluish-purple ray florets and concealed yellow disc florets;
carried in clusters (Jun–Aug). FRUITS are achenes. LEAVES are
spoon-shaped at base, narrow on stem. STATUS Widespread
only in England and Wales.

Blue Fleabane, flower

Sea Mayweed *Tripleurospermum maritimum* Height to 60cm
Spreading plant of coastal shingle and sand. FLOWERS are
borne in clusters of long-stalked heads, 20–40mm across, with
yellow disc florets and white ray florets (Apr–Oct). FRUITS are achenes. LEAVES
are divided into cylindrical fleshy segments. STATUS Widespread and common.

Wormwood *Artemisia absinthium* Height to 80cm
Aromatic, silkily hairy plant of disturbed coastal grassland. FLOWERS are borne in
bell-shaped, nodding yellowish heads, 3–5mm across; in branched spikes (Jul–Sep).
FRUITS are achenes. LEAVES are divided into deeply cut lobes,
silvery-hairy on both sides. STATUS Locally common only in
England and Wales.

Blue Fleabane

Wormwood

Sea Wormwood *Artemisia maritima* Height to 65cm
Aromatic plant of saltmarshes and sea walls; tolerates salt
spray. FLOWERS are borne in egg-shaped yellow heads,
1–2mm across; in dense, branched, leafy spikes (Aug–Oct).
FRUITS are achenes. LEAVES are divided and downy on both
sides. STATUS Locally common only on suitable coasts of
England and Wales.

Least Lettuce *Lactuca saligna* Height to 1m
Slender plant of coastal banks and sea walls. Flowers open
only in sun, between 9am and 11am. FLOWERS in yellow
heads, 1cm across, up stem (Jul–Aug). FRUITS are achenes.
LEAVES are narrow. STATUS Local; Thames Estuary and Rye
Harbour in Sussex only.

Wormwood, flowers

Common Dandelion *Taraxacum officinale* Height to 35cm
Variable grassland plant. FLOWERS in heads, 3–6cm across,
with yellow florets; on hollow 'milk'-yielding stems (Mar–
Oct). FRUITS have a hairy pappus, arranged as a 'clock'.
LEAVES are spoon-shaped and basal. STATUS Widespread
and common.

Sticky Groundsel

Sticky Groundsel *Senecio viscosus* Height to 60cm
Stickily hairy plant of dry, bare places. FLOWERS comprise
conical heads, 12mm long, of yellow disc florets and recurved
ray florets; in open clusters (Jul–Sep). FRUITS are hairless.
LEAVES are pinnately divided. STATUS Locally common.

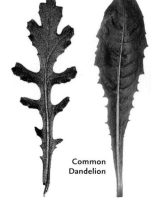

Common Dandelion

Common Dandelion, seedhead

Slender Thistle
Carduus tenuiflorus Height to 1m
Spiny-winged, cottony plant of
dry coastal grassland. FLOWERS
are borne in egg-shaped heads,
5–10mm across, with pinkish-red
florets; carried in clusters (Jun–
Aug). FRUITS have unbranched
hairs. LEAVES are pinnate and
spiny. STATUS Locally common.

Blue Fleabane

Sea Mayweed

Wormwood

Sea Wormwood

Least Lettuce

Common Dandelion

Sticky Groundsel

Slender Thistle

Bluebell *Hyacinthoides non-scripta* Height to 50cm

Bulbous perennial. Sometimes abundant on coastal cliffs. **FLOWERS** are bell-shaped, with 6 recurved lobes at mouth, and bluish purple (rarely pink or white); in 1-sided spikes (Apr–Jun). **FRUITS** are capsules. **LEAVES** are narrow, glossy green and basal. **STATUS** Widespread and locally abundant.

Spring Squill *Scilla verna* Height to 5cm

Compact plant of dry, short coastal grassland. **FLOWERS** are 10–15mm across, bell-shaped and lilac-blue; in upright, short-stalked clusters, each flower with a bluish-purple bract (Apr–Jun). **FRUITS** are capsules. **LEAVES** are wiry, curly, basal and 4–6 in number; appear in early spring, before flowers. **STATUS** Locally common only on coasts of W Britain and E Ireland.

Autumn Squill *Scilla autumnalis* Height to 7cm

Similar to Spring Squill (above) but blooms later and has subtly different flowers. Confined to coastal grassland. **FLOWERS** are 10–15mm across, bell-shaped and bluish purple; in compact, stalked clusters, flowers lacking a bract (Jul–Sep). **FRUITS** are capsules. **LEAVES** are wiry and basal; appear in autumn. **STATUS** Coasts of SW England only.

Bee Orchid *Ophrys apifera* Height to 30cm

Perennial of dry, mainly calcareous grassland; often common near coasts. **FLOWERS** have pink sepals and green upper petals; lower petal is inflated, furry and maroon, with pale yellow markings (vaguely bumblebee-like); in spikes (Jun–Jul). **FRUITS** are egg-shaped. **LEAVES** are green and mostly basal. **STATUS** Locally common only in England, Wales and S Ireland.

Early Spider-orchid

Early Spider-orchid *Ophrys sphegodes* Height to 35cm

Orchid of dry grassland on calcareous soils; mostly coastal. **FLOWERS** comprise green sepals and yellowish-green upper petals; lower petal is 12mm across, expanded, furry and maroon-brown, variably marked with a metallic blue H-shaped mark; in spikes (Apr–May). **FRUITS** are egg-shaped. **LEAVES** are oval; appear as a basal rosette. **STATUS** Local, in S England only.

Common Spotted-orchid *Dactylorhiza fuchsii* Height to 60cm

Grassland orchid, mostly on calcareous or neutral soils. **FLOWERS** range from pale pink to pinkish purple, with darker markings on 3-lobed lower lip; in open spikes (May–Aug). **FRUITS** are egg-shaped. **LEAVES** are dark-spotted; comprise a basal rosette and narrow stem leaves. **STATUS** Locally common.

Common Spotted-orchid

Southern Marsh-orchid *Dactylorhiza praetermissa* Height to 70cm

Southern Marsh-orchid

Orchid of damp grassland, such as wet dune-slacks, mostly on calcareous soils. **FLOWERS** are pinkish purple with a 3-lobed lip; in tall, dense spikes (May–Jun). **FRUITS** are egg-shaped. **LEAVES** are green and unmarked. **STATUS** Common only in the S.

Bluebell

Spring Squill

Autumn Squill

Early Spider-orchid

Bee Orchid

Common Spotted-orchid

Southern Marsh-orchid

Early Marsh-orchid *Dactylorhiza incarnata* Height to 60cm
Orchid of damp grassland, including dune-slacks. FLOWERS are usually flesh-pink, but creamy white or reddish purple in some subspecies; 3-lobed lip is reflexed along mid-line; in spikes (May–Jun). FRUITS are egg-shaped. LEAVES are yellowish green and narrow. STATUS Widespread but local.

Autumn Lady's-tresses *Spiranthes spiralis* Height to 15cm
Charming little orchid of short, dry grassland; often common on coastal turf and dunes. FLOWERS are white and downy; in a distinct spiral up the grey-green stem (Aug–Sep). FRUITS are egg-shaped and downy. LEAVES are oval; appear as basal rosette that withers long before flower stem appears. STATUS Locally common in S England, Wales and SW Ireland.

Autumn Lady's-tresses

Lizard Orchid
Himantoglossum hircinum Height to 1m

Extraordinary orchid of undisturbed grassland and stabilised dunes. Flowers smell of goats. FLOWERS have a greenish-grey hood, marked inside with reddish streaks, and a very long, twisted lip (up to 5cm); in tall spikes (May–Jul). FRUITS form at base of flowers. LEAVES comprise basal leaves that soon wither, and stem leaves that persist. STATUS Regularly seen at Sandwich Bay, Kent.

Lizard Orchid

Fen Orchid *Liparis loeselii* Height to 7cm
Delicate, yellowish-green orchid. Ssp. *ovata* grows in bare, damp dune slacks. FLOWERS are upwards facing with spiky sepals and petals. FRUITS are pear-shaped (Jun–Jul). LEAVES comprise a basal pair. STATUS Dwindling population in S Wales, declining due to habitat degradation.

Marsh Helleborine *Epipactis palustris* Height to 50cm
Attractive orchid of wet dune slacks. FLOWERS have reddish-green sepals,whitish upper petals marked with red, and frilly, whitish lip with red streaks; in open spikes (Jul–Aug). FRUITS are pear-shaped. LEAVES are broad and oval towards base of plant, narrower up stem. STATUS Very locally common in S England, S Wales and S Ireland.

Marsh Helleborine

Dune Helleborine *Epipactis dunensis* Height to 65cm
Understated orchid of dune-slacks. FLOWERS comprise narrow, greenish-white sepals and upper petals, and a broadly heart-shaped lip that is greenish white, pink-tinged towards centre, with a recurved tip; in open spikes, flowers seldom opening fully (Jun–Jul). FRUITS are pear-shaped. LEAVES are oval. STATUS Rare, restricted to Anglesey and N England.

Eelgrass *Zostera marina* Length to 50cm
Grass-like marine plant of sand and silt substrates; usually grows submerged, below low-water mark. FLOWERS are small and greenish; borne in branched clusters, enclosed by sheaths (Jun–Sep). FRUITS are spongy. LEAVES are 1cm wide and up to 50cm long, and with more than 3 veins. STATUS Widespread but local.

Dwarf Eelgrass *Zostera noltii* Length to 12cm
Similar to Eelgrass (above) but smaller; grows in similar habitats, but between mid-water and low-water marks. FLOWERS are small and greenish; borne in branched clusters, enclosed by sheaths (Jun–Sep). FRUITS are spongy. LEAVES are 1.5mm wide and up to 12cm long, and 1-veined. STATUS Widespread but local. SIMILAR SPECIES Narrow-leaved Eelgrass *Z. angustifolia* has leaves up to 15cm long and 1cm wide, with 1–3 veins; it grows in similar habitats but above mid-water mark.

Dwarf Eelgrass

Dwarf Eelgrass

Early Marsh-orchid

Autumn Lady's-tresses

Marsh Helleborine

Fen Orchid

Lizard Orchid

Early Marsh-orchid, var. *coccinea*

Dune Helleborine

Eelgrass

Dwarf Eelgrass

Tasselweed *Ruppia* sp. Length to 1m
Submerged aquatic perennial with slender stems.
Grows in brackish coastal pools and ditches. **FLOWERS**
comprise 2 greenish stamens and no petals; in
pairs, arranged in umbels on stalks that rise
to the surface (Jul–Sep). **FRUITS** are swollen,
asymmetrical and long-stalked. **LEAVES**
are hair-like and less than 1mm wide.
STATUS Local.

Tasselweed

Sea Rush
Juncus maritimus Height to 1m
Upright, stiff perennial
that forms clumps and
grows in drier upper
reaches of saltmarshes and among coastal rocks. **FLOWERS** are pale yellow and borne in
loose clusters below a sharp-pointed bract (Jun–Jul). **FRUITS** are brown, bluntly pointed
and equal in length to sepals. **LEAVES** are sharply pointed. **STATUS** Locally common on
coasts.

Toad Rush *Juncus bufonis* Height to 40cm
Tufted annual; grows on damp, bare ground, including ruts
along tracks and margins of pools; often common on coasts.
FLOWERS are greenish white and borne in branched clusters,
topped by a sharp spine (May–Sep). **FRUITS** are brown,
egg-shaped and shorter than sepals. **LEAVES** are narrow and
grooved. **STATUS** Widespread and common. **SIMILAR SPECIES**
Dwarf Rush *J. capitatus* (height to 5cm) is a reddish annual with
entirely basal leaves. Flowers in terminal clusters with 2 leaf-
like bracts (May–Jun). Grows on bare ground on the Lizard,
Cornwall, the Channel Isles and Anglesey.

Dwarf Rush

Hard Rush *Juncus inflexus* Height to 1.2m
Tufted perennial with stiff, ridged bluish or greyish-green stems. Grows in damp grassy
places but avoids acid soils. **FLOWERS** are brown and borne in loose clusters below a long
bract (Jun–Aug). **FRUITS** are brown and egg-shaped with a tiny point. **LEAVES** are absent.
STATUS Widespread and common except in the N.

Compact Rush *Juncus conglomeratus* Height to 1m
Upright perennial of damp, grazed grassland, mainly on acid soils. Similar to compact-
flowered form of Soft Rush (p. 106) but stems are darker green, ridged, rough and not
glossy. **FLOWERS** are brown and borne in compact clusters
(May–Jul). **FRUITS** are dark brown, egg-shaped and as long
as sepals. **LEAVES** are absent. **STATUS** Locally common.

Saltmarsh Rush *Juncus gerardii* Height to 50cm
Characteristic rush of saltmarshes, often covering
extensive areas. **FLOWERS** are dark brown and borne in
loose clusters, flanked by leaf-like bracts (Jun–Jul). **FRUITS**
are brown, egg-shaped, glossy and equal in length to
sepals. **LEAVES** are dark green, and arise at base of plant
and on stems. **STATUS** Locally common around coasts.

Jointed Rush *Juncus articulatus* Height to 60cm
Creeping or upright perennial of damp dune slacks.
FLOWERS are brown in open, branched clusters
(May–Jun). **FRUITS** are brown, egg-shaped with a pointed
tip. **LEAVES** are curved with a transverse joint. **STATUS**
Locally common.

Jointed Rush

Tasselweed

Sea Rush

Hard Rush

Toad Rush

Compact Rush

Saltmarsh Rush

Soft Rush *Juncus effusus* Height to 1.5m
Typical of overgrazed grassland, mostly on acid soils. Stems are yellowish green, glossy and smooth. FLOWERS are pale brown; in loose clusters near stem tops (Jun–Aug). FRUITS are yellow-brown, egg-shaped, indented at tip and shorter than sepals. LEAVES are absent. STATUS Widespread and common.

Soft Rush

Sea Club-rush *Bolboschoenus maritimus* Height to 1.25m
Creeping, robust perennial that grows at margins of brackish water near sea. Stems are rough and triangular in cross section. FLOWERS comprise a tight terminal cluster of egg-shaped spikelets, flanked by a long, leafy bract (Jul–Aug). FRUITS are dark brown. LEAVES are rough and keeled. STATUS Locally common.

Sea Club-rush

Sand Sedge *Carex arenaria* Height to 35cm
Creeping perennial of sand dunes. Progress of underground stems can be detected by aerial shoots, which appear in straight lines. FLOWERS comprise pale brown spikes, in a terminal head, male flowers above females (May–Jul). FRUITS are yellowish brown and beaked. LEAVES are wiry. STATUS Locally common on most suitable coasts.

Curved Sedge *Carex maritima* Height to 12cm
Distinctive creeping plant of coastal sand. FLOWERS are brown and arranged in dense, egg-shaped terminal heads without bracts; borne on curved stalks (Jun–Jul). FRUITS are beaked and very dark brown. LEAVES are curved, with inrolled margins. STATUS Local, restricted to Scotland and NE England.

Common Reed *Phragmites communis* Height to 2m
Impressive plant of damp ground and marshes. Often forms vast stands. Plant turns brown and persists through winter. FLOWERS are spikelets, purplish brown then fading; in branched, 1-sided terminal clusters (Aug–Sep). FRUITS are brown. LEAVES are broad and long. STATUS Widespread and common.

Lyme-grass *Leymus arenarius* Height to 1.5m
Blue-grey perennial of sand dunes and sandy beaches. FLOWERS are borne in tall heads of paired grey-green spikelets (Jun–Aug). FRUITS are small, dry nutlets. LEAVES are up to 15mm wide, with inrolled margins. STATUS Widespread and common on E coast of Britain; scarce or absent elsewhere.

Marram *Ammophila arenaria* Height to 1m
Perennial of coastal dunes that colonises and stabilises shifting sands by means of its underground stems. FLOWERS are borne in dense spikes, with 1-flowered straw-coloured spikelets (Jul–Aug). FRUITS are small, dry nutlets. LEAVES are tough, grey-green, rolled and sharply pointed. STATUS Widespread and common on suitable coasts.

ABOVE: **Lyme Grass** *Chortodes elymi*, an east coast moth whose larvae feed exclusively on Lyme-grass.
LEFT: **Shore Wainscot** *Mythimna litoralis*, whose larvae feed exclusively on Marram.
BELOW: **L-album Wainscot** *Mythimna l-album*, a largely coastal moth whose larvae feed mainly on Marram.

Soft Rush

Sea Club-rush

Sand Sedge

Curved Sedge

Common Reed

Lyme-grass

Marram

Red Fescue *Festuca rubra* Height to 50cm
Clump-forming perennial of grassy places; common near coasts, on cliffs and on margins of saltmarshes. **FLOWERS** are an inflorescence, the spikelets 7–10mm long and usually reddish (May–Jul). **FRUITS** are small, dry nutlets. **LEAVES** are either narrow, wiry and stiff, or flat (on flowering stems). **STATUS** Widespread and common.

Yorkshire Fog

Yorkshire Fog *Holcus lanatus* Height to 1m
Variable tufted perennial with downy grey-green stems. Grows on disturbed, broken ground and sea cliffs. **FLOWERS** are in heads that are tightly packed at first but then spread; comprise reddish-tipped grey-green 2-flowered spikelets (May–Aug). **FRUITS** are small, dry nutlets. **LEAVES** are grey-green and downy. **STATUS** Widespread and common.

Creeping Soft-grass *Holcus mollis* Height to 60cm
Similar to Yorkshire Fog (above) but more slender; stems are downy only at joints. Grows in grassy areas, mainly on acid soils. **FLOWERS** are borne in heads, compact at first and then spreading, with purplish-green spikelets, each with a bent awn (Jun–Aug). **FRUITS** are small, dry nutlets. **LEAVES** are grey-green. **STATUS** Widespread and common.

Sea Barley *Hordeum marinum* Height to 5cm
Tufted blue-green annual of bare ground and dry grassy places near the sea. **FLOWERS** are borne in long, unbranched spikes, 7–8cm long, the spikelets in 3s, with stiff, spreading awns (Jul–Aug); flowering stems are prostrate at base. **FRUITS** are small, dry nutlets. **LEAVES** are 4–5mm wide. **STATUS** Local and exclusively coastal.

Common Cord-grass *Spartina anglica* Height to 1.3m
Tufted perennial, of hybrid origin, found on mudflats and saltmarshes. **FLOWERS** are borne in a stiff inflorescence of elongated clusters of 3–6 yellowish flower heads, up to 35cm long (Jul–Sep). **FRUITS** are small, dry nutlets. **LEAVES** are grey-green and tough. **STATUS** Widespread on coasts of England, Wales, and E and S Ireland.

Sea Couch *Elytrigia atherica* Height to 1m
Tough perennial that grows in maritime grassland. **FLOWERS** are borne in a stiff, unbranched inflorescence with many-flowered yellowish-green spikelets (Jun–Aug). **FRUITS** are small, dry nutlets. **LEAVES** are green and inrolled, with a sharp terminal point. **STATUS** Widespread and locally common.

Cock's-foot *Dactylis glomerata*
Height to 1m
Tufted perennial of grassy cliffs. **FLOWERS** are borne in an inflorescence of long-stalked, egg-shaped heads that spread, fancifully resembling a bird's foot (Jun–Jul). **FRUITS** are dry nutlets. **LEAVES** are rough with slightly inrolled margins. **STATUS** **NOTE** Some coastal forms are very compact.

Cock's-foot, with compact form inset

Red Fescue

Yorkshire Fog

Creeping Soft-grass

Sea Barley

Common Cord-grass

Sea Couch

Mathew's Wainscot *Mythimna favicolor*, a mainly east coast moth whose larvae feed exclusively on Common Saltmarsh-grass.

Common Saltmarsh-grass
Puccinellia maritima Height to 30cm
Hairless, tufted perennial. Grows in saltmarshes and forms swards. **FLOWERS** are borne in spike-like heads, with spikelets along all the branches, which are mainly upright, not spreading (Jul–Aug). **FRUITS** are small, dry nutlets. **LEAVES** are grey-green and often inrolled. **STATUS** Widespread and locally common.

Reflexed Saltmarsh-grass
Puccinellia distans Height to 30cm
Hairless, tufted perennial. Grows in saltmarshes and forms small colonies. **FLOWERS** are borne in spike-like heads, with spikelets along branches (Jun–Jul); these spread and reflex in fruit. **FRUITS** are small, dry nutlets. **LEAVES** are grey-green and often inrolled. **STATUS** Widespread and locally common.

Stiff Saltmarsh-grass *Puccinellia rupestris* Height to 20cm (often much shorter)
Tough, tufted annual. Grows in saline mud on coastal banks, tracks and muddy shingle. **FLOWERS** are borne in a dense, branched inflorescence, mostly one-sided (May–Aug). **FRUITS** are nutlets. **LEAVES** are relatively wide and hooded. **STATUS** Locally common in S.

Annual Beard-grass *Polypogon monspeliensis* Height to 80cm
Distinctive annual of sparsely vegetated places near the sea, notably margins of drainage channels. **FLOWERS** appear in a dense inflorescence with long awns, green at first, turning silky white later, sometimes partly shrouded by uppermost leaf (Jun–Aug). **FRUITS** are dry nutlets. **LEAVES** are rough and flat. **STATUS** Scarce and local, mainly in coastal SE England.

Hare's-tail Grass *Lagurus ovatus* Height to 50cm
Attractive and distinctive plant of coastal dunes. **FLOWERS** are borne in egg-shaped heads that are softly hairy; awns are bent halfway along length (Jun–Aug). **FRUITS** are dry nutlets. **LEAVES** are grey-green and hairy; upper sheaths are inflated. **STATUS** Naturalised and rare, mainly on S coasts.

Bulbous Foxtail *Alopecurus bulbosus* Height to 25cm
Tufted grey-green perennial whose stems are bulbous at the base. Grows in damp coastal grassland. **FLOWERS** are borne in cylindrical purplish heads, 2–3cm long, the spikelets with long awns and blunt ligules (Jun–Aug). **FRUITS** are small, dry nutlets. **LEAVES** are narrow and smooth below. **STATUS** Locally common in S England and S Wales only.

Fern-grass *Catapodium rigidum* Height to 15cm
Tough, wiry grass with superficially fern-like inflorescences. Grows in dry grassland. **FLOWERS** are borne in a branched inflorescence with short-stalked spikelets, more or less in one plane (May–Jul). **FRUITS** are nutlets. **LEAVES** are narrow and wiry. **STATUS** Locally common in the S. **SIMILAR SPECIES** Sea Fern-grass *C. marinum* is similar but stouter, and exclusively coastal.

Curved Hard-grass *Parapholis incurva* Height to 10cm
Distinctive tough grass of bare coastal ground. **FLOWERS** are borne in a curved purplish inflorescence of compact spikelets (Jun–Aug). **FRUITS** are nutlets. **LEAVES** are narrow. **STATUS** Scarce and local, in S Britain only.

Common Saltmarsh-grass

Reflexed Saltmarsh-grass

Stiff Saltmarsh-grass

Bulbous Foxtail

Annual Beard-grass

Hare's-tail Grass

Fern-grass

Curved Hard-grass

INTRODUCING COASTAL INVERTEBRATES

Naturalists divide living things into distinct groups, the members of which share common characters; this is called classification. The main subdivisions among the invertebrates (animals without backbones) are referred to as phyla (singular, phylum). Some coastal invertebrate phyla are mainly or exclusively marine; others have marine, freshwater and terrestrial representatives; a few are mainly or solely found on land.

SPONGES (PHYLUM PORIFERA)
Sessile, filter-feeding animals whose cells are not differentiated into obvious tissues. There are both vase-shaped and encrusting species. A typical animal has numerous small holes through which sea water enters an inner cavity lined with cells that filter out food particles; filtered sea water then exits via a large pore. Sponges are described on pp. 114–15.

JELLYFISH, SEA ANEMONES AND ALLIES (PHYLUM CNIDARIA)
Sometimes referred to as coelenterates, these soft-bodied animals show radial symmetry. The phylum is introduced in more detail on pp. 116–17.

SEA GOOSEBERRIES AND COMB JELLIES (PHYLUM CTENOPHORA)
These are typically translucent or almost transparent animals, whose soft bodies seem to lack any real substance. They are pelagic, moving by means of rows of beating hairs called cilia, and are seasonally abundant. Ctenophores are bioluminescent. The group is described on pp. 126–7.

SEGMENTED WORMS (PHYLUM ANNELIDA)
Relatives of the familiar earthworm, this diverse group is found in a wide range of habitats, and shows a great range of body forms. The phylum is introduced in more detail on pp. 128–9.

OTHER MARINE WORMS
A range of other elongated animals bearing the word 'worm' in their names are found on the seashore. These include the flatworms (phylum Platyhelminthes), carnivorous creatures that move with a gliding motion; and ribbon worms (phylum Nemertea), unsegmented predators and scavengers, some species of which are extremely long.

CRUSTACEANS (PHYLUM CRUSTACEA)
An arthropod phylum whose representatives are found everywhere in the marine environment. The body form varies, but typically animals have a hard, calcified exoskeleton. The phylum is introduced in more detail on pp. 148–9.

Conventional wisdom used to place arthropods (invertebrates with jointed legs and a hard exoskeleton) in a phylum with representative sub-groups (called classes) including crustaceans, insects, spiders and allies. Modern thoughts on classification now elevate most of these sub-groups to phylum status.

Acorn worms and sea squirts are the link between invertebrates and vertebrates, respectively animals without and with a backbone. Acorn worms (phylum Hemichordata) are worm-like but have a nerve cord in their collar. As adults, sea squirts (or tunicates) may look primitive but they are more closely related to fish than to, say, sponges, which some resemble. They belong to the phylum Chordata, sub-phylum Urochordata, and their larvae have a notochord and dorsal nerve cord in the tail.

TERRESTRIAL ARTHROPODS

Several arthropod groups are widespread in terrestrial habitats, with a few representatives found on coasts and the upper seashore; none has colonised the marine world. They include the following: insects (phylum Hexapoda), which are introduced in more detail on p. 183; centipedes and millipedes (phylum Myriapoda), elongated, segmented animals with paired legs on most segments; and spiders (phylum Chelicerata), predators that have bodies divided into two sections (a fused cephalothorax and an abdomen), with four pairs of legs. Terrestrial arthropods are described on pp. 182–203.

SEA SPIDERS (PHYLUM PYCNOGONIDA)

These are strictly marine arthropod-like animals that superficially resemble true terrestrial spiders. The body is segmented and there are four pairs of segmented legs. Sea spiders are described on pp. 180–1.

MOLLUSCS (PHYLUM MOLLUSCA)

A large and varied group, molluscs are found in all marine habitats. The body form is tremendously variable, many species having ornate, protective shells. The phylum is introduced in more detail on pp. 204–5.

STARFISH, SEA URCHINS AND ALLIES (PHYLUM ECHINODERMATA)

Echinoderms are exclusively marine animals whose body shows radial symmetry, this being most obvious in starfishes and sea urchins. Calcified plates protect the body, and spines are characteristic of many species. The phylum is introduced in more detail on pp. 242–3.

BRYOZOANS (PHYLUM BRYOZOA)

These sessile, colonial animals grow on larger seaweeds, rocks and shells, depending on the species. They feed by means of ciliated tentacles. Many bryozoan species are the favourite food of sea slugs. Bryozoans are described on pp. 254–5.

MINOR INVERTEBRATE PHYLA

There are a number of other exclusively marine invertebrate phyla with relatively few representatives that are seldom seen on the seashore; their relative obscurity is reflected in the fact that most do not have common names, and they are not dealt with in detail in this book. These phyla include the following: Priapula, resembling fat worms with a spiny proboscis at one end and branched structures at the other; Echiura, plump, cylindrical animals with a proboscis; Sipuncula, unsegmented worm-like animals with a tentacle-fringed mouth, many of which live in burrows; Phoronida (horseshoe worms), plump, worm-like animals whose mouth is surrounded by a horseshoe arrangement of tentacles; Brachiopoda (lamp shells), whose body is attached to substrate by a short stalk, and protected by paired, unequal shells like a bivalve mollusc.

Breadcrumb Sponge *Halichondria panicea* Diameter to 15cm (sometimes much more)
Commonest and most familiar sponge of rocky shores. Found on and under rocks on
lower shore, in pools and in sub-tidal zone. BODY forms a spreading mass, with raised
bumps and striking pores (oscula). Typically either green or orange. STATUS Widespread
and common on suitable shores. SIMILAR SPECIES *Myxilla incrustans* is also encrusting,
typically yellow with obvious oscula; surface has pits and ridges and web-like
coat of fine fibres. Slimy and odourless (*Halichondria* smells strongly).
Widespread on lower shore. *Ophlitaspongia papilla* is blood-red
to orange, the smooth surface with regular oscula.

Purse Sponge

Breadcrumb
Sponge, green
form

Estuary Sponge

Purse Sponge
Grantia compressa Length to 25mm
Distinctive sponge that typically grows attached
to larger seaweeds or among short, tufted seaweeds
encrusting rocks on lower shore. BODY is sac-like,
flattened and buffish white. STATUS Widespread
and locally common on suitable coasts.

Estuary Sponge *Hymeniacidon perleve* Diameter to 15cm
Mound- or cushion-forming sponge that grows on rocks on
lower shore, but also on stones, buried or part-buried in silt in
estuaries. Tolerates desiccation. BODY is typically orange, surface
irregularly corrugated with sparse small pores (oscula). STATUS
Widespread and locally common.

Sycon ciliatum Length to 45mm
Distinctive little sponge. Grows attached to seaweeds, and sometimes rocks, on lower shore
and in pools. BODY is irregularly ovoid and buffish white; opening (osculum) has a radiating
fringe of spiny hairs. STATUS Widespread and locally common on suitable coasts.

Boring Sponge *Cliona celata* Diameter to 6cm or more
Encrusting sponge that bores into, and sometimes covers, calcareous rocks and large
mollusc shells. Bored shells are washed up on shoreline during gales, once sponge has
died. BODY (boring form) comprises spongy projections with terminal pore (osculum)
arising from holes bored in substrate; sometimes forms an uneven, spreading mass, with
large pores (oscula). STATUS Widespread and common on suitable shores.

Mermaid's Glove *Haliclona oculata* Height to 20cm
Much-branched sponge. Grows sub-littorally, attached to stones on sheltered shores and
in estuaries. Often washed up bleached, and then not always immediately recognisable
as a sponge. BODY is divided in the manner of a leafless tree. 'Branches' are round in
cross section, orange-yellow with openings in rows. STATUS Widespread and locally
common, especially on S and W coasts.

Leucosolenia botryoides Width to 25mm
Distinctive sponge. Grows attached to seaweeds on lower shore. BODY comprises
numerous bunches of finger-like white tubes with a terminal pore. STATUS Widespread,
commonest on W and NW coasts; almost absent from the SE.

Suberites ficus Width to 12cm
Colourful sponge. Found from lower shore to sub-littoral zone, on rocky coasts. BODY
is variable: sometimes a distorted sphere or fig-shaped (this form previously referred to
as *S. domuncula*); also encrusts shells, notably scallops. Typically orange-yellow. STATUS
Widespread on S and W coasts; generally absent elsewhere.

Dysidea fragilis Width to 15cm
Encrusting or lobe-forming sponge, found under rocks on lower shores on sheltered
coasts. BODY of littoral form typically comprises 2–4cm-long lobes tightly adhering to
rocks. Surface is studded with craters, framed by ragged-tipped cones. Usually buffish
white. STATUS Widespread and locally common.

Ophlitaspongia papilla

Myxilla incrustans

Breadcrumb Sponge

Purse Sponge

Estuary Sponge

Sycon ciliatum

Boring Sponge

Mermaid's Glove

Leucosolenia botryoides

Dysidea fragilis

Suberites ficus

Suberites domuncula

INTRODUCING CNIDARIA

Ranging in size and shape from sea anemones and soft corals to large and impressive jellyfish, Cnidaria is certainly a diverse group of animals. And, armed with stinging cells, some species really pack a punch to the incautious marine biologist.

THE NATURAL HISTORY OF CNIDARIA

Although some cnidarian species are large and superficially complex, in evolutionary terms they are simple animals. They exhibit radial symmetry in their body form. The outer wall of the body comprises two layers, which can be thin, jelly-like or muscular depending on the species. The body layers enclose a body cavity, and this connects with the sea outside via a single opening or mouth. Typically, the mouth is surrounded by rows of tentacles, these coated with stinging cells that, on contact, release a barbed thread armed with toxins. The stinging cells serve both to capture and subdue prey, and as a defence against attack.

In a typical cnidarian, there are two stages in the life cycle. The sexual stage is called a medusa; it is bell-shaped and free-swimming, with a central mouth below and tentacles around the bell margin. The medusa produces sperm and eggs, and the resulting larva eventually settles and forms a sessile polyp stage. Mature polyps produce and bud off small free-swimming medusae, and the cycle repeats itself. In jellyfish, the medusa stage is dominant and the polyp stage is much reduced. In sea anemones, the reverse is the case, the polyp being dominant; fertilisation in this group is internal and there is no medusa stage.

There are many subdivisions within the phylum Cnidaria. The most striking and distinctive representatives are detailed as follows:

JELLYFISH

Although diverse in classification terms, jellyfish can be recognised for what they are by their body form, which comprises an umbrella-like bell with a jelly-like consistency. Depending on the species, the bell can be flattish or domed and almost hemispherical; long tentacles hang around the bell margin in most species. Typical jellyfish are free-swimming and move by means of pulsating contractions of the bell; to a degree, they are also at the mercy of tides and currents.

Pelagia noctiluca,
a typical jellyfish.

STALKED JELLYFISH

These intriguing jellyfish live upside down, the stalk attached by a basal sucker to a seaweed frond or eelgrass leaf. The umbrella has radiating arms that end in groups of tentacles. If the need arises, stalked jellyfish can alter their position, using their tentacles to 'cartwheel' along.

Tubularia indivisa, a typical hydroid.

HYDROIDS

Typically seen as the polyp stage and often in colonial form, hydroids are a diverse and abundant group of marine animals. However, because many species are relatively small and delicate, and collapse out of water, their true abundance and significance is often overlooked. Most hydroids are sessile polyps, but the Portuguese Man-of-war and By-the-wind-sailor (often thought of as jellyfish) are floating, free-swimming animals.

SOFT CORALS

Despite their English name, these are relatively tough animals whose body form is toughened by calcified spines. The coral-like structures are formed of colonies of polyps. The polyps themselves are retractable.

SEA FANS

These colonial relatives of the soft corals form large branched and fan-like structures, the branches arranged more or less in one plane. The individual polyps live along the side branches of the fan.

Red Sea Fingers, a colourful soft coral.

SEA ANEMONES

Sea anemones are solitary animals that comprise a tough, rather rubbery and cylindrical body with an apical mouth surrounded by tentacles. They attach themselves to a substrate using a basal sucker; many species attach themselves to bare rock, while a few burrow into, or rather are mostly concealed by, soft sediment. Cup corals and jewel anemones are not, strictly speaking, true sea anemones; the former are protected by a calcified cup.

Snakelocks Anemone.

Compass Jellyfish
Chrysaora hysoscella
Diameter to 30cm
Impressive and distinctive
jellyfish, found in inshore
waters in summer. **BODY**
comprises a rather flattened
brownish bell marked with 32
marginal lobes and radiating 'V'
markings; has 24 long, trailing
tentacles and 4 mouth arms.
STATUS Widespread and locally
common, mainly Jul–Aug.

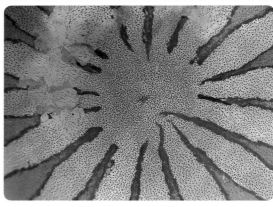

Compass Jellyfish

Rhizostoma octopus
Diameter to 80cm (Not illustrated)
Large and rather solid jellyfish,
found in inshore waters in late
summer. **BODY** comprises a
smooth, domed bluish umbrella without marginal tentacles; there are 8 trailing arms,
these divided terminally. **STATUS** Locally common, mainly Aug–Oct.

Lion's Mane Jellyfish *Cyanea capitata* Diameter to 85cm
Large jellyfish that can deliver a painful sting; found in inshore waters in summer. **BODY**
comprises a rather flattened brown umbrella with slightly undulating margins; there are
65+ slender tentacles, and 4 divided and very frilly arms. **STATUS** Locally common but
mainly in N waters, Jun–Aug.

Blue Jellyfish *Cyanea lamarckii* Diameter to 30cm
Familiar jellyfish of inshore waters in late spring and summer. **BODY** comprises a rather
translucent purplish-blue umbrella with numerous slender, trailing tentacles and 4
thick, lobed arms. **STATUS** Widespread and locally common, mainly Jun–Aug.

Pelagia noctiluca Diameter to 10cm
Relatively small jellyfish; mainly offshore but sometimes inshore in late summer. **BODY**
comprises a translucent domed umbrella covered in knobbly warts; there are marginal
tentacles and trailing, frilly arms. **STATUS** Locally common, mainly in the N and W, Jul–Sep.

Moon
Jellyfish

Moon Jellyfish *Aurelia aurita* Diameter to 35cm
Generally the commonest jellyfish in inshore
waters, and often stranded. **BODY** comprises
a flattened translucent bluish umbrella,
through which 4 dark semicircular rings
(gonads) can be seen (pink when seen
against a dark background); there
are small marginal tentacles and 4
frilly arms. **STATUS** Widespread and
locally common, mainly Jun–Aug.

Sessile Jellyfish
Haliclystus auricula Length to 35mm
Distinctive jellyfish and generally
the commonest stalked species.
Found attached to large seaweeds
and eelgrasses. **BODY** is shaped like
an inverted umbrella, with 8 radiating
'arms' tipped with terminal tentacles;
attached to substrate by stalk. **STATUS**
Widespread and locally common.

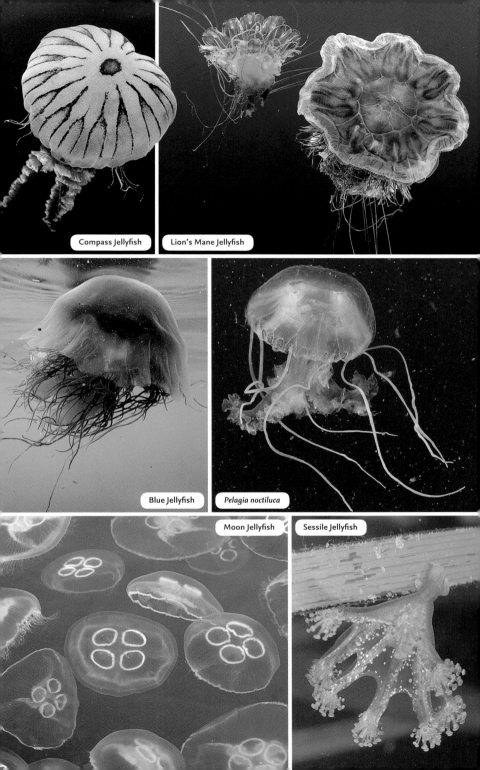

Compass Jellyfish

Lion's Mane Jellyfish

Blue Jellyfish

Pelagia noctiluca

Moon Jellyfish

Sessile Jellyfish

By-the-wind-sailor *Velella velella* Length to 6cm
Distinctive pelagic hydroid. Mainly oceanic, but sometimes blown inshore or beached after gales. BODY is bluish purple and comprises a flattened disc-like float, and an upright fin-like 'sail'; below this hang short tentacles. STATUS Common in the open Atlantic but only occasional inshore, mainly in autumn.

Portuguese Man-of-war *Physalia physalis* Width to 12cm
Unmistakable colonial hydrozoan. Typically pelagic and oceanic, but sometimes blown ashore after gales. BODY comprises an ovoid pinkish float with a pleated crest, and numerous blue and pink trailing, stinging tentacles. STATUS Common in summer in the Western Approaches; occasional on SW shores.

Hydrozoan medusae
Sexually reproducing stages in the hydrozoan life cycle are pelagic and called medusae (singular, medusa). They are sometimes seen in the surface layers of the sea. Almost transparent, they are easiest to pick out at night with torchlight. They are bell-shaped, resembling miniature jellyfish, and swim in a pulsating manner. Most are tiny, but those of *Leuckartiara* can be 1cm or so long. STATUS Widespread.

Oaten Pipes *Tubularia* sp. Length to 15cm
Distinctive hydroids, found in tufted colonies attached to rocks in pools on lower shore and in sub-littoral zone. BODY comprises a long stalk and terminal 'head'; tube-like mouth is surrounded by oral tentacles, fringed below by sub-oral tentacles. *T. indivsa* has 40 or so oral tentacles and 30 or so sub-oral tentacles. *T. larynx* (length to 4cm) is smaller, with branched stems, and head with 20 or so oral tentacles and 20 or so sub-oral tentacles. Both species are widespread and locally common.

Corymorpha nutans Length to 8cm
Distinctive hydroid that recalls a sea anemone. Lives on silty sand and gravel; sub-littoral, very occasionally in pools. BODY comprises a tapering stalk, marked with longitudinal pale lines, and swollen terminally with long tentacles; central mouth is surrounded by shorter tentacles. STATUS Widespread and locally common.

Hydractinia echinata Height to 4mm
Mat-forming colonial hydroid that coats the surface of shells occupied by hermit crabs. Lower shore and sub-littoral zone. BODY comprises a spiny pinkish mat, studded (when immersed) with polyps resembling tiny sea anemones. Out of water, shell looks to have a fuzzy coating. STATUS Widespread and fairly common.

Hydractinia echinata

Aglaophenia pluma Length to 7cm
Colonial hydroid. Grows on seaweeds, notably *Halidrys* sp. BODY comprises a straight yellowish main stem with white side branches, these with tiny cup-like polyps along length. Overall, colony resembles a small feather. STATUS Widespread and locally common, mainly in the S and SW.

Obelia geniculata Length to 5cm
Small but distinctive hydroid. Grows in masses on seaweeds, notably *Fucus* and *Laminaria*. BODY comprises a zigzag pinkish-red main stem; short side branches arise from angles, bearing terminal polyps with tentacles. STATUS Widespread and locally common, except in the SE. SIMILAR SPECIES **Dynamena pumila** (length to 25mm) comprises hair-like chains (sometimes branched) of paired polyps. Epiphytic on *Fucus* and *Laminaria* seaweeds. Widespread and common.

Ventromma halecioides Length to 4cm
Branching colonial hydroid found growing on eelgrasses and stones in sheltered lagoons. BODY comprises a straight central main stem with alternate side branches, on which sit 3–5 polyps, each with tentacles. Overall, colony recalls a leaf skeleton or feather. STATUS Widespread but local.

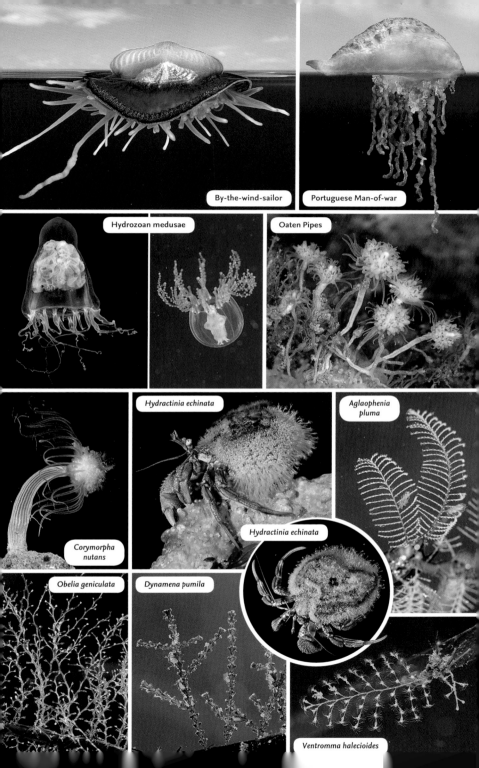

By-the-wind-sailor

Portuguese Man-of-war

Hydrozoan medusae

Oaten Pipes

Hydractinia echinata

Aglaophenia pluma

Corymorpha nutans

Hydractinia echinata

Obelia geniculata

Dynamena pumila

Ventromma halecioides

ABOVE: **Beadlet Anemone colony, at low tide in sea cave;** BELOW: **Beadlet Anemone giving birth.**

Beadlet Anemone *Actinia equina* Diameter to 5cm
Our most familiar sea anemone. Found on a wide range of rocky shores, at mid- to low-tide levels, and in pools and caves. **BODY** is either uniformly red or green. When expanded, comprises a broad-based column with ring of blue 'beads' at top, just below the numerous tentacles. Contracts into a blob when disturbed or out of water. **STATUS** Widespread and locally common.

Strawberry Anemone
Actinia fragacea Diameter to 8cm
Superficially similar to Beadlet Anemone (above) but larger and distinctively marked. Lives on lower shore on shaded rocks and in gullies. **BODY** is red overall, the column adorned with pale spots. **STATUS** Local; commonest in SW England.

Snakelocks Anemone
Anemonia viridis Diameter to 5cm
Familiar and distinctive sea anemone whose tentacles do not retract completely when disturbed or out of water. Lives attached to rocks and in pools on lower shore. **BODY** has a stout column and numerous long tentacles, sometimes uniformly grey-brown but usually greenish with purple tips. **STATUS** Widespread and locally common.

Snakelocks Anemone, grey-brown form

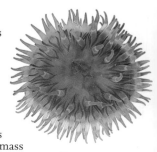

Gem Anemone
Aulactinia verrucosa Diameter to 5cm
Squat, well-marked sea anemone. Lives attached to rocks on lower shore, and in pools. **BODY** comprises up to 48 stout tentacles, banded with grey-brown and white; column has longitudinal rows or warts, 6 rows of which are whitish. **STATUS** Locally common only in SW Britain.

Dahlia Anemone *Urticina felina* Diameter to 15cm
Impressive and colourful sea anemone. Lives attached to rocks, typically below low-tide mark, but sometimes in pools. **BODY** comprises short, stout column armed with adhesive warts, to which debris is invariably attached. Tentacles are relatively short and arranged in 10s; range in colour from white to pink or peachy yellow, depending on individual. **STATUS** Widespread and locally common.

Horseman Anemone *Urticina eques* Diameter to 30cm
Similar to Dahlia Anemone (above) but larger; column lacks adhesive warts and consequently remains clear of debris. Lives attached to rocks on lower shore; also sub-littoral. **BODY** comprises a stout column and rather long tentacles; overall colour is yellowish orange, but often with flushes of red. **STATUS** Widespread and locally common.

Plumose Anemone *Metridium senile* Length to 25cm
Impressive and distinctive sea anemone. Lives attached to rocks; mainly sub-littoral but also in pools. **BODY** comprises tall, stout, smooth column with terminal collar, and frothy mass of tentacles. Column is usually either white or orange, tentacles are typically white. **STATUS** Widespread and locally common.

Horseman Anemone

Beadlet Anemone

Snakelocks Anemone, green and purple form

Strawberry Anemone

Gem Anemone

Dahlia Anemone

Horseman Anemone

Plumose Anemone

Daisy Anemone *Cereus pedunculatus* Diameter to 12cm
Burrowing sea anemone that lives in mud and silty sand. Found from lower shore into deeper water. **BODY** comprises a long column, attached to buried stone and completely covered by sediment. Only terminal end is visible, with up to 200 shortish tentacles, marbled and mottled blue-grey, buff and white. **STATUS** Widespread and locally common. **SIMILAR SPECIES** *Peachia cylindrica* (diameter to 10cm) lives buried in gravel and sand from low-tide zone into deeper water. Only terminal end is visible, with a broad disc (grey-brown or white) and 12 stout tentacles with 'V' markings. Commonest in the W.

Sagartia troglodytes

Sagartia troglodytes Diameter to 5cm
Burrowing sea anemone that lives in sand, fine gravel and mud. Found on lower shore and sub-littoral zone. **BODY** comprises a slender column, attached to buried stone and covered in sediment. Only terminal end is visible, with up to 200 rather long tentacles, typically banded and marbled grey-brown and buff. **STATUS** Widespread and locally common.

Elegant Anemone *Sagartia elegans* Diameter to 4cm
Attractive but variable sea anemone. Lives on rocks, sometimes in crevices or holes, into which it retreats if disturbed. Found from lower shore into deeper water. **BODY** comprises a column with non-adhesive pale suckers, and terminal array of up to 200 tentacles. Several colour forms exist, including: pure white; pale tentacles and orange-yellow disc; marbled grey, brown and buff; pinkish tentacles and pale disc. **STATUS** Widespread and locally common.

Fountain Anemone *Sagartiogeton laceratus* Height to 6cm
Attractive anemone. Sub-littoral, often part-buried in silt, attached to stones; occasionally on shells of large whelks. In areas where it is common, sometimes hauled in by fisherman, attached to weights and rigs. **BODY** comprises a smooth orange-buff column, often with pale longitudinal lines. Disc is orange with up to 200 slender tentacles. Reproduces by division, hence it can appear damaged. **STATUS** Widespread and locally common, mainly in the W.

Sandalled Anemone *Actinothoe sphyrodeta* Diameter to 5cm
Attractive sea anemone, found on rocks in relatively exposed spots, from lower shore into deeper water. **BODY** comprises a smooth column, often marked with longitudinal lines but lacking suckers; terminal array of up to 100 slender tentacles. Overall colour can be either pure white, or white with yellow oral disc. **STATUS** Widespread and locally common.

Calliactis parasitica

Calliactis parasitica Length to 10cm
Extraordinary and distinctive sea anemone, invariably found attached to Common Whelk shells occupied by Common Hermit Crab (p. 164). Relationship is commensal, possibly symbiotic, but not parasitic. **BODY** comprises a rough-looking orange-buff column and up to 700 rather small buffish tentacles. **STATUS** Widespread but encountered only occasionally. **SIMILAR SPECIES Cloak Anemone** *Adamsia carciniopados* (width to 5cm) lives symbiotically on shells occupied by hermit crab *Pagurus prideaux* (p. 164). Body is creamy white with pink spots. Mainly sub-littoral.

Diadumene cincta Length to 6cm
Colourful anemone. Grows on kelp holdfasts and among sponges; lower shore and sub-littoral zone. **BODY** has smooth column and up to 200 slender tentacles. Usually orange. **STATUS** Local, S Britain only.

Daisy Anemone

Sagartia troglodytes

Elegant Anemone

Fountain Anemone

Sandalled Anemone

Calliactis
parasitica

Diadumene cincta

Starlet Sea Anemone

Starlet Sea Anemone
Nematostella vectensis Diameter to 1cm
Worm-like, burrowing sea anemone found in silty mud in undisturbed saline lagoons. **BODY** comprises a slender, unattached column, up to 2cm long and mostly buried in sediment; and 16 slender, translucent tentacles. **STATUS** Very local, mainly around the Solent and East Anglian coast. Protected by law.

Devonshire Cup-coral
Caryophyllia smithii Diameter to 3cm
A hard coral with a calcified external skeleton. Grows attached to rock, usually below low water, sometimes in pools on lower shore. **BODY** comprises pale pinkish or peachy knob-tipped tentacles atop a hard base; terminal end is oval with radiating ridges, and animal withdraws inside if disturbed. **STATUS** Widespread and locally common only in the W and N.

Scarlet-and-gold Star-coral *Balanophyllia regia* Diameter to 2cm
Colourful little hard coral. Grows in rock crevices, usually below low water, sometimes in pools on lower shore. **BODY** comprises up to 48 blunt-ended tentacles, dotted with pale warts, and a deep orange oral disc. **STATUS** Local, restricted to SW Britain.

Jewel Anemone *Corynactis viridis* Length to 4cm
Attractive and distinctive sea anemone-like soft coral. Grows attached to rock, sometimes in dense groups, usually below low water or occasionally in pools on lower shore. **BODY** comprises a column and tentacles with pale, knobbed tips. Colour varies, but often pinkish purple or green. **STATUS** Widespread and locally common in W and N Britain.

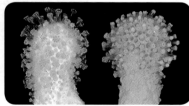

Dead-Man's Fingers (*left*) and Red Sea Fingers (*right*)

Dead-man's Fingers
Alcyonium digitatum Length to 15cm
Fleshy soft coral. Grows on rocks, usually below low water, sometime in pools on lower shore. Dislodged specimens are sometimes washed up. **BODY** branches into finger-like lobes; usually either orange or white, the surface studded with translucent polyps that can withdraw if disturbed. **STATUS** Widespread and locally common.

Red Sea Fingers

Red Sea Fingers *Alcyonium glomeratum* Diameter to 20cm
Similar to Dead-man's Fingers (above) but with more slender, redder 'fingers'. Grows on rocks, usually below low water. **BODY** branches into finger-like lobes; red, with contrasting white polyps that can withdraw if disturbed. **STATUS** Local, mainly SW Britain.

Sea Gooseberry *Pleurobrachia pileus* Length to 2cm
Generally the commonest sea gooseberry. Pelagic and mainly oceanic, but seasonally abundant inshore, mainly in spring and summer. **BODY** comprises a transparent ovoid structure with 8 rows of beating and shimmering, iridescent hairs for swimming. Two fishing tentacles trail below. **STATUS** Occasionally common, mainly in the W and N.

Comb Jelly *Beroe cucumis* Length to 12cm
Distinctive pelagic animal, occasionally common inshore in summer months. **BODY** comprises a transparent bag-like structure, open at mouth end and with longitudinal lines of beating hairs. The commensal amphipod crustacean *Hyperia galba* (p. 158) often lives inside. **STATUS** Commonest in the W and N.

Starlet Sea Anemone

Devonshire Cup-coral

Jewel Anemone, typical form

Dead-man's Fingers

Scarlet-and-gold Star-coral

Red Sea Fingers

Sea Gooseberry

Comb Jelly

Jewel Anemone, green form

INTRODUCING MARINE SEGMENTED WORMS

Segmented worms may not be the most glamorous of marine creatures, but their importance in marine ecology cannot be overstated. Burrowing, filter-feeding species help consolidate silty substrates, while almost all segmented worms are food for a wide range of predators, from crustaceans to fish and birds.

SEGMENTED WORM STRUCTURE AND CLASSIFICATION

As their common name suggests, the long, usually cylindrical bodies of members of the phylum Annelida are segmented. In many species the segments are conspicuous, while in some groups they are covered and obscured by soft plates or hairs. The mouth is near the head end and the gut runs the entire length of the body. Some annelid worm groups have bristles and outgrowths on the segments.

In the marine world, familiar representatives of the phylum Annelida are placed in three sub-groups: class Oligochaeta (whose best-known members are terrestrial earthworms) – small, easily overlooked and relatively unspecialised worms, including the Bloodworm *Tubifex* sp., a denizen of organic-rich silt; class Hirundinea – leeches, marine species of which suck the blood of fish and have distinct suckers at both ends; and class Polychaeta – the most diverse and well-represented class of segmented worms in the marine world. The range of polychaete worms found on the seashore is too diverse to discuss fully in a book of this size, but the following are some of the most distinctive groups:

Bloodworm *Tubifex* sp.

Ragworms – active, predatory worms that burrow in mud and silt. The body comprises 100 or so segments and can be slightly flattened depending on the species. There are antennae, tentacles and eyes at the head end; at the front of the gut is an eversible pharynx that can be projected out of the mouth. Almost all segments have an upper and lower pair of bristles that aid locomotion, and a pair of filaments is present at the tail end.

King Ragworm.

Catworms – active, predatory worms, rather similar to ragworms. The body comprises 100 or so segments. The head is relatively small, and at the front end of the gut is an eversible pharynx that can be projected out of the mouth. Almost all segments have an upper and lower pair of bristles with a gill in between. There is a single filament at the tail end. Agitated animals swim in a sinuous manner.

Catworm *Nephtys caeca.*

Paddleworms – long worms comprising several hundred segments. There are tentacles and antennae at the head end, and most of the remaining segments bear a pair of flattened, paddle-like appendages. Paddleworms are active carnivores.

Phyllodoce groenlandica.

Scaleworms – unusual-looking polychaete worms whose dorsal surface is mostly or entirely covered with overlapping scales; in most species, the body is very flattened. In the case of the Sea Mouse and its relatives, the scales are covered in a dense mat of hair-like bristles that completely covers the dorsal surface.

Alentia gelatinosa.

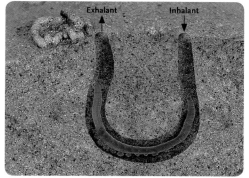

Blow Lug in its burrow.

Lugworms – sedentary worms that live in U-shaped burrows in mud and silty sand. Segments at the front end of the body are armed with bunches of bristles; segments in the middle section have feathery gills; and the tail end is narrower than the rest of the body. Lugworms feed in situ in their burrows: silt and detritus is ingested via the mouth, food particles are digested, and sand is excreted at the tail end, building up as little mounds of tubular 'casts'.

Sand Mason and relatives – plump-bodied worms with a swollen front section and narrower, tapering tail section. At the head end are conspicuous tentacles and branched gills. Many species live in unsophisticated burrows under stones and other objects, the tentacles collecting detritus from the nearby seabed. The Sand Mason constructs a protective tube of stones and small shells, and lives part-buried in silty sand.

Sand Mason removed from its tube.

Fanworms – intriguing worms that have a funnel-shaped arrangement of fairly stiff tentacles at the head end. When feeding, these tentacles project beyond the mouth of the tube in which the worm lives and assist with filter-feeding. Movement or sudden changes in light intensity, detected by sensitive eye-spots, cause the tentacles to be withdrawn.

Peacock Worm.

Tubeworms – interesting worms that live inside calcified tubes, these attached along their length to a solid object; this might be a stone or shell in some species, or a broad seaweed frond in others. A fan-shaped arrangement of tentacles can be protruded outside the mouth of the tube, allowing filter-feeding. In some species the mouth of the tube can be sealed by a modified tentacle.

Ficopomatus enigmaticus.

Neoamphitrite figulus

Polycirrus caliendrum

Neoamphitrite figulus
Length to 20cm
Soft-bodied worm. Lives in burrows on muddy shores and in estuaries; sometimes found under stones. ADULT has 100 or so segments, anterior 24 swollen and with chaetae. Head has mobile brown feeding tentacles and 3 pairs of divided red gills. STATUS Widespread and locally common.

Eupolymnia nebulosa
Length to 15cm
Soft-bodied worm. Lives in a slimy tube, often under stones on lower shore. ADULT has 100 segments, anterior 17 with chaetae; body is brown with white spots. Head has brownish feeding tentacles marked with narrow pale bands, and shortish red gills. STATUS Widespread and locally common.

Polycirrus caliendrum
Length to 8cm
Extremely colourful and distinctive worm. Lives in a mucous tube, under stones and debris on sheltered muddy shores. ADULT is bright orange with 70–90 segments; much of head end is often obscured by tangled mass of tentacles. STATUS Local, mainly in W Britain.

Thelepus cincinnatus Length to 15cm
Tube-dwelling worm. Tube is encrusted with debris and located under stones and holdfasts on sheltered shores. ADULT has 100 or so segments, anterior 30 or more with chaetae. Head end has pale tentacles and short, branched red gills. STATUS Widespread and locally common.

Cirratulus cirratus Length to 10cm
Slender worm with fairly uniformly sized segments. Lives mostly buried in mud beneath stones or among eelgrass roots. ADULT is orange-red with 140 or so segments. Head is blunt and bears 2 groups of 2–8 tentacles; these are often all that can be seen of the worm. Slender, tentacle-like gills appear on other segments. STATUS Widespread and locally common.

Cirriformia tentaculata Length to 15cm
Colourful worm. Found under stones in muddy gravel, on lower shore. Thread-like red tentacles are sometimes visible in shallow water. ADULT has 300 or so segments and is reddish (breeding male is yellow, breeding female greenish). Head is pointed and lacks eyes; has 2 bunches of numerous red tentacles arising behind head and red tentacle-like gills along much of body. STATUS Widespread and locally common.

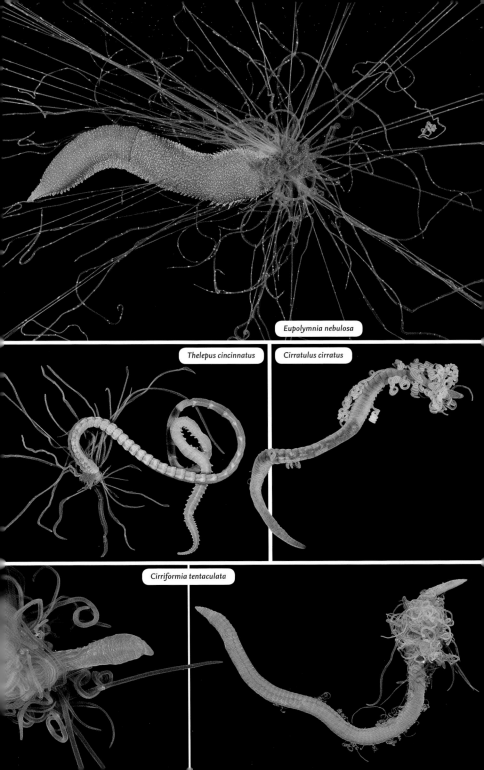

Eupolymnia nebulosa

Thelepus cincinnatus

Cirratulus cirratus

Cirriformia tentaculata

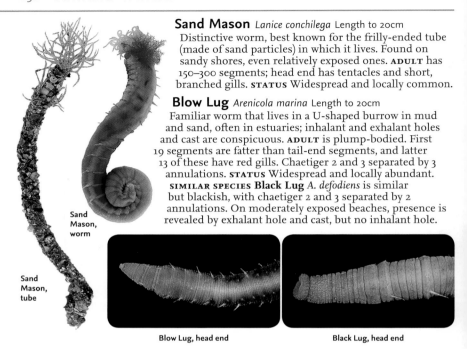

Sand Mason *Lanice conchilega* Length to 20cm
Distinctive worm, best known for the frilly-ended tube (made of sand particles) in which it lives. Found on sandy shores, even relatively exposed ones. **ADULT** has 150–300 segments; head end has tentacles and short, branched gills. **STATUS** Widespread and locally common.

Blow Lug *Arenicola marina* Length to 20cm
Familiar worm that lives in a U-shaped burrow in mud and sand, often in estuaries; inhalant and exhalant holes and cast are conspicuous. **ADULT** is plump-bodied. First 19 segments are fatter than tail-end segments, and latter 13 of these have red gills. Chaetiger 2 and 3 separated by 3 annulations. **STATUS** Widespread and locally abundant. **SIMILAR SPECIES Black Lug** *A. defodiens* is similar but blackish, with chaetiger 2 and 3 separated by 2 annulations. On moderately exposed beaches, presence is revealed by exhalant hole and cast, but no inhalant hole.

Sand Mason, worm

Sand Mason, tube

Blow Lug, head end

Black Lug, head end

Arenicolides branchialis Length to 20cm
Similar to Blow Lug (above) but tail end is not noticeably narrower. Lives in crevices in, and gaps between, rocks lodged in muddy sand. **ADULT** has bristles of some sort on all segments, and gills on segments 13–40 or so. **STATUS** Widespread and locally common. **SIMILAR SPECIES** *A. ecaudata* has gills on segments 16–50 or so.

Scoloplos armiger Length to 12cm
Slender worm that burrows in muddy sand on lower shore. **ADULT** is reddish; front 20 or so segments are flattened, the remainder rounded. Head end is pointed, tail end has 2 slender appendages, and most segments except anterior 12 or so have gills. **STATUS** Widespread and locally common.

Glycera tridactyla Length to 10cm
Slender worm, found in muddy sand on lower shore. Rolls into a tight corkscrew when disturbed. **ADULT** is pearly pink with up to 170 annulated segments. Head end is pointed with 4 minute antennae; tail end has 2 projections. **STATUS** Widespread and locally common.

Glycera alba Length to 6cm
Slender worm, found among and under rocks on lower shore. **ADULT** is whitish, palest towards head end, with 120 or so segments. Head end is pointed, with 4 tiny antennae arranged in star-like fashion. Parapods are armed with bristles. **STATUS** Local, mainly in SW and W Britain.

Glycera tridactyla, head end

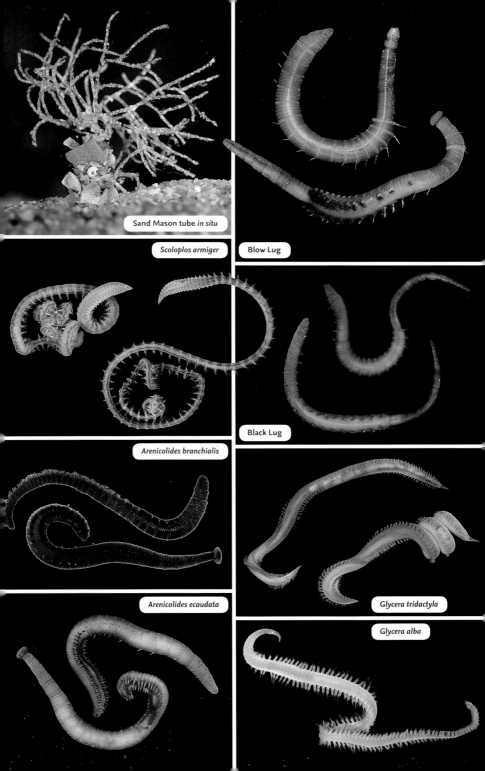

Sand Mason tube *in situ*

Scoloplos armiger

Blow Lug

Arenicolides branchialis

Black Lug

Arenicolides ecaudata

Glycera tridactyla

Glycera alba

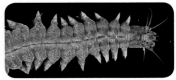

Estuary Ragworm
Hediste diversicolor Length to 12cm

Active, flattened worm; feels 'flabby' when handled – if lifted midway with a pencil, body goes completely flaccid. Lives in a burrow in muddy sand, often in estuaries. **ADULT** is reddish or greenish, with 120 or so segments. Head has 2 small antennae, 2 palps and 4 tentacles on each side; tail end has 2 appendages. Red blood vessel runs dorsal length of body. **STATUS** Widespread and locally common.

ABOVE: **Ragworm**; BELOW: *Nereis pelagica*

Ragworm *Perinereis cultrifera* Length to 20cm
Familiar worm, found under stones, and in crevices and laminarian holdfasts. **ADULT** has 120 or so segments, slightly domed in cross section. Body is greenish brown, with red dorsal blood vessel; parapods are reddish. Head has 2 anterior antennae, 2 palps and 4 tentacles on each side; posterior pair is longest. Tail has 2 appendages. **STATUS** Widespread and locally common.

Nereis pelagica Length to 12cm
Active worm, similar to Estuary Ragworm (above) but favouring different habitat: lives in a mucous tube among laminarian holdfasts. **ADULT** is more cylindrical than flattened, with 120 or so segments. Body is reddish brown or greenish, with a metallic sheen. Head has 2 small antennae, 2 palps and 4 tentacles on each side; tail end has 2 appendages. **STATUS** Widespread and locally common.

King Ragworm *Alitta virens* Length to 25cm
Impressive worm, unmistakable when adult because of its size. Burrows in muddy sand, often in estuaries or sheltered bays. **ADULT** has up to 200 broadly flattened segments and is green with a metallic sheen. Head has 2 antennae, 2 palps and 4 tentacles on each side; tail end has 2 appendages. **STATUS** Widespread and locally common.

ABOVE: **King Ragworm**; BELOW: *Nephtys caeca*

Catworms *Nephtys* sp. Length to 20cm
Active worms that burrow in muddy sand on sheltered shores and in estuaries. Swim in a sinuous manner. Several species are widespread but specific identification is hard in the field. Regularly encountered species include *N. caeca* (in muddy gravel and sand, *see also* p. 128), *N. hombergii* (in muddy sand) and White Catworm *N. cirrosa* (in clean sand). **ADULTS** are flattened, with up to 200 segments, pinkish grey with a pearly iridescence. Head is tiny, with 4 tiny antennae (appears to lack antennae to naked eye). Tail has 1 tiny projecting appendage. **STATUS** Widespread and locally common.

Marphysa sanguinea Length to 50cm
Impressive worm. Superficially ragworm-like, but head appendages and presence of gills allows separation. Lives in a tube under stones and in mud on lower shore. **ADULT** is pinkish red with 250 or so segments. Head has 5 short appendages, tail end has 2 appendages, and segments on latter half of body have paired red gills. **STATUS** Local in S Britain.

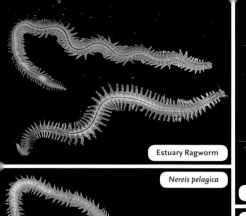

Estuary Ragworm

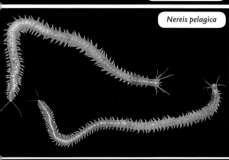

Nereis pelagica

free-swimming, reprodutive stage
(known as an epitoke) of *Nereis* sp.

Marphysa sanguinea

head end

tail end

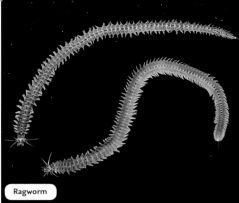

Ragworm

King Ragworm

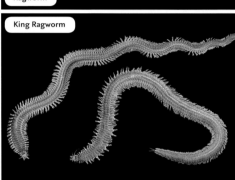

Nephtys caeca

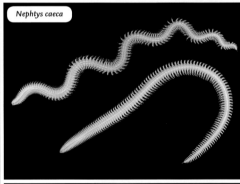

Nephtys hombergii

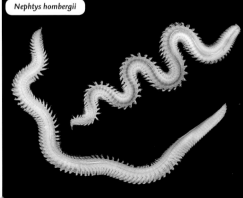

Gallery Worm

Gallery Worm *Capitella capitata* Length to 8cm
Earthworm-like marine worm and one of several
similar, related *Capitella* species. Lives buried in
muddy sand on lower shore. **ADULT** is pinkish
red and yellow, with 100 or so segments. Body is
extremely contractile. Head end is conical and lacks
appendages. Segments bear simple chaetae and
have a 'ribbed' appearance. **STATUS** Widespread and
locally common.

Lysidice ninetta Length to 5cm
Intriguing worm, sometimes found crawling over
rocks in pools on lower shore. **ADULT** has rather
rounded body. Head bears 3 small, bluntly pointed tentacles that are pale and
contrast with otherwise darker, mostly reddish-purple body; segment 4 is
contrastingly pale. **STATUS** Local, mainly in the S and SW.

Phyllodoce lamelligera Length to 50cm
Colourful paddleworm, found under rocks on lower
shore. Secretes mucus if disturbed. **ADULT** has several
hundred segments. Dorsal surface is bluish green,
paddles are greenish or brownish. Head has 4 pairs
of long tentacles. **STATUS** Locally common in S and
SW Britain.

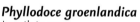

Phyllodoce
lamelligera

Phyllodoce groenlandica
Length to 30cm
Impressive paddleworm, found under
rocks and in crevices on lower shore. **ADULT** has several hundred
segments. Dorsal surface is yellowish green, paddles are green
with brown markings. Head has 4 pairs of long tentacles.
STATUS Widespread and locally common.

Phyllodoce maculata Length to 7cm
Slender, easily overlooked paddleworm. Lives
on shores with muddy sand, often around
mussel beds; seen in shallow pools at low tide.
ADULT has up to 250 yellowish-brown segments,
each with dark central marking; yellowish
paddles also have dark central mark. **STATUS**
Widespread and locally common.

Phyllodoce
groenlandica

Greenleaf Worm *Eulalia viridis* Length to 10cm
Slender, very colourful paddleworm. Lives on rocky
shores; found under stones and in laminarian holdfasts. **ADULT** has up to
200 green segments and leaf-like, pointed green paddles. Head has 5
antennae (2 lateral pairs and 1 on dorsal surface) plus 4 pairs
of tentacles. **STATUS** Widespread and fairly common.

Flabelligera affinis Length to 3cm
Unusual and distinctive worm. Lives permanently
inside a sheath of secreted mucus, to which
particles adhere, hence easily overlooked. Found
under stones on lower shore; sometimes among
spines of sea urchins. **ADULT** has 40–50 segments,
with 2 palps and fringe of delicate gills at head end.

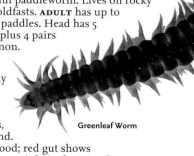

Greenleaf Worm

Body is rather transparent, tinged by greenish blood; red gut shows
through. **STATUS** Widespread but generally scarce, mainly in the W and N.

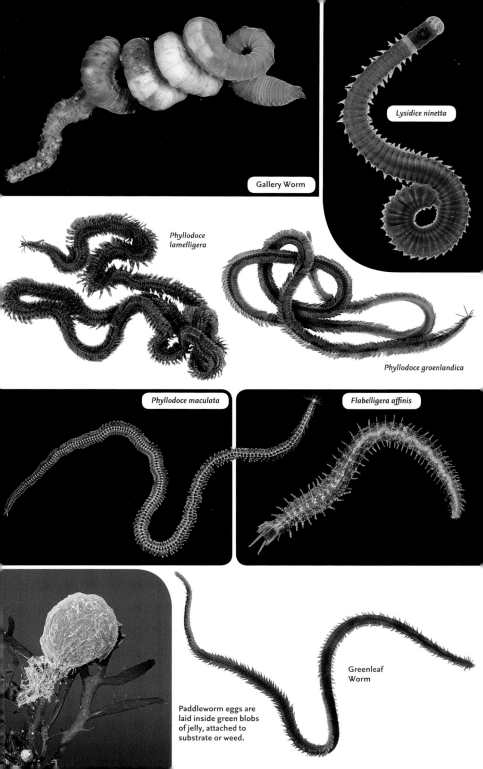

Gallery Worm

Lysidice ninetta

Phyllodoce lamelligera

Phyllodoce groenlandica

Phyllodoce maculata

Flabelligera affinis

Greenleaf Worm

Paddleworm eggs are laid inside green blobs of jelly, attached to substrate or weed.

diagram showing Parchment Worm, *in situ* in its tube

Parchment Worm
Chaetopterus variopedatus Length to 20cm
Bizarre and unmistakable worm. Lives in a tough U-shaped tube made of parchment-like material encrusted with sand and debris. Found on relatively sheltered shores, in muddy sand at low water and sub-littoral zone. Easily overlooked. **ADULT** has body in 3 sections: head end is fleshy with palps; middle region is concerned with processing food; tail end has numerous chaetae. **STATUS** Widespread and very locally common, except in the SE.

Owenia fusiformis Length to 9cm
Distinctive worm. Lives in a tough tube, tapering at both ends and coated with neatly 'tiled' flattish sand grains. Found buried in clean sand at mid-tide level on extensive beaches. **ADULT** is green with around 30 segments. Head end has short, frilly tentacles. **STATUS** Widespread and locally common, except in the SE.

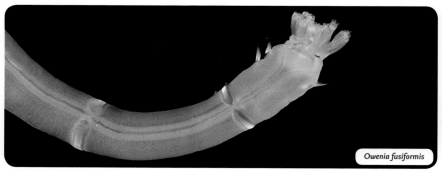
Owenia fusiformis

Gattyana cirrosa Length to 5cm
Impressive scaleworm, always living commensally in tubes of *Chaetopterus* or terebellid worms. **ADULT** has 15 pairs of semi-opaque scales that do not cover last 4–5 segments of body. **STATUS** Widespread and very locally common.

Alentia gelatinosa Length to 8cm
Delicate scaleworm, found under rocks on sheltered shores. Looks gelatinous. **ADULT** has 18 pairs of translucent yellowish-brown scales, covering whole body. **STATUS** Widespread and fairly common.

Adyte assimilis Length to 20mm
Delicate worm that readily sheds scales. Found on *Echinus* sea urchins and in kelp holdfasts, usually where echinoderms are present. **ADULT** has 15 pairs of almost transparent, subtly yellowish-buff scales, covering most of body. **STATUS** Widespread but local and hard to detect.

Sigalion mathildae Length to 12cm
Rather atypical scaleworm with a cylindrical body. Rolls into a spiral when disturbed, recalling a miniature Slow-worm. Found in sand at low water. **ADULT** is creamy white with around 200 segments and 150 or so scales, covering whole body. **STATUS** Widespread but local, mainly in the W and NW. **SIMILAR SPECIES Sthenelais boa** (length to 15cm) has a slender but slightly flattened, tapering body and snake-like appearance. Head has a median antenna, 2 lateral antennae and 2 long palps. Mainly in the W, in muddy sand.

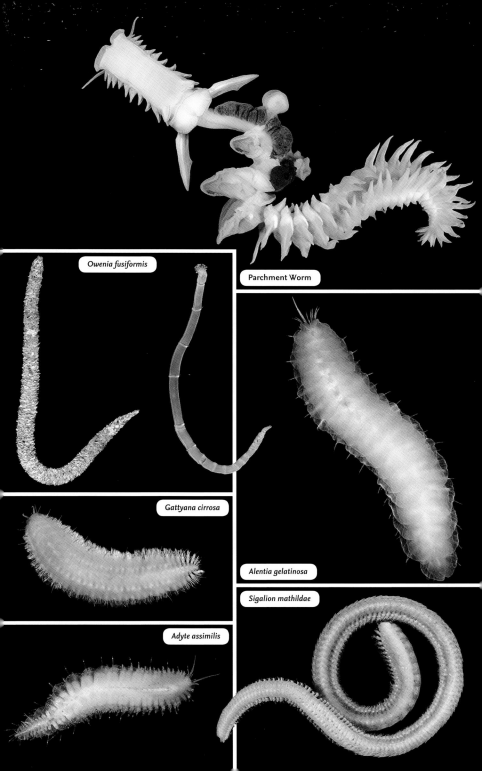

Owenia fusiformis

Parchment Worm

Gattyana cirrosa

Alentia gelatinosa

Sigalion mathildae

Adyte assimilis

Lepidonotus clava Length to 25mm
Well-marked scaleworm, found under rocks on lower shore. ADULT is parallel-sided with 12 pairs of round scales; these do not overlap down mid-line. STATUS Widespread and locally common.

Lepidonotus squamatus Length to 5cm
Scaleworm found under rocks on lower shore. ADULT is parallel-sided with 12 pairs of round, textured scales; these are yellowish, marbled with brown, often with a dark central spot. Scales overlap down mid-line. STATUS Widespread and locally common.

Lagisca extenuata Length to 35mm
Active scaleworm, found under rocks at low tide. ADULT has 15 pairs of scales covering anterior part of body; posterior 10 or so segments are not covered. STATUS Widespread and fairly common.

Harmothoe imbricata Length to 45mm
Active scaleworm, found under rocks and in laminarian holdfasts, at low water. ADULT has 15 pairs of scales covering whole dorsal surface. Scales are coated in granules and have hair-fringed margins; often yellowish brown with a metallic sheen, sometimes dark-centred. Frontal horns and dorsal cirri are fairly long. STATUS Widespread and locally common.

Harmothoe impar Length to 25mm
Well-marked scaleworm, found under stones at low water. ADULT has 15 pairs of scales covering whole dorsal surface. Scales are textured, fringed and variably marbled brown with a yellowish central spot. Front horns and dorsal cirri are long. STATUS Widespread and locally fairly common.

Harmothoe glabra Length to 55mm
Distinctive scaleworm, found at low water, usually in association with terebellid worms and their tubes. ADULT has 15 pairs of overlapping scales. Scales are slightly translucent yellow with a chestnut margin. Front horns and dorsal cirri are long. STATUS Widespread but scarce; mainly in the W.

Harmothoe lunulata Length to 35mm
Well-marked scaleworm, sometimes found under rocks at low water but more usually in tubes of Sand Mason (p. 132) and other worms. ADULT has 15 pairs of overlapping scales. Scales are smooth and unfringed, pale yellowish with a dark sub-marginal crescent and central spot. Frontal horns are long, dorsal cirri are short. STATUS Widespread but local, mainly in the W and N.

Sea Mouse Aphrodita aculeata Length to 20cm
Atypical but unmistakable scaleworm; hardly recognisable as a worm. Found part-buried in sand at extreme low water; sometimes stranded. ADULT has oval body, scales hidden by a dense coat of bristly hairs; dorsal hairs are flattened, lateral ones are iridescent. STATUS Widespread; locally common but seen only occasionally.

Lepidonotus clava

Lepidonotus squamatus

Lagisca extenuata

Harmothoe imbricata

Harmothoe impar

Harmothoe glabra

Harmothoe lunulata

Janua pagenstecheri Diameter to 2mm

Small worm that lives inside a calcified, sinistrally spiral tube attached to seaweed, particularly Serrated Wrack (p. 34); often in small groups. ADULT has tentacles on its head that project when immersed in sea water. Tube is white; entrance can be sealed by operculum at low tide. STATUS Widespread and locally common.

Limpet shell coated with *Janua pagenstecheri*

Spirorbis spirorbis Diameter to 4mm

Small worm that lives inside a calcified, dextrally spiral tube, attached to a range of objects including coralline seaweeds, shells and crab carapaces. ADULT has tentacles on its head that project when immersed. Tube is grubby white and usually with 3 ridges; entrance can be sealed by operculum. STATUS Widespread and locally common.

Serpula vermicularis tube

Serpula vermicularis Tube length to 70mm

Worm that lives in a sinuous calcareous tube (round in cross section), usually with 3 longitudinal ridges; attached to rocks and bivalve mollusc shells at low water. ADULT has 60–70 tentacles. Tube is pinkish white; entrance can be plugged with funnel-shaped operculum, the end fringed with rounded teeth. STATUS Widespread and locally common.

Pomatoceros lamarcki tube

Pomatoceros triqueter Tube length to 25mm

Worm that lives inside a calcareous tube (triangular in cross section) with a single longitudinal ridge; tube is attached along its length to rock or other hard substrate. Mostly sub-littoral, sometimes found at low tide. ADULT has feathery tentacles at head end, which extend when immersed. Entrance can be plugged by cup-shaped calcareous plate. STATUS Widespread and locally common. SIMILAR SPECIES *P. lamarcki* is similar but tube has 3 longitudinal ridges along its length; entrance can be plugged by bulb-shaped operculum. Found on rocks on lower shore.

BELOW:
Hydroides dianthus tube

Hydroides norvegica Tube length to 30mm

Worm that lives in a calcareous tube (round in cross section); sometimes several entwined. ADULT has 2 groups of 8 or so tentacles. Tube is sometimes spiral at base, mostly brownish but white terminally. Entrance can be plugged with funnel-shaped, spine-tipped operculum; spine array is radiating and symmetrical. STATUS Widespread and locally common. SIMILAR SPECIES *Filograna implexa* (tube length to 25mm) lives in a more delicate and slender tube (round in cross section), usually in entwined masses. Has 8 tentacles and plugs tube with 2 cup-shaped opercula. Widespread and locally common.

Hydroides dianthus Tube length to 30mm

Similar to *H. norvegica* (above) but separable by studying operculum. Lives in calcareous tube. ADULT has 2 groups of 8 or so tentacles. Tube is white, sometimes stained brown. Entrance can be plugged with funnel-shaped, spine-tipped operculum; spine array is asymmetrical, some spines incurved. STATUS Introduced from North America, first discovered in 1970 in the Solent. Now locally common there and may be spreading.

Ficopomatus enigmaticus Tube length to 25mm

Worm that lives in a calcareous tube (round in cross section), typically in dense masses (several tubes deep) encrusting stones and other solid objects; often in estuaries and tidal lagoons. ADULT has 12–20 feathery tentacles. Tube is often flared at mouth, mostly yellowish brown but whitish terminally; entrance can be plugged by swollen, flat-ended, spine-tipped operculum. STATUS Widespread and locally common.

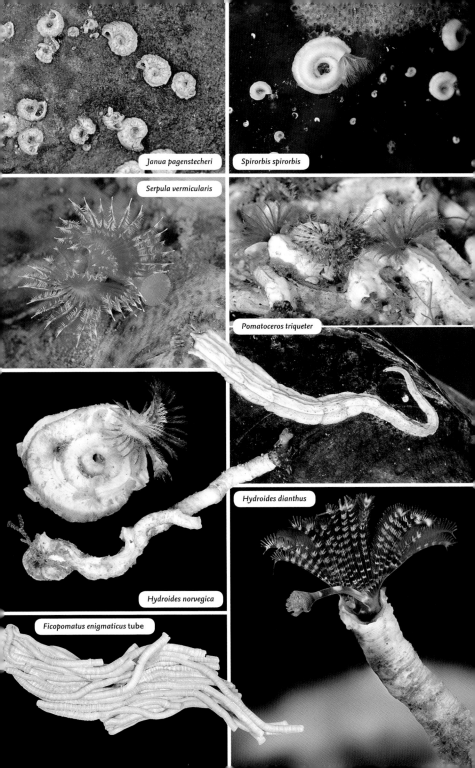

Janua pagenstecheri

Spirorbis spirorbis

Serpula vermicularis

Pomatoceros triqueter

Hydroides dianthus

Hydroides norvegica

Ficopomatus enigmaticus tube

Peacock Worm *Sabella pavonina* Tube length to 25cm

Distinctive worm that lives inside a tough, rubbery tube covered with silt particles. Lives part-buried in silty mud (5–7cm of tube protrude), often in eelgrass beds. Tentacles are visible only when worm is undisturbed and immersed. **ADULT** has several hundred segments. Head bears 2 arrays of up to 50 tentacles; these are banded with colour and, when spread, form a daisy-like array. **STATUS** Widespread and locally common. **SIMILAR SPECIES *Megalomma vesiculosum*** (tube length to 12cm) lives inside a tough tube, to which debris is attached; only 3cm or so of tube protrude. Adult has 100–200 segments and up to 50 banded tentacles; each has a terminal eye-spot, those on central 2 tentacles largest. Locally common in the S and SW.

Honeycomb Worm *Sabellaria alveolata*
Tube length to 4cm

Worm that lives in a sandy tube. Tubes form tightly packed masses, attached basally to part-buried rocks in muddy sand, on lower shore. Overall effect of colony resembles honeycomb. **ADULT** has up to 30 segments, a reflexed 'tail' and a crown of very short tentacles at head that protrude from tube end when immersed. **STATUS** Very locally common, mainly in the S and SW.

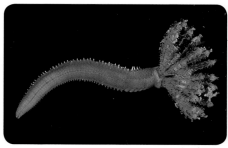

Bispira volutacornis Length to 10cm

Worm that lives in a mud tube, usually mostly under rocks or in a crevice on lower shore. **ADULT** has up to 100 segments, head end with 2 spiral whorls of 90 or so whitish tentacles that protrude when immersed. **STATUS** Locally common in the S and SW.

Pseudopotamilla reniformis Length to 10cm

Worm that lives in a slightly translucent membranous tube, usually mostly protected in a rock crevice or hole. When worm withdraws, end of tube folds over, making it hard to spot. **ADULT** has up to 100 segments, head end with 20 or so translucent greenish tentacles, each marked with 3 dark eye-spots. **STATUS** Widespread and locally common.

Branchiomma bombyx Length to 45mm

Worm that lives in a membranous tube, lodged among epiphytic sea squirts and other colonists of seaweeds, holdfasts and rock undersides. Small individuals are relatively mobile and move around if dislodged. **ADULT** has up to 25 feathery tentacles on each side; each with several pairs of tiny eyes and paired projections (like curled tongues). Tentacles retract into tube if animal is disturbed. **STATUS** Widespread but local.

Polydora ciliata Length to 25mm

Slender worm, easily overlooked. Worm's tube is in hole in limestone rock or coralline seaweeds. When undisturbed, 2 long palps protrude. **ADULT** has 150 or so segments, most with chaetae. Head is blunt, with 2 palps; body ends in a funnel. **STATUS** Widespread, except in the far N.

Euclymene lumbricoides Length to 10cm

Slender worm that lives in a particle-encrusted mucous tube in muddy sand at low water, often in eelgrass beds. **ADULT** is reddish with rather uniform segmentation; 19 segments bear chaetae, and the front ones are banded. Head has notched plate and tail end has fringed funnel. **STATUS** Widespread and locally common in the W.

close up of
tube entrances

Honeycomb Worm

colony

close up of worm
at tube entrance

Peacock Worm

Pseudopotamilla reniformis

Branchiomma bombyx

Bispira volutacornis

tubes, *in situ*

Polydora ciliata

Euclymene lumbricoides

worm

tube

Pygospio elegans Length to 15mm
Distinctive but tiny worm, easily overlooked; tubes, constructed from small sand particles, are more obvious. Lives in blackish mud, in estuaries and mudflats. ADULT has thread-like body with 55 or so segments. Head is blunt-ended with 2 long palps; rear end is fringed by leaf-like projections. STATUS Widespread and locally very common.

Malacoceros fuliginosus Length to 50mm
Tube-dwelling worm, found under stones on muddy sand, at low water. ADULT is slender, with finger-like red gills on dorsal surface of each segment. Head has 2 long palps and lobe with frontal 'horns'. Tail end is fringed with 8 or so petal-like lobes. STATUS Widespread and locally common.

Odontosyllis gibba Length to 25mm
Active, slender worm. Found under stones and in seaweed holdfasts on lower shore; swims in surface layers of sea at night. ADULT has body comprising 40 or so segments, each marbled brown and white. Head has 4 red eyes, 3 antennae (1 median) and paired palps. STATUS Widespread but local, mainly in the S and W.

Typosyllis krohni Length to 30mm
Active worm, found in holdfasts and under stones. ADULT has slender body. Cirri alternate in length; longer ones are also thick and often curl up. Eyes are red. STATUS Local, mainly in the SW and W.

Amblyosyllis formosa Length to 15mm
Active, distinctive worm. Found among algal holdfasts on lower shore. ADULT has 15 roughly triangular segments and long cirri that often curl at tip. Eyes are red. STATUS Local, mainly in the SW and W.

Flatworms (phylum Platyhelminthes)
Small, flat carnivorous worms, unrelated to annelids; glide over substrates by means of cilia. Found under stones on lower shore. Head end has mouth; sometimes eye-spots and simple tentacles too. Most are hard to identify to specific level, but sub-littoral species *Prosthecereaus vittatus* has unique pattern of black stripes on a creamy-white body.

Arrow Worms Parasagitta sp. (phylum Chaetognatha) Length to 10mm
Predatory worms, unrelated to annelids. Present in plankton and rock pools. Hard to detect; easiest to observe after dark using a torch. BODY is arrow-shaped and almost transparent. Head has fringe of hairs. Fins aid movement. STATUS Widespread and common but easily overlooked.

Nemertean Worms (phylum Nemertea)
Sometimes referred to as ribbon worms, nemerteans are not related to segmented annelid worms. Most species have elongate, smooth and rather flat bodies. The tail end usually tapers, and the head end is usually swollen, sometimes with visible eye-spots. Nemerteans are active predators of smaller invertebrates. Although some are well marked, most nemerteans are hard to identify to species level.

Bootlace Worm

Bootlace Worm Lineus longissimus Length to 10m
Distinctive nemertean worm and a contender for Britain's longest animal. Body is fragile. Found in coiled mass under rocks and in crevices on lower shore. ADULT has soft, slimy, dark brown body. Head end is slightly swollen and marked with longitudinal grooves. STATUS Widespread and locally common.

BELOW: *Golfingia elongata*

Golfingia elongata (phylum Sipuncula) Length to 12cm
Unusual tubular animal, unrelated to segmented annelid worms. Lives buried in muddy sand on lower shore and in sub-littoral zone. ADULT is cylindrical and creamy white, tinged pink. Main part of body has a granular surface. Rear end tapers; has retractile fringe of 20–30 tentacles at front end. STATUS Widespread but local, mainly in the W and NW; probably overlooked.

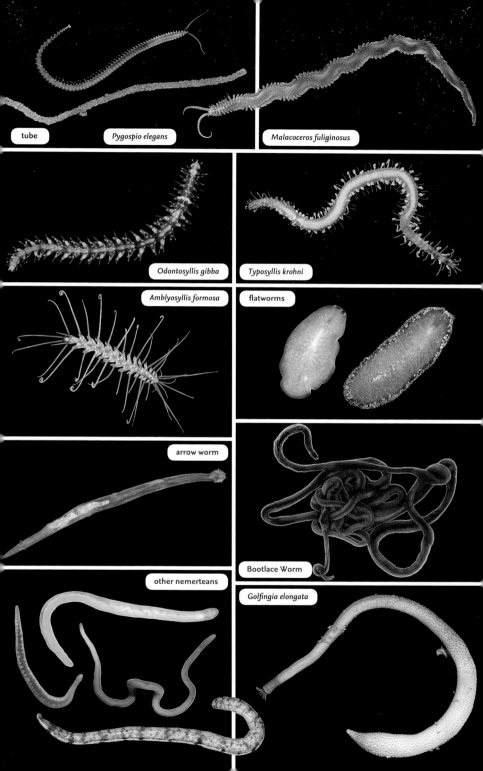

tube

Pygospio elegans

Malacoceros fuliginosus

Odontosyllis gibba

Typosyllis krohni

Amblyosyllis formosa

flatworms

arrow worm

Bootlace Worm

other nemerteans

Golfingia elongata

INTRODUCING COASTAL ARTHROPODS

Arthropods are among the most numerous creatures on the planet. A huge diversity of species can be found in the sea and on the seashore, as well as in coastal terrestrial habitats.

THE RANGE OF ARTHROPODS

Until recently, arthropods were, in classification terms, assigned their own phylum. Nowadays, many biologists elevate each of the various arthropod groups to this status and the term 'arthropod' has become a more general one relating to animals that have a hard outer skeleton and jointed limbs.

Terrestrial arthropod groups, found on the coast, include insects (phylum Hexapoda), centipedes and millepedes (phylum Myriapoda), and spiders (phylum Chelicerata); these groups are dealt with elsewhere in the book, and insects in particular are introduced on p. 183. When it comes to the marine environment (both seashore and open sea), by far the most important and diverse arthropod group is the crustaceans (phylum Crustacea).

INTRODUCING COASTAL CRUSTACEANS

Although a few crustaceans are found on land (woodlice, for example) and in fresh water, the vast majority of species occur in the marine environment. Representatives can be found on rocky and sandy shores, among seaweed holdfasts, in open water, and even as parasites. In fact, almost every conceivable marine habitat will harbour a great diversity of crustacean species, often in abundance.

The archetypal crustacean has a body divided into three sections: head, thorax and abdomen. Each section is segmented, although the segments are often fused and can be hard to discern. Each segment bears a pair of appendages, which are typically modified according to their location and function. Those on the head segments are often modified to serve as sensory organs or mouthparts; elsewhere, they can function as gills or legs (either for walking or swimming, or both). The outer skeleton of a crustacean is typically calcified and hard. In order for the animal to grow, the skin must be shed periodically. Prior to moulting, a crustacean typically resorbs the calcium in its skin, making it soft for a short period. In most crustaceans, there are separate sexes and the larvae are planktonic and free-swimming; the larva becomes more adult-like each time it moults.

Crustaceans are divided into four main subdivisions (classes), three of which are easily found on the shore: copepods (class Copepoda); barnacles (class Cirripedia); and class Malacostraca, which includes the bulk of the classic seashore crustaceans. The fourth, ostracods (class Ostracoda), are very small (to 1mm or so) bivalved creatures and hard to detect. Within the Malacostraca are further subdivisions, called orders; these include mysid shrimps (order Mysidacea), isopods (order Isopoda), amphipods (order Amphipoda), and shrimps, prawns, crabs and lobsters (order Decapoda, which literally means 'ten legs').

Calanus finmarchius, a planktonic copepod.

Copepods – tiny animals. Free-swimming forms are a significant component of zooplankton; they typically swim in a jerky manner (in short spurts), have a pear-shaped body and often carry a pair of egg sacs. There are several parasitic species of copepod, which usually have unusual body forms compared to those of their free-swimming relatives.

Barnacles – atypical and sessile crustaceans with highly modified bodies. They live attached to rocks and other hard substrates, either directly or via a long stalk in the case of goose barnacles. The barnacle body is protected by calcified plates. Barnacles feed by filter-feeding; specialised fan-shaped appendages called cirri beat through the water and collect food particles.

LEFT:
Filter-feeding barnacle *Balanus crenatus*, showing cirri.

RIGHT: *Pranus flexuosus*, a typical mysid shrimp.

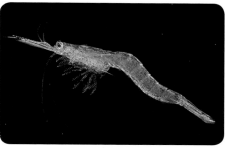

Mysid shrimps – sometimes called opossum shrimps, these are slender animals with delicate appendages and a mostly transparent body; typically, only the eyes appear dark. Many species are seasonally abundant and important as food for larger marine creatures.

Sea Slater, a typical isopod.

Isopods – varied group of small crustaceans, typically with a flattened body that appears distinctly segmented thanks to the dorsal plates. The head is usually obvious, with relatively distinct eyes, and movement is achieved in most species by paired legs on the middle (thoracic) segments of the body. The tail end (telson) is sometimes modified to aid swimming.

Amphipods – small crustaceans with laterally flattened bodies. Typically, the head has obvious paired antennae and eyes; the segmented remainder of the body comprises sections called the pereon, pleon and urosome. Each segment bears specialised appendages; some assist feeding while others are used for walking and swimming.

Beach-hopper, a typical amphipod.

Shrimps and prawns – as with all decapods, the head and thorax are fused, and covered with a plate called the carapace. The body is elongated and a prominent rostrum projects forward between the eyes. There are 10 pairs of legs: five pereopods, the first typically bearing pincers; and five pleopods. At the tail end, the telson is modified to form a fan, used for rapid propulsion through the water.

Common Prawn.

Crabs and lobsters – the head and thorax are fused, and covered with a plate called the carapace. The body is flattened but the shape varies: crabs mostly have a broad carapace, while in lobsters and squat lobsters it is more elongate and slightly cylindrical. There are 10 pairs of legs: five pereopods, the first typically bearing pincers; and five pleopods. At the tail end of lobsters and squat lobsters, the telson is modified to form a fan, used for rapid propulsion through the water.

Green Shore Crab.

Hermit crabs are highly modified animals; the long, coiled, soft abdomen is protected by the empty mollusc shell in which the crab lives.

Common Shiny Woodlouse *Oniscus asellus* Length to 14mm
Found under beach debris above high-tide line. ADULT is shiny; marbled grey and brown, with rows of yellow patches. Head has lateral lobes, and jointed end of antennae comprises 3 sections. STATUS Common and widespread.

Common Rough Woodlouse *Porcellio scaber* Length to 10mm
Found under strandline debris above high-tide line. ADULT is narrower than Common Shiny Woodlouse (above) and greyer, the surface rough not shiny; jointed end of antennae comprises 2 sections. STATUS Common and widespread.

Pill Woodlouse *Armadillidium vulgare* Length to 11mm
Intriguing woodlouse: can roll into a ball when disturbed. Found under stones and debris above high-tide line. ADULT is slate-grey and rounded in cross section. STATUS Commonest in the S.

Sea Slater *Ligia oceanica* Length to 30mm
Large, fast-moving woodlouse-like crustacean. Mostly nocturnal but easily found by turning boulders and large stones on rocky shore; also found in crevices in harbour walls. ADULT has flattened grey body with long antennae and conspicuous appendages at tail end. STATUS Widespread and common.

Nebalia bipes Length to 12mm
Almost transparent crustacean, found when stones are turned on lower shore, often trapped in surface film of water. ADULT is laterally flattened; head, thorax and anterior part of abdomen are visible through bivalve carapace. Rest of abdomen is slender and ends in a forked appendage. Eyes are red. Male has long 2nd antennae. STATUS Widespread but easily overlooked.

Sea Slater

Dynamene bidentata Length to 8mm
Segmented isopod with oval body; uropod has distinctive lateral projections. Rolls into a ball if disturbed. Found in rock crevices and empty barnacle shells on sheltered shores. ADULT is greyish. Male has backward-projecting spines on 6th thoracic segment. STATUS Widespread and fairly common.

Lekanesphaera rugicauda Length to 9mm
Vaguely woodlouse-like isopod. Found in clustered groups under stones in estuaries and brackish water; swims well but rolls into a ball if disturbed. ADULT is oval in outline; yellowish brown, textured with tubercles. Has broad telson and splayed uropods. STATUS Widespread and locally common.

Sphaeroma serratum Length to 10mm
Plump-bodied isopod that curls up if disturbed. Found under rocks on lower shore. ADULT is oval in outline, hemispherical in cross section. Tail end is rounded; outer uropod has serrated margin. STATUS Local, mainly in the SW.

Cymodoce truncata Length to 10mm
Similar to *Sphaeroma serratum* (above) but separable by studying shape of tail end. Found under rocks and among kelp holdfasts, on lower shore. ADULT is oval in outline, hemispherical in cross section. Telson is often slightly hairy, with posterior projections and lateral uropods. Body is yellowish or pinkish, with granular texture to tail end. STATUS Locally common, mainly in the SW.

Jaera sp. Length to 5mm
Woodlouse-like isopods. Several similar species are common. Found in water; most tolerate brackish or low-salinity conditions. In estuaries or under stones on mid- to upper shore. ADULT is oval with relatively long antennae. STATUS Widespread and locally common.

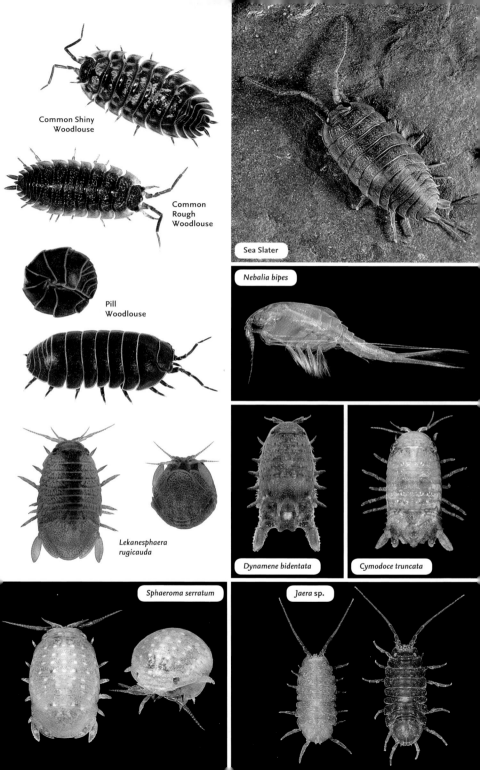

Common Shiny
Woodlouse

Common
Rough
Woodlouse

Pill
Woodlouse

Sea Slater

Nebalia bipes

Lekanesphaera rugicauda

Dynamene bidentata

Cymodoce truncata

Sphaeroma serratum

Jaera sp.

Gribble *Limnoria lignorum* Length to 5mm
Small isopod whose signs of activity are more easily observed than the animal itself: bores holes into soft, submerged wood and causes decay of pilings of piers and jetties. **ADULT** has elongate-oval body outline, obvious segments, and broad telson. **STATUS** Widespread and common, but animal itself is found only by careful searching.

Synisoma acuminatum Length to 25mm
Distinctive elongate isopod. Well camouflaged when resting among Sea Oak fronds (p. 35). Found on sheltered rocky shores and in pools. **ADULT** has slender, segmented body with long antennae and relatively long legs. **STATUS** Widespread and fairly common but easily overlooked.

Astacilla longicornis Length to 25mm
Unusual elongate isopod. Hard to find when resting among seaweeds and hydroids; occurs on sheltered rocky shores and in pools. **ADULT** is cylindrical with very long pereon segment 4. Second antennae have very long basal segments. **STATUS** Widespread and locally common in W only.

Synisoma acuminatum

Idotea linearis Length to 40mm
Elongate isopod with parallel-sided body. Found on sandy shores. **ADULT** is brown and flattened, with long antennae. Rear margin of telson is smoothly concave. **STATUS** Locally common. **SIMILAR SPECIES** *I. chelipes* is smaller (length to 15mm), with pointed telson tip. Restricted to brackish pools.

Idotea granulosa Length to 20mm
Isopod with narrowly oval outline to body. Found on rocky shores, usually among *Fucus* and *Ascophyllum* seaweeds. **ADULT** has a flattened brown body. Telson is large and tapers; tip is incurved, ending in a narrow, blunt tip. **STATUS** Widespread and locally common.

Idotea baltica Length to 30mm
Narrowly oval isopod. Mainly sub-littoral, sometimes in rock pools and among drifting seaweed. **ADULT** colour is variable but usually either brown or greenish; typically has white spots down centre of dorsal surface. Telson is broad and relatively large, with 3 points at tip. **STATUS** Widespread and locally common.

Idotea baltica, in floating seaweed raft.

Idotea emarginata Length to 30mm
Isopod with narrow, almost parallel-sided outline. Mainly sub-littoral but also in pools and among drifting seaweed. **ADULT** has flattened brownish body and a dark dorsal stripe. Telson is broad; outer margins curve gently, rear margin is concave. **STATUS** Widespread and common.

Idotea neglecta Length to 30mm
Isopod with a narrowly oval outline. Mainly sub-littoral but also found in pools and among drifting seaweed. **ADULT** has a flattened body; usually brown, but sometimes has bold white markings. Telson has curving sides and ends in a distinct point. **STATUS** Widespread and locally common.

Idotea pelagica Length to 11mm
Small, narrow isopod. Associated with barnacles and mussels on fairly exposed rocky shores. Swims actively. **ADULT** has a proportionately large head and stout antennae (flagellum shorter than basal segments). Telson has parallel sides but tapers to a point. Body is brown with white marks. **STATUS** Widespread but local, mainly W.

Idotea emarginata   *Idotea neglecta*

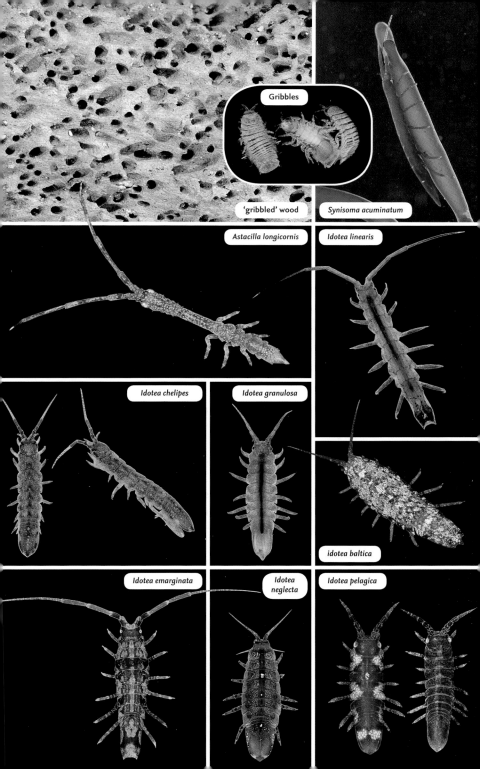

Gribbles

'gribbled' wood

Synisoma acuminatum

Astacilla longicornis

Idotea linearis

Idotea chelipes

Idotea granulosa

idotea baltica

Idotea emarginata

Idotea neglecta

Idotea pelagica

Speckled Sea Louse *Eurydice pulchra* Length to 8mm

Compact isopod. Lives buried in intertidal sand when tide is out, but emerges and swims actively with rising tide, particularly after dark. ADULT has narrow, streamlined body, with rounded dorsal surface. Dark chromatophores expand and contract according to ambient light levels. STATUS Widespread and locally common; easiest to find by torchlight after dark. SIMILAR SPECIES *E. affinis* is smaller and paler. Found on lower shore of sandy beaches, emerging into surf on rising tides. Widespread and locally common on suitable coasts.

Orchomene nana Length to 5mm

Intriguing little amphipod, often found in clustered groups inside empty crab and heart-urchin shells, and the like. ADULT has a compact greyish-white body, through which orange-brown organs show in larger animals; eyes are red and kidney-shaped. First antennae are thick-based and stubby; 2nd antennae are long. STATUS Widespread and locally common, but easily overlooked.

Chaetogammarus marinus Length to 25mm

Laterally flattened amphipod with a curved dorsal outline. Out of water, jerks along on its side. Found on sandy shores, under stones and seaweed at low tide. ADULT has greenish body and elongate eyes. Last 3 segments of body have dorsal clusters of spines. Has 2 pairs of antennae; 1st has a short accessory flagellum. STATUS Widespread and common.

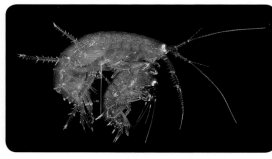

Gammarus locusta, mating pair

Gammarus locusta

Length to 35mm

Laterally flattened amphipod. Out of water, jerks along on its side. Found on rocky and mixed shores, under stones and seaweed at low tide. ADULT has olive-brown body and kidney-shaped eyes. Last 3 segments of body have dorsal clusters of spines. Has 2 pairs of antennae; 1st has a short accessory flagellum. STATUS Widespread and common.

Gammarus duebeni Length to 17mm

Laterally flattened amphipod with a curved dorsal outline. Out of water, jerks along on its side. Found in brackish water and shores with freshwater run-off (also in river mouths). ADULT is olive-brown with kidney-shaped eyes. Last 3 segments of body have dorsal clusters of spines. Has 2 pairs of antennae; 1st has a short accessory flagellum. STATUS Locally common.

Gammarellus homari Length to 10mm

Well-marked, sculptured amphipod. Mainly sub-littoral but sometimes found in pools or among beached seaweed. ADULT is laterally flattened, with sharp dorsal keels on coxal segments. Pale ground colour is suffused orange-brown and studded with pale spots. Has red kidney-shaped eyes and accessory flagellum on 1st antenna. STATUS Widespread but local.

Dexamine spinosa Length to 12mm

Well-marked amphipod. Lives on lower shore in eelgrass beds and seaweed holdfasts. ADULT is mottled reddish brown and grey, adorned with pale spots; dorsal spines on last 4 segments. Antenna pair 1 is longer than 2, and lacks accessory flagellum. STATUS Widespread but local.

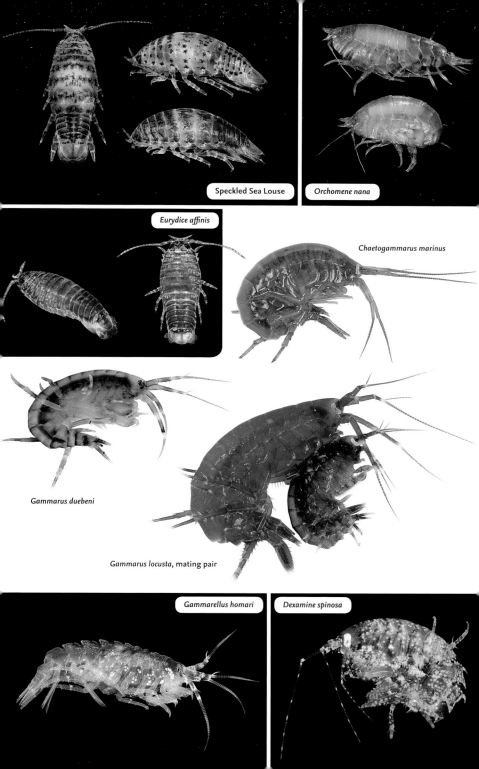

Speckled Sea Louse

Orchomene nana

Eurydice affinis

Chaetogammarus marinus

Gammarus duebeni

Gammarus locusta, mating pair

Gammarellus homari

Dexamine spinosa

Maera grossimana Length to 10cm
Slender amphipod, found by turning rocks on sheltered shores. **ADULT** is yellowish, flushed pink; antenna pair 1 is long, with accessory flagellum. Gnathopod 2 is large and subchelate. **STATUS** Locally common only in the SW.

Apherusa jurinei Length to 8mm
Found in tangled masses of seaweed and laminarian holdfasts. **ADULT** has curved dorsal outline. Antenna pair 1 lacks accessory flagellum and is slightly longer than antenna pair 2. Eyes are red and kidney-shaped. **STATUS** Local, mainly in the W.

Jassa falcata Length to 9mm
Tube-dwelling amphipod. Colonies of tubes often cloak mooring ropes and submerged rocks by late summer. **ADULT** has well-marked, slender body and long antennae (particularly basal segments). Male has large, articulating 2nd gnathopod with basal spine. **STATUS** Widespread but rather local. Commonest in the W; most easily found in summer. **SIMILAR SPECIES** *Parajassa pelagica* (length to 10mm) has oval gnathopod and whorls of long hairs on antenna pair 2. Lives in tubes, often on kelp holdfasts. Locally common, mainly in the W.

Ericthonius sp. Length to 8mm
Tube-dwelling amphipods. Several superficially similar species make tubes on eelgrass and seaweed stems on sheltered shores. **ADULT** has slender body and long antennae (particularly basal segments). Male has large, articulating 2nd gnathopod with basal spine. **STATUS** Widespread but rather local. Commonest in the W; most easily found in summer.

Erichthonius sp. in tube on Eelgrass

Haustorius arenarius
Length to 12mm
Bizarre, unmistakable amphipod whose digging abilities earn it the nickname 'Bulldozer Shrimp'. Lives buried in clean sand on middle shore, on extensive beaches. If disturbed, swims upside down. **ADULT** has domed whitish body with large, flattened hind legs used for digging; leg segments are fringed with spiny hairs. Eyes are small, yellowish and hard to discern. **STATUS** Locally common only on coasts of Wales, and NW and NE England.

Urothoe sp. Length to 8mm
Burrowing amphipods. Several superficially similar species are found in muddy sand from middle shore to sub-littoral zone. **ADULTS** have plump, rounded body. Head and eyes are relatively conspicuous; 1st antenna has accessory flagellum. Hind legs are large and adapted for digging. **STATUS** Widespread and locally common, except in the SE.

Bathyporeia pilosa Length to 7mm
Distinctive plump-bodied amphipod. Lives buried in sand, from middle shore downwards. **ADULT** has domed body with powerful hind legs for digging; 1st antenna has thickened basal segment. **STATUS** Widespread and locally common, except in the SE.

Ampithoe rubricata Length to 20mm
Laterally flattened amphipod. Lives in a tube fixed to seaweed or under rocks. **ADULT** is reddish or greenish with darker speckling. Antennae are relatively long and similar in length; flagellum is absent. **STATUS** Widespread and common but overlooked.

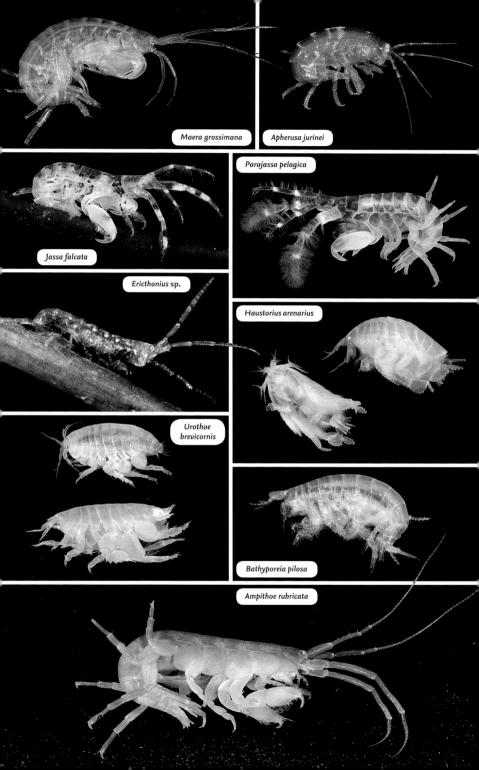

Maera grossimana

Apherusa jurinei

Parajassa pelagica

Jassa falcata

Ericthonius sp.

Haustorius arenarius

Urothoe brevicornis

Bathyporeia pilosa

Ampithoe rubricata

Sand-hopper *Talitrus saltator* Length to 25mm
Plump-bodied, slightly laterally flattened amphipod. Out of water, jerks along on its side. Found on sandy beaches. Mostly nocturnal; in daytime, usually buried in sand. ADULT has a marbled grey and whitish body and striking eyes. First antennae are short; 2nd antennae are long, with very long basal segments, and tinged orange. STATUS Widespread and common.

Beach-hopper *Orchestia gammarellus* Length to 18mm
Laterally flattened amphipod whose outline is curved towards rear end. Hops frantically when disturbed, typically ending up on its side. Found by turning strandline debris on beaches with coarse sand and stones. ADULT has a reddish-brown body, sometimes tinged green. First antennae are short; 2nd antennae are long, with very long basal segments. Eyes are rounded. Male has large 2nd gnathopods. STATUS Widespread and common. SIMILAR SPECIES *Hyale* sp. (length to 8mm) are hopping amphipods that live intertidally on rocky shores, mainly in the W. Second antennae are longer than 1st but relatively shorter than those of Beach-hopper, with short basal segments.

Atylus swammerdamei Length to 10mm
Pale, laterally flattened amphipod. Lives among sub-littoral seaweeds and on sand; active in surface waters after dark. ADULT is mostly white, stained yellowish brown in patches. Dorsal surface has 2 sharp teeth with notch between. Eyes are large, kidney-shaped and red. Antennae are long, 1st pair marginally shorter than 2nd and without accessory flagellum. STATUS Widespread and locally common, except in the SE.

Hyperia galba Length to 10mm
Plump-bodied pelagic amphipod. Usually lives inside Comb Jelly (p. 126), or jellyfish *Rhizostoma octopus* and *Pelagia noctiluca* (p. 118). ADULT is usually brownish (sometimes pale), with large head and greenish eyes. STATUS Widespread and fairly common given specific habitat requirements.

Corophium volutator Length to 10mm
Unusual amphipod with dorso-ventrally flattened body. Lives in burrows in estuary mud, but only where consistency allows this, and where diatoms (food) coat the silt surface. ADULT has elongate yellowish body with brown markings, and very long and thickened 2nd antennae. STATUS Widespread and very locally common; absent from many seemingly suitable areas. Important food for Dunlin (p. 336) and other waders. SIMILAR SPECIES *C. arenarium* is smaller and found in sand rather than silty mud.

Chelura terebrans Length to 6mm
Minute amphipod, found in timber riddled with Gribbles (p. 152). ADULT is brownish and not markedly flattened. Margins of body segments and legs have bristles; these collect sediment, creating 'hairy' or 'fuzzy' appearance. Third abdominal segment has backward-projecting spine. Has backward-pointing jointed tail appendage, larger in male than female. STATUS Locally common but associated only with Gribbles.

Caprella linearis Length to 22mm
Bizarre slow-moving, elongate amphipod. Well camouflaged when resting among seaweeds on sheltered shores. ADULT has slender brownish body with long antennae, large 2nd gnathopod, and long posterior pereopods, used for clinging to seaweeds and other substrates. STATUS Widespread and fairly common, but easily overlooked. SIMILAR SPECIES *C. acanthifera* is smaller (length to 15mm), with a swollen skull-like head and spiny outgrowths on dorsal surface. Widespread in the W.

Caprella linearis

Cyathura carinata Length to 13mm
Slender, rather cylindrical isopod. Found mainly in estuaries, often in areas of run-off or streams. ADULT has rather transparent elongate body with relatively short antennae. STATUS Widespread in S Britain.

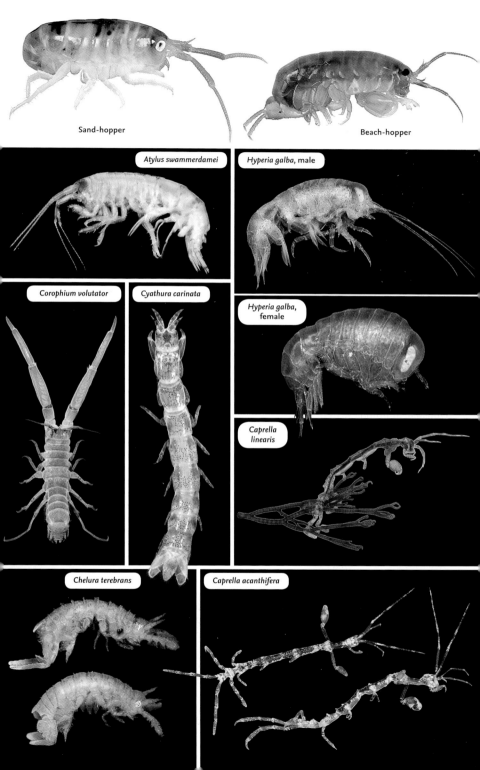

Sand-hopper

Beach-hopper

Atylus swammerdamei

Hyperia galba, male

Corophium volutator

Cyathura carinata

Hyperia galba, female

Caprella linearis

Chelura terebrans

Caprella acanthifera

Edible Crab *Cancer pagurus* Carapace width to 20cm
Familiar and unmistakable crab. Smaller individuals are found under stones and seaweeds
on lower shore; larger individuals are typically in deeper water. **ADULT** is reddish overall.
Carapace is oval with a 'piecrust' margin. Pincers are large and black-tipped.
STATUS Widespread and common.

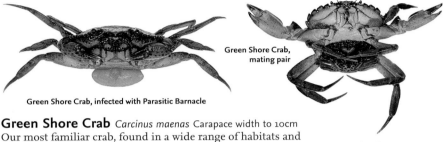

Green Shore Crab,
mating pair

Green Shore Crab, infected with Parasitic Barnacle

Green Shore Crab *Carcinus maenas* Carapace width to 10cm
Our most familiar crab, found in a wide range of habitats and
salinities. **ADULT** has an angular-oval carapace with 5 teeth on
each side (lateral to the eyes), and 3 equal lobes between the
eyes. Carapace colour is variable, but typically marbled
green, brown or reddish. **STATUS** Widespread and
common. **NOTE** Females carry yellowish egg mass on
underside of abdomen for several weeks or months.
Some individuals are infected with Parasitic
Barnacle (p. 178), which appears as orange ball on
underside of abdomen, recalling an egg mass.

Green Shore Crab,
female with eggs

Hairy Crab *Pilumnus hirtellus* Carapace width to 15mm
Small but distinctive crab; extremely hairy, particularly on legs and margins of
carapace. Found on rocky and mixed shores. **ADULT** has angular-oval carapace, with
5 sharp teeth on each side (lateral to eyes); leading edge between eyes is straight with
central notch. Legs and upper surface of carapace are marbled dark grey and white,
with reddish suffusion in places. **STATUS** Widespread and locally common.

Furrowed Crab or **Montagu's Crab** *Xantho incisus* Carapace width to 30mm
Distinctive crab with sculptured upper surface to carapace and proportionately large
pincers. Found on sheltered rocky shores. **ADULT** is usually reddish overall. Carapace has
5 blunt teeth on each side (lateral to eyes); leading edge, between eyes, is straight. Pincers
are usually black but can be brown. Legs are sparsely hairy at most. **STATUS** Widespread
and locally common.

Risso's Crab,
female with eggs

Risso's Crab *Xantho pilipes* Carapace width to 30mm
Similar to Furrowed Crab (above), with sculptured
upper surface to carapace, but legs and sides of
carapace are fringed with hairs. On lower shore
of rocky coasts. **ADULT** is usually reddish overall.
Carapace has 5 pointed teeth on each side (lateral
to eyes); leading edge, between eyes, is undulate.
Pincers are usually brown but can be black.
STATUS Widespread and locally fairly common.

Pirimela denticulata Carapace width to 15mm
Dainty, colourful little crab. Mostly sub-littoral but
found under rocks at extreme low water. Quickly
scuttles between stones and under rocks when disturbed.
ADULT has rather diamond-shaped carapace, very pointed between eyes, with sharp
lateral teeth. Colour often matches background, and can be pinkish, or green and
brown. **STATUS** Widespread but local and easily overlooked.

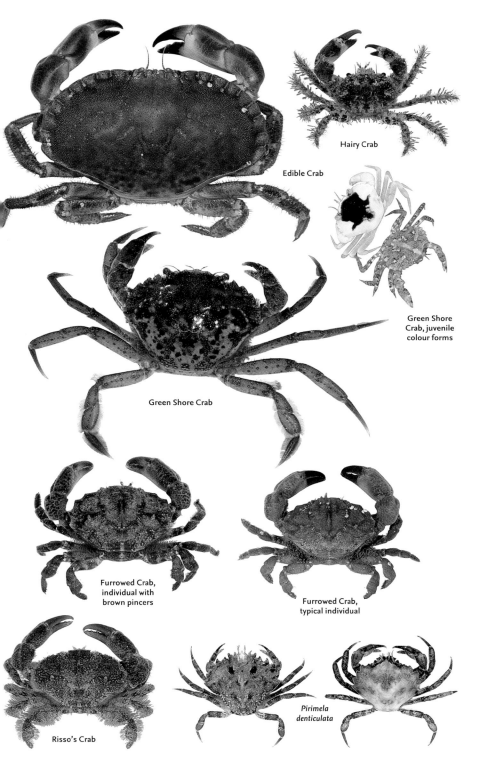

Edible Crab

Hairy Crab

Green Shore Crab, juvenile colour forms

Green Shore Crab

Furrowed Crab, individual with brown pincers

Furrowed Crab, typical individual

Risso's Crab

Pirimela denticulata

Velvet Swimming Crab *Necora puber* Carapace width to 60mm

Impressive and distinctive crab with a well-deserved reputation for being aggressive when threatened. Favours sheltered rocky shores. ADULT has an angular carapace with 5 teeth on each side (lateral to eyes) and 10 small teeth between eyes. Upper surface of carapace is brownish with velvety texture. Eyes and joints on front legs are red. Pincers are tinged blue and red. End segments of hind legs are flattened and paddle-like, used for swimming. STATUS Widespread and locally common.

Portumnus latipes Carapace width to 20mm

Dainty little swimming crab, found on sandy substrates. ADULT has rather shield-shaped carapace, usually marbled brown and buff. Hind pereopods have flattened end segment, used for swimming. STATUS Widespread and locally common.

Portumnus latipes

Harbour Crab *Liocarcinus depurator* Carapace width to 40mm

Distinctive swimming crab. On muddy sand of lower shore and sub-littoral zone. ADULT has angular carapace with 5 teeth on each side (lateral to eyes), and 3 rounded teeth between eyes. Colour is reddish overall, but paddle-like end segment to hind legs is tinged violet. STATUS Widespread and locally common.

Arch-fronted Swimming Crab *Liocarcinus arcuatus* Carapace width to 35mm

Active swimming crab. On gravelly sand of lower shore and sub-littoral zone. ADULT has carapace with 5 sharp teeth on each side (lateral to eyes) and untoothed, curved margin between eyes. Pincers are relatively small. STATUS Locally common, mainly in the SW.

Marbled Swimming Crab *Liocarcinus marmoreus* Carapace width to 35mm

Boldly patterned swimming crab. On sand and gravel of lower shore and sub-littoral zone. ADULT has marbled red, brown and greenish carapace. Three blunt teeth present between eyes, middle one smallest. Segment behind pincers does not have tooth on outer edge. STATUS Locally common, mainly in the SW and NW.

Flying Crab *Liocarcinus holsatus* Carapace width to 40mm

Active swimming crab. Often swims vigorously in surface water if disturbed or placed in bucket. On gravel and coarse sand. ADULT has 3 blunt teeth present between eyes, middle one largest. Segment behind pincers has tooth on outer edge. STATUS Widespread and locally common around coasts of England and Wales.

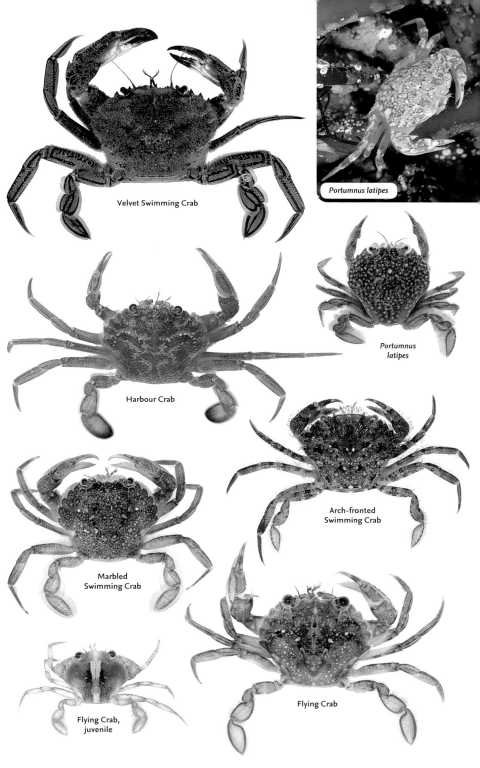

Velvet Swimming Crab

Portumnus latipes

Harbour Crab

Portumnus latipes

Marbled Swimming Crab

Arch-fronted Swimming Crab

Flying Crab, juvenile

Flying Crab

Masked Crab *Corystes cassivelaunus* Carapace length to 40mm
Unmistakable crab. Seldom seen alive because it lives buried in sand; dead specimens often washed up on strandline. **ADULT** is pinkish brown, with an oval carapace and very long antennae; male has very long front legs. **STATUS** Widespread and locally common.

Sponge Crab *Dromia personata* Carapace width to 60mm
Distinctive crab that often has sponge on back of carapace, held in place by hind legs. Sub-littoral, sometimes seen by snorkellers or found in crab pots. **ADULT** is deep-bodied with large front legs and pink pincers. Entire body is covered by dense velvety 'fur'. **STATUS** Widespread but local and recorded only occasionally.

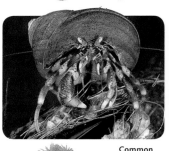

Common Hermit Crab

Pagurus bernhardus Carapace length to 30mm
Our commonest and most familiar hermit crab. Small individuals occupy empty shells the size of periwinkles; larger animals occupy Common Whelk shells (p. 216). **ADULT** is seen as hardened head end, including carapace, legs and pincers; soft-bodied abdomen is hidden inside, and protected by, the mollusc shell it inhabits. Alarmed animal retreats inside shell, sealing entrance with pincer. Right pincer is larger than left. Has sharp-pointed rostrum between eyes. **STATUS** Widespread and common in most coastal habitats. **NOTE** Large individuals (usually in whelk shells) sometimes have anemone *Calliactis parasitica* (p. 124) living on shell. **SIMILAR SPECIES** *P. prideaux* (carapace length to 15mm) usually has Cloak Anemone (p. 124) covering shell and has rounded rostrum between eyes. Locally common but mainly sub-littoral.

Common
Hermit Crab

Common Hermit
Crab, adult with
Calliactis parasitica

Pagurus cuanensis Carapace length to 15mm
Small but distinctive hermit crab. Found in pools and sheltered rocky coasts on lower shore and in sub-littoral zone. **ADULT** is extremely hairy, with colourful eyes and slender eye stalks. Right pincer is larger than left. **STATUS** Widespread and locally common on S and W coasts.

South-claw Hermit Crab

Diogenes pugilator Carapace length to 15mm
Small hermit crab, identified by studying relative sizes of left and right pincers. Lives mainly in Netted Dog Whelk shells (p. 216) on lower shores of sandy beaches. **ADULT** has left claw larger than right when viewed from above (*Pagurus* sp. have right claw larger than left). **STATUS** Widespread and locally common in the SW but easily overlooked.

Common
Hermit Crab
without shell

South-claw Hermit Crab

South-claw
Hermit Crab
without shell

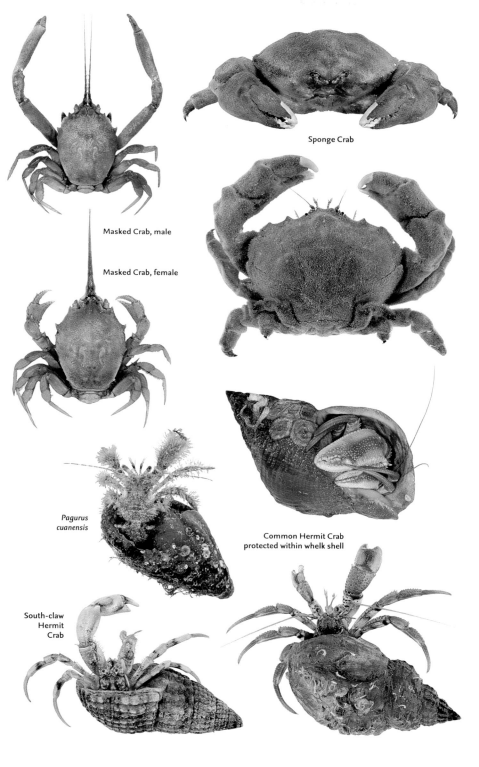

Masked Crab, male

Masked Crab, female

Sponge Crab

Pagurus cuanensis

Common Hermit Crab
protected within whelk shell

South-claw
Hermit
Crab

Chinese Mitten Crab *Eriocheir sinensis* Carapace length to 5cm

Distinctive crab with specific habitat requirements. Lives in fresh water for most of life, burrowing into muddy banks; adults migrate to estuaries to breed. ADULT has squarish-circular carapace with widely spaced eyes; typically marbled reddish green. In adults, base of pincer segment has diagnostic 'mitten' coating of hairs. STATUS Introduced from Far East, now locally common (and an environmental problem) in Thames and Medway.

Pea Crab

Pinnotheres pisum Carapace width to 8mm

Delicate, dainty little crab. Lives inside bivalve molluscs, particularly Common Mussel (p. 226). ADULT has pale legs and almost circular carapace that is pale yellowish with reddish markings. STATUS Fairly common but only inside host molluscs.

Pea Crab

Common Spider Crab

Maja squinado Carapace length to 20cm

Impressive crab with relatively slender legs. Found on mixed shores; usually in deep water but sometimes in pools and gullies at low tide. ADULT is pinkish orange overall. Carapace is teardrop-shaped in outline and covered with large, angular spines on dorsal surface. Legs have rather long segments and pincers are narrow. STATUS Widespread and locally common.

Great Spider Crab *Hyas araneus* Carapace length to 10cm

Bulky and impressive spider crab. Carapace is often coated with attached seaweeds, tubeworms and hydroids, making precise shape and texture hard to discern. On gravel and rocky shores, but mostly sub-littoral. ADULT is reddish brown with teardrop-shaped carapace and pointed rostrum divided down middle. Legs and pincers are rather slender. STATUS Widespread and fairly common, least so in the SW and commonest in the NW.

Four-horned Spider Crab *Pisa tetraodon* Carapace length to 4cm

Distinctive crab, easily overlooked since it adorns carapace and legs with seaweeds. Found on sheltered rocky and mixed shores; mostly sub-littoral but sometimes in pools. ADULT is reddish buff overall but colour is often obscured by hydroid colonies, seaweeds and encrusting silt. Carapace is sculptured and roughly diamond-shaped, broadest towards rear end; note lateral spines, rear pair of which projects at right angles. Has rostral spines ('horns') at front of carapace. Legs are slender and relatively small. STATUS Widespread and fairly common. SIMILAR SPECIES *P. armata* (carapace length to 4cm) has diamond-shaped carapace with velvety texture. Carapace has fewer spines on dorsal surface, no lateral teeth, 2 teeth in front of eyes, 2 slightly backward-pointing teeth at rear and 1 at far rear. Legs are stout and knobbly. Mainly Dorset to Sussex, and NW Wales.

Eurynome aspera Carapace length to 15mm

Small, short-legged spider crab. Mostly sub-littoral, among algal holdfasts and stones; sometimes in lower-shore pools or on lifted crab pots. ADULT is pinkish buff, oval with frontal horns and dorsal tubercles. Colour and texture usually obscured by hydroid growth and detritus. STATUS Widespread but local, in the S and W.

Eurynome aspera

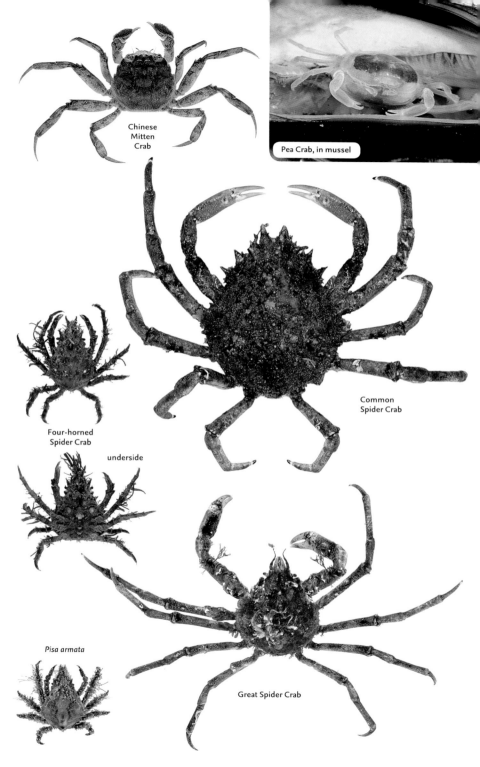

Chinese
Mitten
Crab

Pea Crab, in mussel

Four-horned
Spider Crab

Common
Spider Crab

underside

Pisa armata

Great Spider Crab

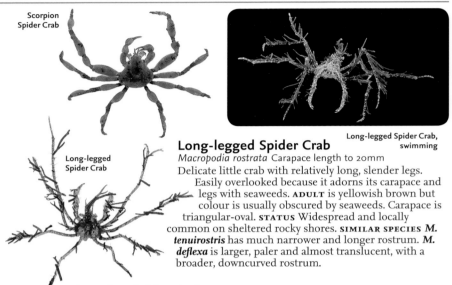

Scorpion
Spider Crab

Long-legged
Spider Crab

Long-legged Spider Crab,
swimming

Long-legged Spider Crab
Macropodia rostrata Carapace length to 20mm
Delicate little crab with relatively long, slender legs.
Easily overlooked because it adorns its carapace and
legs with seaweeds. ADULT is yellowish brown but
colour is usually obscured by seaweeds. Carapace is
triangular-oval. STATUS Widespread and locally
common on sheltered rocky shores. SIMILAR SPECIES *M.
tenuirostris* has much narrower and longer rostrum. *M.
deflexa* is larger, paler and almost translucent, with a
broader, downcurved rostrum.

Scorpion Spider Crab *Inachus dorsettensis* Carapace length to 15mm
Dainty little crab. Distinguished from *Macropodia* sp. by more robust front legs
and pincers, and presence of spine behind eye. Found on mixed shores, sometimes
among seaweeds in pools. ADULT is yellowish buff overall, carapace with tubercles;
colour and texture often obscured by coating of sponges and hydroids. STATUS
Widespread and locally common.

Broad-clawed Porcelain Crab
Porcellana platycheles Carapace length to 15mm
Distinctive little crab, usually found under rocks and
boulders; can be overlooked until it moves because its
flattened, hairy body (pressed flat to rock surface) is
typically coated with silt. ADULT is greyish brown
overall above, white and porcelain-like below.
Carapace is rounded and fringed with hairs, as are
legs. Pincers are broad. STATUS Widespread and
locally common.

Broad-clawed Porcelain Crab

Long-clawed Porcelain Crab *Pisidia longicornis*
Carapace length to 10mm
Recalls Broad-clawed Porcelain Crab (above) but body is hairless. Found on sheltered
rocky shores. ADULT is usually reddish brown overall. Carapace is circular and legs and
pincers are relatively slender. STATUS Widespread but local.

Common Squat Lobster *Galathea squamifera* Carapace length to 35mm
Our commonest squat lobster. If disturbed, shoots backwards by snapping abdomen
against thorax. Found under stones on rocky shores, on mid- to lower shore. ADULT is
greenish brown overall, with a flattened carapace. Abdomen is curved under carapace,
and legs and pincers are slender. STATUS Widespread and locally common.

Spiny Squat Lobster *Galathea strigosa* Carapace length to 80mm
Colourful squat lobster. Usually sub-littoral but sometimes rock pools. ADULT has red and
blue banding. Legs are red and spiny. STATUS Widespread and locally common in deep
water; scarce in intertidal zone. SIMILAR SPECIES *G. intermedia* is smaller (length to 10mm)
and reddish overall; slender legs have fine spines. Widespread but mainly sub-littoral.

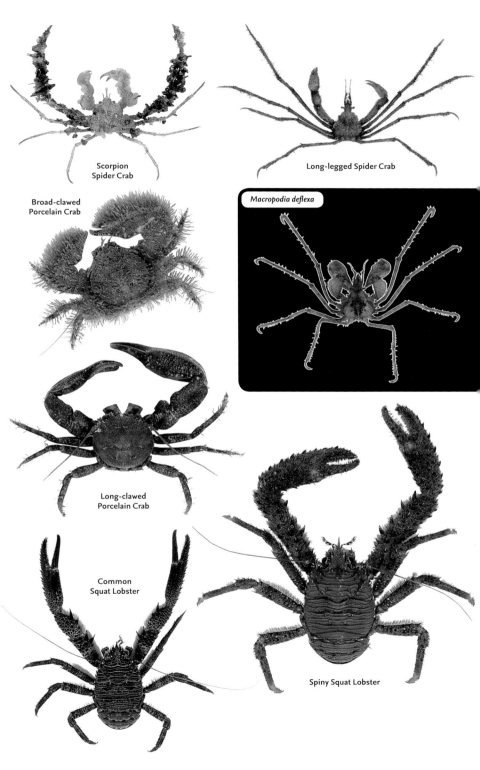

Scorpion
Spider Crab

Long-legged Spider Crab

Broad-clawed
Porcelain Crab

Macropodia deflexa

Long-clawed
Porcelain Crab

Common
Squat Lobster

Spiny Squat Lobster

Rugose Squat Lobster *Munida rugosa* Carapace length to 30mm
Distinctive squat lobster. Lives on rocky coasts. Mostly sub-littoral but occasionally found at low water. ADULT is reddish with corrugated carapace and very long pincers and pincer legs. STATUS Locally common only in W and N Scotland.

Norway Lobster *Nephrops norvegicus* Carapace length to 20cm
Slender-bodied lobster-like crustacean. Lives in burrows excavated in soft mud. Commercially exploited and often sold as Scampi or Dublin Bay Prawn. ADULT is reddish pink overall with parallel-sided body. Carapace and pincers bear spines. STATUS Widespread; formerly common but now local and generally scarce due to overfishing.

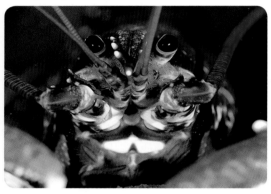

Common Lobster
Homarus vulgaris Length to 40cm
Impressive and unmistakable crustacean. Can grow much larger than quoted size, but commercial exploitation prevents this in most places. Favours rocky and mixed shores; scarce intertidally but sometimes found in pools. Resides in rock crevices and emerges to feed. ADULT is bluish purple overall, fringed on segments and telson with orange. Pincers are massive and unequal. STATUS Widespread and still fairly common.

Hooded Prawn *Athanas nitescens* Length to 20mm
Small but robust crustacean with a passing resemblance to a miniature Common Lobster (above). Found under stones on sheltered rocky shores, and in pools with gravel and stones. ADULT is usually bluish or greenish (sometimes reddish), but almost always with a pale dorsal strip. Front legs and pincers are relatively large. STATUS Widespread and locally common, least so in the N.

Crawfish *Palinurus elephas* Length to 40cm
Distinctive lobster relative that lacks obvious pincers. Heavily exploited commercially, affecting adversely both size and abundance. Found on mixed shores; usually sub-littoral but sometimes in pools and gullies. ADULT is reddish brown overall. Carapace and abdomen are armed with sharp spines, as is swollen base to antennae. STATUS Widespread but generally scarce.

Snapping Prawn *Alpheus macrocheles* Length to 35mm
Unmistakable prawn with hugely enlarged pincers. 'Snapping' sound (like popping popcorn) is audible when emitted by *in situ* animals under rocks at very low water. ADULT is yellowish orange. One pincer (left or right) is larger than the other, with swollen pinkish-orange articulation that creates snapping sound. Eyes are flush with carapace. STATUS Local and generally scarce in the S, mainly Dorset to Isle of Wight.

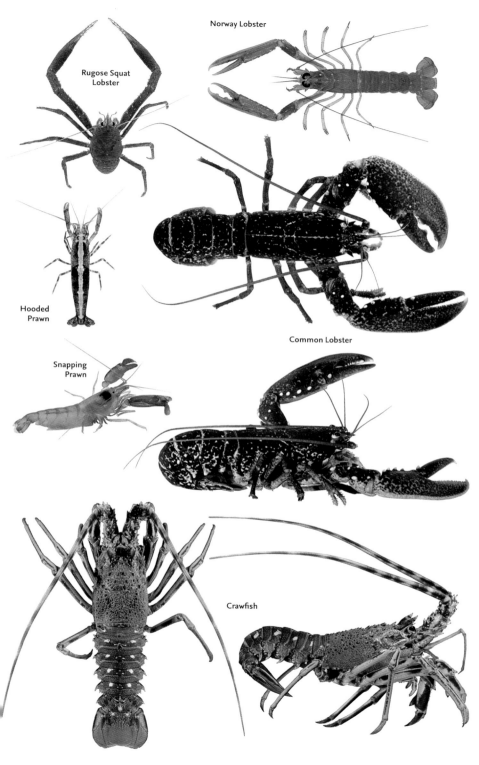

Rugose Squat Lobster

Norway Lobster

Hooded Prawn

Common Lobster

Snapping Prawn

Crawfish

Mysids

Sometimes known as opossum shrimps, mysids are small shrimp-like crustaceans with slender, almost transparent bodies. They are often abundant and ecologically very important (as food for other animals), but their colourless bodies make them hard to spot and even harder to identify. Often their

presence can be detected only by looking for their opaque eyes, which appear disembodied as the animals move through the water. Three fairly typical species are covered here, but there are plenty of others that require an expert eye. **Chameleon Shrimp** *Praunus flexuosus* (length to 25mm) is widespread and swarms in sheltered rock pools and estuaries, often hanging motionless in mid-water; it has a 'hunchback' profile, divided telson and antennal scale (plate-like structure seen alongside base of antennae) 8 times longer than broad, with a sub-terminal spine on outer margin. **P. inermis** (length to 15mm) is found on sheltered rocky shores and in pools; has a 'hunchback' profile, telson is divided at tip, and antennal scale is 4 times longer than broad, with a sub-terminal spine on outer margin. **Leptomysis sp.** (length to 15mm) are usually found offshore in mid-water, but come to surface and inshore after dark; body is slender, antennal scale is rather short and rounded, and telson is undivided.

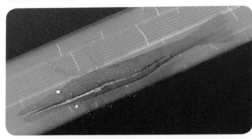

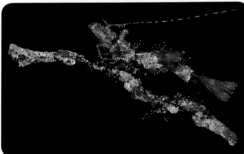

TOP: *Hippolyte inermis*; ABOVE: *Hippolyte longirostris*

Chameleon Prawn

Hippolyte varians Length to 30mm
Small, colourful prawn. Found in pools and under seaweeds on sheltered rocky shores. **ADULT** is often bright green or yellow (sometimes red or brown). Rostrum has 1 dorsal tooth, just in front of eye. First 2 pairs of legs have minute pincers; these are hard to discern. **STATUS** Widespread and locally common. **SIMILAR SPECIES H. inermis** (length to 40mm) is typically green, often with a pale dorsal line at head end. Rostrum is relatively long, slightly downcurved and lacks a dorsal tooth. SW only, often in eelgrass beds. **H. longirostris** (length to 20mm) is partly transparent and variably marked with pink and brown, creating superb camouflage. Rostrum has 2–4 dorsal teeth. Body has tufts of hairs. Scarce in pools on lower shore, SW only.

Thoralus cranchii Length to 45mm

Robust little prawn. Found in pools and under rocks at low water. **ADULT** is marbled and mottled brown and reddish. Dark stippling and yellowish bands on legs and tail end enhance camouflage among seaweeds. Rostrum is short, with 3 dorsal and 2 terminal teeth. **STATUS** Widespread but local, mainly in S Britain.

Eualus occultus Length to 25mm

Compact, partly transparent prawn. Found in pools and under rocks at low water. **ADULT** is variably colourful, with blue and yellow dots, and sometimes pink patches. Rostrum is rather short, with 2–4 dorsal and 2 terminal teeth. **STATUS** Widespread but local, SW only.

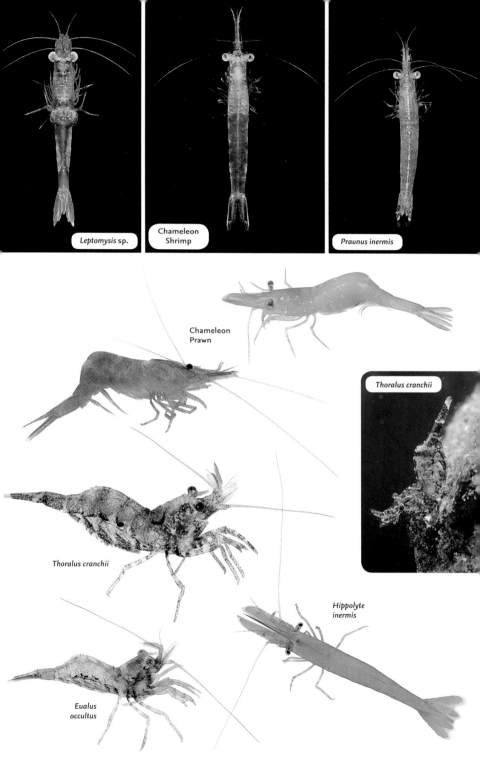

Leptomysis sp.

Chameleon Shrimp

Praunus inermis

Chameleon Prawn

Thoralus cranchii

Thoralus cranchii

Thoralus cranchii

Hippolyte inermis

Eualus occultus

ABOVE: *Philocheras fasciatus*; BELOW: **Brown Shrimp**

Philocheras fasciatus Length to 20mm
Well-marked little shrimp. In common
with its close relatives, it has no obvious
pincers. Favours pools on sandy and mixed
shores. ADULT has stout body banded black
and white; in good light, patches of bright
colours are seen on carapace and telson.
Carapace has single dorsal spine and
straight-margined projection between eyes.
STATUS Widespread and locally common.

Brown Shrimp
Crangon crangon Length to 8cm
Widespread and familiar shrimp of sandy
shores. Well camouflaged against its
favoured substrate; swims well and burrows
with ease. Obvious pincers are absent.
ADULT has a pale body, suffused buffish
brown and stippled with dark dots. STATUS
Widespread and locally very common.

Common Prawn *Palaemon serratus* Length to 70mm
Our commonest prawn. Found in pools and among seaweeds on rocky and mixed
shores, from mid-tide level into sub-littoral waters. ADULT is classic prawn shape:
elongate body, fan-shaped telson and slender legs, first 2 pairs with slender pincers.
Rostrum profile is diagnostic: 6–7 dorsal teeth and elongated, upcurved tip. STATUS
Widespread and locally common.

Palaemon elegans Length to 60mm
Similar to Common Prawn (above) but separable using rostrum profile. Found in pools
and under seaweed on sheltered rocky shores. ADULT is typical prawn shape. Rostrum is
more or less straight along dorsal margin, with typically 8–9 teeth, 2–3 of which lie
behind eye socket. STATUS Widespread, commonest in the S.

Palaemon longirostris Length to 75mm
Similar to Common Prawn (above) but separable using rostrum profile. Found in
estuaries and brackish water, sometimes penetrating up rivers to limits of tidal influence.
ADULT is typical prawn shape. Rostrum is more or less straight along dorsal margin,
with 7–8 teeth, 2 of which lie behind eye socket. STATUS Local, in the S and SE only.

Palaemon adspersus Length to 70mm
Similar to Common Prawn (above) but separable using rostrum profile. Found in pools
and under seaweeds on sheltered, mixed shores. ADULT is typical prawn shape. Rostrum is
more or less straight along dorsal margin, with 5–6 teeth, 1 of which lies behind eye socket;
rostrum tip is usually minutely divided. STATUS Locally common, in the S and SE only.

Palaemonetes varians Length to 50mm
Recalls *Palaemon adspersus* (above) but shape is more compact, pincers are relatively
smaller and rostrum tip is usually undivided. Found in estuaries and brackish water,
including sites with very low salinity. ADULT is prawn-shaped and body is almost
transparent. Dorsal margin of rostrum is almost straight, with 4–6 teeth, 1 of which lies
behind eye socket. STATUS Widespread and locally common.

Aesop Prawn *Pandalus montagui* Length to 45mm (Not illustrated)
Recalls *Palaemon* sp. (notably Common Prawn, above) in terms of overall shape, but pincers
are minute and rostrum shape is distinctive. Body is flushed with pink, hence alternative
common name of Pink Shrimp. Mostly sub-littoral. ADULT has long, slender rostrum,
with narrow, upswept tip; upper margin has 10–12 teeth (4 lying behind eye socket), and
tip is divided. STATUS Widespread and locally common offshore; rare inshore.

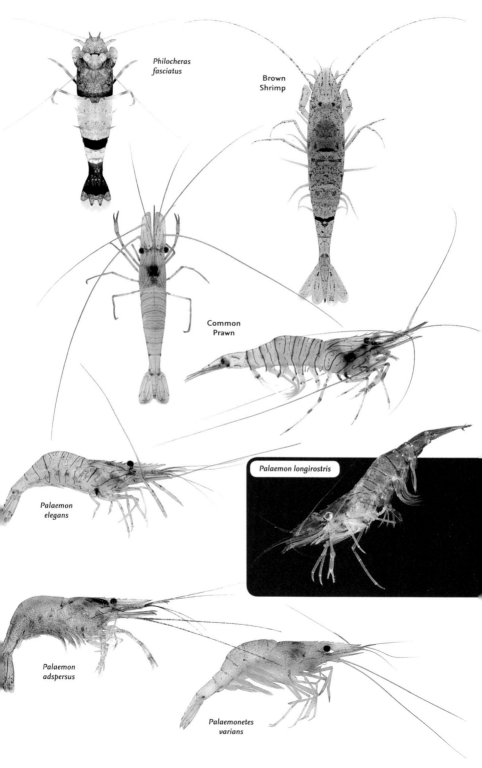

Philocheras
fasciatus

Brown
Shrimp

Common
Prawn

Palaemon
elegans

Palaemon longirostris

Palaemon
adspersus

Palaemonetes
varians

Poli's Stellate Barnacle *Chthamalus stellatus* Diameter to 15mm
Broad-based, slightly flattened-conical barnacle, found on exposed rocky shores at mid-tide level and below. ADULT has 6 distinctly ridged greyish-white shell plates. Aperture opening is oval; tergal plates are roughly same length as scutal plates and suture between them is kinked. STATUS Locally common on suitable shores in SW England and S Ireland.

Poli's Stellate Barnacle
Montagu's Stellate Barnacle

Montagu's Stellate Barnacle
Chthamalus montagui Diameter to 10mm
Broad-based, slightly flattened-conical barnacle, found in large colonies on moderately exposed rocky shores, usually above mid-tide level. ADULT has 6 distinctly ridged grey-brown shell plates. Aperture opening is kite-shaped; plates are bluish, tergal ones shorter than scutal ones and with a kinked suture between. STATUS Locally common on suitable shores in S and W Britain.

Acorn Barnacle   *Balanus balanus*

Acorn Barnacle *Semibalanus balanoides* Diameter to 10mm
Shell shape varies according to exposure and crowding, from flattened-conical to columnar. Found on rocky shores: mid-tide level on moderately exposed shores; higher up with increasing exposure. ADULT has 6 shell plates; aperture is diamond-shaped; tergal plates are much shorter than rostral plates, the suture between them straight but stepped. STATUS Widespread and locally common.

Balanus perforatus

Balanus balanus Diameter to 30mm
Large, conical barnacle of rocky coasts; lower shores and sub-littoral. ADULT has 6 deeply ridged greyish-white shell plates. Tergal plates narrow compared to scutal plates; suture between them forms acute angle. STATUS Mainly northern; almost absent from S and SW.

Balanus perforatus Diameter to 30mm
Volcano-shaped, grey-brown (sometimes purple-tinged) barnacle of rocky shores; lower shore and sub-littoral. ADULT has 6 shell plates (not immediately obvious owing to deeply ridged surface). Tergal and scutal plates are concealed within aperture. STATUS Locally common, in SW only.

Balanus crenatus Diameter to 20mm
Robust barnacle with steep-sided conical profile, and offset opening. Found on sheltered rocky coasts, lower shore and sub-littoral zone. ADULT has 6 smooth whitish shell plates. Tergal and scutal plates are concealed within aperture. STATUS Locally common only in the W.

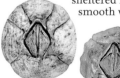

Balanus improvisus Diameter to 15mm
Broadly conical barnacle. Restricted to brackish water, attached to stones and algae. ADULT has 6 smoothish shell plates, forming a low conical tower. Tergal and scutal plates, speckled white and purple, cover diamond-shaped opening. STATUS Widespread but local, mainly in the S.

Balanus improvisus   *Elminius modestus*

Elminius modestus Diameter to 10mm
Flattish barnacle found in sheltered waters, including estuaries. ADULT has 4 shell plates (unusual amongst British barnacles). Aperture is diamond-shaped; suture between the tergal and scutal plates acute. STATUS Introduced from New Zealand, now locally common.

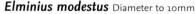

Wart Barnacle

Wart Barnacle *Verruca stroemia* Diameter to 5mm
Distinctive but unobtrusive. Found on algal holdfasts and under rocks on lower shore. ADULT has flattened, irregular shape, with 4 ridged shell plates; whitish or brownish. STATUS Locally common, except in SE.

Montagu's Stellate Barnacle

Acorn Barnacle

underside, showing calcified base

Balanus crenatus

Balanus perforatus

Elminius modestus

Wart Barnacle

Common Goose Barnacle *Lepas anatifera* Length to 50cm

Distinctive and unusual pelagic barnacle, found in groups (often 100s) attached to flotsam. **ADULT** comprises a head section, up to 5cm long, with a whitish shell plate embedded in brownish skin, and a long blackish stalk. Feathery cirri protrude between shell plates when immersed and often in dead specimens. **STATUS** Occasionally beached on shores in W Britain; less frequent in the E. **SIMILAR SPECIES** *L. pectinata* (length to 4cm) comprises a stalk and 15mm head section, the plates greyish buff and strongly ribbed. Pelagic, attached to floating objects, often with Common Goose Barnacle. Washed ashore after gales, mainly in the SW.

Common Goose Barnacle

Pollicipes pollicipes

BELOW:
Buoy Barnacle

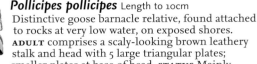

Pollicipes pollicipes Length to 10cm

Distinctive goose barnacle relative, found attached to rocks at very low water, on exposed shores. **ADULT** comprises a scaly-looking brown leathery stalk and head with 5 large triangular plates; smaller plates at base of head. **STATUS** Mainly S species; range extends to SW Britain, where rare.

Buoy Barnacle *Dosima fascicularis* Length to 3cm

Pelagic barnacle, sometimes washed up after W gales. **ADULT** has translucent body plates and short stalk attached initially to floating feather or other flotsam, sometimes aided by barnacle's own secreted white float; also attaches to dislodged mooring floats and buoys. **STATUS** Occasional on storm beaches in SW Britain, usually in summer and early autumn.

Caligus elongatus

Parasitic Barnacle *Sacculina carcini* Width to 25mm

Unrecognisable as a barnacle relative. Parasite of crabs, notably Green Shore Crab (p. 160). **ADULT** comprises a branching network within crab's body; visible external sign of parasite's presence is sac-like structure (orange, maturing to brown) containing reproductive organs, located on underside of crab's abdomen (could be mistaken for egg sac). **STATUS** Fairly common in Green Shore Crab populations.

Lernaeocera branchialis Length to 50mm

Bizarre and atypical copepod. Juvenile is pear-shaped, parasitic on flatfish. Adult is parasite of Atlantic Cod (p. 266) and related fish, living with 1 end permanently embedded in gill arch. **ADULT** comprises a swollen, contorted red sausage-shaped mass, with paler egg mass. Attachment end is much divided, branches penetrating host's blood vessels and body cavity. **STATUS** Widespread and fairly common.

Lepeophtheirus pectoralis Length to 4mm

Unusual copepod, parasitic on flatfish, notably Plaice (p. 284). **ADULT** has a flattened, elongate body and lives adpressed to skin on upperside of fish. **STATUS** Widespread and generally common.

Caligus elongatus Length to 12mm

Distinctive parasitic copepod of fishes, notably Atlantic Cod (p. 266), Pollack (p. 266) and various flatfish. **ADULT** has pale, rather flattish body and is usually attached to gills, or beneath tongue of host. **STATUS** Widespread and fairly common.

Clavella adunca Length to 8mm

Unusual parasitic copepod of fishes, notably Atlantic Cod (p. 266) and related species. **ADULT** has rather amorphous-looking buffish-white body, with tube- or handle-like structure attached. Recognisable as a copepod when paired egg sacs are present. **STATUS** Widespread and fairly common.

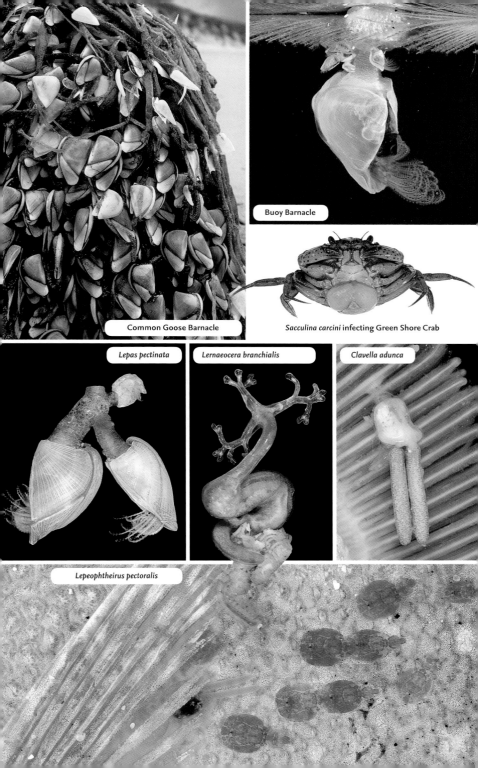

Buoy Barnacle

Common Goose Barnacle

Sacculina carcini infecting Green Shore Crab

Lepas pectinata

Lernaeocera branchialis

Clavella adunca

Lepeophtheirus pectoralis

PLANKTON

Plankton are minute organisms that drift in sea currents. As individuals they can be hard to discern with the naked eye (other than as small dots and specks), but collectively they can transform otherwise crystal-clear sea water into a rich, organic soup. Although plankton is, to a degree, at the mercy of currents and tides, many species possess considerable mobility, including diurnal movements though the water column: some are present in surface waters only after dark.

In general terms, there are 2 types of plankton: phytoplankton, which are microscopic plants; and zooplankton, the term applied to planktonic animals. The importance of plankton in ecological terms cannot be overstated. As photosynthetic organisms, phytoplankton deplete carbon dioxide from the atmosphere and produce oxygen. Together with the zooplankton, they form the basis of the food chain in the marine environment.

Zooplankton is a collective term that embraces a wide range of animal groups, although in inshore British waters crustaceans are often the dominant creatures. Many small copepods are planktonic throughout their lives, but most familiar seashore

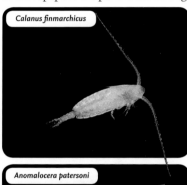

Calanus finmarchicus

Anomalocera patersoni

crustaceans (crabs and squat lobsters, for example) have planktonic larval stages, whose role is to colonise new habitats. Alongside these can be seen larval stages of other groups, including starfish. Most plankton cannot be identified to species level in the field. However, a couple of groups, and a couple of individual species, can be recognised with the aid of a hand lens.

Calanus finmarchicus Length to 3mm

By plankton standards, a large and distinctive copepod. Lives in open water; only easily found in surface layers after dark by torchlight. Important food for larval fish, notably Herring (p. 262). ADULT has narrowly pear-shaped body, whitish with reddish central patch. Note long antennae and 'tail' appendages. STATUS Widespread and abundant in summer, but easily overlooked.

Anomalocera patersoni Length to 2mm

Colourful planktonic copepod. Lives in open water but active in surface layers mainly at night. ADULT has vivid green body and long 'tail' appendages. Right antenna is modified for reproduction. STATUS Widespread and locally common but easily overlooked.

SEA SPIDERS

Sometimes placed in their own phylum (Pycnogonida), sea spiders superficially resemble their terrestrial cousins; they eat hydroids and sea anemones. Segmented body has 4 pairs of segmented legs. Most are hard to identify but 2 extreme forms can be distinguished, and are regularly found. **Nymphon sp.** (length to 10mm) are found under stones from mid- to low water, and have a slender body and legs. Move in apparent 'slow motion' and curl up when disturbed. Widespread and locally common. **Pycnogonum littorale** (length to 20mm) is found under stones and among seaweed holdfasts on lower shore, and has a relatively stout body and thick, segmented legs. Widespread but local.

Nymphon sp.

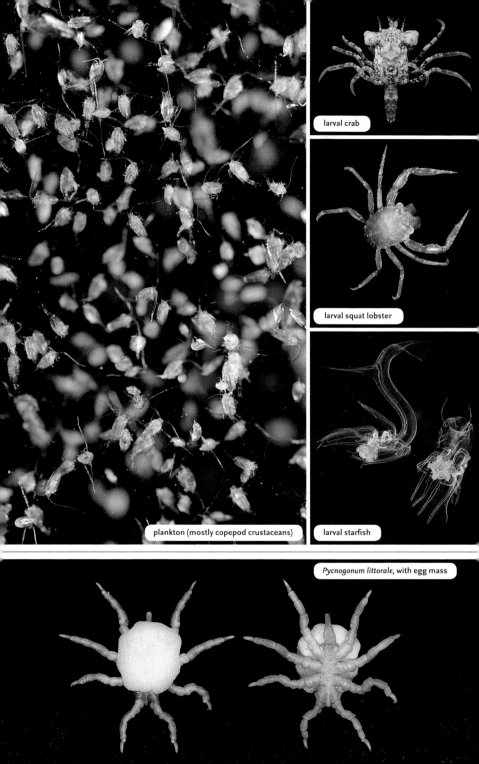

larval crab

larval squat lobster

larval starfish

plankton (mostly copepod crustaceans)

Pycnogonum littorale, with egg mass

INTRODUCING TERRESTRIAL INVERTEBRATES

A wide range of terrestrial invertebrates is found around our coasts, providing a wealth of wildlife in addition to that found on the seashore. Some groups have marine relatives that also live on the seashore, while others are strictly tied to land.

THE RANGE OF TERRESTRIAL INVERTEBRATES

Some invertebrates are found only in the sea, such as sponges, jellyfish and starfish. Many groups have relatives from both the marine and terrestrial worlds, including annelid worms, crustaceans and molluscs. However, a few invertebrate groups are strictly terrestrial, with many coastal, but no truly marine, representatives.

COASTAL INVERTEBRATES

Invertebrates, and insects in particular, are among the most numerous and diverse groups of organisms on the planet. Little wonder then that they are well represented on the coast. Most widespread species of terrestrial invertebrates are found both inland and near the coast; in a book of this size it would be impossible to include all these representatives, and it would divert the book's function away from its coastal core. Some invertebrates are, however, strictly coastal while others thrive best within sight of the sea; these species are included. Terrestrial invertebrates covered by this book include the following: groups with both marine and terrestrial representatives – crustaceans and molluscs; and strictly terrestrial invertebrates – insects, centipedes, millipedes and spiders.

INSECTS (*see* opposite) – well represented in coastal habitats; the Green Tiger Beetle *Cicindela campestris* is a typical and showy representative.

CENTIPEDES (*see* p. 202) – *Strigamia maritima* is a typical strandline species.

CRUSTACEANS (*see* p. 150) – the Pill Woodlouse *Armadillidium vulgare* is a common strandline representative of a group with numerous marine relatives.

MILLIPEDES (*see* p. 202) – although widespread inland, the Striped Millipede *Ommatoiulus sabulosus* is common and obvious under strandline debris.

MOLLUSCS (*see* pp. 238–9) – snails, and slugs such as this orange form of the Large Black Slug *Arion ater*, are common in coastal grassland.

SPIDERS (*see* p. 202) – the Zebra Spider *Salticus scenicus* is widespread inland but common on coastal timber and stones, along with several similar species.

COASTAL INSECTS

Insects are the most conspicuous of our terrestrial invertebrates, and the most diverse. It is slightly odd then that they have never colonised the marine world. In classification terms, insects are invertebrates (animals without backbones) belonging to a subdivision called Arthropoda, animals that have an external skeleton and paired, jointed limbs; muscles allowing movement are internal.

An adult insect's body is divided into three main regions: the head, which supports many sensory organs as well as the mouthparts; the abdomen, to which three pairs of legs and paired wings are attached (wings are absent in some insects); and the segmented abdomen, within which many of the main body organs are contained.

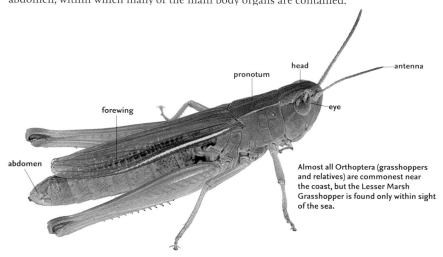

pronotum — head — antenna

forewing

eye

abdomen

Almost all Orthoptera (grasshoppers and relatives) are commonest near the coast, but the Lesser Marsh Grasshopper is found only within sight of the sea.

A Silver Y moth, newly arrived from France.

RESIDENTS AND MIGRANTS

Some insects lead rather sedentary lives but, as a whole, the presence of wings and many species' ability to fly actively means that many are extremely mobile. Flight is particularly characteristic of butterflies and moths. Most species are rather territorial and do not stray far from their favoured habitats. A few, however, are long-distance migrants, reaching British shores from mainland Europe; understandably, they are commonest on the coast, their first point of arrival. In the case of some species, migrants boost resident populations already established here. But any Painted Lady butterfly and Silver Y moth you see on the coast is likely to have migrated from mainland Europe.

Clouded Yellow *Colias croceus* Wingspan 50mm

Fast-flying, active butterfly that seldom settles for long. **ADULT** has dark-bordered upperwings that are yellow in female, orange-yellow in male. Both sexes have yellow underwings with few dark markings. **LARVA** is green and feeds on Lucerne *Medicago sativa*. **STATUS** Summer migrant in varying numbers. Very common on coasts in some years.

Large White *Pieris brassicae* Wingspan 60mm

Our largest 'white' butterfly. **ADULT** has yellowish underwings. Upperwings are creamy white with a black tip to forewing; female also has 2 spots on forewing. Flies May–Sep. **LARVA** is black and yellow, and feeds on cabbage family members. **STATUS** Common and widespread; migrants boost numbers on S coasts in summer.

ABOVE: Large White, larva
LEFT: Large White, male

Small Tortoiseshell

Aglais urticae Wingspan 42mm
Wayside species and common on coasts. Sun-loving and fond of basking. **ADULT** has upperwings marbled orange, yellow and black; underwings are smoky brown. Flies Mar–Oct with 2 or 3 broods; last brood hibernates. **LARVA** is yellow and black; gregarious, and feeds on Common Nettle (p. 56). **STATUS** Has declined in many areas but still common on coasts in the S.

ABOVE: Small Tortoiseshell, larvae
LEFT: Small Tortoiseshell

Peacock, larva

Peacock *Inachis io* Wingspan 60mm

Distinctive and familiar visitor to coastal flowers. **ADULT** has smoky-brown underwings and maroon upperwings with bold eye markings. Flies Jul–Sep and again in spring after hibernation. Sometimes hibernates indoors or in sheds and outbuildings. **LARVA** is blackish with spiky bristles; lives in clusters on Common Nettle (p. 56). **STATUS** Common and widespread except in the N.

Painted Lady *Vanessa cardui* Wingspan 60mm

Active, fast-flying butterfly. **ADULT** has upperwings marbled pinkish buff, white and black; underwings are buffish with a similar pattern to upperwing. **LARVA** is blackish with spiky bristles; feeds on thistles. **STATUS** Summer migrant in variable numbers; most numerous near coasts. Sometimes breeds but does not survive winter.

Red Admiral *Vanessa atalanta* Wingspan 60mm

Sun-loving wayside butterfly. **ADULT** has marbled smoky-grey underwings, and black upperwings with red bands and white spots. Seen in many months but commonest Jul–Aug. **LARVA** is blackish with spiky bristles; feeds on Common Nettle (p. 56) and lives within a tent of stitched-together leaves. **STATUS** Seen mostly as a summer migrant, and commonest near coasts; adults hibernate in small numbers.

Red Admiral, newly-emerged Adult

Small Copper

Small Copper

Lycaena phlaeas Wingspan 25mm
Attractive open-country species. **ADULT** has variable orange and dark brown pattern on upperwings; underwings have a similar pattern to upperwings but dark brown is replaced by grey-buff. Flies May–Sep in 2 or 3 broods. **LARVA** is green and feeds on Sheep's Sorrel (p. 56). **STATUS** Locally common.

Clouded Yellow, underwing

Large White, female

Small Tortoiseshell

Peacock

Painted Lady

Red Admiral

Small Copper

Common Blue *Polyommatus icarus* Wingspan 32mm
Our most widespread blue butterfly. **ADULT** male has blue
upperwings; female's are usually brown, but sometimes tinged
blue in middle. Underwings of both sexes are grey-brown
with dark spots. Flies Apr–Sep in successive broods. **LARVA** is
green and feeds on trefoils. **STATUS** Common in grassy places,
especially near coasts in the S.

Common Blue

Glanville Fritillary
Melitaea cinxia Wingspan 40mm
Beautifully marked butterfly. **ADULT**
has orange-brown upperwings;
underwings are creamy white and orange-buff. Flies May–Jun
but active only in sunshine. **LARVA** feeds gregariously on Sea
Plantain (p. 98). **STATUS** Very locally common on undercliffs
on the Isle of Wight and in S Hampshire.

Glanville Fritillary

Dark Green Fritillary
Argynnis aglaja Wingspan 60mm
Fast and powerful flier; visits
thistles and knapweeds. **ADULT** has orange-brown upperwings;
underside of hindwing has greenish scaling. Flies Jul–Aug.
LARVA feeds on violets. **STATUS** Widespread but local on sand
dunes and grassy cliffs in Britain and Ireland.

Dark Green Fritillary

Wall Brown

Wall Brown
Lasiommata megera Wingspan 45mm
Colourful, sun-loving butterfly.
ADULT has orange-brown
upperwings and a fritillary-like
appearance, but shows small
eye-spots on wings. Double-brooded,
flying Apr–May and Jul–Sep. **LARVA**
feeds on grasses. **STATUS** Widespread
but declining and now rather scarce;
least so on coasts in S Britain.

Grayling *Hipparchia semele* Wingspan 50mm
Sun-loving butterfly that sits with its wings folded and
angled to the sun to cast the least shadow. **ADULT** has
beautifully patterned underwings with an orange forewing
showing 2 eye-spots. Flies Jun–Aug. **LARVA** feeds on grasses.
STATUS Widespread, favouring warm, dry places, especially
sparsely vegetated rocky coasts in SW Britain.

Grayling

Meadow Brown *Maniola jurtina* Wingspan 50mm
Classic grassland butterfly. **ADULT** has brown upperwings;
male has a small orange patch on forewing containing an
eye-spot; orange patch is larger in female. Flies Jun–Aug.
LARVA is green and feeds on grasses. **STATUS** Common and
widespread, often locally abundant in coastal grassland.

Small Heath *Coenonympha pamphilus* Wingspan 30mm
Small grassland butterfly. **ADULT** seldom reveals upperwings.
Underside of forewing is orange with an eye-spot; hindwing
is marbled grey, brown and buff. Double-brooded, flying
May–Jun and Aug–Sep. **LARVA** Feeds on grasses. **STATUS**
Widespread, but restricted to unimproved grassland and
locally common only in the S, especially near coasts.

Meadow Brown,
underwing

Common Blue, male

Common Blue, female

Glanville Fritillary

Dark Green Fritillary

Wall Brown

Grayling

Meadow Brown, female

Small Heath

Small Skipper *Thymelicus sylvestris* Wingspan 25mm
Has an active, buzzing flight; often visits grassland thistles. Rests with wings held at an angle. **ADULT** has orange-brown upperwings and orange-buff underwings. Brown underside to antennal tip allows separation from similar Essex Skipper (below). Flies Jul–Aug. **LARVA** is green; feeds on various grasses. **STATUS** Common and widespread.

Essex Skipper *Thymelicus lineola* Wingspan 25mm
Similar to Small Skipper (above) but underside to antennal tips is black. Has a similar buzzing flight. **ADULT** has orange-brown upperwings and orange-buff underwings. Flies Jun–Jul. **LARVA** is green; feeds on various grasses. **STATUS** Locally common in the S.

Lulworth Skipper *Thymelicus acteon* Wingspan 28mm
Subtly attractive skipper with an active, buzzing flight. **ADULT** has khaki-brown upperwings. Forewing has a crescent of pale spots like a paw-print; markings are brighter on female than on male. Flies Jun–Jul. **LARVA** feeds on grasses. **STATUS** Very local in coastal grassland from Purbeck in Dorset to E Devon.

Large Skipper, underwing

Large Skipper *Ochlodes faunus* Wingspan 34mm
Active butterfly that often holds its wings at an angle at rest. **ADULT** has dark brown upperwings with pale markings. Underwings are buffish orange with paler spots. Flies Jun–Jul. **LARVA** is green; feeds on grasses. **STATUS** Common and widespread in coastal grassland in England and Wales.

Thrift Clearwing
Synansphecia muscaeformis Length 12–15mm
Day-flying moth that is active only in sunshine. Rests on flowers of its larval foodplant; males are attracted to specific pheromone lures. **ADULT** has a dark body with yellow markings. Wings are partly transparent. Flies Jun–Jul. **LARVA** feeds on roots of Thrift (p. 90). **STATUS** Locally common on sea cliffs in W England and Wales with extensive areas of Thrift.

Hummingbird Hawkmoth
Macroglossum stellatarum Wingspan 45mm
Day-flying species that hovers with an audible hum and collects nectar using its long tongue. **ADULT** has brown forewings and an orange patch on hindwings; note white on sides of abdomen. Flies May–Oct. **LARVA** is pale green with a longitudinal white line, white spots and a relatively small bluish 'horn' at tail end. Feeds on bedstraws. Seen only occasionally in Britain, mostly in the S. **STATUS** Migrant visitor from mainland Europe in summer, in variable numbers; in some years it is common in coastal areas.

Hummingbird Hawkmoth

Convolvulus Hawkmoth
Agrius convolvuli Wingspan 100–110mm
Impressive moth. Rests on fences and posts in daytime. Feeds by hovering at large-mouthed flowers (such as ginger lilies *Hedychium* sp.), drinking nectar through its long proboscis. Feeds from dusk onwards on warm nights. **ADULT** has a marbled grey forewing. Pink-flushed hindwings and pink-barred abdomen are hidden at rest but exposed if moth is alarmed. Flies Jun–Oct. **LARVA** is green or brown with diagonal stripes and a 'horn' at tail end. Feeds on bindweeds. **STATUS** Regular migrant, mostly seen near coasts.

Convolvulus Hawkmoth

Small Skipper

Essex Skipper

Lulworth Skipper

Large Skipper

Thrift Clearwing

Convolvulus Hawkmoth

Hummingbird
Hawkmoth

Brown-tail *Euproctis chrysorrhea* Wingspan 35–40mm
Distinctive moth. **ADULT** is white and fluffy-looking. Abdomen is tipped with brown hairs. Flies Jul–Aug. **LARVA** is hairy and brown with red and white tufts. Hairs cause skin rash. Feeds in a communal web on Common Hawthorn *Crataegus monogyna* and Blackthorn *Prunus spinosa*. **STATUS** Locally common on S and E coasts of England.

Garden Tiger *Arctia caja* Wingspan 50–65mm
Broad-winged moth. **ADULT** has a variable brown and white pattern on forewings; dark-spotted orange hindwings are revealed in alarm. Flies Jul–Aug. **LARVA** is hairy; feeds on herbaceous plants. **STATUS** Once widespread, now only locally common, mainly in rough coastal grassland.

Cream-spot Tiger *Arctia villica* Wingspan 55mm
Attractive moth. **ADULT** has black and white forewings; these conceal yellow and black hindwings unless moth is disturbed. Flies May–Jul. **LARVA** is brown and hairy, and feeds on herbaceous plants. **STATUS** Locally common in coastal grassland.

Six-spot Burnet
Zygaena filipendulae Length 18–22mm
Distinctive day-flying moth. **ADULT** has metallic greenish-blue forewings with 6 red spots, and red hindwings. Flies Jul–Aug. **LARVA** is yellowish with black dots; feeds on bird's-foot trefoils. **STATUS** Locally common, sometimes abundant, on grassy sea cliffs and dunes.

Silver Y
Autographa gamma Length 20–22mm
Distinctive moth. Flies by day as well as after dark. **ADULT** has marbled grey-brown forewings with a diagnostic white 'Y' marking. Flies May–Oct. **LARVA** feeds on low-growing plants. **STATUS** Widespread and common migrant from S Europe.

Six-spot Burnet, larva and pupal cocoon

Bristletail
Petrobius maritimus Length 15–20mm
Wingless, scuttling insect. **ADULT** has an elongate, rather flattened and segmented body, covered in metallic scales. Rear end has 3 long, bristly 'tails'. **STATUS** Locally common on rocky shores above the high-tide line, in sea caves and on damp, shady rock overhangs.

Springtail

Springtails Order Collembola Length 2–4mm
Minute wingless insects whose specific identification is best left to experts. **ADULTS** have a rather hunchbacked body, relatively long antennae and a forked appendage at rear end with which they can spring into the air to escape danger. **STATUS** Locally common under strandline debris.

Dusky Cockroach *Ectobius lapponicus* Length 10–12mm
Flattened, scuttling insect. Flies in sunny weather. **ADULT** has long antennae and tough grey-brown forewings that cover abdomen. Seen mainly Jun–Aug. **STATUS** Locally common in coastal grassland; easily overlooked.

Common Earwig *Forficula auricularia* Length 13mm
Unmistakable flightless insect. **ADULT** has a shiny brown body. Pincer-like cerci are curved in male but straight in female. **STATUS** Locally common. Mostly nocturnal. Found under strandline debris during daytime.

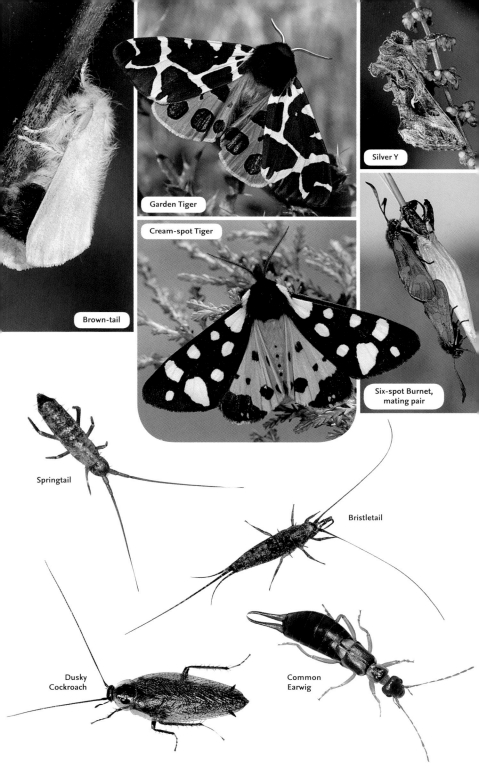

Brown-tail

Garden Tiger

Silver Y

Cream-spot Tiger

Six-spot Burnet, mating pair

Springtail

Bristletail

Dusky Cockroach

Common Earwig

Cepero's Groundhopper *Tetrix ceperoi* Length 9–13mm

Tiny grasshopper relative. Hops well and can fly. **ADULT** has broad 'shoulders' and long wings that extend beyond long pronotum. Colour is variable but typically marbled grey and brown. **STATUS** Coastal; restricted to bare, damp ground in S England and S Wales.

Mottled Grasshopper

Myrmeleotettix maculatus Length 15–18mm

Small, stout grasshopper. **ADULT** colour varies from green to brown (sometimes tinged red) but body always looks marbled. Has inflected, angular lines on pronotum. Tips of antennae are clubbed in male, swollen in female. Male is smaller than female. **STATUS** Locally common on dunes.

Mottled Grasshopper, female

Meadow Grasshopper

Chorthippus parallelus Length 17–23mm

Distinctive grasshopper. **ADULT** has a gently incurved pronotom. Female is much larger than male and has very short forewings (less than half abdomen length). Male's wings are only marginally shorter than abdomen. **STATUS** Widespread and common in grassy places.

Lesser Marsh Grasshopper *Chorthippus albomarginatus* Length 15–21mm

Distinctive coastal species. **ADULT** has a gently incurved pronotum. Recalls Meadow Grasshopper (above) but forewing is much longer (still does not reach tip of abdomen) and shows a bulge near base on anterior margin. Female is much larger than male. **STATUS** Restricted to coastal grassland and dunes.

Grey Bush-cricket *Platycleis albopunctata* Length 20–24mm

Distinctive insect. **ADULT** has a mainly marbled grey-brown body with a yellow underside to abdomen; female has an upcurved blackish ovipositor. Wings are fully formed. **STATUS** Favours warm coastal grassland, often on S-facing slopes. Restricted mainly to S England and S Wales. Often remains hidden during daytime.

Great Green Bush Cricket, female

Great Green Bush-cricket

Tettigonia viridissima Length 45–55mm

Our largest bush-cricket. Male's song is loud but hard to pinpoint. **ADULT** is bright green except for brown dorsal stripe. Female has a long, straight ovipositor. Both sexes have long wings. **STATUS** Local in coastal scrub and commonest on S coast from Dorset to Cornwall.

Roesel's Bush-cricket *Metrioptera roeselii* Length 15–18mm

Well-marked insect. Male's high-pitched, buzzing song is inaudible to many people. **ADULT** is usually brown with pale margins to sides of pronotum; sides of abdomen are sometimes yellowish but 3 yellow spots are always present. Most adults are short-winged and flightless; a few have fully formed wings and can fly. **STATUS** Formerly almost exclusively coastal, but species is now spreading inland. Favours rank grassland.

Long-winged Conehead *Conocephalus discolor* Length 17–20mm

Furtive and easily overlooked insect. **ADULT** has a slender body, mostly bright green except for brown stripe on dorsal surface of head and pronotum; brown wings are as long as abdomen and female has a straight ovipositor. **STATUS** Formerly exclusively coastal, but species is now spreading inland. Favours dense grassy habitats.

Short-winged Conehead *Conocephalus dorsalis* Length 16–18mm

Slender, furtive insect. When alarmed, aligns body, antennae and legs along stems and moves to opposite side from observer. **ADULT** has a green body with a brown dorsal stripe; forewings are reduced. Female has an upcurved ovipositor. **STATUS** Locally common only in S England and S Wales in coastal grassland; often associated with clumps of rushes.

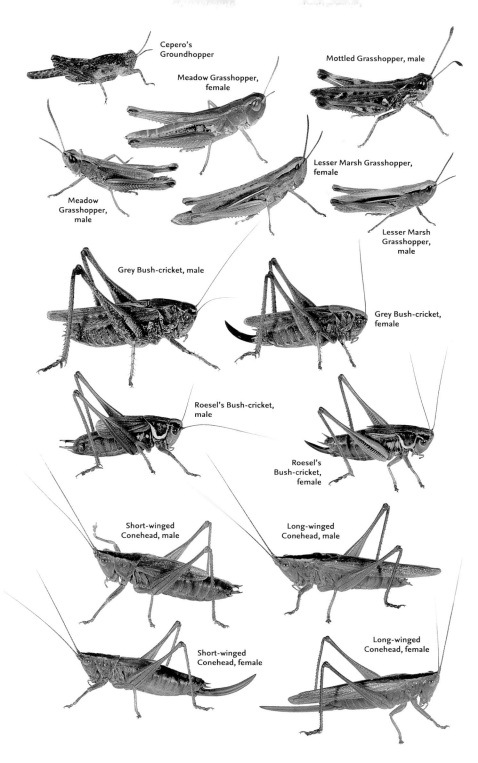

Cepero's Groundhopper

Mottled Grasshopper, male

Meadow Grasshopper, female

Meadow Grasshopper, male

Lesser Marsh Grasshopper, female

Lesser Marsh Grasshopper, male

Grey Bush-cricket, male

Grey Bush-cricket, female

Roesel's Bush-cricket, male

Roesel's Bush-cricket, female

Short-winged Conehead, male

Long-winged Conehead, male

Short-winged Conehead, female

Long-winged Conehead, female

Green Tiger Beetle *Cicindela campestris* Length 14mm
Active predator. Runs fast on the ground and flies well in sunshine. ADULT has green upperparts with pale spots on elytra, and shiny bronze legs and thorax margins. Seen May–Jul. STATUS Locally common on dune and coastal heaths.

Northern Dune Tiger Beetle *Cicindela hybrida* Length 15mm
Similar to Green Tiger Beetle (above). ADULT has bronzy upperparts with broad creamy-white marks on elytra. Seen Jun–Jul. STATUS Scarce, restricted to dunes on the Sefton coast in NW England. SIMILAR SPECIES **Dune Tiger Beetle** *C. maritima* is found in dunes around the Bristol Channel, and in N Wales and N Norfolk.

Sulphur Beetle *Ctenopius sulphureus* Length 8–11mm
Distinctive species. Usually seen on flowers and feeds on pollen. ADULT is bright yellow (the only pure yellow British beetle). Seen mainly May–Aug. STATUS Locally common in dry coastal habitats, particularly dunes and bare cliffs.

Shore Sexton Beetle *Necrodes littoralis* Length 21–23mm
Impressive beetle. ADULT has a black body; antennae are mostly dark, palest towards tip. Hind tibiae are incurved; both elytra bear a 'pimple'. Seen mostly May–Oct. STATUS Common and widespread. Mainly nocturnal but sometimes found by turning over rotting tideline debris, especially animal corpses.

Burying Beetle *Nicrophorus vespilloides* Length 18–21mm
Distinctive beetle. ADULT is mostly black but with orange markings on elytra; anterior pair form a band, posterior pair often reduced to large spots. Antennae are clubbed and dark. Seen mostly May–Oct. STATUS Common and widespread. Mostly nocturnal; sometimes found by turning over animal corpses.

Paederus littoralis Length 8–9mm
One of several so-called rove beetles. ADULT has an elongated black and red body. STATUS Widespread and common in open coastal habitats and on cliffs. Seen mainly May–Oct. An active hunter but also found under strandline debris or by turning over stones.

Rose Chafer *Cetonia aurata* Length 17mm
Colourful beetle, often found in flowers. Moves in a cumbersome manner. ADULT has a shiny bronzy-green body; parallel-sided elytra are flecked with white lines and marks. Seen May–Sep. LARVA lives in rotting wood. STATUS Widespread and locally common, except in Scotland.

Seven-spot Ladybird *Coccinella 7-punctata* Length 6–7mm
One of our most familiar and common ladybirds. ADULT has reddish-orange elytra and 7 black spots; head and thorax are black and white. Seen Mar–Oct. LARVA is blackish with orange spots; body has a spiky appearance. Active on plants, feeding on aphids. STATUS Found in a wide range of habitats; often common on coasts.

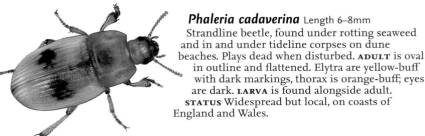

Phaleria cadaverina Length 6–8mm
Strandline beetle, found under rotting seaweed and in and under tideline corpses on dune beaches. Plays dead when disturbed. ADULT is oval in outline and flattened. Elytra are yellow-buff with dark markings, thorax is orange-buff; eyes are dark. LARVA is found alongside adult. STATUS Widespread but local, on coasts of England and Wales.

Phaleria cadaverina

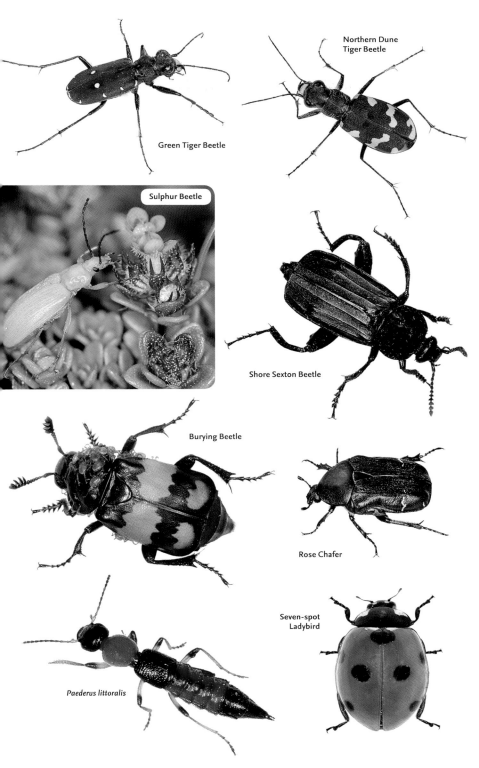

Green Tiger Beetle

Northern Dune Tiger Beetle

Sulphur Beetle

Shore Sexton Beetle

Burying Beetle

Rose Chafer

Paederus littoralis

Seven-spot Ladybird

Oil Beetle *Meloe proscarabeus* Length 26mm
Unmistakable fat-bodied insect. Produces pungent oil when alarmed. **ADULT** has a shiny bluish-black body with small elytra that do not cover swollen abdomen. Seen Apr–Jun. **LARVA** lives inside nest of a solitary bee. **STATUS** Widespread but local in dry coastal grassland.

Dor Beetle *Geotrupes stercorarius* Length 15mm
Rotund beetle, often seen trundling across paths. **ADULT** has a shiny blue-black lozenge-shaped body and spiky-margined legs. **LARVA** feeds in horse or cow dung. Seen May–Jul. **STATUS** Locally common throughout, in grassland where grazing animals are kept.

Bloody-nosed Beetle *Timarcha tenebricosa* Length 20mm
Lumbering, flightless beetle, often seen plodding across paths. When disturbed, exudes drops of bright red blood-like fluid from mouth. **ADULT** is blackish and shiny, with proportionately large legs and 'feet', and an ovoid abdomen. Seen Apr–Jun. **STATUS** Widespread and fairly common in coastal grassland.

Broscus cephalotes Length 18–20mm
Ground beetle and an active predator. **ADULT** has a flattened black body. Elytra and thorax are smooth and slightly matt. **STATUS** Locally common in dunes and dry sandy soil near the coast.

Kelp Fly *Coelopa frigida* Length 10–15mm
One of several specialist flies associated with the strandline. Reluctant to fly more than a short distance. **ADULT** has a flattened body, allowing it to live among layers of rotting weed in strandline debris. **LARVA** feeds on rotting organic matter in strandline. **STATUS** Common, sometimes abundant, wherever seaweed collects.

Broscus cephalotes

Sand Wasp *Ammophila sabulosa* Length 20mm
Active insect with a 'twitching' gait when walking. Adult catches, immobilises and buries caterpillars (in a burrow in sand) as food for its larvae. **ADULT** has a slender, mostly black body with orange on anterior half of abdomen. Seen May–Aug. **STATUS** Locally common on coastal dunes.

Red-tailed Bumblebee

White-tailed Bumblebee
Bombus lucorum Length 12–22mm
Usually the commonest of several bumblebee species seen near coasts. Nests in holes in the ground. **ADULT** has a bright yellow collar and band at front of abdomen. All individuals have a white-tipped abdomen. Seen Apr–Oct. **STATUS** Widespread and fairly common in coastal grassland. **SIMILAR SPECIES Red-tailed Bumblebee** *B. lapidarius* has a red-tipped abdomen.

Colletes succinctus Length to 12mm
One of several mining bees (genera *Colletes* and *Andrena*) that are found on coasts. Solitary, but lives in large aggregations, each bee mining a burrow in soft coastal banks and cliffs. Burrow (containing larva) is stocked with pollen from heathers (*Erica* and *Calluna*). **ADULT** has yellow-brown hairs on thorax and whitish bands on otherwise dark abdomen. **STATUS** Associated with coastal heathlands, in W and S Britain.

Oil Beetle

Dor Beetle

Broscus cephalotes

Bloody-nosed Beetle

Sand Wasp

Kelp Fly

White-tailed Bumblebee, mating pair

Colletes succinctus

Migrant Hawker *Aeshna mixta* Length 60mm

Well-marked dragonfly. **ADULT** has blue markings on abdomen but dark upper surface to thorax; note also yellow triangle at front end of abdomen. Flies Jun–Oct. **STATUS** Local resident; common around coastal freshwater pools. Numbers are boosted by influxes of migrants from Europe.

Southern Hawker *Aeshna cyanea* Length 70mm

Large, active species. **ADULT** has broad green stripes on thorax and abdomen, with markings of similar coloration except for last 3 segments of male, where markings are blue. Flies Jun–Oct. **STATUS** Common near coastal freshwater pools in S England.

Brown Hawker *Aeshna grandis* Length 74mm

Easily recognised, even in flight. **ADULT** has a brown body and bronze wings; male also has blue spots on 2nd and 3rd segments of abdomen. Flies Jul–Sep. **STATUS** Commonest in SE England, near well-vegetated coastal freshwater pools. Patrols regular hunting territory around margins.

Hairy Dragonfly *Brachytron pratense* Length 55mm

Well-marked dragonfly. **ADULT** male has blue eyes, a hairy thorax and blue spots on abdomen. Adult female has greenish eyes, yellow spots on abdomen, and a hairy thorax and abdomen. Flies May–Jun. **STATUS** Local, near coastal freshwater pools, mainly in SE England.

Broad-bodied Chaser *Libellula depressa* Length 43mm

Actively hawks for insects but also perches for long periods. **ADULT** has a broad, flattened abdomen; sky-blue with small yellow spots on sides in mature male, brown with yellow spots on sides in female and immature male. Wings have dark brown bases. Flies May–Aug. **STATUS** Common near coastal freshwater pools in S England.

Yellow-winged Darter

Red-veined Darter

Common Darter *Sympetrum striolatum* Length 36mm

Frequently rests on ground but also uses perches. **ADULT** has a narrow body. Abdomen is deep red in mature male, orange-brown in immature male and female. Flies Jun–early Nov. **STATUS** Commonest dragonfly in many parts. Breeds in still fresh water; often feeds well away from water. **SIMILAR SPECIES** **Yellow-winged Darter** *S. flaveolum* has bright orange-yellow flush at base of wings. Regular migrant from mainland Europe, mainly to S and SE England, sometimes in good numbers. Breeds occasionally but colonies seldom persist. **Red-veined Darter** *S. fonscolombii* is a migrant visitor to S coasts. Male has bright red body and base of wing veins; female has yellow body.

Ruddy Darter *Sympetrum sanguineum* Length 35mm

Often perches with wings depressed slightly. **ADULT** is similar to Common Darter (above), but mature male has a markedly constricted, bright red abdomen; female and immature male have black legs (variably brown in Common) and a yellow patch at base of hindwing. Flies Jul–Sep. **STATUS** Locally common near coastal freshwater pools.

Migrant Hawker

Southern Hawker

Brown Hawker

Hairy Dragonfly

Broad-bodied Chaser, female

Broad-bodied Chaser, male

Common Darter, mating pair

Ruddy Darter

Emerald Damselfly *Lestes sponsa* Length 35mm

Colourful damselfly that often rests with wings slightly open. **ADULT** male has a mainly shiny green body with sky-blue eyes, central band and abdomen tip; inner abdominal appendages are straight. Female has shiny green eyes and body. Flies Jun–Aug. **STATUS** Widespread but local beside coastal pools; commonest in the S.

Scarce Emerald Damselfly, female

Scarce Emerald Damselfly

Lestes dryas Length 35mm
Very similar to Emerald Damselfly (above). Also often rests with wings slightly open. **ADULT** male has a mainly shiny green body with sky-blue eyes, central band and abdomen tip; inner abdominal appendages are curved. Female has shiny green eyes and body. Flies Jun–Aug. **STATUS** Generally scarce but very locally common near freshwater and slightly brackish channels and ditches in Ireland and SE England.

Azure Damselfly

Coenagrion puella Length 33mm
Familiar colourful species. **ADULT** has 2 black lines on side of abdomen (1 in Common Blue Damselfly, below). Male is sky-blue with black bands on abdomen and a black 'U' marking on segment 2; female is mostly black but with a blue tip to abdomen. Flies May–Aug. **STATUS** Widespread and common except in the N; favours ditches and ponds, and generally common near coasts.

Common Blue Damselfly *Enallagma cyathigerum* Length 32mm

Dainty species. **ADULT** has a single black line on side of thorax (2 in Azure Damselfly, above). Male is blue with black bands on abdomen and a mushroom cloud-shaped dot on segment 2. Green and black female has a diagnostic ventral spine near abdomen tip. Flies May–Sep. **STATUS** Common near vegetated still water around coasts.

Blue-tailed Damselfly *Ischnura elegans* Length 32mm

Distinctive damselfly. **ADULT** is easily identified by mainly black body with sky-blue segment 8 of abdomen. Flies May–Aug. **STATUS** Common and widespread except in the far N. Tolerates moderate pollution and slightly brackish conditions.

Red-eyed Damselfly *Erythromma najas* Length 35mm

Distinctive species. **ADULT** has striking red eyes and a blue-tipped blackish abdomen; thorax of male is black above and blue on sides, female's is black and yellow. Flies May–Sep. **STATUS** Locally common only in central and S England, favouring ponds and channels.

Large Red Damselfly *Pyrrhosoma nymphula* Length 35mm

Distinctive damselfly with a rather weak flight. **ADULT** is mainly bright red but abdomen is marked with black, more extensively on female than male. Note the black legs. Flies May–Aug. **STATUS** Common and widespread in a range of coastal freshwater habitats, including ponds, channels and ditches.

Common Blue Damselfly, abdominal segment 2

ABOVE: Blue-tailed Damselfly, tip of abdomen

LEFT: Red-eyed Damselfly, tip of abdomen

Emerald Damselfly, male

Scarce Emerald Damselfly, male

Azure Damselfly

Common Blue Damselfly, mating pair

Blue-tailed Damselfly

Red-eyed Damselfly

Large Red Damselfly

Strigamia maritima Length to 12cm
Exclusively coastal centipede. Found under stones and among strandline debris on shores. **ADULT** has an extremely slender, segmented body, orange-red in colour with a pair of antennae at head end. Seen mainly Apr–Oct. **STATUS** Widespread on coasts in W Britain.

Lithobius forficatus Length 30mm
Familiar centipede, found under stones and shoreline debris in the daytime. **ADULT** has a shiny orange-brown body that is relatively broad and flattened. Legs, antennae and fangs are obvious. Seen mainly Apr–Oct. **STATUS** Common and widespread.

Wasp Spider *Argiope bruennichi* Length to 14mm (female); to 5mm (male)
Unmistakable spider. Constructs an orb web with a zigzag of silk. **ADULT** female is larger and plumper than male; in both, abdomen has yellow, black and white bands. Seen mainly May–Sep. **STATUS** Probably introduced from Europe; now locally common in coastal grassland in S England.

Purse-web Spider, purse webs

Purse-web Spider *Atypus affinis* Length 12mm
Extraordinary spider that lives inside a mainly subterranean silken tube. Prey is captured if it walks over part of the tube that lies on the soil surface. **ADULT** is dark brown with a plump abdomen, shiny carapace and long, downward-pointing fangs. Seen year-round. **STATUS** Very locally common in dry, well-draining soil, but silken tubes are easily overlooked.

Dysdera crocata Length 12mm
Attractive and distinctive spider that hides under stones during daytime. Found in coastal sites with numerous woodlice; these are captured using its relatively large, opposable fangs. **ADULT** has reddish legs and cephalothorax, and a buffish-brown abdomen. Seen mainly Apr–Oct. **STATUS** Locally common and widespread.

Metellina merianae Length 9mm
Typical cave spider that shuns light and spends its life in caves and cellars. **ADULT** has a marbled brown and black abdomen, while its shiny legs are marked with irregular bands of reddish brown and black. Seen May–Jul. **STATUS** Widespread, particularly common near coasts.

Zebra Spider *Salticus scenicus* Length 7mm
Well-marked and aptly named jumping spider. Moves restlessly up sunny rocks and walls; spots potential prey using its large eyes and then stalks to within leaping range. Seen mainly Jul–Oct. **ADULT** has black and white stripes. **STATUS** Common and widespread.

Common Garden Spider
Araneus diadematus Length to 12mm (female); to 5mm (male)
Familiar spider. Constructs a sophisticated orb web. **ADULT** varies from grey-brown to reddish brown; abdomen has a central row of white dots and transverse white streaks that form a cross. Male is much smaller than female. Seen Jul–Oct. **STATUS** Common and widespread in coastal grassland.

Common Garden Spider, web

Strigamia maritima

Lithobius forficatus

Wasp Spider

Dysdera crocata

Metellina merianae

Purse-web Spider

Common Garden Spider

Zebra Spider

INTRODUCING MOLLUSCS

Molluscs are among the most familiar of all seashore invertebrates and also one of the most diverse. Many species are known for their shell, but in some species this is small or internal; in a few molluscs, the shell is absent altogether. Taken as a group, they occupy almost every conceivable niche in the coastal environment.

WHAT ARE MOLLUSCS?

Although molluscs are a diverse group, all have a body that comprises a head, a region called the visceral mass that contains the vital organs, and a muscular foot. The visceral mass is shrouded by tissue called the mantle; in a typical mollusc, the mantle margin secretes the shell. The mantle also encloses a cavity, connecting with the marine world, and inside which are located the gills as well as openings to the excretory and reproductive systems.

THE RANGE OF MOLLUSCS

Molluscs are divided in classification terms into several sub-groups. Those regularly found on the seashore include the following: chitons (class Polyplacophora); gastropod molluscs (class Gastropoda); bivalves – molluscs with paired shells (class Bivalvia); tusk shells (class Scaphopoda); and cuttlefish, squid and octopuses (class Cephalopoda). The gastropods are the largest class of molluscs and the group is separated further into a number of subdivisions that embrace everything from winkles and limpets to sea slugs and terrestrial snails.

Lepidochitona cinerea

upperside   underside

Chitons – unusual and distinctive molluscs, oval in outline, whose shell comprises eight interlocking dorsal plates. The plates provide protection and a degree of flexibility; this allows the animal to clamp down onto irregular rock surfaces with the aid of its muscular foot.

Winkles, whelks, top shells and limpets (class Gastropoda, sub-class Prosobranchia) – a large and very varied mollusc group. The head bears eyes and tentacles, and the mouth has a rasping, tongue-like radula, used in feeding. Movement is achieved by a muscular foot, and the body is protected by a shell that is spiral in most prosobranchs, limpets being an exception. As with other gastropods, the latter half of the mantle cavity undergoes a process called torsion during larval development, whereby it twists through 180 degrees; facing forward, it provides a chamber into which the vulnerable head can be withdrawn.

Painted Top Shell

Sea slugs and sea hares (class Gastropoda, sub-class Opisthobranchia) – not closely related to terrestrial slugs, these molluscs typically have no shell, or one that is greatly reduced. Their soft bodies are protected by noxious secretions and most species advertise the fact that they are distasteful with striking colours. In many sea slugs, gills are external and there are obvious tentacles at the head end. Movement is achieved by the muscular foot.

Elysia viridis

Terrestrial snails (class Gastropoda, subclass Pulmonata) –

most familiar as land and freshwater snails (and slugs too), a few species are found on the seashore; fewer still have returned to the marine environment. In terrestrial species, the mantle cavity is filled with air and functions as a lung. The head has eyes and tentacles, and the mouth has a rasping radula for feeding. Movement is achieved by a muscular foot, and the body is protected by a shell that typically is spiral. As with other gastropods, torsion occurs during larval development.

Mouse-eared Snail

Bivalves – in these molluscs, a hinged pair of shells protects the soft body. When the shell valves are open, siphons allow the flow of water through the mantle cavity and over the gills, where food particles are filtered out. The foot is often relatively large and muscular, while the head is absent. Many bivalves live buried, or part-buried, in sediment, while others attach themselves to rocks. There are also species that are free-living and a few can even swim by snapping their shells together to create propulsion.

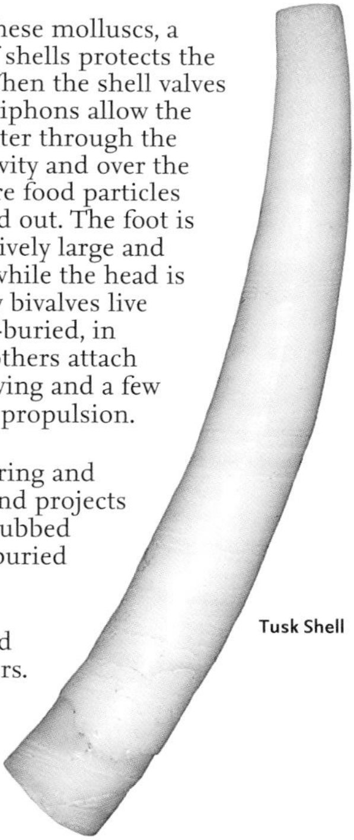

Common Cockle

Tusk shells – unusual molluscs with a cylindrical, tapering and slightly curved shell that is open at both ends. The head end projects slightly from the broader end of the cylinder, and bears clubbed tentacles that are used in feeding; in life, the head end is buried in sediment.

Cuttlefish, squid and octopuses – highly modified and distinctive molluscs, most of which are active predators. To facilitate this way of life, most have large eyes and sophisticated behaviour. In cephalopods, the mollusc foot has been modified to form long, muscular tentacles, armed with suckers for grasping prey.

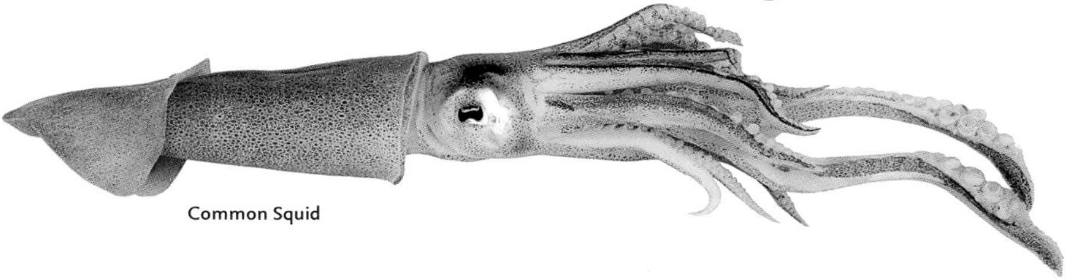

Tusk Shell

Common Squid

Leptochiton asellus Length to 18mm

Rather plain chiton, found under stones on lower shore. **ADULT** is oval and yellowish. Shell plates show growth lines, keel and posterior 'beak'; surface is finely granular in middle, coarser towards margins. Girdle is relatively narrow, with rectangular scales and marginal spines. **STATUS** Widespread and locally common on S and W coasts.

Lepidochitona cinerea

Lepidochitona cinerea Length to 25mm

Our commonest chiton, usually found under stones on lower shore. **ADULT** has rather narrow girdle, covered in small granules and fringed with large, blunt spines. Shell plates are granular, with shallow keel and posterior 'beak'; head plate has 9 or so notches. Colour variable, often greenish grey or yellowish, with bands on girdle. **STATUS** Widespread and locally common, least so on E England coast.

Callochiton septemvalvis Length to 3cm

Well-marked chiton, found under stones on lower shore. **ADULT** is oval and greenish or reddish, variably marbled with white. Shell plates show growth lines, keel and posterior 'beak'; surface is finely granular in middle, coarser towards margins. Girdle is relatively broad, coated with dense, low spines and with marginal spines. **STATUS** Local and rather scarce, mainly on S and W coasts. **SIMILAR SPECIES** *Tonicella rubra* (length to 2cm) Colourful chiton, found under stones on lower shore. Adult has rather broad girdle, covered in oval granules and fringed with spines. Shell plates are smooth. Widespread and locally common.

Acanthochitona crinita Length to 3cm

Distinctive oval chiton. Found on rocks on lower shore. **ADULT** has rather broad girdle with 18 tufts of bristles and fringe of spines. Shell plates have unevenly scattered, relatively large pear-shaped granules. Colour variable, often marbled brown, reddish or yellow. **STATUS** Widespread and locally common. **SIMILAR SPECIES** *A. fascicularis* (length to 6cm) has shell plates coated with fine, even granulation. Colour is variable but sometimes has dorsal row of pale V markings; locally common only in S and SW.

Tusk Shell Antalis entalis Length to 4cm

Tusk-like. Lives buried, head down, in offshore sand; sometimes washed up on beaches. **SHELL** is white, cylindrical, curved and tapering (broadest at head end). Open both ends; posterior end has circular aperture. **STATUS** Widespread and locally common, least so in the S. **SIMILAR SPECIES** *A. vulgare* is larger (length to 6cm), with oval posterior aperture; in the SW only.

Slit Limpet Emarginula fissura Length to 1cm

Cap-shaped mollusc, found on rocks on lower shore. Feeds on sponges. **SHELL** is buffish yellow and conical, with swept-back profile when seen side on. Has distinct slit in anterior margin. **STATUS** Widespread and locally common.

Common Keyhole Limpet

Diodora graeca Length to 7mm

Distinctive mollusc, found on rocks on lower shore. Feeds on sponges. **SHELL** is flattened-conical in profile; viewed from above, outline is oval and note narrowly oval apical hole. **STATUS** Locally common only in the N and W.

Common Keyhole Limpet

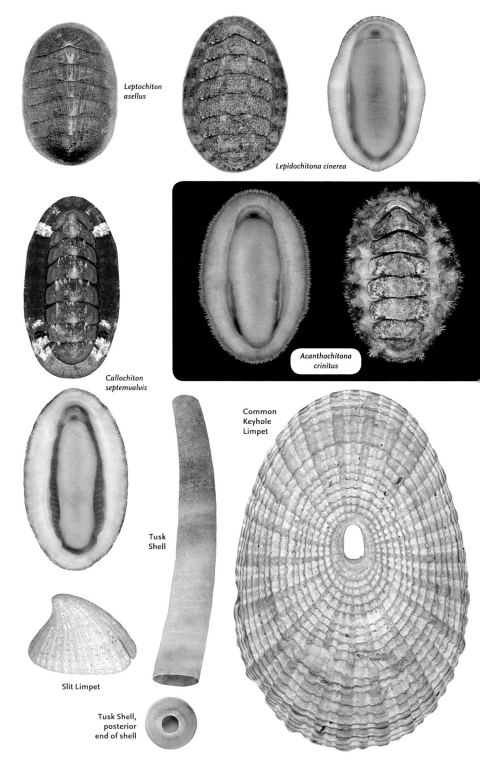

Leptochiton asellus

Lepidochitona cinerea

Callochiton septemvalvis

Acanthochitona crinitus

Common Keyhole Limpet

Tusk Shell

Slit Limpet

Tusk Shell, posterior end of shell

ABOVE: **Common Limpets;**
RIGHT: **Common Limpet, underside, showing foot**

Green Ormer *Haliotis tuberculata* Length to 9cm
Unmistakable ear-shaped mollusc, found on rocky shore at low water. Feeds on small red seaweeds. SHELL is oval with a small spiral and marginal row of holes through which mantle protrudes. Outer surface is rough and marbled green and brown; inner surface has mother-of-pearl lining. STATUS Restricted to Channel Islands but locally common there.

Common Limpet
Patella vulgata Length to 6cm
Familiar mollusc and our commonest limpet. Found on rocks between mid- and low water. SHELL is conical with radiating ridges; shells on higher shore have steeper cone than those lower down. Inside of shell is greenish grey and sole of foot is orange. STATUS Widespread and locally abundant.

Black-footed Limpet
Patella depressa Length to 3cm
Well-marked limpet, found on exposed rocky sites on lower shore. SHELL is flattened-conical with radiating ridges. Inner surface is yellowish with marginal dark rays; sole of foot is black. STATUS Restricted to the SW.

Black-footed Limpet, underside, showing foot

Black-footed Limpet, inside of shell

China Limpet, underside, showing foot

China Limpet
Patella ulyssiponensis Length to 5cm
Distinctive limpet, found on exposed rocky sites on lower shore. SHELL is flattened-conical with radiating ridges. Inner surface is porcelain-white, tinged yellow towards centre; sole of foot is orange. STATUS Commonest in the W, absent from the SE.

Common Tortoiseshell Limpet *Tectura testudinalis* Length to 3cm
Beautifully patterned limpet, found on lower shore on rocks encrusted with small red seaweeds. SHELL is flattened-conical and rather smooth; typically whitish, marbled with brown and grey. STATUS A mainly N species, absent from the SE.

White Tortoiseshell Limpet *Tectura virginea* Length to 1cm
Delicate-looking limpet, found on lower shore on rocks encrusted with small red seaweeds. SHELL is flattened-conical and smooth; typically whitish or pale pinkish, with radiating, subtly darker rays (these can be absent). STATUS Widespread and locally common.

Slipper Limpet, mass of animals

Slipper Limpet *Crepidula fornicata* Length to 5cm
Familiar mollusc, found on muddy and gravelly shores, often washed up alive. Arching stacks of several animals are common. SHELL is oval and cap-shaped, with small, shallow spire; outer surface is pinkish brown. STATUS Accidentally introduced from North America, now locally abundant in the S.

Blue-rayed Limpet *Helcion pellucidum* Length to 15mm
Distinctive limpet, typically found on fronds and stipes of *Laminaria* seaweeds. SHELL is cap-shaped and domed, with eccentric apex; surface is smooth, translucent and chestnut-brown with radiating lines of blue spots. Older animals may have worn chalky shells with a 'ledged' profile. STATUS Widespread and locally common.

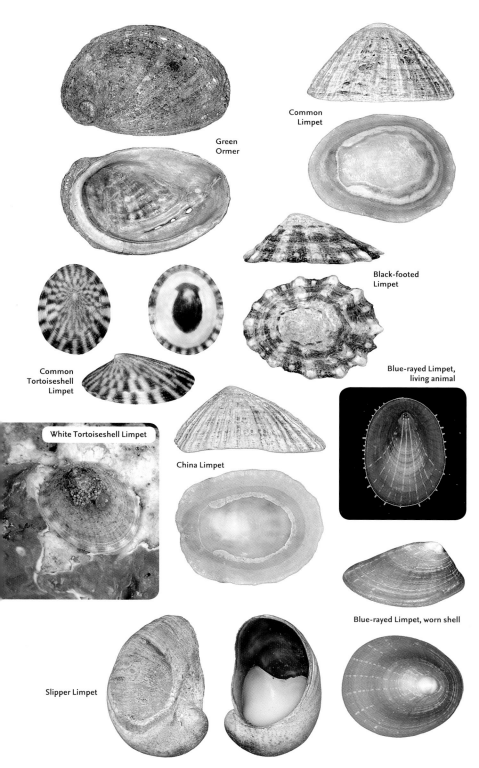

Common
Limpet

Green
Ormer

Black-footed
Limpet

Common
Tortoiseshell
Limpet

Blue-rayed Limpet,
living animal

White Tortoiseshell Limpet

China Limpet

Blue-rayed Limpet, worn shell

Slipper Limpet

Grooved Top Shell *Jujubinus striatus* Height to 10mm
Attractive mollusc, found at low water among eelgrasses and *Codium* seaweeds. SHELL is
conical and flat-sided (not 'stepped'), with 8–10 whorls and 8–10 shallow ridges per
whorl. Usually whitish with dark brown markings. STATUS Mainly in the SW.

Thick Top Shell *Osilinus lineatus* Height to 30mm
Robust, heavy-shelled mollusc, found on sheltered rocks on lower
shore. SHELL is rounded-conical in outline with 5–6 whorls;
aperture has obvious tooth. Typically rufous brown with darker
zigzag markings; worn areas reveal mother-of-pearl colours.
STATUS Locally common, mainly in the W and SW.

Painted Top Shell *Calliostoma zizyphinum* Height to 30mm
Elegant shell, found on sheltered rocky shores; usually sub-littoral, sometimes at
low-water mark. SHELL is conical with pointed apex and 10–12 subtly ribbed whorls.
Usually marbled pinkish brown and white. STATUS Widespread but rather local.

Grey Top Shell *Gibbula cineraria* Height to 15mm
Well-marked shell, familiar on strandline; in life, found on rocky shores at extreme low
water and in pools. SHELL is rounded-conical with 5–6 finely ridged whorls. Usually
buffish grey with narrow reddish-brown bands. STATUS Widespread and locally common.

Flat Top Shell *Gibbula umbilicalis* Height to 20mm
Similar to Grey Top Shell (above) but flatter, and with more convex profile. Found on
rocky shores, from mid- to low water into sub-littoral zone. SHELL is bluntly conical, the
5–6 whorls with fewer ridges than Grey Top Shell. Usually greenish with widely spaced
reddish-purple bands. STATUS Widespread in the W; absent from much of the E coast.

Turban Top Shell *Gibbula magus* Height to 30mm
Stout, robust shell. Found on lower shore on rocky and mixed
substrates. SHELL is rounded overall with 8 ridged whorls; shells
are pinkish brown, patchily suffused with orange, and typically
worn and damaged. STATUS Locally common in the S and NW;
absent from most of the E coast.

Turban Top Shell

Pheasant Shell *Tricolia pullus* Height to 8mm
Colourful and beautifully patterned shell. Associated with red
seaweeds on sheltered shores. SHELL is ovoid with up to 6 whorls,
yellowish with intricate red patterning. STATUS Locally common
in the S and W; absent from the E coast.

Least Chink Shell *Lacuna parva* Height to 4mm
Minute shell. Found on *Fucus* seaweeds on middle and lower
shore. SHELL has globular shell with low spire. Head has long,
slender tentacles. STATUS Widespread and locally common,
except in the SE.

Least Chink Shell

Banded Chink Shell *Lacuna vincta* Height to 10mm
Well-marked shell. Found on seaweeds, notably Serrated Wrack (p. 34), and eelgrasses.
SHELL is ovoid with a pointed spire and 5 whorls; yellowish buff with brown spiral bands.
STATUS Widespread and locally common, although absent from much of the SE.

Rissoa parva Height to 5mm
Small, well-marked shell. Often abundant among red seaweeds on sheltered rocky shores.
SHELL is ovoid with a pointed spire, sometimes with low ridges on the whorls; usually
buffish white with dark bands. Aperture can be closed with an operculum. STATUS
Widespread and locally common, except in the E. NOTE There are several very similar
Rissoa species. SIMILAR SPECIES *Cingula trifasciata* (height to 4mm) has tiny shell. Found
on rocky shores, under seaweed and rocks at low tide. Shell is rather ovoid with a conical
spire. Usually buffish with dark spiral stripes (3 on largest whorl). Widespread and
commonest in the W and N.

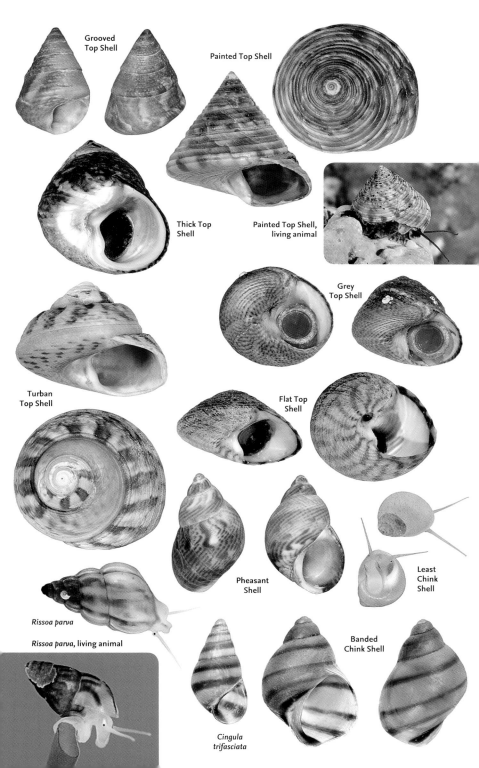

Grooved Top Shell

Painted Top Shell

Thick Top Shell

Painted Top Shell, living animal

Grey Top Shell

Turban Top Shell

Flat Top Shell

Pheasant Shell

Least Chink Shell

Rissoa parva

Rissoa parva, living animal

Cingula trifasciata

Banded Chink Shell

Laver Spire Shell *Hydrobia ulvae* Height to 6mm

Small, ecologically important species. Found mainly in estuaries. **SHELL** is a conical spire with almost straight-sided whorls. Typically grey-brown but often coated with mud. Head has pale tentacles with dark sub-terminal band. **STATUS** Widespread and common on suitable coasts. **SIMILAR SPECIES** *H. ventrosa* has rounded whorls and tentacles without dark band. *H. neglecta* has rounded whorls and tentacles with dark marks close to tip. **New Zealand Mudsnail** *Potamopyrgus antipodarum* has slightly rounded whorls and tentacles with pale central line.

Assorted *Hydrobia* species

Black-lined Periwinkle *Littorina nigrolineata* Height to 30cm

Distinctive shell; found on rocky shores, typically amongst *Ascophyllum* and *Fucus* seaweeds. **SHELL** is rounded with a short spire and 5 or 6 whorls; yellowish with dark spiral lines. **STATUS** Locally common, mainly in W Britain.

Small Periwinkle *Littorina neritoides* Height to 8mm

Tiny shell, easy overlooked when lodged in crevices, empty barnacle cases, etc. Found on rocky shores, usually above mid-tide level. **SHELL** is ovoid with a pointed spire; usually dark grey. **STATUS** Widespread and locally common, except in the E.

Common Periwinkle

Common Periwinkle *Littorina littorea* Height to 30mm

Familiar shell; found on sheltered rocky shores, across intertidal zone. **SHELL** is ovoid with a pointed spire and rough, sculptured whorls; usually grey-brown, appearing blackish when damp and out of water. **STATUS** Widespread and locally very common, least so on the E coast.

Flat Periwinkle *Littorina obtusata* Height to 10mm

Distinctive shell. Found on sheltered rocky shores; associated with brown seaweeds, notably *Ascophyllum* and Bladder Wrack (p. 35). **SHELL** is ovoid, with a low, flat spire and rounded aperture; often yellow, but orange, grey-brown and even chequered shells occur in different habitats. **STATUS** Widespread and locally very common, least so on the E coast.

Littorina mariae Height to 10mm

Very similar to Flat Periwinkle (above). Found on rocky shores, typically on Serrated Wrack (p. 34). **SHELL** is globular, with a low, flat spire and very large, oval aperture. **STATUS** Widespread and locally common, mainly in the W and SW.

Flat Periwinkle, colour forms

Rough Periwinkle *Littorina saxatilis* Height to 17mm

Solid shell; found on upper shore, usually among seaweeds, in habitats ranging from rocky shores to estuaries. **SHELL** is globular with a pointed spire and ridged whorls; colour is variable but often orange or brown. **STATUS** Widespread and generally common. **SIMILAR SPECIES** Several very similar species exist: *L. rudis* is found on Channel Wrack (p. 33); *L. tenebrosa* has a thinner, less sculptured and more rounded shell and occurs in estuaries; *L. arcana* is found on upper zones of exposed rocky shores, among *Verrucaria* lichens.

Littorina neglecta Height to 5mm

Tiny, easily overlooked shell. Usually found on exposed rocky shores, in crevices and empty barnacle shells. **SHELL** is globular and thin, with a short, blunt spire; usually yellowish brown with a dark spiral band or dark patterns. **STATUS** Locally common, mainly in the W and N.

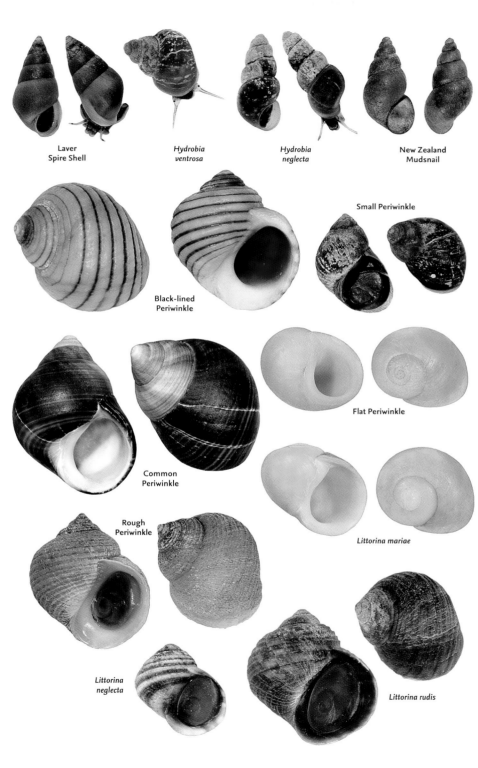

Laver
Spire Shell

*Hydrobia
ventrosa*

*Hydrobia
neglecta*

New Zealand
Mudsnail

Small Periwinkle

Black-lined
Periwinkle

Common
Periwinkle

Flat Periwinkle

Rough
Periwinkle

Littorina mariae

*Littorina
neglecta*

Littorina rudis

Auger Shell *Turritella communis* Height to 55mm
Almost unmistakable. Sub-littoral on sandy shores; in life, buries itself, but empty shells are often washed up. SHELL is an elongate and sharply pointed spire with sculptured whorls. STATUS Widespread and locally common, although absent from the SE.

Common Wentletrap *Epitonium clathrus* Height to 40mm
Beautiful, distinctive shell. Sub-littoral on soft substrates, feeding on sea anemones; empty shells sometimes washed up. SHELL is a tall spire with up to 15 strongly ribbed whorls. Buffish white, sometimes with brown spiral bands. STATUS Widespread but very local.

Needle Whelk *Bittium reticulatum* Height to 10mm
Small shell, easily overlooked. Found on muddy sand in sheltered spots, often amongst eelgrasses. Empty shells are best found by sieving. SHELL is a slender spire with 12–15 whorls, evenly sculptured with criss-crossing spiral and longitudinal ridges. STATUS Widespread and fairly common on the S coast; more local in the W and absent from the E.

Cerithiopsis tubercularis Length to 7mm
Sculptured shell with a sinistral spiral. Found on sponges (on which it feeds), often with coralline seaweeds, under rocks on lower shore. SHELL is slender, tapering towards conical tip. Whorls bear spiral rows of tubercles. STATUS Commonest along S England coast and W Wales.

Violet Snail

Violet Snail *Janthina janthina* Width to 35mm
Unmistakable mollusc. Pelagic and oceanic but sometimes blown onshore during prolonged gales. Empty shell is fragile and breaks easily. SHELL is pale violet and almost spherical, with a large outer whorl and aperture. In life, dark violet-brown animal can be seen attached to 'float' of mucus-trapped bubbles. STATUS Occasionally washed up on W coast beaches in summer, typically when large numbers of By-the-wind-sailor (on which it feeds; p. 120) are also stranded.

Pelican's Foot *Aporrhais pespelecani* Height to 40mm
Elegant and unmistakable shell. Sub-littoral, ploughing through surface of muddy sand. Empty shells often washed up. SHELL comprises a spire with ridged whorls and outer lip of aperture extending as projecting points. STATUS Widespread and locally common in the S and W; virtually absent from the E coast.

Hungarian Cap Shell *Capulus ungaricus* Width to 25mm
Distinctive shell. In life, clamps onto other mollusc shells, notably those of scallops and Horse-mussels. SHELL is broad, flattened and ridged, with an apical spire; usually yellowish brown. STATUS Local, mainly in the W.

Chinaman's Hat *Calyptraea chinensis* Width to 15mm
Flattened, limpet-like shell. Found on lower shore, usually on stones among soft substrates. SHELL is a low yellowish cone; plate-like partition is seen inside shell. STATUS Local, on the S coast and SW Wales.

Spotted Cowrie, juvenile

Spotted Cowrie *Trivia monacha* Length to 12mm
Distinctive shell. Found on rocky shores, feeding on ascidians, notably Star Ascidian and *Botrylloides leachii* (p. 252). SHELL is flattened-ovoid and glossy, with a ribbed surface and slit-like aperture; pinkish buff with 3 dark spots. In life, mantle wraps around most of shell. Juveniles have a short spire. STATUS Widespread and locally common; commonest in the S, and scarce or absent from the E coast.

Arctic Cowrie *Trivia arctica* Length to 10mm
Similar to Spotted Cowrie (above) but shell is unspotted. Found on lower shore on rocky coasts; feeds on ascidians. SHELL is flattened-ovoid, glossy and whitish. In life, mantle wraps around most of shell. STATUS Widespread and locally common except on E coast.

Auger
Shell

Common
Wentletrap

Needle
Whelk

Cerithiopsis tubercularis

Pelican's Foot

Violet Snail

Hungarian
Cap Shell

Spotted Cowrie,
living animal

Chinaman's Hat

Arctic Cowrie

Spotted Cowrie

Necklace Shell *Euspira catena* Height to 30mm

Attractive and distinctive shell. In life, animal ploughs through sand searching for bivalve mollusc prey. Drills neat hole in shell (*see* p. 235); empty prey shells (and those of Necklace Shell) are found washed up on suitable shores. **SHELL** is orange-brown, shiny and rather spherical, with large final whorl and aperture. **STATUS** Locally common in the S and on the Welsh coast; rather scarce elsewhere.

European Sting Winkle

European Sting Winkle *Ocenebra erinacea* Length to 50mm

Distinctive sculptured shell. Predator of bivalve molluscs and barnacles found on lower shore, on rocky and mixed coasts. **SHELL** has conical spire and broad aperture, with whorls bearing ribs and projections. **STATUS** Widespread and locally common in S and SW England and Wales; scarce elsewhere.

Common Whelk *Buccinum undatum* Length to 10cm

Large, familiar whelk of rocky and mixed shores; feeds on worms and bivalve molluscs. **SHELL** has broadly oval aperture and conical spire, with ridged whorls and slightly 'stepped' outline. Typically pale brown. **STATUS** Widespread and locally common. **NOTE** Lays yellowish egg masses under rocks; these are often washed up.

Red Whelk *Neptunea antiqua* Length to 15cm

Recalls Common Whelk (above), but smoothly rounded whorls give it a 'smoother' outline. Found on rocky and mixed shores; feeds on carrion and a predator of marine worms. **SHELL** has narrowly oval aperture, flushed orange-red inside, and rounded whorls with fine spiral ridges. Typically grey-buff. **STATUS** Locally common, mainly in the N and NW.

Colus gracilis Length to 70mm

Distinctive narrow shell. Usually sub-littoral on sand and mud, but shells are washed up. **SHELL** has narrowly oval aperture and slender, conical spire, sharply pointed at tip. Whorls are finely ridged but outline is flat-sided. Usually buffish white; aperture mouth is pale. **STATUS** Mainly in the N.

Dog Whelk *Nucella lapillus* Length to 40mm

Familiar seashore mollusc. Found on rocky shores, especially sheltered sites, and feeds on barnacles and mussels. **SHELL** is oval in outline with spirally ridged whorls; spire is conical and pointed, aperture is oval with thickened, ribbed outer lip. Colour influenced by food, but often greyish or yellowish, sometimes with dark spiral bands. **STATUS** Widespread and locally very common. **NOTE** Clusters of yellowish egg capsules (like large wheat grains) are laid on rocks in spring.

Thick-lipped Dog Whelk *Hinia incrassata* Length to 12mm

Robust shell, found on rocky and mixed shores, often under boulders and in pools at low tide. **SHELL** is brown and ovoid, with ribbed and spirally grooved whorls; aperture is smallish and rounded with thick, toothed outer lip. **STATUS** Widespread and locally common, but scarce on the E England coast.

ABOVE: **Dog Whelk, adult with eggs;** BELOW: **Netted Dog Whelk**

Netted Dog Whelk *Hinia reticulata* Length to 30mm

Robust, compact shell. Usually found on sand and muddy substrates among rocks. **SHELL** is rather pear-shaped in outline, with ribbed and spirally grooved whorls; aperture is elongate-oval with fine-toothed inner margin to outer lip. **STATUS** Widespread and locally common only on S and W coasts. **SIMILAR SPECIES Small Dog Whelk** *H. pygmaea* (length to 14mm) is less 'netted' in appearance and has wider aperture. Sub-littoral on sand; sometimes washed up. NW and SW Britain; absent from Irish and North seas.

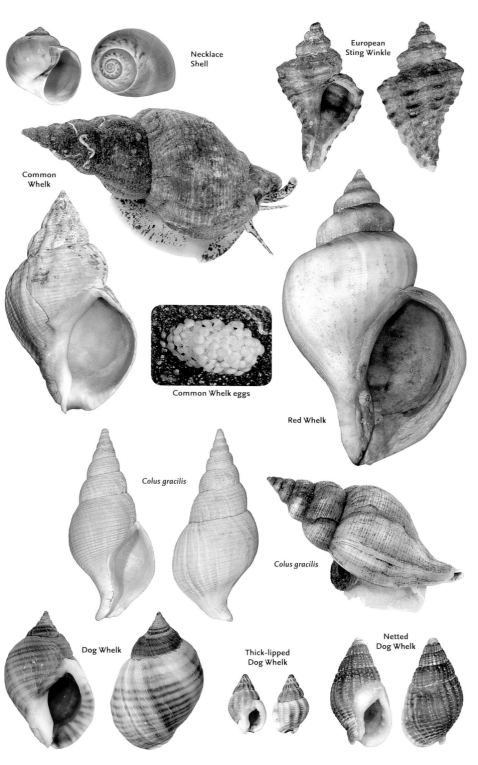

Necklace Shell

European Sting Winkle

Common Whelk

Common Whelk eggs

Red Whelk

Colus gracilis

Colus gracilis

Dog Whelk

Thick-lipped Dog Whelk

Netted Dog Whelk

Sea Lemon *Archidoris pseudoargus*
Length to 10cm

Our most familiar sea slug. Found on rocky shores, often under rocks at low tide. Feeds on encrusting sponges. ADULT has warty texture, with lamellate rhinophores at head end, and ring of frilly gills at tail end. Colour is variable but typically blotchy yellow and brown. STATUS Widespread and locally common only on S and W coasts.

Geitodoris planata Length to 60mm
Can be confused with Sea Lemon (above). Found on rocky shores at low tide and in pools. ADULT is brownish yellow (darker than Sea Lemon), with 5–6 star-shaped patches (acid glands) on each side of mantle. In addition to rhinophores, has oral tentacles (lacking in Sea Lemon). STATUS Local, SW Britain only.

Onchidoris bilamellata Length to 40mm
Well-marked sea slug. Found on rocky shores; feeds on barnacles. ADULT is blotched brown and white; mantle is covered in relatively long, blunt tubercles. Has lamellate rhinophores and up to 29 rather short gills arranged in a wide circle. STATUS Widespread but local; mainly in the S and NW.

Goniodoris nodosa Length to 25mm
Distinctive sea slug, found on sheltered rocky shores at low water and in pools. Feeds on encrusting bryozoans and ascidians. ADULT has a translucent white mantle, studded with white spots, sometimes with pinkish body showing through. Has rhinophores, oral tentacles and up to 13 tentacles. STATUS Widespread but local; absent from much of the E England coast.

Acanthodoris pilosa

Acanthodoris pilosa, mating pair and eggs

Acanthodoris pilosa Length to 30mm
Distinctive sea slug. Found at low water on rocky shores where bryozoan prey are common; easiest to find in spring. ADULT is usually white, mantle with rather long, pointed tubercles. Has stalked lamellate rhinophores and up to 9 feathery gills. STATUS Widespread, commonest in the S and W, scarce on the E coast.

Jorunna tomentosa Length to 50mm
Unobtrusive sea slug. Feeds on encrusting sponges on lower rocky shore and in sub-littoral zone. ADULT is whitish or yellowish (sometimes with dark paired dorsal spots), with a woolly or velvety texture, a ring of pale retractile gills and brownish lamellate rhinophores. STATUS Widespread and locally common.

Greilada elegans Length to 30mm
Colourful and unmistakable sea slug. Found on rocky coasts; usually sub-littoral but sometimes in pools. ADULT is orange with blue spots. Has lamellate rhinophores, short oral papillae and up to 7 dorsal gills. STATUS Local and scarce; restricted to the SW.

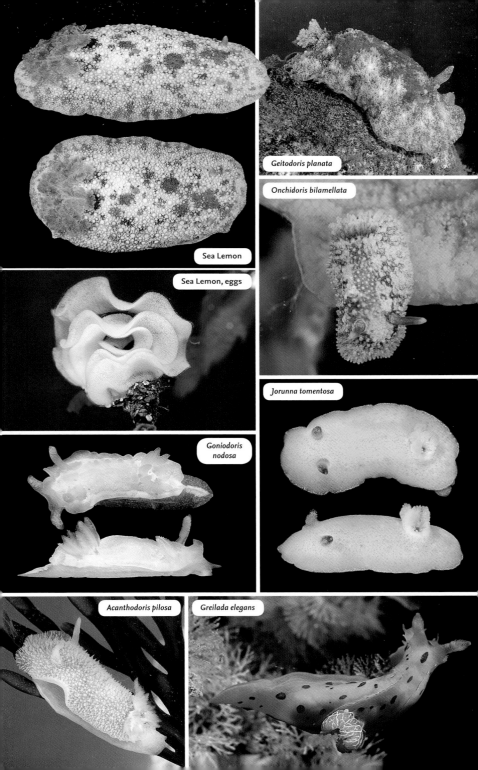

Geitodoris planata

Onchidoris bilamellata

Sea Lemon

Sea Lemon, eggs

Jorunna tomentosa

Goniodoris
nodosa

Acanthodoris pilosa

Greilada elegans

Ancula gibbosa Length to 30mm

Attractive little sea slug. Found on sheltered rocky shores; feeds on ascidians. ADULT is translucent white (internal organs can sometimes be discerned), with orange-tipped projections and rhinophores, and dorsal gills surrounded by projections. STATUS Widespread but local, mainly in the S and NW.

Ancula gibbosa

Orange-clubbed Sea Slug

Limacia clavigera Length to 15mm

Small, colourful sea slug. Found on rocky shores at low water and in pools. Feeds on bryozoans. ADULT is white with orange-yellow spots, marginal projections and lamellate rhinophores. STATUS Locally common on SW and W coasts; absent from much of the E coast.

Orange-clubbed Sea Slug

Polycera quadrilineata Length to 35mm

Attractive sea slug. Found near its food (encrusting bryozoans) in pools and at low water on sheltered rocky shores. ADULT is translucent white, with rows of orange-yellow patches and lines on body. Head has 4 terminal projections; these and rhinophores are tipped orange-yellow. STATUS Locally common, especially in the W.

ABOVE: **Sea Hare, young animal;** BELOW: *Elysia viridis*

Sea Hare Aplysia punctata Length to 70mm

Familiar sea slug. Found in a wide range of habitats; probably commonest on sheltered rocky shores. Feeds on seaweeds. ADULT is usually reddish (sometimes brown or green), marked with numerous white spots. Head has long rhinophores and oral tentacles, giving it a fancifully horse- or hare-like appearance. Note wing-like flaps along body length. STATUS Widespread and locally common in the W and SW; virtually absent from the E coast.

Elysia viridis Length to 35mm

Colourful and distinctive sea slug, but well camouflaged among green seaweeds, notably Velvet Horn (p. 28), on which it feeds. Found on sheltered rocky shores. ADULT is usually green with bright blue and red spots. Has smooth paired rhinophores and wing-like parapodial flaps along most of body. STATUS Widespread and locally common on S and NW coasts; scarce or absent elsewhere.

Facelina auriculata Length to 35mm

Slender sea slug. Feeds mainly on *Tubularia indivisa* (p. 120); lower-shore pools and sub-littoral zone. ADULT has pinkish-flushed pale body and ringed brown rhinophores. Body has whorls of white-tipped purple cerata; oral tentacles are long. STATUS Widespread but local.

Facelina bostoniensis Length to 50mm

Relatively broad sea slug. Feeds on *Tubularia* hydroids, on lower shore and in sub-littoral zone. ADULT has translucent white body, tinged pink, and white-tipped ringed rhinophores. Body has overlapping, white-tipped brown cerata. Curls into ball when agitated. STATUS Widespread and locally common, mainly from SW England to NW Scotland.

Facelina bostoniensis, disturbed animal

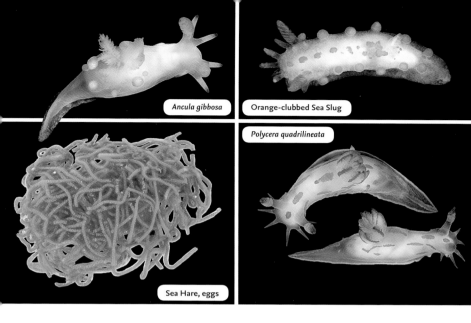

Ancula gibbosa

Orange-clubbed Sea Slug

Polycera quadrilineata

Sea Hare, eggs

Elysia viridis

Sea Hare

Facelina auriculata

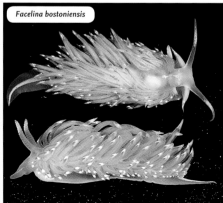

Facelina bostoniensis

Flabellina pedata Length to 45mm
Colourful sea slug. Feeds on hydroids; lower shore and sub-littoral zone. ADULT has purple body and pinkish-red cerata; tentacles, ribbed rhinophores and cerata are white-tipped. STATUS Widespread, commonest in the S and W.

Catriona gymnota Length to 20mm
Elegant sea slug. Feeds on *Tubularia* hydroids; lower-shore pools and sub-littoral zone. ADULT has whitish body, oral tentacles and rhinophores. Cerata are swollen, orange and white-tipped. STATUS Local, mainly in the SW.

Grey Sea Slug *Aeolidia papillosa* Length to 10cm
Impressive and distinctive sea slug. Found on rocky shores where sea anemones (its food) are common. ADULT is greyish white or brownish white, with long, soft projections arranged in rows down sides, leaving dorsal surface bare. Head has smooth rhinophores and oral tentacles. STATUS Locally common on S and W coasts; scarce or absent elsewhere.

ABOVE: **Grey Sea Slug**; INSET: *Aeolidiella alderi*

Aeolidiella alderi Length to 30mm
Recalls Grey Sea Slug (above) but smaller. Found on rocky and mixed shores, usually in vicinity of prey (sea anemones, notably Daisy Anemone, p. 124), and under stones at low tide. ADULT is mostly pale yellow, flushed orange towards head. Has soft projections in rows down sides, those at head end whitish. STATUS Local, mainly in the S and W.

Palio nothus Length to 20mm
Well-marked sea slug found on sheltered rocky shores. ADULT is olive-green with a network of pale patches and tubercles. Has lamellate rhinophores and 5 frilly gills. STATUS Widespread but rather scarce.

Cadlina laevis Length to 30mm
Small, compact sea slug, found on sheltered rocky shores. Feeds on sponges. ADULT is translucent creamy white, studded with paler tubercles and yellow spots near margins, and with yellowish mantle fringe. Has yellow-tipped lamellate rhinophores and, usually, 5 frilly gills. STATUS Widespread in the N and NW, scarce in the SW and absent elsewhere.

Celtic Sea Slug *Onchidella celtica* Length to 15mm
Unusual mollusc, more closely related to land snails than true sea slugs. Found on rocks in the splash zone, often hiding among barnacles or in rock crevices. Active in damp weather. ADULT has blackish-grey dorsal surface, covered in knobbly tubercles. Tentacles visible when active. STATUS Local, mostly in Cornwall and N Devon.

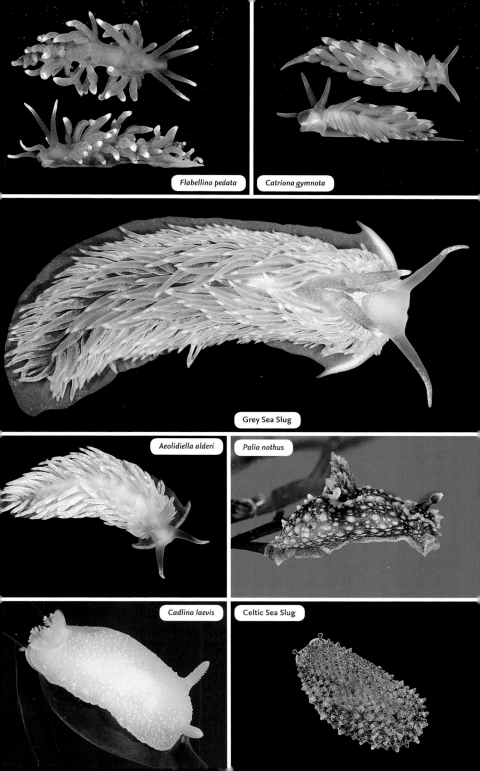

Flabellina pedata

Catriona gymnota

Grey Sea Slug

Aeolidiella alderi

Palio nothus

Cadlina laevis

Celtic Sea Slug

Yellow-plumed Sea Slug
Berthella plumula Length to 40mm

Yellow-plumed
Sea Slug

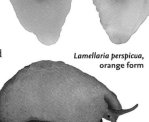

Colourful sea slug with internal shell; easily overlooked out of water as it contracts to a flattened blob. Found on rocky shores, feeding on Star Ascidian (p. 252) and other ascidians. **ADULT** has subtle reticulate pattern. Rhinophores and oral tentacles are inrolled. **STATUS** Widespread on SW and W coasts only.

Lamellaria perspicua Length to 25mm

Lamellaria perspicua,
orange form

Unusual mollusc with internal shell, recalling but unrelated to true sea slugs. Found on sheltered rocky shores; feeds on ascidians. **ADULT** is unevenly domed, with subtle reticulate pattern; colour variable, often marbled greyish white, but sometimes white or orange. Mantle forms tubular opening at front. **STATUS** Widespread but local on S and W coasts.

Velvet Shell *Velutina velutina* Width to 20mm
Unusual mollusc. Found on stony and mixed substrates; usually sub-littoral but empty shell is sometimes washed up. **SHELL** is ear- or cap-shaped with extremely large outer whorl. Outer coating (periostracum) is brown and slightly furry. **STATUS** Widespread but local.

Runcina coronata Length to 6mm
Small sea slug with internal shell. Found on sheltered rocky shores, often on Velvet Horn (p. 28), on which it feeds. Easily overlooked. **ADULT** has a dark brown mantle with numerous small, pale spots and orange margin. Head has yellow margin and white-spotted 'collar'. Yellowish foot is visible posteriorly. **STATUS** Widespread but local, mainly in the SW and W.

Lobe Shell *Philine aperta* Length to 60mm
Strange-looking sea slug with an internal shell. Found on lower zones of sandy beaches; feeds on polychaete worms and bivalve molluscs. **ADULT** is creamy white and 4-lobed. **STATUS** Widespread and locally common on S and W coasts.

Haminoea navicula Length to 60mm
Unusual shelled sea slug. Found in saline lagoons and sheltered eelgrass beds in estuaries. Empty shells are easier to find than living animals. **ADULT** has spotted brown body; mantle and lateral flaps envelop shell. Shell is fragile and ovoid; aperture runs entire length of shell; whorls are not visible when viewed end on. **STATUS** Local, mainly restricted to Hampshire and Dorset.

Akera bullata Length to 50mm
Unusual shelled sea slug. Found in saline lagoons and sheltered eelgrass beds. **ADULT** has brown body with pale spots. Head has shield-like cover and lateral flaps are occasionally used for swimming. In life, mantle and flaps partly envelop shell. Shell is ovoid; aperture runs length of shell; whorls are visible when viewed end on. **STATUS** Very local, with a scattered distribution, mostly in Hampshire and Dorset, and NW coast.

Acteon tornatilis Length to 25mm
Unusual sea slug. Has shell into which animal can withdraw. Found on sandy shores, burrowing and feeding on marine worms, including Sand Mason (p. 132). Empty shells often washed up. **ADULT** has an ovoid shell, pink with pale spiral bands. In life, mantle flaps are broad. **STATUS** Widespread, mainly on W coasts; perhaps commonest in Wales.

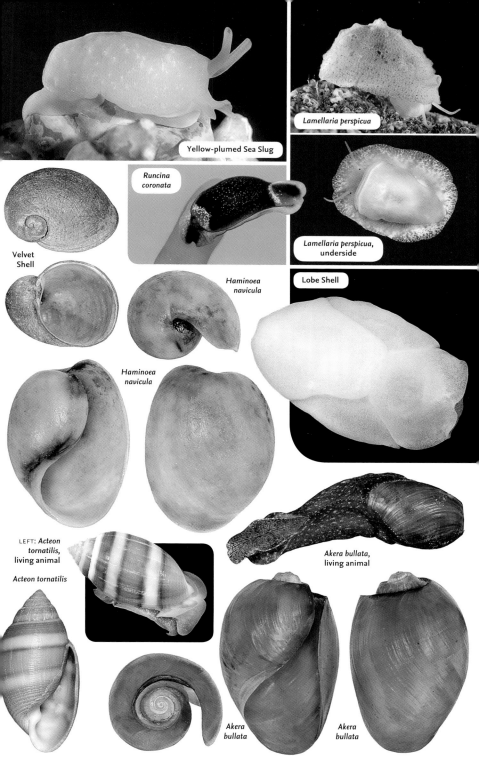

Yellow-plumed Sea Slug

Lamellaria perspicua

Runcina coronata

Lamellaria perspicua, underside

Velvet Shell

Haminoea navicula

Lobe Shell

Haminoea navicula

LEFT: *Acteon tornatilis,* living animal

Acteon tornatilis

Akera bullata, living animal

Akera bullata

Akera bullata

Ark-shell *Arca tetragona* Length to 45mm
Unmistakable bivalve, attached by byssus threads to rocks. On lower shore and
sub-littoral zone. SHELL is rectangular in outline, with angular sides and radiating ribs.
STATUS Mainly in the N, locally common only in Hebrides and Orkney.

Dog Cockle *Glycymeris glycymeris* Width to 60mm
Beautifully patterned bivalve. Sub-littoral in sand; empty shells often washed up. SHELL
is circular in outline, usually yellowish buff with concentric reddish-brown zigzag lines.
STATUS Locally common in the S and W; absent from much of the E.

Common Mussel
Mytilus edulis Width to 60mm
Familiar bivalve. Lives attached to rocks
and other hard substrates in areas of
fast-flowing water on lower shore,
attached by byssus threads. SHELL is
oval to fan-shaped, pointed at one end.
Typically tinged bluish purple but can
look blackish. STATUS Widespread and
locally common. SIMILAR SPECIES
Nucula nucleus (length to 10mm) is a
small bivalve, found in gravel and
coarse sand. Mostly sub-littoral but
shells are washed up. Shell is brown with concentric growth ridges and bands; outline is
broadly triangular with 1 curved edge. Commonest off the S England coast and Wales.

Horse-mussel *Modiolus modiolus* Width to 100mm
Similar to Common Mussel (above) but larger. Mostly sub-littoral but shells often
washed up. SHELL is oval to fan-shaped in outline; umbo is rounded. Typically rusty
brown. STATUS Widespread and locally common.

Bearded Mussel *Modiolus barbatus* Width to 60mm
Distinctive bivalve. Mainly sub-littoral but empty shells sometimes washed up. SHELL is
angular-oval in outline, pointed at 1 end. Typically brown, broader part of shell with
stout bristles. STATUS Local, mainly on S and W coasts, north to N Wales. SIMILAR
SPECIES Bean Mussel *Modiolula phaseolina* (width to 20mm) is a tiny, distinctive mussel
found lodged in kelp holdfasts and under rocks on lower shore. Oval brown shell has
spiny outgrowths on periostracum. Local, mainly in the W and N.

Zebra Mussel *Dreissena polymorpha* Width to 30mm
Unwelcome introduction from Russia. Mainly in fresh water but also in upper tidal
reaches of a few large rivers, including the Exe and Thames. Attaches to stones and other
mussel species by byssus threads. SHELL has fan-shaped outline; typically buffish with
concentric brown zigzag lines. STATUS Widespread in England; local in Wales and Scotland.

Marbled Crenella *Modiolarca tumida* Width to 20mm
Small, well-marked bivalve. Lives in kelp holdfasts and embedded in large tunicates.
SHELL is oval and ribbed; usually yellowish green, marbled with reddish brown. STATUS
Widespread and locally common, except on the E coast.

Green Crenella *Musculus discors* Width to 12mm
Tiny bivalve with unusual habits: moves using its muscular foot, with long siphon
protruding. Found on lower shore on rocky coasts. SHELL is angular-oval, often white
but sometimes tinged greenish. STATUS Widespread but almost absent from the E.

Musculus costulatus Width to 15mm
Well-marked bivalve. Lives attached to rocks and algal holdfasts by byssal threads, but
capable of reorientation using muscular foot. SHELL has ribbed valves, yellowish overall
but with bold reddish-brown markings, many of which are V-shaped. STATUS
Widespread but local, mainly in the SW.

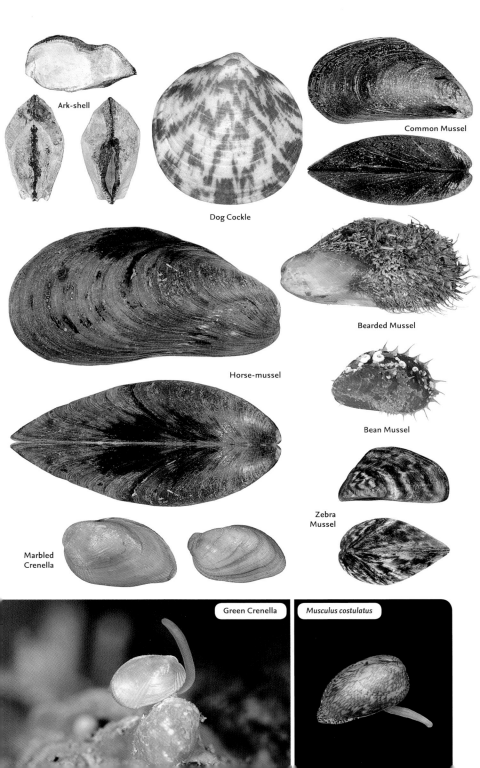

Ark-shell

Dog Cockle

Common Mussel

Bearded Mussel

Horse-mussel

Bean Mussel

Zebra
Mussel

Marbled
Crenella

Green Crenella

Musculus costulatus

Heteranomia squamula

Saddle Oyster *Anomia ephippium* Width to 50mm
Unusual bivalve. Attaches to rocks and encrusting weeds on lower shore of sheltered rocky coasts. SHELL is rounded in outline, with 2 dissimilar valves: lower (right) valve is flat with oval hole at base and is attached to substrate; upper (left) valve is domed. Has 3 muscle scars on inner surface of upper valve. STATUS Widespread and locally common, least so on the E coast. SIMILAR SPECIES *Heteranomia squamula* (width to 15mm) is more delicate, with 2 muscle scars on inner surface of upper valve.

Great Scallop *Pecten maximus* Width to 12cm
Iconic free-living bivalve. Sub-littoral on sand and gravel substrates, but shells often washed up. SHELL is circular in outline, with up to 17 radiating ribs and square-cut 'ears' at base (almost equal). In life, cupped right valve lies on substrate, flat left valve is uppermost. Swims freely. STATUS Widespread on S and W coasts; fairly common, although badly depleted by commercial fishing.

Queen Scallop *Aequipecten opercularis* Width to 90mm
Similar to Great Scallop (above) but with subtle differences in outline and 'ears'. Found on lower shore and sub-littorally on mixed shores; young animals are attached by byssus threads. SHELL is rounded-oval in outline, with up to 20 radiating ridges. Both valves are cupped (left more so than right), with 1 'ear' longer than the other (especially on right valve). STATUS Widespread on S and W coasts; fairly common, although badly depleted by commercial fishing.

Variegated Scallop *Chlamys varia* Length to 60mm
Well-marked scallop. Found on rocky shores, attached by byssus threads or free-living. SHELL is elongate-oval, marbled reddish brown and with 25–35 spiny ridges; spines are often worn in strandline shells. Ribbed basal 'ears' are much longer on 1 side than other; 'ear' on right valve has byssal notch. STATUS Fairly common, least so on the E coast.

Humpback Scallop *Chlamys distorta* Length to 50mm
Distinctive distorted bivalve, often hard to recognise as a scallop. Found on lower shore on rocky coasts. SHELL is elongate-oval with up to 70 radiating ribs. One basal 'ear' is larger than other but these are not always pronounced. Right valve is attached to rock and shape moulds to substrate. STATUS Commonest in the S and NW.

Tiger Scallop *Palliolum tigerinum* Width to 25mm
Small, fairly distinctive scallop. Found on sheltered shores, on gravel and coarse sand; at low water and in sub-littoral zone. SHELL is rounded-oval, marbled reddish brown and with concentric growth rings, usually smooth but sometimes with 30 or so subtle ribs. Ribbed basal 'ears' are much longer on one side than the other; 'ear' on right valve has byssal notch. STATUS Widespread; commonest in the W, mostly absent from the E.

Common Oyster *Ostrea edulis* Width to 90mm
Distinctive and iconic bivalve. Found on muddy gravel seabeds; mostly sub-littoral but shells sometimes washed up. SHELL is circular to oval in outline with concentric scaly ridges. Outside colour is greyish white; shell interior has mother-of-pearl coating. Left valve is cupped, right valve is flattish. STATUS Still fairly common on S and W coasts but locally depleted or destroyed by commercial exploitation. SIMILAR SPECIES **Portuguese Oyster** *Crassostrea gigas* (length to 25cm) is mostly sub-littoral, on gravel and mixed substrates. Shell is irregularly oval. Outer surface has irregular concentric, flaky ridges; inner surface has mother-of-pearl coating. Introduced, now established in the S.

Gaping File Shell *Limaria hians* Length to 25mm
Constructs a 'nest' of debris on lower shore in crevices and under rocks. SHELL is narrowly oval, recalling a slender scallop in outline; in profile, gap between valves is diagnostic. In life, orange tentacles project. STATUS Local and scarce, least so in the NW.

Saddle Oyster

Heteranomia squamula

Variegated Scallop

Great Scallop

Great Scallop

Queen Scallop

Humpback Scallop

Queen Scallop

Tiger Scallop

inside

Portuguese Oyster

Common Oyster

Gaping File Shell

Lasaea adansoni Width to 3mm
Tiny bivalve, recognised by its size, colour and location: lives on upper shore and in splash zone on rocky coasts, among *Lichina* clumps and empty barnacle shells. SHELL is reddish brown, rounded in outline and plump in profile. STATUS Widespread and locally common in the S and W, but mostly absent from the E coast. SIMILAR SPECIES **Turtonia minuta** (width to 3mm) has 3 small teeth on inside of shell below umbo (*Lasaea* sp. have lateral teeth but only 1 tooth below umbo). Yellow-brown and oval with a prominent umbo. Found on rocky shores, in crevices and empty barnacle shells. Commonest in the N and NW.

Hard-shell Clam *Mercenaria mercenaria* Width to 11cm
Robust bivalve. Lives in muddy substrates, mostly sub-littoral but sometimes at low-tide level. SHELL is thick and roughly triangular, with rounded outer margins. Surface has numerous concentric bands; typically grey-brown, tinged violet towards margin. STATUS Introduced from North America (where known as Qahog); now local on the S coast.

Icelandic Cyprine *Arctica islandica* Width to 11cm
Robust bivalve. Sub-littoral in muddy sand but shells often washed up. SHELL is thick and rounded-oval. Periostracum is dark brown but peels and wears in empty shells. Inside is white with 3 cardinal teeth and 1 lateral tooth. STATUS Widespread and common, except in the SE. NOTE Contender for world's longest living animal – can live for several hundred years.

Pullet Carpet Shell *Tapes corrugata (Venerupis senegalensis)* Length to 50mm
Well-marked bivalve. In life, lives in sub-littoral sand and gravel; empty shells often washed up. SHELL is elongate-oval, with numerous concentric ridges and radial striations. STATUS Scattered and local, mainly on S and W coasts. SIMILAR SPECIES **Manila Clam** *Ruditapes philippinarum* (length to 60mm) is more rounded and has dark rays; introduced, now local on S coast.

Rayed Artemis *Dosinia exoleta* Width to 50mm
Striking bivalve. Lives buried in muddy sand and gravel; empty shells often washed up. SHELL is almost circular in outline, but with fairly prominent umbo. Outer surface has numerous concentric ridges and is usually buffish brown with radiating darker brown bands; inner surface is shiny. STATUS Widespread but local, mainly in the S and W.

Warty Venus *Venus verrucosa* Width to 60mm
Robust bivalve with a sculptured shell. Sub-littoral in gravel and coarse sand; empty shells are washed up. SHELL is oval with 20 or so raised concentric ridges. On posterior part of shell, ridges are 'cut', forming wart-like projections; these wear in beached shells. STATUS Scattered distribution, mainly in Hampshire and Dorset coast, and N Wales.

Striped Venus *Chamelea gallina* Width to 40mm
Well-marked bivalve. On sandy shores, mainly sub-littoral but empty shells often washed up. SHELL is broadly triangular with curved margin. Surface is buffish brown, with concentric ridges and radiating (often interrupted) darker brown rays. STATUS Widespread and fairly common on suitable coasts; absent from most of SE England.

Thin Tellin *Angulus tenuis* Width to 26mm
Thin, rather delicate bivalve. Lives in sand on lower shore. SHELL is angular-oval; anterior margin is rounded, posterior margin pointed. Outer margin has fine concentric ridges; colour variable but often yellow-brown with reddish bands. STATUS Widespread and locally common on suitable coasts.

Baltic Tellin *Macoma balthica* Width to 25mm
Small, plump bivalve. Lives in muddy sand on lower shore, often in estuaries. SHELL is rounded-oval; anterior margin rounded, posterior margins more angular. Colour variable but often yellowish brown with reddish bands. STATUS Widespread and common.

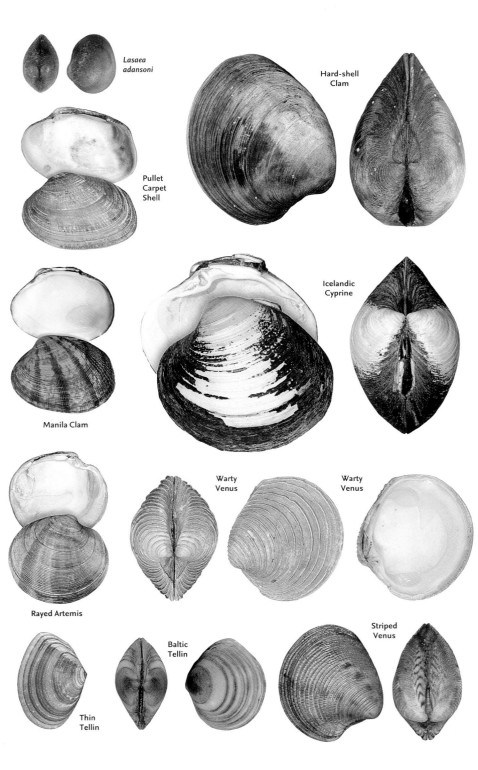

Lasaea
adansoni

Hard-shell
Clam

Pullet
Carpet
Shell

Icelandic
Cyprine

Manila Clam

Warty
Venus

Warty
Venus

Rayed Artemis

Striped
Venus

Thin
Tellin

Baltic
Tellin

Common Cockle *Cerastoderma edule* Width to 45mm
Iconic bivalve and our commonest cockle species. Lives in sand and muddy sand; tolerates a range of salinities. SHELL is rounded-oval and thick. Outer surface is grey-brown with 24 or so radiating ribs; inner surface is whitish, with ribs showing on outer margin only (not extending beyond pallial line). STATUS Widespread and locally common on suitable coasts.

Lagoon Cockle *Cerastoderma glaucum* Width to 35mm
Similar to Common Cockle (above) but with angular outline and thin shell. Favours brackish lagoons. SHELL is rounded-oval in outline with straight (not curved) posterior margin. Outer surface is grey-brown with 24 or so radiating ribs; inner surface is whitish, with ribs visible across whole shell. STATUS Local, mainly in the S and SE; occurrence is limited by its specialised habitat requirements.

Rough Cockle *Acanthocardia tuberculata* Width to 90mm
Plump bivalve. Lives in muddy sand on lower shore and below. SHELL is rounded-oval. Outer surface is grey-brown with 18–20 ridged, radiating ribs, these armed with spines and tubercles (worn in beached shells); inner surface is whitish, with ribs showing on outer margin only (not extending beyond pallial line). STATUS Very locally common on the S coast only.

Rough Cockle

Spiny Cockle *Acanthocardia aculeata* Width to 95mm
Distinctive bivalve. Sub-littoral in muddy sand and gravel; empty shells washed up. SHELL is angular-oval with straightish posterior margin. Outer surface is grey-brown with 20 or so ridged, radiating ribs, these armed with spines (worn in beached shells); inner surface is whitish, with ribs visible across whole shell. STATUS Very local on the S coast.

Prickly Cockle *Acanthocardia echinata* Width to 70mm
Plump bivalve. Sub-littoral in muddy sand and gravel; empty shells washed up. SHELL is rounded-oval. Outer surface is grey-brown with 20–23 ridged, radiating ribs, these armed with spines (worn in beached shells); inner surface is whitish, with ribs visible across whole shell. STATUS Widespread and locally common, least so on the E coast.

Norway Cockle *Laevicardium crassum* Length to 70mm
Distinctive cockle. Sub-littoral in sand and gravel; empty shells washed up. SHELL is oval, pointed at hinge end. Outer surface is brown with 50 or so indistinct ribs; inner surface is whitish, tinged pink, with ribs creating crenulated margin. STATUS Widespread and locally common, except on the E coast.

Thick Trough Shell *Spisula solida* Width to 50mm
Robust bivalve. Found in sand, on lower shore and sublittoral. SHELL is triangular in outline with curved outer margin, distinct umbo and fine concentric lines. Outer surface is yellowish-brown but worn shells are paler. Inside, note serrated lateral teeth. STATUS Widespread and locally common, least so on E coast.

Common Otter Shell, living animal

Rayed Trough Shell *Mactra stultorum* Width to 50mm
Distinctive bivalve. Lives in sand on lower shore; empty shells often washed up. SHELL is triangular with a curved outer margin and concentric lines on outer surface. Typically pale brown with darker radiating 'rays'. STATUS Widespread and fairly common but absent from much of NW and SW Britain.

Common Otter Shell *Lutraria lutraria* Width to 125mm
Large bivalve. Lives in sand on lower shore; buries deep and seen only as washed-up shells. SHELL is elongate-oval. Outer surface has concentric lines and ridges; typically pale brown with flaky, dark brown coating around margin. STATUS Widespread but scattered; commonest in S England, Wales and N Scotland.

Common
Cockle

Lagoon
Cockle

Spiny Cockle

Rough
Cockle

Spiny Cockle

Prickly
Cockle

Norway
Cockle

Rayed Trough
Shell

Thick
Trough
Shell

Common
Otter Shell

Banded Wedge Shell *Donax vittatus* Width to 35mm

Attractive bivalve. Lives in sand, on lower shore and in sub-littoral zone; empty shells often washed up. SHELL is elongate-triangular. Outer surface has numerous fine, radiating and concentric lines and concentric bands of colour; inner surface has patches of violet-blue. Both surfaces have crenulated outer margin. STATUS Widespread but scattered; commonest on S and NW coasts of England, and Welsh coast.

feeding trails

Peppery Furrow Shell

Scrobicularia plana Width to 60mm
Characteristic bivalve of estuaries. Tolerates brackish water and buries in mud; siphons create characteristic star-shaped patterns on surface when feeding. SHELL is oval with pointed umbo. Outer surface has numerous fine, concentric lines and is often greyish white, tinged yellow around margin; inner surface is shiny. STATUS Widespread and locally common only in the S.

Faroe Sunset Shell *Gari fervensis* Width to 50mm

Attractive bivalve. Mostly sub-littoral in sand, but often washed up. SHELL is elongate-oval to oblong. Outer surface has concentric rings, and ridge running diagonally from umbo to posterior margin; typically pinkish lilac with darker concentric bands and radiating 'rays'. Inner surface is shiny pinkish lilac. STATUS Widespread and locally common.

Sand Gaper *Mya arenaria* Width to 14cm

Robust, thick-shelled bivalve. Lives buried in muddy sand on lower shore and below; often found in estuaries. Empty shells are often washed up. SHELL is oval in outline, anterior end rounded, posterior end more pointed. Outer surface has concentric ridges; brown in life but strandline shells often worn white. Left valve has spoon-shaped projection near hinge. STATUS Widespread and locally common on suitable shores.

Blunt Gaper *Mya truncata* Width to 70mm

Robust, thick-shelled bivalve. Lives buried in clean muddy sand, typically in shallow sub-littoral zone, but empty shells are washed up. SHELL has rectangular outline with truncate posterior margin. Outer surface has rough concentric ridges. STATUS Widespread and locally common on suitable shores.

Basket Shell *Corbula gibba* Width to 15mm

Small, robust bivalve found in muddy sand; lower shore and sub-littoral. SHELL has unequal oval valves, flattish left valve fitting inside lip of convex right valve. STATUS Widespread and locally common; particularly on S England and S Wales coasts, scarce and patchy on E coast.

Pandora inaequivalvis Length to 25mm

Unusual and distinctive bivalve. Mainly sub-littoral in sand but sometimes washed up alive or as empty shells. SHELL comprises unequal, slightly translucent white valves. Lower valve is shallowly concave, upper is almost flat. STATUS Local and generally scarce; sites include Studland Bay and Bracklesham Bay.

Norway Shipworm *Nototeredo norvegica*

Tube length to 50cm
Atypical bivalve, hardly recognisable as a mollusc. Lives in a cylindrical (often U-shaped) calcified tube in floating timber (once boats, nowadays usually driftwood). SHELL comprises paired, angular, plate-like valves used for boring into wood. Animal's worm-like body ends in 2 siphons that appear at open end of tube; can be closed using calcified paddle-shaped plates (pallets). STATUS Records are scattered and patchy, mostly from beaches in the S and W. SIMILAR SPECIES **Great Shipworm** *Teredo navalis* is similar but with straight-sided pallets.

Norway Shipworm, tubes *in situ*

pallet   shell

Banded
Wedge
Shell

Faroe Sunset Shell
with hole drilled
by Necklace Shell
(*see* p. 216)

Peppery
Furrow
Shell

Faroe Sunset Shell

Sand Gaper

Blunt Gaper

Basket Shell

Pandora inaequivalvis

animal *in situ*

Norway Shipworm

tube

Pod Razor Shell *Ensis siliqua* Length to 20cm

Distinctive bivalve. Lives buried, vertically, in fine sand on lower shore and in shallows; dead shells often washed up. SHELL is almost straight, with parallel sides and truncate ends; siphons protrude from anterior end, muscular foot from posterior end. STATUS Widespread; some populations have been ruined by exploitation, but still locally common on some suitable shores.

Common Razor Shell *Ensis ensis* Length to 12cm

Distinctive bivalve. Lives buried, vertically, in fine sand on lower shore and in shallows; dead shells often washed up. SHELL is evenly curved in outline, with parallel sides; anterior end is curved, posterior end truncate. STATUS Widespread; many populations have been ruined by exploitation, but still locally common on some suitable shores.

Pod Razor Shell, empty shells washed up after storm

ABOVE: **Grooved Razor Shell, living animal**
LEFT: **Common Razor Shell, living animal**

Grooved Razor Shell *Solen marginatus* Length to 12cm

Elongate bivalve. Burrows in sand; lower shore and sub-littoral zone. Dead shells often washed up. SHELL has straight, parallel sides and truncate ends; note distinct marginal groove near anterior end of both valves. STATUS Locally common on the S coast, NW Norfolk and W coast N to Lancashire.

Pharus legumen Length to 12cm

Pod-like bivalve. Burrows in fine sand; lower shore and sub-littoral zone. SHELL is elongate-rectangular in outline; posterior end is blunt, anterior end tapers. STATUS Locally common only off coasts of Wales and NW England.

Wrinkled Rock Borer *Hiatella arctica* Length to 4cm

Robust bivalve that bores into soft rocks and attaches by byssal threads in rock crevices; lower shore and sub-littoral zone. SHELL is rectangular in outline. Valve outer surface is ridged and often worn. STATUS Widespread and locally common except off coasts of E England.

Common Piddock *Pholas dactylus* Length to 14cm

Robust bivalve that bores into soft rock, compacted clay and peat; lower shore and sub-littoral zone. SHELL is narrowly oval in outline, pointed at 1 end. Valves 'gape' and outer surfaces have toothed, concentric ridges that aid boring. STATUS Widespread but local; commonest in the S, absent from the N.

Oval Piddock *Zirfaea crispata* Length to 9cm

Distinctive bivalve that bores into soft rocks, submerged wood, peat and clay; lower shore and sub-littoral zone. SHELL is angular-oval in outline. Valves 'gape' and outer surfaces have concentric, toothed ridges and transverse ridge from umbo. STATUS Widespread but local; absent from much of the SW and NW.

White Piddock *Barnea candida* Length to 6cm

Recalls Common Piddock (above) but shell is narrower and gapes only at posterior end. Bores into peat and soft rocks; lower shore and sub-littoral zone. SHELL is elongate-oval with concentric, toothed ridges. STATUS Widespread and locally common, mainly in SE and NW England, and Wales.

White Piddock, living animal *in situ*

American Piddock *Petricola pholadiformis* Length to 8cm

Boring bivalve, found in compacted clay and mud; lower shore and sub-littoral zone. SHELL is narrowly rectangular in outline. Outer surface is strongly ridged and often stained orange by sediment. STATUS Introduced North American species, now locally common, mainly in the SE.

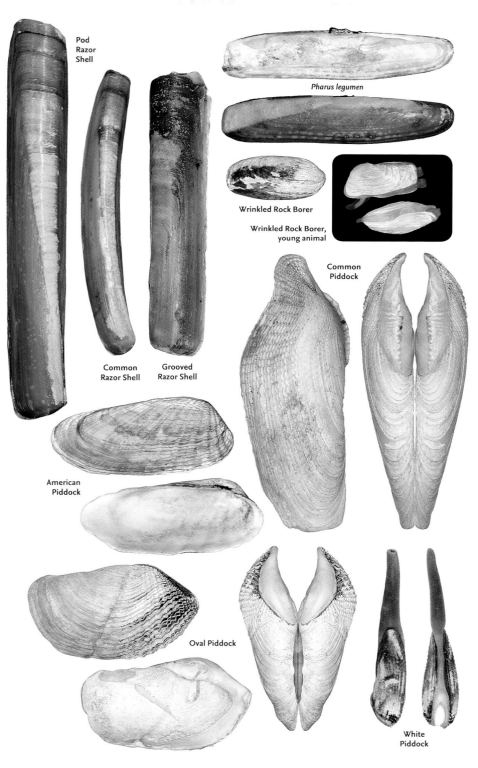

Pod Razor Shell

Pharus legumen

Wrinkled Rock Borer

Wrinkled Rock Borer, young animal

Common Piddock

Common Razor Shell

Grooved Razor Shell

American Piddock

Oval Piddock

White Piddock

Looping Snail
Truncatella subcylindrica Height to 5mm
Small but distinctive shell. Found on upper shore
of estuaries and mudflats, typically in interstices
between pebbles. SHELL is cylindrical; spire tip
is snapped off except in small, young animals.
Walks by using foot in a 'looping' manner.
STATUS Very local, from Cornwall to Essex.

Looping Snail, living animal

BELOW: Mouse-eared
Snail, living animal

Mouse-eared Snail *Myosotella myosotis* Length to 8mm
Small snail, found on upper reaches of estuaries and just
above splash zone on sheltered shores. Usually lives
under rotting seaweed and eelgrass debris. SHELL is
narrowly oval and pointed at apex. Shell mouth is oval
with thickened outer and inner lips, each with 3 or more
'teeth'. STATUS Widespread and locally common except
in the N.

Two-toothed
White Snail

Two-toothed White Snail *Leucophytia bidentata* Length to 6mm
Distinctive small snail. Lives among stones and under seaweed
debris on upper shore, on sheltered rocky coasts. SHELL is narrowly
oval and creamy white. Shell mouth is narrowly oval, inner lip thickened with 2
'teeth'. STATUS Local, mainly in the S.

Lagoon
Snail

Pointed
Snail

Lagoon Snail
Paludinella littorina Length to 2mm
Minute snail. Lives in caves and
crevices, just above high-tide line.
Easily overlooked or mistaken for juvenile periwinkle. SHELL is
rounded, glossy, semi-transparent and yellowish grey. STATUS
Local, in the SW only, from the Isle of Wight to S Wales.

Pointed Snail *Cochlicella acuta* Length to 15mm
Distinctive shall. Found in dunes and coastal calcareous
grassland. SHELL is narrowly pointed. Markings are variable:
sometimes whitish with narrow dark band on
bottom whorl; or with much more extensive brown markings.
STATUS Widespread and locally common in the S and W;
absent from the E.

Heath Snail *Helicella itala* Diameter to 18mm
Well-marked snail of dunes and coastal calcareous grassland.
SHELL is a flattened spiral, variably marked with spiral brown
bands. STATUS Widespread and locally common except in the
NE.

Heath
Snail

Banded Snail *Cernuella virgata* Diameter to 18mm
Variably marked snail of dunes and coastal calcareous
grassland. SHELL is rather globular in outline, with tight
spiral whorls; usually marked with a dark spiral band
(sometimes several on largest whorl).
STATUS Widespread and locally
common except in the N.

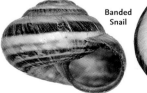

Banded
Snail

Kentish Snail
Monacha cantiana Diameter to 15mm
Wayside snail, common in coastal
habitats, especially in dunes in the
N of its range. SHELL is rather
globular, mainly pale buff and

flushed darker brown towards mouth (inside and out). **STATUS** Widespread and locally common in England; scarcer and almost exclusively coastal in Wales.

Wrinkled Snail

Candidula intersecta Diameter to 12mm
Distinctive snail of dunes and coastal grassland. **SHELL** is flattened-globular with tightly packed whorls; these are marked with spirally radiating ridges and dark lines, creating a 'wrinkled' appearance. **STATUS** Widespread and locally common except in the NW.

White-lipped Snail

Cepaea hortensis Diameter to 18mm
Distinctive snail; 1 of 2 very similar species. Found in dunes, coastal grassland and scrub. **SHELL** is globular with variable forms: typically either uniform yellow or yellow with dark spiral bands. Note the diagnostic white lip to shell mouth. **STATUS** Widespread and locally common; exclusively coastal in the N.
SIMILAR SPECIES Brown-lipped Snail *C. nemoralis* has similarly variable markings but diagnostic dark brown lip. Widespread and locally common, but absent from much of the N.

Garden Snail *Cornu aspersum*

Diameter to 40mm
Familiar large snail. Found in dunes, coastal grassland and scrub. **SHELL** is marbled brown and black, often rather worn in older specimens. **STATUS** Widespread and generally common, but local and scarce in the far N.

Great Black Slug

Arion ater Length to 10cm
Large and distinctive slug, seen in 2 main colour forms. Occurs in a wide range of habitats inland, but particularly common on coastal cliffs, paths and dunes. **ADULT** is usually either uniformly black or orange-brown. **STATUS** Widespread and common throughout.

Kentish Snail

Wrinkled Snail

White-lipped Snail

White-lipped Snail, living animal

Brown-lipped Snail

Garden Snail

Great Black Slug, brown form

Great Black Slug

Common Cuttlefish, eggs

LEFT: **Common Cuttlefish,
young animals**

Cuttlebone

Common Cuttlefish *Sepia officinalis* Length to 35cm
Impressive and distinctive cephalopod mollusc. Found on sandy and gravel substrates, mainly sub-littoral but inshore (for spawning) in late spring and summer. Cuttlebones (internal shell) often washed up. **ADULT** has oval body with lateral fins, large eyes, and arms with 4 rows of suckers. **STATUS** Locally common off coasts of S and SW England, and Wales.

Little Cuttlefish
Sepiola atlantica
Length to 20mm
Beautiful little cephalopod mollusc. Found in shallows at low tide on sandy shores, also in pools. **ADULT** has compact, rather rounded body, with rounded, slightly frilly fins and relatively large head, eyes and tentacles. Head is fused to mantle on dorsal surface, between eyes. Ability to change colour is impressive. **STATUS** Widespread but local; commonest in the S and W. **SIMILAR SPECIES Stout Bobtail** *Rossia macrosoma* (length to 6cm) has rounded fins and head is not fused, dorsally, to mantle. In the NW only.

ABOVE: **Little Cuttlefish, resting**
LEFT: **Little Cuttlefish, swimming**

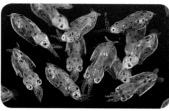

ABOVE: **Common Squid, young animals**
LEFT: **Common Squid, eggs**

Common Squid
Loligo vulgaris Length to 70cm
Slender, fast-swimming cephalopod mollusc. Usually in open sea but sometimes in shallow inshore waters in spring and summer. **ADULT** has elongate, torpedo-shaped body with triangular fins and large eyes. Most tentacles are rather short; 2 are long and clubbed, with very large median suckers. **STATUS** Locally common only on S and W coasts. **SIMILAR SPECIES Long-finned Squid** *L. forbesi* is slightly smaller (length to 60cm); median suckers on tentacle club are only marginally larger than lateral ones. Range is similar to that of Common Squid.

Curled Octopus *Eledone cirrhosa* Length to 50cm
Our most commonly encountered octopus. Lives on rocky coasts. Usually sub-littoral, but sometimes found in pools or brought up in crab pots. **ADULT** has a smooth, sac-like body and large eyes, mantle cavity opening via a siphon. Tentacles are long and very mobile, often curling at tip; tentacles have single row of suckers. Animal can change colour rapidly to match background. **STATUS** Locally common only in the SW and on W coasts. **SIMILAR SPECIES Common Octopus** *Octopus vulgaris* (length to 90cm) has a warty texture, relatively smaller eyes and 2 rows of suckers on tentacles. Very local on S and W coasts.

Common Cuttlefish

Little Cuttlefish

Common Squid

Curled Octopus

Curled Octopus, swimming

INTRODUCING ECHINODERMS

An exclusively marine group of invertebrates, the echinoderms are striking and distinctive creatures. All are slow-moving and some are virtually sedentary. Representatives of all the main groups are easily found on the seashore.

WHAT ARE ECHINODERMS?

Echinoderms are characterised by having bodies that exhibit radial symmetry; this feature is obvious in most groups, but less so in the sea cucumbers, which have elongated bodies. The collective common name for the group, echinoderm, literally means 'spiny skin', and indeed this is the most distinctive feature of the sea urchins in particular. All echinoderms have an outer skeleton of calcified plates, which range in complexity from a few scattered plates embedded in the skin in sea cucumbers, to a rigid, calcified dome in sea urchins. Tube feet protrude from pores, located in radiating rows (typically, five rows); these are used for movement or anchoring, depending on the species, and are operated by an internal hydraulic system. There is a central mouth; some echinoderms are grazers while others are active predators.

THE RANGE OF ECHINODERMS

The phylum Echinodermata is divided into a number of sub-groups. Those found regularly on the seashore, or in shallow coastal seas, include the following: feather stars (class Crinoidea); starfish, sea stars and cushion stars (class Asteroidea); brittlestars (class Ophiuroidea); sea urchins (class Echinoidea); and sea cucumbers (class Holothuroidea).

Feather Star.

Feather stars – unusual echinoderms that comprise ten delicate, flexible arms radiating from a central cup; the cup is attached to a rock or other substrate by a branched 'stalk'. The feather star mouth is located in the centre of the cup on the upper side.

Common Starfish.

Starfish, sea stars and cushion stars – distinctive echinoderms that are typically star-shaped, usually with five radiating arms. The upper surface is tough and usually covered with tubercles or short spines. Underneath, rows of tube feet line grooves along the arms; between the feet are tiny gills and pincer-like cleaning appendages. Most starfish species have slender arms, usually five in number but sometimes more. Sea stars have a broad central body with many relatively short, radiating arms; cushion stars are overall pentagonal in outline, the projecting arms being reduced in length.

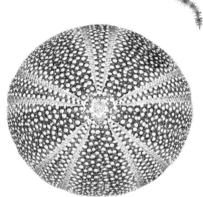

Brittlestars – easily recognised by the five slender, brittle, flexible arms that radiate from a central rounded disc. There are two rows of tube feet on the underside of each arm; the arms themselves comprise numerous spiny segments.

Common Brittlestar.

Sea urchins – distinctive echinoderms whose skeletal plates are linked to form a rigid case called a 'test'; depending on the species, this can be spherical, ovoid or flattish. The test is typically covered in spines, between which lie appendages. Tube feet are found on the underside, aligned in five rows and radiating from the central mouth; the mouth contains a five-jawed structure called 'Aristotle's lantern'.

ABOVE: **Edible Sea Urchin test, with spines removed.**
RIGHT: **Underside of *Psammechinus miliaris*, showing the mouth, tube feet and spines.**

Cotton Spinner, a typical sea cucumber.

Sea cucumbers – sausage-shaped echinoderms with a mouth at one end, surrounded by retractile tentacles, and the anus at the other. The tough, leathery skin is embedded with skeletal plates; in some species, the skin is covered in spikes. There are five rows of tube feet, running the length of the body; three are on the ventral surface and two on the dorsal surface.

Common
Starfish

Common Starfish *Asterias rubens* Diameter to 30cm
Our most familiar starfish. Found on a wide range of shores
but usually near prey (including polychaete worms and molluscs,
often mussels). Seashore individuals are usually rather small. **ADULT**
is usually orange-brown overall with 5 stout arms, each with white
spines in a central row and in irregularly scattered clumps.
STATUS Widespread and often locally common.

Leptasterias muelleri Diameter to 6cm
Small, well-marked starfish. Found on sheltered rocky coasts, on lower shore. **ADULT** has
5 stout arms. Seashore individuals are usually greenish (sometimes pinkish purple in
deeper water). Arms have pale tips and margins, and rows of star-shaped clusters of pale
spines. **STATUS** Locally common only in the N and NW.

Seven-armed Starfish
Luidia ciliaris Diameter to 50cm
Impressive and distinctive starfish. Found on sheltered rocky coasts, on lower shore.
Seashore individuals are usually relatively small. **ADULT** usually has diagnostic 7 arms
(sometimes lost or partly regrown), orange with a fringe of white spines. **STATUS** Locally
common only in the W, from Devon to N Scotland.

Spiny
Starfish

Spiny Starfish *Marthasterias glacialis* Diameter to 65cm
Impressive and distinctive starfish. Found on rocky coasts, on lower
shore. Seashore individuals are usually relatively small. **ADULT** has 5
rather slender arms, greenish or greenish brown with longitudinal
rows of spines, each spine arising from a swollen, minutely
spiny base. **STATUS** Locally common only in the W,
from Devon to N Scotland.

Common Sun Star *Crossaster papposus* Diameter to 35cm
Unmistakable starfish. Usually found on rocky and mixed coasts;
generally sub-littoral but sometimes on lower shore, or washed
up after gales. Active predator of other echinoderms. **ADULT**
comprises a large central disc and usually 11–13 rather slender arms.
Reddish orange with paler margin to disc. **STATUS** Widespread, but
commonest N from Wales and N Norfolk; easiest to find on shores in the NW.

Purple Sun Star *Solaster endeca* Diameter to 35cm
Large, striking starfish. Found on rocky and mixed coasts; usually sub-littoral but
sometimes washed up after gales. **ADULT** has a relatively smaller central disc than
Common Sun Star (above), with usually 9–11 slender, long arms. Usually purplish but
can be yellowish orange. Arms are rather rounded in cross section, with numerous small
spines. **STATUS** Mainly N species, locally common only on coasts of NW and N Scotland.

Sand Star *Astropecten irregularis* Diameter to 20cm
Distinctive starfish. Found on sandy coasts, buried on lower shore and in sub-littoral
zone. Sometimes washed up after gales. **ADULT** is very flat; the 5 stiff arms have marginal
plates and spines, and a leathery upper surface. Usually orange or pinkish orange, arms
often tipped violet. **STATUS** Widespread but locally common only off SW and W coasts.

Henricia sanguinolenta Diameter to 20cm
Attractive starfish. Found on sheltered rocky coasts, on lower shore.
Seashore individuals are usually relatively small. **ADULT** has 5 narrow
arms, rather rounded in cross section, with regular clusters of spines on
upper surface. Usually reddish violet but often yellowish orange.
STATUS Locally common on SW, W and N coasts; easiest to find
on shores in the NW. **SIMILAR SPECIES Bloody Henry Starfish** H.
oculata is very similar. Examine skin surface for certain identification:
spines are covered by skin, creating a pock-marked texture. More
widespread than *H. sanguinolenta* but mainly sub-littoral.

Sand
Star

Common Starfish

Leptasterias muelleri

INSET: Seven-armed Starfish eating a Thick Top Shell

Seven-armed Starfish

Spiny Starfish

Common Sun Star

Sand Star

Henricia sanguinolenta

Purple Sun Star

Bloody Henry Starfish

Bloody Henry Starfish

Cushion Star *Asterina gibbosa* Diameter to 5cm
Distinctive starfish relative, found under rocks on lower
shore. **ADULT** is shaped like a nativity star. Body is fleshy,
usually mottled dark green or reddish brown. **STATUS**
Locally common only in the SW and on W coasts. **SIMILAR**
SPECIES *A. phylactica* is similar but smaller (diameter to
15mm), typically buffish overall with a dark central star-shaped
pattern. Restricted to upper-shore pools with coralline algae, in the SW only.

Red Cushion Star *Porania pulvillus* Diameter to 10cm
Unmistakable. Found on rocky and mixed coasts; usually sub-littoral, sometimes washed
up after storms. **ADULT** has a thick, fleshy body with relatively short, triangular arms.
Reddish orange, adorned with white spots. **STATUS** Locally common only in the NW.

Feather Star *Antedon bifida* Length to 10cm
Feathery and delicate echinoderm. Found attached to undersides of rocks and in rocky
gullies; lower shore and sub-littoral zone. Able to move around and attach itself at will.
ADULT has 5 pairs of feathery arms arising from basal disc. Below this, 20–25 cirri attach
animal to rock. Arms are usually reddish and banded. **STATUS** Locally common only in
the W, from Devon to N Scotland.

Common Brittlestar
Ophiothrix fragilis Disc diameter to 20mm
Well-marked and often colourful brittlestar. Found
under stones on sheltered rocky shores. **ADULT** has
spiny disc with pair of triangular plates (radial
shields) at base of each leg; has distinct gap between
each pair. Legs are fragile, roughly 5× disc diameter,
and armed with spines. Colour overall is usually
reddish, legs often banded. **STATUS** Widespread but
commonest in the W. **SIMILAR SPECIES Crevice**
Brittlestar *Ophiopholis aculeata* (disc diameter to
20mm) has angular disc with scales and granules (not
spines) on surface; radial shields are not visible. Each
leg segment has dorsal oval plate fringed by small
scales. Mainly in the W, commonest in the NW.

ABOVE: **Feather Star;** BELOW: **Common**
Brittlestar; BOTTOM: **Small Brittlestar**

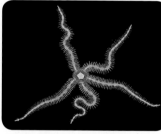

Ophiocomina nigra Disc diameter to 25mm
Distinctive dark brittlestar. Found on rocky coasts;
lower shore and sub-littoral zone. **ADULT** has
uniform granular disc (lacking radial shields) and
relatively slender legs, roughly 5× disc diameter, with
fine spines. **STATUS** Locally common only in the W,
from Devon to N Scotland; commonest in the NW.

Small Brittlestar
Amphipholis squamata Disc diameter to 5mm
Small, easily overlooked brittlestar. Found under
stones and rocks on lower shore. **ADULT** has disc
covered in small scales, with pale, closely abutting
pair of radial shields at base of each leg. Legs are
slender, roughly 4× disc diameter, with short spines.
STATUS Widespread and locally common.

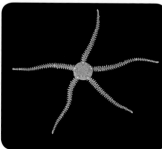

Amphiura brachiata Disc diameter to 12mm
Distinctive brittlestar. Lives buried in sand on lower
shore, sometimes with leg tips projecting. **ADULT** has
disc covered in scales, with prominent radial shields.
Legs are species' most striking feature: up to 15×
longer than disc diameter. **STATUS** Local, mainly in W.

Cushion Star

Asterina phylactica

Red Cushion Star

Feather Star

Common Brittlestar

Ophhiocomina nigra

Small Brittlestar

Amphiura brachiata

Edible Sea Urchin
Echinus esculentus Diameter to 12cm
Unmistakable sea urchin, found on rocky coasts; lower shore and shallow sub-littoral zone. **ADULT** has domed outline, pinkish overall with radial bands tinged green or purple. Spines usually red and white, tipped violet. **STATUS** Widespread and locally common, but absent from most of the SE, from Dorset to Norfolk.

Psammechinus miliaris Diameter to 5cm
Distinctive little sea urchin. Found under rocks and among seaweeds on lower shore. **ADULT** is relatively flattened in outline and greenish overall. Spines are green with purple tips. **STATUS** Widespread and locally common.
SIMILAR SPECIES Northern Sea Urchin *Strongylocentrotus droebachiensis* (diameter to 7cm) has numerous rather fine spines, red, green or purple, but usually white-tipped; restricted to Shetland Isles. **Purple Sea Urchin** *Paracentrotus lividus* has numerous purple or green spines and often bores cavities in limestone rocks, where it resides; very locally common in W Ireland (mainly Co. Clare), rare in SW England.

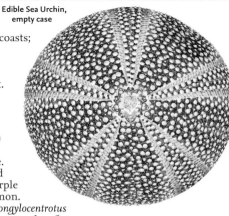

Edible Sea Urchin, empty case

Psammechinus miliaris, empty case

Sea Potato, empty case

Sea Potato
Echinocardium cordatum Length to 5cm
Unmistakable sea urchin. Lives buried in muddy sand on lower shore. Empty shells often washed up. **ADULT** is oval to heart-shaped in outline, with numerous close-packed buffish spines. **STATUS** Widespread and locally common.

Purple Heart Urchin *Spatangus purpureus* Length to 6cm
Distinctive sea urchin. Lives buried in sand and gravel. Occasionally found exposed at surface on very low tides, or washed up after gales. **ADULT** is heart-shaped in outline with numerous spines, shorter than those of Sea Potato (above), and purplish. **STATUS** Widespread and very locally common, mainly in the W and SW.

Green Sea Urchin *Echinocyamus pusillus* Length to 10mm
Tiny sea urchin. Lives buried in sand and is easily overlooked. **ADULT** is oval and flattened. Spines are short and closely packed. Empty shell shows 2 holes (mouth and anus) on ventral surface. **STATUS** Widespread but local; absent from much of the SE.

Edible Sea Urchin

ventral surface showing mouth

Psammechinus miliaris

Purple Sea Urchin

Sea Potato

Green Sea Urchin

Purple Heart Urchin

Sea Gherkin *Pawsonia saxicola* Length to 12cm

Striking sea cucumber, found under rocks and among seaweed holdfasts on lower shore. **ADULT** has a smooth white body, with 5 rows of tube feet (ventral rows are double). Tentacles are branched; main stems are grey, tips flecked yellowish buff. **STATUS** Widespread and locally common, mainly in the SW and W, from Dorset to Shetland. **SIMILAR SPECIES** *Ocnus lactea* is smaller (length to 4cm). Body is white and smooth, with irregular rows of single tube feet; tentacles are yellowish buff. Local, mainly in the W.

Brown Sea Cucumber *Aslia lefevrei* Length to 12cm

Rather undistinguished-looking sea cucumber, found under rocks and in crevices on lower shore. **ADULT** has wrinkled brown body with tube feet in 5 double rows. Tentacles are branched and dark. **STATUS** Widespread and locally common, mainly in the SW and W, from Dorset to Shetland.

Cotton Spinner *Holothuria forskali* Length to 25cm

Unmistakable large sea cucumber, found in rock crevices on lower shore of rocky coasts. When disturbed, can eject a mass of sticky cotton-like threads that entangle would-be predators. **ADULT** is soft and brown to black, paler below than above. Has 3 ventral rows of tube feet and relatively short, branched tentacles. **STATUS** Widespread and locally common only in the W.

Leptosynapta inhaerens Length to 12cm

Slender, delicate sea cucumber. Lives buried in sandy mud on lower shore. **ADULT** is pink and worm-like, body capable of great contraction and extension. Has 12 much-branched tentacles. **STATUS** Widespread but scattered; absent from much of the SE. **SIMILAR SPECIES** *Labidoplax digitata* is also worm-like and lives buried in sandy mud; each of its 12 tentacles have just 2 pairs of branches at tip. Scattered and local, mainly in the W.

Ciona intestinalis,
orange form

Ciona intestinalis Length to 12cm

Striking sea squirt. Solitary, but often in groups on suitable substrates: attaches basally to rocks, large seaweeds and pier pilings. **ADULT** has soft, tubular, retractile body with 2 openings close together. Typically translucent whitish (sometimes orange) with yellow around rim of openings. **STATUS** Widespread and locally common, except in E England.

Ascidiella aspersa Length to 10cm

Tough, gristly sea squirt, attached on 1 side to rocks and seaweeds on lower shore. **ADULT** is irregularly ovoid and usually milky white; surface is rough, often with attached and embedded debris. Has 2 siphons, 1 at top, the other ⅓ way down body. **STATUS** Widespread and locally common, except in the E.

Ascidiella scabra Length to 4cm

Small sea squirt; lives attached to seaweeds, notably Serrated Wrack (p. 34), on lower shore. **ADULT** is roughly ovoid and slightly translucent white, sometimes tinged pink; surface is wrinkled but smooth. Has 2 siphons, 1 at top, the other ¼ way down body; openings sometimes flushed red. **STATUS** Widespread, commonest in the W and NW.

Leathery Sea Squirt *Styela clava* Length to 10cm

Tough, strange-looking sea squirt. Lives attached to rocks and hard substrates, but often washed up after gales. **ADULT** is irregularly club-shaped, with a leathery, warty surface and tough, slender stalk. **STATUS** Alien and introduced. Now locally common in the S and SE, particularly around harbours.

Neptune's Heart Sea Squirt *Phallusia mammillata* Length to 14cm

Large and distinctive sea squirt. Lives attached on 1 side to rocks on lower shore in silty areas. **ADULT** is whitish and irregularly flask-shaped, with a knobbly surface. **STATUS** Locally common only in Dorset and S Devon.

Sea Gherkin

Ocnus lactea

Ciona intestinalis

Brown Sea Cucumber

underside

upper surface

Cotton Spinner

Ascidiella aspersa

Leptosynapta inhaerens

Neptune's Heart Sea Squirt

Ascidiella scabra

Leathery Sea Squirt

Ascidia mentula Length to 15cm

Tough sea squirt, attached on 1 side to rocks and *Laminaria* holdfasts on lower shore.
ADULT is rubbery and elongate. Usually reddish but much of surface can be coated with
detritus. Has 1 terminal siphon, the other ¾ way down body; siphon lobes are often
marked with white. **STATUS** Widespread and locally common only on S and W coasts.
SIMILAR SPECIES *A. conchilega* has a flattened-ovoid greenish-
white body; 1 siphon is apical, the other 2/3 way down
body; both usually point upwards. Widespread,
commonest on S and W coasts.

Baked Bean Ascidian
on Common
Whelk

Baked Bean Ascidian

Dendrodoa grossularia Length to 15mm
Distinctive sea squirt. Attaches singly or in
aggregates to rocks, holdfasts and larger
mollusc shells. **ADULT** is irregularly
spherical, surface often encrusted; has
2 siphons. **STATUS** Widespread and
locally common, least so on E coasts.

Morchellium argus Length to 40mm

Intriguing sea squirt, attached to rocks on lower
shore. **ADULT** colony comprises club-shaped lobes with distinct flat-topped head and
stalk. Zooids are embedded inside; apical inhalant siphons have 8 lobes. **STATUS**
Widespread on S and W coasts.

Aplidium punctum Length to 20mm

Compact sea squirt. Lives attached to seaweeds on rocky shores. **ADULT** comprises
irregularly rounded lobes, zooids with 6 lobes around siphons and apical red spot.
STATUS Locally common, mainly in S and W. **SIMILAR SPECIES** *Polyclinum aurantium*
(length to 25mm) comprises rounded, flat-topped and sand-encrusted lobes. Widespread
but scattered, mainly S and W.

Lightbulb Sea Squirt *Clavelina lepadiformis* Length to 20mm

Distinctive colonial sea squirt. Lives attached to rocks and seaweeds; mainly sub-littoral.
ADULT comprises groups of transparent zooids, each with internal yellow-white and
brown lines, recalling lightbulb filaments. **STATUS** Widespread and locally common,
least so on coasts of E England.

Orange Lights Sea Squirt *Pycnoclavella aurilucens* Length to 6mm

Smaller than Lightbulb Sea Squirt (above), with different markings. Attaches to rocks
and seaweeds from lower shore to sub-littoral zone. **ADULT** comprises groups
of semi-transparent buffish zooids with orange-yellow internal lines.
STATUS Locally common, in SW England and Wales only.

Star Ascidian *Botryllus schlosseri* Width to 8cm or more

Distinctive colonial ascidian. Forms encrusting sheets on rocks
and large seaweeds on rocky coasts. **ADULT** colony comprises
star-shaped groups of narrowly oval zooids; these are
typically yellowish buff and set in a colourful test,
usually blue, purple or orange-brown. **STATUS**
Widespread and locally common, least so
on coasts of E England.

Botrylloides leachi

Botrylloides
leachi

Length to 8cm or more
Striking ascidian. Forms fleshy,
encrusting sheets and masses on seaweeds and rocks, on
lower shore. **ADULT** colony colour is variable but often orange or
grey. Zooids are paler than test and arranged in convoluted parallel chains.
STATUS Widespread and locally common, least so on coasts of SE and E England.

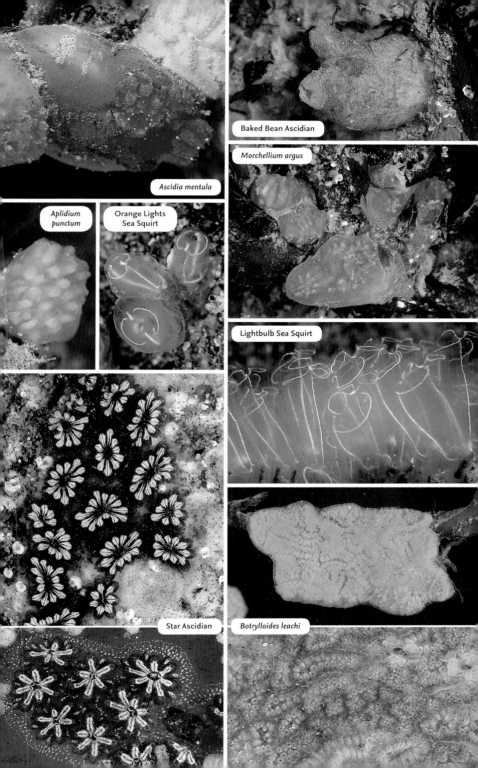

Ascidia mentula

Baked Bean Ascidian

Morchellium argus

Aplidium punctum

Orange Lights Sea Squirt

Lightbulb Sea Squirt

Star Ascidian

Botrylloides leachi

Sea Mat *Membranipora membranacea* Length to 7cm or more
Distinctive bryozoan. Forms flat, encrusting mats on fronds of *Laminaria* seaweeds. ADULT colony is white and lacy-looking, with zooids arranged in regimented grid; individual openings are rectangular. STATUS Widespread and locally common, least so in E England.

Electra pilosa *Length to 5cm*
Striking bryozoan. Forms flat, encrusting mats on seaweeds, notably Irish Moss and Grape Pip Weed (p. 36). ADULT colony is whitish and irregularly circular to star-shaped. Individual zooid openings are oval, the combined effect vaguely recalling miniature chainmail. STATUS Widespread and locally common, least so on coasts of E England.

Tubulipora plumosa *Diameter to 20mm*
Encrusting, calcified bryozoan, found on seaweed fronds, notably *Laminaria* and *Saccorhiza*. ADULT colony is roughly circular but lobed, the individual zooids forming fan-shaped radiations of tiny upswept pipes. STATUS Local, in the SW only.

Disporella hispida *Length to 10mm*
Encrusting, calcified bryozoan, found under rocks at low water. ADULT colony resembles a flattened cup, encrusting on rocks, often among coralline seaweeds. Close view reveals spiky texture, with zooids opening via tiny pores and tubes. STATUS Widespread but local, mainly on S and W coasts.

Alcyonidium hirsutum *Length to 8cm*
Superficially sponge-like, encrusting bryozoan, often with a lobed appearance. Found on Serrated Wrack (p. 34) and Grape Pip Weed (p. 36). ADULT colony is tough, gelatinous and usually buffish. Out of water, surface is slightly textured. In water, zooids emerge (like tiny sea anemones), each with 16–20 tentacles. STATUS Widespread and locally common in the W and N, scarce or absent elsewhere.

ABOVE: *Alcyonidium hirsutum*, close-up of polyps

Flustrellidra hispida *Length to 30mm*
Encrusting bryozoan found on seaweeds, mainly Serrated Wrack (p. 34). ADULT colony out of water resembles a gelatinous patch, like a blob of dried glue; close inspection reveals tightly packed zooid chambers with tiny spikes around each opening. In water, zooids emerge (like tiny sea anemones), each with 28 tentacles. STATUS Widespread and locally common, mainly in the W and N.

Flustrellidra hispida, colony out of water

Hornwrack *Flustra foliacea* Length to 15cm
Branched, colonial bryozoan with a passing resemblance to tough, leathery seaweed. Sub-littoral, attached to rocks; living and bleached dead specimens often washed up. Fresh specimens smell of lemon. ADULT colony appears bushy, with much-divided *Fucus*-like lobes that twist irregularly. STATUS Widespread and locally common.

Bugula turbinata *Length to 5cm*
Bushy, rather seaweed-like colonial bryozoan. Lives attached to stones and rocks on lower shore. ADULT has main 'stems' branching from base, along which are arranged spiral whorls of smaller branches that bear zooids. STATUS Widespread and locally common, mainly in the S and SW.

Cellepora pumicosa

Cellepora pumicosa *Diameter to 5cm or more*
Colonial bryozoan. Encrusts rocks and kelp holdfasts on lower shore. ADULT colony forms nodular patches; circular openings are seen with hand lens. Texture is hard and coarse, and will graze human skin. Typically orange-red. STATUS Widespread and locally common.

Sea Mat

Electra pilosa

Alcyonidium hirsutum

Tubulipora plumosa

Disporella hispida

Hornwrack

Flustrellidra hispida

Bugula turbinata

Cellepora pumicosa

INTRODUCING FISH

Fish are the most diverse group of vertebrates in inshore waters, and it is usually possible to discover a dozen or more species on almost any stretch of coast. Each species is adapted to a particularly niche, thus minimising competition for food. Consequently, many of our seashore fish look strikingly different from one another.

FISH CLASSIFICATION

Marine fish belong to a subdivision of the phylum Chordata (vertebrates) called Pisces. Within this class are two basic forms: elasmobranchs (sharks, rays and relatives), which have a cartilaginous skeleton; and teleosts, or bony fish, whose skeletons are calcified. In general terms though, the basic layout is broadly similar, given the variability in fish form generally.

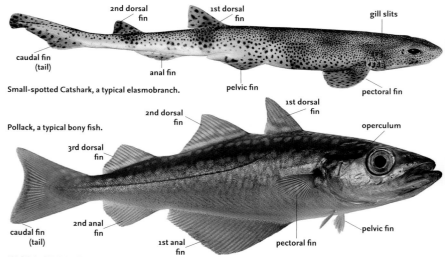

Small-spotted Catshark, a typical elasmobranch.

2nd dorsal fin · 1st dorsal fin · gill slits · caudal fin (tail) · anal fin · pelvic fin · pectoral fin

Pollack, a typical bony fish.

2nd dorsal fin · 1st dorsal fin · operculum · 3rd dorsal fin · caudal fin (tail) · 2nd anal fin · 1st anal fin · pectoral fin · pelvic fin

FISH STRUCTURE

Most open-water coastal fish species are streamlined. Typically, their body is torpedo-shaped, deeper in profile than it is wide, and the thin fins can be raised or lowered to suit the animal's requirements. Seen side on, a fish's caudal (tail) fin is striking and is the main means of propulsion. The remaining fins aid directional control and stability: on the dorsal surface is the dorsal fin (or fins in some species); on the ventral surface are pelvic fins at the front and an anal fin at the back; and on the side, just behind the gill opening, are pectoral fins. Most bony fish have an internal swim bladder that aids buoyancy.

Many seashore fish species, such as this Tompot Blenny, are not free-swimming and their shape reflects their habits: some rest on rocks or sand, and a few species (clingfish being good examples) have suckers that allow them to grip onto substrates. In terms of general form, if not appearance, the arrangement of fins in these species is similar to that of their open-water cousins.

Flatfish, such as this Plaice, are an exception to the rule in terms of fish structure. In their early stages they resemble conventional species. But during their development the head shape distorts so that, although they lie and swim on their sides, both eyes are on top.

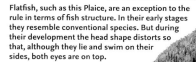

SKIN AND SCALES
The body of a fish is covered with a tough skin, and in most species small plates (called scales) are embedded in this to form an additional protective layer. Because the scales are not connected to one another, the body's flexibility is not compromised; in many bony fish the scales are large and overlap. Fish scales get bigger as the animal grows, new scale material being laid down in layers by the fish's skin.

STAYING ALIVE
Like air-breathing animals, fish need oxygen in order to survive. Dissolved oxygen is extracted from the water in which they live using gills; these are sited in chambers that connect with the back of the mouth and exit via openings on the side of the body. The comb-like structures that comprise the gills are covered in blood-filled tissues that absorb oxygen.

Ray's Bream scales.

SHOALING AND REPRODUCTION
Although some fish species lead essentially solitary lives, many live in single-species shoals, particularly when young; each shoal usually contains fish of a similar size. This behaviour benefits individuals on the principle of safety in numbers – there are more eyes on the lookout for potential danger, and if a predator attacks a shoal the chances of an individual becoming its meal are reduced.

Most open-water marine fish form shoals when breeding, producing vast numbers of eggs to allow for heavy predation. Inshore species often attach their eggs to rocks or weeds, and some make a nest. Many cartilaginous fish (catsharks and skates) protect their eggs and developing young within a tough, horny case attached to seaweed, called a 'mermaid's purse'. Although the eggs of these species are laid in deep water, mermaid's purses are often found washed up on the shoreline; sometimes they still contain a live embryo.

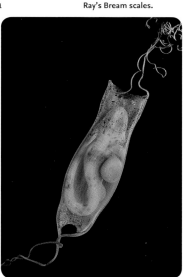

Egg case of Small-spotted Catshark with embryo inside.

Basking Shark

Cetorhinus maximus Length to 12m

Basking Shark

Our largest fish, and 2nd largest on the planet. Filter-feeds surface plankton in summer. ADULT has typical shark shape but disproportionately large mouth. Above water, nose, dorsal fin and top of tail fin are often visible. STATUS Most records are from SW England, N Irish Sea and NW Scotland, Jun–Sep. Scarce in some years if plankton is poor.

Blue Shark *Prionace glauca* Length to 2m

Large predatory shark. Feeds mainly on squid and fish. Tagging records indicate most British individuals are immature females that migrate long distances. ADULT is blue-grey above and whitish below. STATUS Scarce seasonal visitor, mainly to the SW.

ABOVE LEFT: Small-spotted Catshark, juvenile in daytime
ABOVE RIGHT: Small-spotted Catshark, juvenile after dark

ABOVE: Small-spotted Catshark, embyro inside egg case
BELOW: Starry Smooth Hound

Small-spotted Catshark or Dogfish

Scyliorhinus canicula Length to 75cm

Familiar inshore fish. Found in inshore waters, on mixed substrates. ADULT is slender and buffish yellow above with darker spots. Skin is rough – like sandpaper. Eye has slit-like pupil. Lays eggs, protected in a tough case, a so-called mermaid's purse (p. 369). STATUS Widespread and locally common, except along the E coast.

Starry Smooth Hound

Mustelus asterias Length to 1.2m

Elegant shark relative, found in inshore waters over sand and gravel; feeds mainly on crabs. ADULT is slender and streamlined. Buffish grey above with numerous white spots; underside is pale. Eye has round pupil. Gives birth to live young. STATUS Widespread and locally common in the S and W only; mainly in summer. SIMILAR SPECIES Smooth Hound *M. mustelus* (length to 1.5m) is less frequently caught in inshore waters. Dorsal surface is uniformly grey-brown and lacks white spots. Widespread but generally scarce, in the S and SW only.

Basking Shark

Blue Shark

Small-spotted Catshark

Small-spotted Catshark

Starry Smooth Hound

Smooth Hound

Thornback Ray

Thornback Ray

Thornback Ray *Raja clavata* Length to 90cm
The most familiar inshore ray. **ADULT** has flat, roughly
diamond-shaped body with short snout. Dorsal surface of
long tail has thorny spines with swollen bases; these continue
in a line along dorsal surface of body. Upper body surface is
grey-brown with dark stripes or pale and dark spots; lower
surface is pale. Tail looks banded. Lays eggs, protected in a
tough case (p. 369). **STATUS** Widespread and locally common in
the S and W only. **SIMILAR SPECIES Common Skate** *Dipturus
batis* (length to 2m) is larger, with a more elongate snout
and spines only on tail; upper surface is uniformly dark
grey-brown. Generally rare due to overfishing.

Thornback Ray,
juvenile underside

Spotted Ray *Raja montagui* Length to 75cm
Similar to Thornback Ray (above) but separable
using pattern and structure. Fairly common in shallow inshore waters over sand. **ADULT**
has roughly diamond-shaped body and short, pointed snout. Upper surface is grey-brown
with dark spots that do not extend to wing margins. Tail is long and does not look banded.
Has spines along dorsal surface of tail and along centre of body; these lack swollen bases.
Lays eggs, protected in a tough case (p. 368). **STATUS** Widespread and locally common in
the S and W only. **SIMILAR SPECIES Blonde Ray** *R. brachyura* (length to 1m) has dark spots
on upper surface that extend to wing margins. Widespread but
rather scarce, in the S and W only.

Small-eyed Ray *Raja microocellata* Length to 75cm
Well-marked ray. Found in mouths of estuaries and sandy
bays. **ADULT** has typical ray shape with rather short snout.
Upper surface is grey-brown with pale lines and spots. Lays
eggs, protected in a tough case (p. 369). **STATUS** Widespread
and locally common in the S and W only. **SIMILAR SPECIES**
Undulate Ray *R. undulata* (length to 1m) is grey-brown above,
with dark lines bordered by white dots. Scarce, mainly in the S.

Small-eyed Ray,
juvenile underside

Common Stingray *Dasyatis pastinaca* Length to 1.2m
Fairly distinctive ray, renowned for its ability to
inflict a painful wound. Favours estuary mouths
and shores with muddy sand. **ADULT** has
shield-shaped body outline with long,
tapering tail, armed dorsally with single 'stinging' spine. Upper surface of body is uniformly
yellowish grey. Gives birth to live young. **STATUS** Generally scarce, mainly in the S.

Marbled Electric Ray *Torpedo marmorata* Length to 1.5m
Unusual ray, capable of delivering a powerful shock (up to 220V) from organs in pectoral
fins. **ADULT** has unmistakable rounded outline; tail is relatively short with rounded
dorsal fins. Body upper surface is mottled and marbled grey-brown. **STATUS** Scarce,
mainly in the W and SW.

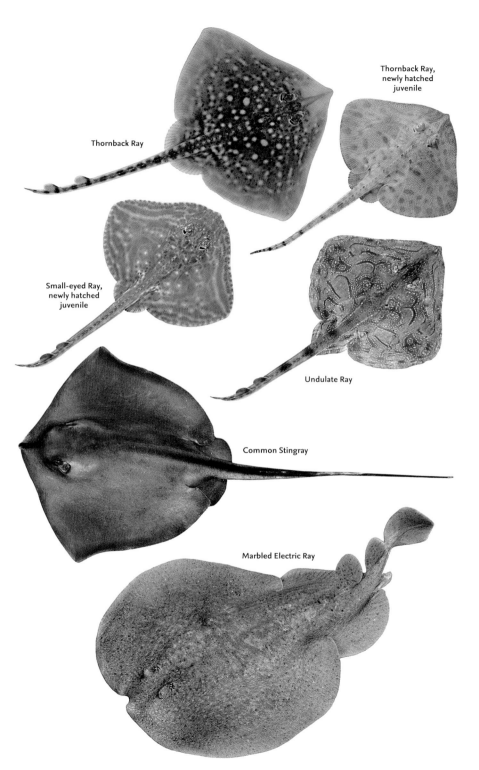

Thornback Ray

Thornback Ray, newly hatched juvenile

Small-eyed Ray, newly hatched juvenile

Undulate Ray

Common Stingray

Marbled Electric Ray

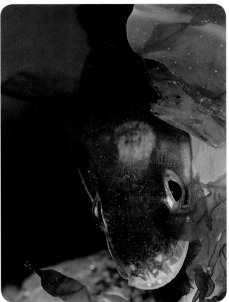

Conger Eel

Sea Lamprey
Petromyzon marinus Length to 1.2m
Parasitic eel-like fish with a cartilaginous backbone. Lacks jaws; toothed sucker is used to latch onto live fish. Sometimes found on rocky coasts; migrates to fresh water to spawn. ADULT has a slender body, reduced fins for swimming and line of round gill openings behind eye. STATUS Widespread but generally scarce.

Conger Eel
Conger conger Length to 1.8m
Impressive eel. Large individuals favour wrecks and rocky crevices, and are sometimes seen when snorkelling. Smaller animals are found under rocks at low water. ADULT has slender body, blue-grey above, paler below. Eyes are relatively large, upper jaw protrudes and dorsal fin starts just behind pectoral fins. STATUS Widespread and generally common, least so on E coasts.

Common Eel
Anguilla anguilla Length to 1m
Similar to Conger Eel (above) but with subtle structural differences. Found in fresh water for much of life but also on rocky shores and in estuaries. ADULT is yellowish for much of life, but turns silvery blue as adult before migration. Compared to Conger, note relatively smaller eyes, protruding lower jaw and dorsal fin that starts way down body. STATUS Widespread but rather scarce, numbers much reduced in recent years.

Herring
Clupea harengus Length to 40cm
Shoal-forming, economically important fish. Favours open seas but sometimes found inshore. ADULT is streamlined, blue-grey above and silvery on sides. Dorsal fin starts in front of pelvic fin. STATUS Widespread but rather scarce, numbers much reduced in recent years due to overfishing.

Sprat
Sprattus sprattus Length to 16cm
Shoal-forming relative of Herring

Common Eel, migrating across coastal mudflat.

(above). Found in open seas but comes inshore in summer in particular. ADULT is streamlined, blue-grey above and on sides, silvery white below. Dorsal fin lies above pelvic fins. Belly has rough, saw-scaled outline. STATUS Widespread and fairly common.

Pilchard
Sardina pilchardus Length to 25cm
Shoal-forming fish. Found in open seas, often inshore in summer. ADULT is streamlined, bluish above and silvery on sides and below. Scales are relatively large. Dorsal fin starts in front of pelvic fins. STATUS Widespread but rather scarce, mainly in the SW; numbers much reduced in recent years due to overfishing.

Sea Lamprey

Conger Eel

Common Eel

Herring

Sprat

Pilchard

Atlantic Salmon *Salmo salar* Length to 1.5m

Distinctive large fish. Found in open seas for much of life, but migrates into fresh water to spawn. **ADULT** has streamlined, powerfully muscular body. At sea, silvery grey above and silvery white below, with dark spots on back and flanks; spawning individuals become duller and more yellow. **STATUS** Widespread and locally, and seasonally, fairly common, least so in the E and SE.

Sea Trout *Salmo trutta* ssp. *trutta* Length to 1.3m

Migratory subspecies of Brown Trout; found in opens seas for much of life but spawns in fresh water. Similar to Atlantic Salmon (above) but separable with care. **ADULT** is silvery blue above and pale below at sea, but acquires reddish-yellow hues in fresh water. All individuals have dark spots on back and flanks; these are proportionately larger and more intense than on Atlantic Salmon. **STATUS** Widespread and locally, and seasonally, fairly common, least so in the E and SE.

Angler Fish *Lophius piscatorius* Length to 2m

Large, flattened and unmistakable fish. Favours sandy substrates; sometimes seen in shallows, but also in deeper water. **ADULT** has a proportionately large head and tapering tail end. Lies in wait for prey, attracted by slender fishing 'lure'; these are engulfed by huge mouth, armed with sharp teeth. Marbled brown and buff colours provide good camouflage on seabed. **STATUS** Widespread and fairly common only in the W and SW.

Shore Clingfish *Lepadogaster lepadogaster* Length to 8cm

Distinctive intertidal fish, found under rocks and in pools on lower shore. **ADULT** is overall tadpole-shaped and broadly flattened, with a pointed snout. Colour is variable, but typically yellow or orange with a pattern of pale lines and dark spots, and 2 blue eye-spots behind real eyes. Note also feathery tentacles in front of eyes. Pelvic fins are modified to form sucker, used for clinging to rocks. **STATUS** Widespread but local, commonest in the SW from Dorset to N Wales.

Connemara Clingfish *Lepadogaster candollii* Length to 7cm

Similar to Shore Clingfish (above) but separable with care. Found under rocks and in pools on lower shore. **ADULT** has a flattened body and large head. Typically green with reddish marbling. Lacks eye-spots but note 2 red spots present at base of dorsal fin. Eyes are relatively large, with radial bands of colour. Dorsal and anal fins are not connected to tail fin (they are in Shore Clingfish); this feature is hard to discern. **STATUS** Local and rather scarce, mainly in the SW and NW.

Small-headed Clingfish

Apletodon dentatus Length to 4cm

Small clingfish. Found in pools and sub-littoral zone on rocky shores; sometimes inside bulbous *Saccorhiza* holdfasts. Easily overlooked: well camouflaged and often remains motionless when exposed. **ADULT** has slender, rather flattened but angular body with pointed snout. Colour is variable: usually marbled greenish (sometimes reddish), with pale patches on back. Has dark patch at base of dorsal and anal fins. Anal fin lies below dorsal. **STATUS** Widespread but local in the W and SW. **SIMILAR SPECIES Two-spotted Clingfish** *Diplecogaster bimaculata* (length to 4cm) is usually reddish. Position of anal fin is slightly staggered behind dorsal fin. Male has 2 dark spots on flanks behind pectoral fins. Widespread but local in the W.

Atlantic Salmon

Sea Trout

Angler Fish

Shore Clingfish

Shore Clingfish,
underside

Connemara Clingfish

Connemara Clingfish,
underside

Small-headed Clingfish

Whiting
Merlangius merlangus Length to 70cm
Streamlined pelagic fish. Young in
particular often occur in shallow inshore
waters. **ADULT** is brown (can appear bluish)
above, silvery below. Note dark spot at
base of pectoral fin. Has 3 dorsal fins and
2 anal fins. Lower jaw is slightly shorter
the upper; tiny barbel on lower jaw is
sometimes present but usually absent.
STATUS Widespread,
commonest in the
S and W.

ABOVE: **Whiting**; BELOW: **Pollack**

Pollack
Pollachius pollachius
Length to 1.25m
Classic fish of rocky
coasts. **ADULT** is
beautifully patterned:
tinged golden overall,
marbled with silvery-grey spots. Lower jaw protrudes; barbel is absent. Has 3 dorsal fins
and 2 anal fins. **STATUS** Widespread and generally common, least so on E coasts.

Saithe *Pollachius virens* Length to 75cm
Northern cousin to Pollack (above), found on rocky coasts. **ADULT** is dark greenish black
above, paler on sides and below. Lower jaw is only slightly longer than upper; barbel is
absent. Has 3 dorsal fins and 2 anal fins. **STATUS** Widespread and generally common in
the N; scarce in the SW, absent from the SE.

Bib or Pout
Trisopterus luscus Length to 40cm
Attractive, rather deep-bodied fish
with relatively tall fins. **ADULT** is golden
brown above, silvery blue below. Fins are
yellowish, dorsal and tail fins with dark
margins. Has 3 dorsal fins and 2 anal fins.
Lower jaw is slightly shorter than upper,
with long barbel. Note dark spot at base
of pectoral fin. **STATUS** Widespread and
generally common in S and W Britain;
absent from much of the NE.

Poor-cod *Trisopterus minutus* Length to 25cm
Streamlined but rather deep-bodied pelagic fish with proportionately very large eyes.
Young in particular venture into inshore waters. **ADULT** is brown above, silvery below.
Has 3 dorsal fins and 2 anal fins. Lower jaw is roughly same length as upper, with delicate
barbel. **STATUS** Widespread and locally common although absent from much of the NE.

Atlantic Cod *Gadus morhua* Length to 120cm
Distinctive fish with a proportionately large head. Young in particular venture into
inshore waters, especially in winter. **ADULT** is brown above and silvery below, marbled
with golden spots and a yellowish hue on flanks. Has 3 dorsal fins and 2 anal fins. Lower
jaw is shorter than upper, with long barbel. **STATUS** Widespread and fairly common,
least so where fished commercially.

Three-bearded Rockling *Gaidropsarus vulgaris* Length to 50cm
Attractive, well-marked fish. Mostly sub-littoral but sometimes found in pools on lower
shore. **ADULT** is pinkish orange, marbled with darker patches; overall, darker above than
below. Head has 3 barbels. **STATUS** Widespread and locally common in the SW and W only.

Whiting

Pollack

Saithe

Bib

Poor-cod

Cod

Three-bearded
Rockling

Shore Rockling, juvenile (so-called 'Mackerel Midge') amongst floating seaweed.

Shore Rockling
Gaidropsarus mediterraneus
Length to 45cm
Found on lower shore, under rocks and in pools. ADULT is dark brown overall, paler below than above. Head has 3 barbels. First dorsal fin has long ray at front; 2nd dorsal fin continues almost to tail. STATUS Local, in the SW only. NOTE Young of this species, and other rocklings, are known as 'mackerel midges' and are greenish above, silvery below; they are found among drifting seaweed rafts, and tangled hiding places on the seabed.

Five-bearded Rockling
Ciliata mustela Length to 30cm
Elongate, rather cylindrical fish. Similar to Shore Rockling (above) but with 5 barbels. Found in pools and under rocks on lower shore; adept at slithering into crevices to escape capture. ADULT is overall brown above, paler below. Head has 5 barbels. Fin arrangement is similar to that of Shore Rockling. STATUS Widespread and fairly common, except in the N.

Horse Mackerel or Scad *Trachurus trachurus* Length to 70cm
Pelagic open-water fish. Ventures into inshore waters in summer; young fish associate with floating seaweed rafts. ADULT often looks pale and silvery overall; close view reveals green tinge to upperparts. Note also striking curve in lateral line. Eyes are proportionately large. STATUS Fairly common in the S and SW only.

Black Sea-bream *Spondyliosoma cantharus* Length to 55cm
Deep-bodied fish with a steep head profile. Ventures into inshore waters in summer. ADULT is bluish grey overall, darker above than below, and tinged reddish on head and underparts. Dorsal fin has spiny rays; pectoral fins are relatively long. STATUS Widespread and fairly common in the S and W; commonest from Dorset to Sussex. SIMILAR SPECIES **Gilthead** *Sparus aurata* (length to 70cm) has diagnostic yellow band across steep forehead and dark patch at anterior end of lateral line. Small numbers move into shallow waters and estuary mouths on S coast in summer.

Blackspot Sea-bream or Red Sea-bream *Pagellus bogaraveo* Length to 60cm
Young in particular venture into inshore waters in summer months. ADULT is deep-bodied with a blunt head. Typically reddish overall with a black spot above base of pectoral fin. Dorsal fin has spiny rays. STATUS Occasional in the S.

Ray's Bream *Brama brama* Length to 80cm
Fast-swimming predator. Typically favours deep waters off W coasts, but regularly beached (sometimes alive) on the E coast, notably in N Norfolk in winter. ADULT is laterally flattened, oval in side profile; tall dorsal and anal fins, long pectoral fins and forked tail. Forehead is steep and mouth has numerous fine teeth. Overall, appears silvery; has rainbow colours on dorsal surface in life. STATUS Recorded annually, seemingly in increasing numbers.

Striped Red Mullet *Mullus surmuletus* Length to 40cm
Striking, colourful fish. Sometimes found inshore, on sandy and muddy substrates. ADULT has a powerful, thickset body. Head is relatively large and blunt, with 2 barbels. Overall colour is red, with darker and yellow longitudinal stripes on sides. First dorsal fin is striped. STATUS Fairly common in the S and SW.

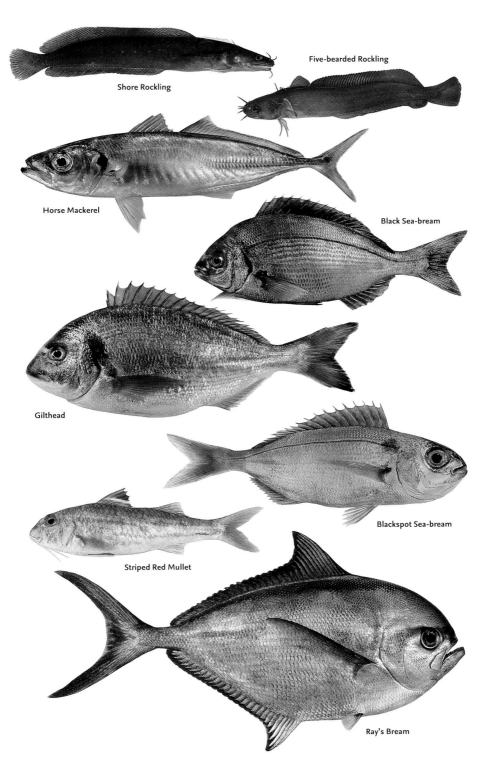

Shore Rockling

Five-bearded Rockling

Horse Mackerel

Black Sea-bream

Gilthead

Blackspot Sea-bream

Striped Red Mullet

Ray's Bream

Three-spined Stickleback
Gasterosteus aculeatus Length to 10cm
Familiar freshwater 'tiddler' that also occurs in
estuaries and brackish lagoons. **ADULT** has slender
body, elongate tailstock, and 3 spines (2 long, 1 short)
in front of dorsal fin. Mostly yellowish green above,
silvery below; breeding male has red belly and blue
eyes. **STATUS** Widespread and locally common.

non-breeding adult

SIMILAR SPECIES Nine-spined Stickleback *Pungitius pungitius* (length to 10cm) has 9–10
dorsal spines; yellowish green above, silvery below. Locally common, except in the SW.

Fifteen-spined Stickleback

Fifteen-spined Stickleback
Spinachia spinachia Length to 15cm
Truly marine stickleback, found in sheltered seas
among seaweeds and eelgrass. **ADULT** has a slender
body, elongate tailstock and 14–16 dorsal spines.
Greenish above, silvery below. **STATUS** Widespread
and locally common except in the SE.

Greater Pipefish *Syngnathus acus* Length to 50cm
Relatively large and robust by pipefish standards.
Found among seaweeds and eelgrass. **ADULT** has
long, slender body, with pectoral fins and small tail
and dorsal fins. Head is angular-looking with 'hump' behind eye; snout is long with
concave profile. Typically brown above, paler below, often with dark bands down back.
STATUS Widespread and locally common in the S and W only. **SIMILAR SPECIES Deep-
snouted Pipefish** *S. typhle* (length to 35cm) has head and long snout that form continuous
straight profile. Typically marbled yellowish green. Local, mainly in the SW. **Nilsson's
Pipefish** *S. rostellatus* (length to 15cm) has shorter snout (roughly same length as rest of
head) and lacks 'hump' behind eye. Favours sandy estuaries and bays.

Snake Pipefish *Entelurus aequoreus* Length to 40cm
Similar to Greater Pipefish (above) but separable by studying markings and head profile.
Found among seaweeds and eelgrass. **ADULT** has slender body, with small dorsal fin and
tiny caudal fin; pectoral fins absent. Usually yellowish brown with vertical dark-bordered
pale lines along body, and dark line through eye. Head is not angular; snout is long with
straight, or very gently concave, profile. **STATUS** Widespread but local; absent from much
of the E.

Worm Pipefish *Nerophis lumbriciformis* Length to 15cm
At first glance, hard to recognise as a living creature, let alone a fish. Found among
seaweeds and under rocks at low water, but easily overlooked. **ADULT** has very slender,

Short-snouted Seahorse

stiff body with small dorsal fin; pectoral and tail fins absent.
Snout is short and upcurved, creating a 'pug-nosed' look.
Usually dark yellowish brown. **STATUS** Widespread and locally
common in the SW and W; mostly absent from E England.
SIMILAR SPECIES Straight-nosed Pipefish *N. ophidion* (length to
25cm) has straighter, longer snout (roughly same length as rest
of head). Found among seaweeds and eelgrass, but mainly
sub-littoral.

Short-snouted Seahorse
Hippocampus hippocampus Length to 15cm
Enigmatic, unmistakable fish. Extremely hard to observe and
protected by law. **ADULT** has classic seahorse shape; profile is
angular and body lacks slender projections. **STATUS** Local,
mainly along S coast of England. **SIMILAR SPECIES Long-
snouted Seahorse** *H. guttulatus* (length to 14cm) has body
adorned with spiny projections. Local, mainly in the S and W.

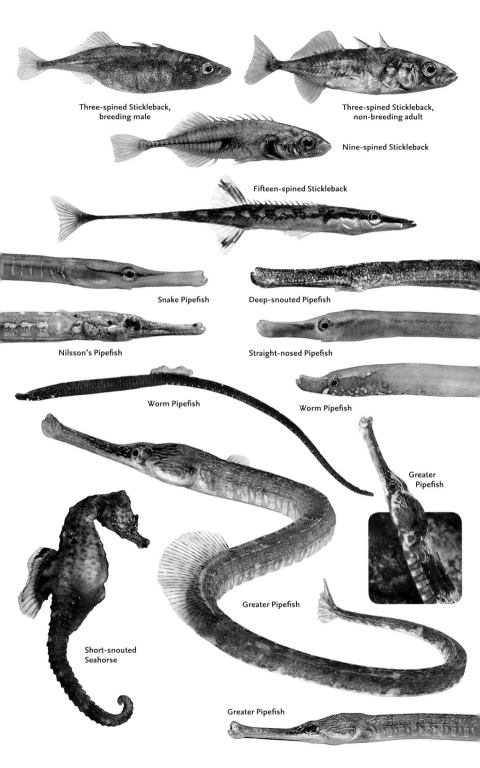

Three-spined Stickleback, breeding male

Three-spined Stickleback, non-breeding adult

Nine-spined Stickleback

Fifteen-spined Stickleback

Snake Pipefish

Deep-snouted Pipefish

Nilsson's Pipefish

Straight-nosed Pipefish

Worm Pipefish

Worm Pipefish

Greater Pipefish

Greater Pipefish

Short-snouted Seahorse

Greater Pipefish

Sand Smelt

Atherina presbyter Length to 15cm
Slender, silvery-looking fish. Swims in shoals, often in inshore waters in summer. **ADULT** is yellowish green above, pale below with silver scales along flanks. Has 2 dorsal fins, sited above pelvic and anal fins, respectively. **STATUS** Local and seasonal, mainly in the S and SW.

juvenile

Garfish *Belone belone* Length to 90cm

Unmistakable pelagic fish. Ventures into inshore waters in summer, along with Mackerel (p. 278). **ADULT** has a very slender body, and long, pointed jaws armed with sharp teeth. Dorsal, anal and tail fins are set far back on body. Green above, silvery on sides and white below. **STATUS** Locally, and seasonally, common, mainly in the S and W.

Grey Gurnard *Eutrigla gurnardus* Length to 45cm

Distinctive fish. Favours sandy and mixed substrates; found in inshore waters in summer. **ADULT** has large head and eyes, and sloping forehead. Pectoral fin does not reach vent; lowest 3 rays lack webbing and are tactile. First dorsal fin often has dark spot. Lateral line is spiny. Overall usually grey-brown with swirly pattern of pale lines and spots on lower flanks. **STATUS** Locally common in the S and W; scarce or absent from the E.

Red Gurnard *Aspitrigla cuculus* Length to 30cm

Stunning fish. Favours sandy and mixed substrates; found in inshore waters in summer. **ADULT** has large head and eyes; sloping forehead has more concave profile than that of Grey Gurnard (above). Pectoral fins extend beyond vent; lowest 3 rays lack webbing and are tactile. Lateral line is not spiny. Overall red, grading to pinkish white on belly. **STATUS** Locally common in the S and W; scarce or absent from E coasts.

juvenile

Tub Gurnard

Chelidonichthys lucerna
Length to 55cm
Attractive fish. Favours sandy and mixed substrates; found in inshore waters in summer. **ADULT** has large head and eyes; forehead slopes abruptly. Pectoral fins extend beyond vent; lowest 3 rays lack webbing and are tactile. Lateral line is not spiny. Overall orange-brown; pectoral fins are often yellow with a blue margin. **STATUS** Locally common in the S and W; scarce or absent from E coasts.

Sea Scorpion *Taurulus bubalis* Length to 20cm

Any rockpool fish with a large spiny head is likely to be this species. **ADULT** has an angular, almost lizard-like head; operculum is armed with 4 spines. Lateral line is spiny. Has white barbels at corners of mouth. Colour and patterning are variable and match background; often marbled reddish brown, with dark banding. **STATUS** Widespread and locally common, least so in the SE. **SIMILAR SPECIES Bull Rout** *Myoxocephalus scorpius* (length to 25cm) has 2 (not 4) obvious spines on operculum, and lacks white barbels at corners of mouth. Lateral line is not spiny. Range is similar to that of Sea Scorpion; seldom intertidal except in the far N. **Pogge** *Agonus cataphractus* (length to 15cm) is elongate, with an 'armoured' look about it; broad, flattened head is armed with spines and barbels. Inshore waters, commonest in the W.

Sand Smelt

Garfish

Grey Gurnard

Red Gurnard

Tub Gurnard

Sea Scorpion

Bull Rout

Pogge

Montagu's Sea Snail, swimming

Montagu's Sea Snail, clinging to stone

Montagu's Sea Snail *Liparis montagui* Length to 5cm
Unusual species, recalling a plump tadpole. At first glance, hard to recognise as a fish at all. Found in pools and under stones on lower shore. **ADULT** is slimy and scaleless, with skin that wrinkles. Head is bulbous. Dorsal and anal fins do not overlap tail fin. Colour variable, often yellowish but sometimes dark reddish brown. **STATUS** Widespread but local; mainly in the S and W. **SIMILAR SPECIES** **Common Sea Snail** *L. liparis* (length to 10cm) is widespread but occurs mainly offshore and is seldom observed. Dorsal and anal fins overlap tail fin.

Lumpsucker *Cyclopterus lumpus* Length to 55cm
Unmistakable fish. Usually offshore, but males, guarding eggs, sometimes found in rocky shallows. Young sometimes occur in pools on lower shore, and among floating rafts of seaweed. **ADULT** is size and shape of a rugby ball. Skin is lumpy and sometimes covered in parasites. Typically bluish black above, marbled reddish below. Young are often uniformly red or yellow. **STATUS** Widespread but local; commonest in the N.

European Sea Bass
Dicentrarchus labrax Length to 1m
Fast-swimming, streamlined predator and a popular sportfish. Often occurs close inshore. **ADULT** is silvery grey overall, darkest on dorsal surface, almost white on belly. Has 2 dorsal fins; 1st is spiny. **STATUS** Widespread but locally common only in S Britain.

Lumpsucker, juveniles among floating seaweeds

Thick-lipped Grey Mullet *Chelon labrosus* Length to 60cm
The commonest of our grey mullet species. Ventures into estuaries and bays in summer. **ADULT** is cigar-shaped overall, with a thick tailstock and narrowly tapering head. At its broadest, upper lip width equals or exceeds eye diameter. Overall colour is silvery grey, darker above than below. **STATUS** Widespread and locally common in S Britain; scarce or absent elsewhere. **SIMILAR SPECIES** **Thin-lipped Grey Mullet** *Liza ramada* (length to 50cm) is silvery grey with a dark spot at base of pectoral fins. At its broadest, upper lip width is less ½ diameter of eye. **Golden Grey Mullet** *Liza aurata* (length to 40cm) is silvery grey with a golden patch on gill cover. At its broadest, upper lip width is roughly diameter of eye.

Ocean Sunfish *Mola mola* Length to 1.5m or more
Massive, unmistakable fish. Sometimes seen at surface inshore, usually from W coast headlands or ferries, in late summer and autumn. **ADULT** is flattened laterally and roughly circular in side profile. Has tall, narrow dorsal and anal fins, and frilled fringe at tail end. **STATUS** Occasional; mainly in W Britain.

Montagu's
Sea Snail

Montagu's
Sea Snail

Lumpsucker,
male

Montagu's Sea
Snail, underside,
showing sucker

European Sea Bass

Thick-lipped Grey Mullet

Ocean Sunfish

Grey Trigger-fish
Balistes capriscus Length to 60cm
Bizarre fish with the look of a
tropical species about it. Found
on rocky coasts, sometimes
around harbour walls. ADULT is
oval in outline with relatively
small eyes and mouth set far
apart. Overall buffish brown;
dorsal, anal and tail fins are
marbled with blue. STATUS
Locally common in the S and
SW, occasional elsewhere.

Grey Trigger-fish

Ballan Wrasse
Labrus bergylta Length to 50cm
Our most familiar and
colourful wrasse. Found
inshore on rocky coasts. ADULT
has a thickset body and long
dorsal fin characteristic of all wrasse. Colour is variable but often marbled reddish brown
or green. STATUS Widespread and locally common except off the coast of E England.

Cuckoo Wrasse *Labrus mixtus* Length to 30cm
Colourful, distinctive wrasse. Found on rocky coasts, venturing inshore in summer
months. ADULT has a rather slender body. Male is mostly blue on head, flanks and tail,
and pinkish orange elsewhere. Female is orange with black spots at base of dorsal fin.
STATUS Widespread and locally common in the S and W; almost absent from the coast of
E England.

Rock Cook *Centrolabrus exoletus* Length to 15cm
Colourful wrasse with a relatively small mouth. Found on rocky coasts and around pier
pilings. ADULT is variably colourful, often with reddish-brown, blue and yellowish
reticulations. Note diagnostic dark band across base of tail. STATUS Widespread and
locally common in the S and W; almost absent from the coast of E England.

Corkwing Wrasse *Symphodus melops* Length to 15cm
Another colourful wrasse. Found on rocky shores with abundant seaweeds. ADULT has
variable colouring, but often yellowish or reddish with blue and red banding, especially
on head. Dark spot at base of tail is diagnostic. STATUS Widespread and locally common
in the S and W.

Corkwing Wrasse

Goldsinny *Ctenolabrus rupestris* Length to 17cm
Distinctive wrasse. Found on rocky coasts with plenty of seaweed cover; usually in
shallow sub-littoral zone. ADULT is rather slim-bodied; mostly pinkish buff, with a
diagnostic dark spot at front of dorsal fin and another at top of tail base. STATUS
Widespread and locally common only on S and W coasts.

Grey Trigger-fish

Ballan Wrasse, juvenile

Ballan Wrasse

Cuckoo Wrasse, male

Cuckoo Wrasse, female

Rock Cook

Corkwing Wrasse

Goldsinny

Dragonet *Callionymus lyra* Length to 20cm

Distinctive fish, broad and flattened at head end, slender and tapering behind. Favours shallow inshore seas; sometimes found in pools on lower shore. **ADULT** has rather long, tapering snout. Breeding male is distinctive: marbled reddish brown with blue spots; 1st dorsal fin is very tall, 2nd marked with blue and yellow. Immatures and females are marbled yellow-brown; 1st dorsal fin is much shorter. **STATUS**

Widespread, but commonest on S and W coasts. **SIMILAR SPECIES Spotted Dragonet** *C. maculatus* (length to 12cm) has a steep, short snout and rather short, almost colourless 1st dorsal fin; this and pectoral fins sometimes have small white spots. SW England and Wales, and Irish Sea coasts. **Reticulated Dragonet** *C. reticulatus* (length to 10cm) also has a steep snout. First dorsal fin is also short but often blackish. Breeding male is patterned with red patches and blue spots. S and W coasts, as far N as Orkney.

Lesser Weever *Echiichthys vipera* Length to 15cm

Notorious fish, capable of inflicting a painful sting to a bather's foot. Found on sandy beaches, mostly buried in substrate during daytime with just eyes visible. **ADULT** has elongate, laterally flattened body with upturned mouth and eyes on top of head. First dorsal fin (with venomous spines) has black membrane; fin is raised in defence. Body is marbled reddish and yellow-grey above, paler below. **STATUS** Widespread and locally common, mainly in S half of Britain.

Greater Weever *Trachinus draco* Length to 40cm

Appreciably larger and more colourful than its Lesser cousin (above). Found on sandy substrates but usually sub-littoral. **ADULT** has elongate, laterally flattened shape with upturned mouth and eyes on top of head. Upperparts marbled with yellow, brown and blue; underparts pale. **STATUS** Widespread but local, mainly in S half of Britain.

Mackerel *Scomber scombrus* Length to 55cm

Fast-swimming predatory fish, popular with anglers. Shoals frequent inshore waters in summer. **ADULT** has streamlined body, pointed head and rather small dorsal fins. Small 'finlets' extend along top and bottom of narrowly tapering tailstock. Body is greenish with black bands above, silver on sides and whitish below; green colour fades to blue after death. **STATUS** Widespread; locally and seasonally common, especially in the S and W.

Boar Fish *Capros aper* Length to 25cm

Bizarre and unmistakable fish. Typically lives near seabed in deep water, but occasionally occurs inshore (or beached, dead), especially in winter, possibly after surviving trawling by-catch. **ADULT** is laterally flattened, rhomboid in side-on profile, with a tall, spiny 1st dorsal fin and very large eyes. **STATUS** Scarce in inshore waters, in the SW only.

John Dory *Zeus faber* Length to 80cm

Another bizarre and unmistakable fish. Regular inshore; usually in fairly deep water but sometimes near surface. **ADULT** is incredibly laterally flattened and angular-oval in side-on profile. Dorsal fin is tall and spiny; other fins are also relatively large. Overall colour is silvery yellow with diagnostic central black spot. **STATUS** Widespread, mainly in the S and W.

Wolf Fish *Anarhichas lupus* Length to 90cm

Unmistakable, superficially eel-like fish. Mostly sub-littoral, usually hiding in crevices in daytime. But sometimes found in deep pools on lower shore. **ADULT** is elongate with large, bulbous head and visible, peg-like teeth. Skin is typically blue-grey but young animals are marbled and banded brown. **STATUS** Locally common in E and NE Scotland only.

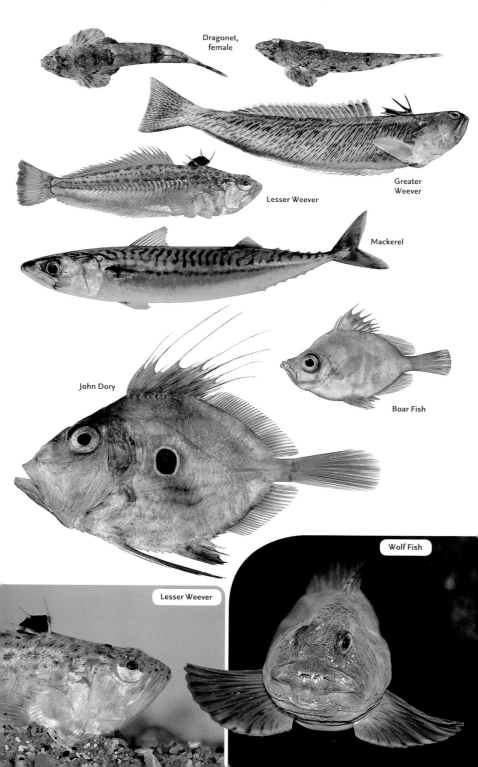

Dragonet,
female

Greater
Weever

Lesser Weever

Mackerel

John Dory

Boar Fish

Wolf Fish

Lesser Weever

Butterfish *Pholis gunnellus* Length to 25cm

Distinctive and unmistakable fish. Found under rocks and seaweed on lower shore. ADULT is superficially eel-like but laterally compressed, yellow body with 15 pale-margined dark spots down dorsal surface. Scales are tiny and embedded in skin; fish is very slippery. STATUS Widespread and locally common; least so in E England.

Sand Eels

Extremely slender fish. Easily recognised as sand eels but specific identification is challenging. Two species are widespread and generally common, more so in the S than N. Both swim in shoals (sometimes both species together), and can burrow into sand and disappear almost instantly if alarmed. Both appear silvery in water; out of water, upper half is greyish yellow and lower half silvery white. In **Lesser Sand Eel** *Ammodytes tobianus* (length to 20cm), dorsal fin starts above pectoral fin; in **Greater Sand Eel** *Hyperoplus lanceolatus* (length to 35cm), dorsal fin starts behind pectoral fin.

Shanny *Lipophrys pholis* Length to 13cm

The commonest blenny on British shores. Found in pools and under rocks on lower shore. Moves around in short bursts, seldom swimming far. Typically props itself up on pectoral fins. ADULT is elongate, smooth and scaleless, with proportionately large head. Has single long dorsal fin with dip in middle. No tentacles on head. Usually mottled and marbled brown and buff. STATUS Widespread and locally common, except in the SE.

Tompot Blenny *Parablennius gattorugine* Length to 25cm

Impressive and colourful blenny. Found on rocky coasts, on lower shore and in sub-littoral zone. ADULT has similar shape overall to Shanny (above), but with stouter body and striking dorsal fin that starts further forward and lacks obvious dip in middle. Head bears pair of frilly tentacles. Colour is variable, but usually marbled reddish brown and buff with dark bands. STATUS Locally common, in the SW only.

Montagu's Blenny
Coryphoblennius galerita Length to 8cm

Colourful and distinctive blenny. Found in pools on rocky coasts, usually on mid-shore. ADULT has similar shape overall to Shanny but with more obvious dip in

middle of dorsal fin and diagnostic tall, frilly tentacle on centre of forehead, with smaller ones behind. Colour is variable but often marbled black, reddish and blue with pale spots. STATUS Locally common but mainly in the S and W.

FAR LEFT: **Tompot Blenny**
LEFT: **Montagu's Blenny**

Butterfish

Lesser Sand Eel

Greater Sand Eel

Shanny

Tompot Blenny

Montagu's Blenny

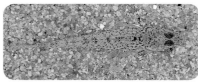

ABOVE: **Sand Goby**; BELOW: **Common Goby**

Small Bottom-dwelling Gobies

Three confusingly similar gobies are recognised by experts. These are notoriously difficult to identify and you could be forgiven for doubting the validity of calling them separate species. Colours and markings are variable and change according to background, and immature animals often lack characters needed for accurate identification. Their 2 dorsal fins are clearly separate (distinguishing them from small Rock and Black gobies, below). But beware confusion with Two-spotted Goby (below), whose spots can 'fade' if fish is kept in a pale container. The following descriptions apply to well-marked animals only. **Sand Goby** Pomatoschistus minutus (length to 65mm) is the most likely small goby you will come across on the shore. Favours sandy coasts and estuaries, and is usually buff, marbled and mottled darker; adult male has a blue-ringed black spot on 1st dorsal fin and scales are present dorsally in front of 1st dorsal fin. Eyes are relatively large and body tapers evenly.

Common Goby P. microps (length to 70mm) is patchily distributed and absent from much of the NE; it favours estuaries and brackish water. Scales are absent dorsally in front of 1st dorsal fin; body has slightly 'hunchback' appearance, and snub nose makes head look almost frog-like. Adult male has dark spot at bases of 1st dorsal and pectoral fins. **Painted Goby** P. pictus (length to 55mm) (not illustrated) is usually sub-littoral on gravelly substrates; there are 4–5 dark patches on flanks and back is subtly banded; 1st dorsal fin has 2 rows of dark spots and dorsal fins have red, blue and yellow hues.

Two-spotted Goby

Gobiusculus flavescens Length to 6cm
Well-marked fish that spends more time swimming in water column than most other gobies. Found among seaweeds and eelgrass beds in shallow water. ADULT has rather streamlined body; marbled brown and buff, with blue spots and pale dorsal patches.
Typically, there is a dark spot at base of tail; male has 2nd dark spot behind pectoral fin.
STATUS Locally common except along the E coast.

Rock Goby Gobius paganellus Length to 12cm

Robust goby. Found in pools and under rocks on lower shore. ADULT has relatively large head and tail; head is rounded in profile and lacks visible lines of papillae seen in Black Goby (below). Typically, body is marbled brown, buff and grey. Some individuals are very dark, leading to confusion with Black Goby. First dorsal fin is short in relative terms (cf. Black Goby); pale yellowish-orange outer margin is diagnostic. Dorsal fins abut one another. Head lacks lines of sensory papillae. STATUS Locally common in the S and W.

Black Goby Gobius niger Length to 16cm

Similar proportions to Rock Goby (above), and often with similar coloration. Favours estuaries and sheltered coasts with muddy substrates; often in eelgrass beds. ADULT has more angular head than Rock Goby, with steeper forehead. Some individuals are uniformly black, but typical colour is marbled brown and grey-buff, sometimes with 4 or 5 dark spots on flanks. First dorsal fin is typically tall and pointed (middle rays are tallest), and lacks a pale margin. Both dorsal fins usually show a dark spot at front; the fins abut one another. Head has lines of sensory papillae. STATUS Locally common, in the S and W.

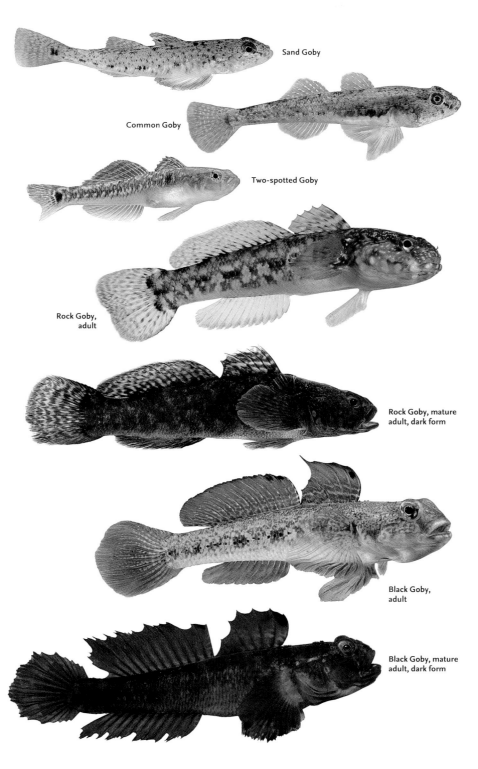

Sand Goby

Common Goby

Two-spotted Goby

Rock Goby, adult

Rock Goby, mature adult, dark form

Black Goby, adult

Black Goby, mature adult, dark form

Lemon Sole *Microstomus kitt* Length to 60cm
Well-marked flatfish, found on sand and gravel; sub-littoral. **ADULT** lives with right side, and eyes, facing uppermost. Outline is oval and head is rather small and rounded. Dorsal and anal fins almost reach tail, which is relatively long. Upper surface is marbled grey and yellowish brown. **STATUS** Widespread and locally common, except in the N and NE.

Dab *Limanda limanda* Length to 25cm
Robust flatfish, found on sandy coasts. **ADULT** lives with right side, and eyes (which are relatively large), facing uppermost. Lateral line on upper surface makes a curving detour above pectoral fin. Upper surface is rough, marbled orange-brown and grey. **STATUS** Widespread and locally common except in the N and NE; declining everywhere.

Flounder *Platichthys flesus* Length to 50cm
One of our most widespread and familiar flatfish. Found on sandy substrates, young animals often inshore. Ventures into freshwater mouths of estuaries. **ADULT** lives with right side, and eyes, facing uppermost. Outline is elongate-oval, and head, tail and tailstock are proportionately large. Mottled patterning resembles sand and gravel. **STATUS** Widespread and locally common.

Plaice *Pleuronectes platessa* Length to 50cm
Well-marked flatfish. **ADULT** lives with right side, and eyes, facing uppermost. Outline is oval-rhomboid with a pointed head and slender tail. Marbled patterning on upper surface is a good match for sand; note the dark-centred red spots. **STATUS** Widespread and locally common.

Plaice, swimming

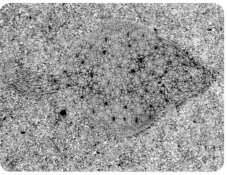

Plaice

Plaice

Lemon Sole

Dab

Flounder

Plaice

Sole *Solea solea* Length to 50cm

Distinctive flatfish whose outline recalls the sole of a shoe. Found on sandy substrates on coasts and in estuaries. **ADULT** lives with right side, and eyes, facing uppermost. Mouth is not terminal, upper pectoral fin has a black spot. Skin is rough and patterned to look like sand and gravel. Anal fin has 61–74 rays. **STATUS** Widespread and locally common in S half of Britain; scarce further N.

displaying pectoral fin

NOTE Black spot on upper pectoral fin is 'flashed' as fin is erected in alarm. This looks very similar to 'warning' issued by Lesser Weever (p. 278), whose fin spines are venomous.

Solenette *Buglossidium luteum* Length to 12cm

Small flatfish, similar to Sole (above) but separable with care. Typically sub-littoral, on sand and gravel, but sometimes in shallows. **ADULT** is narrowly oval, living with right side, and eyes, facing uppermost. Upper pectoral fin lacks a black spot and blind-side pectoral fin is vestigial (fully formed in Sole). Has black line marks every 5th or 6th ray of dorsal and anal fins (those that fringe body). Anal fin has 49–63 rays. Moves in a distinctive, seemingly shuffling manner: ripples the dorsal and anal fins, the black rays looking like slender feet. **STATUS** Locally common, in S Britain only.

Brill *Scophthalmus rhombus* Length to 55cm

Beautifully patterned flatfish. Superbly camouflaged against the sandy substrates it favours. **ADULT** lives with left side, and eyes, facing uppermost. Outline is broadly oval. Anal and dorsal fins are broadest towards tail, and anterior rays of dorsal fin are separated into filaments. **STATUS** Locally common only in the S and SW, N to the Irish Sea.

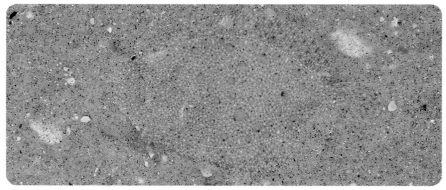

Brill

Topknot *Zeugopterus punctatus* Length to 20cm

Distinctive fish. Unusually for a flatfish, it favours rocky coasts and happily clings onto vertical sides of rock faces. **ADULT** lives with left side, and eyes, facing uppermost. Outline is rounded-oval. Anal and dorsal fins almost meet at head end, and are continuous with tail. Upper surface is typically marbled reddish brown. **STATUS** Widespread and locally common, except on the E coast.

Turbot *Psetta maxima* Length to 70cm

Large flatfish, only juveniles of which are found inshore. Favours sandy substrates. **ADULT** lives with left side, and eyes, facing uppermost. Outline is rhomboid-diamond-shaped with a pointed head and long tail. Upper surface is typical mottled grey with pale and black spots. **STATUS** Locally common in the S and SW.

Sole

Solenette

Brill

Topknot

Turbot

AMPHIBIANS AND REPTILES

Amphibians and reptiles are vertebrate animals. The former have soft skins and breed in water; the latter have a protective layer of scales and lay eggs independent of water. Both groups hibernate during the winter months.

Adder *Vipera berus* Length to 60cm
Well-marked venomous snake. Found in coastal dunes, heath and grassland. **ADULT** is plump-bodied, typically reddish brown or creamy buff with dark zigzag dorsal marking and inverted 'V' on head. Eye has vertical red iris. **STATUS** Widespread but local on mainland coasts.

Adder

Slow-worm

Slow-worm *Anguis fragilis* Length to 40cm
Legless lizard, found in coastal grassland and dunes. **ADULT** has slender, shiny body. Usually coppery brown overall. **STATUS** Widespread but local on mainland coasts, absent from far N and NE; introduced to a few islands.

Common Lizard *Zootoca vivipara* Length to 15cm
Our most widespread lizard. Found on coastal dunes and grassland heaths. **ADULT** is slender with angular, pointed snout. Typically brown with dorsal rows of dark spots, and parallel rows of dark and pale spots on flanks. Juvenile is often all dark. **STATUS** Widespread but local, on mainland coasts.

Common Lizard

Wall Lizard

Common Toad

Natterjack
Toad

Wall Lizard *Podarcis muralis* Length to 17cm
Has a proportionately longer tail than Common
Lizard (facing page). **ADULT** is usually brown with dark
dorsal stripe, incomplete dark stripes on sides defining
brown flanks, and variable dark and white marbling. **STATUS** Native
to Jersey; introduced and locally established on S English coast,
mainly Dorset.

Common Toad *Bufo bufo* Length to 9cm
Familiar toad, found in damp coastal habitats. **ADULT** is olive-
brown to greenish buff; eye has red iris. **STATUS** Widespread
but local on mainland coasts, except in the far N.

Natterjack Toad *Epidalea calamita* Length to 7cm
Unusual toad that burrows freely, and walks rather than hops. Favours dunes
and stabilised saltmarshes with pools. **ADULT** has warty yellowish-brown skin
and diagnostic yellow vertebral stripe. **STATUS** Local populations on coasts of
Dorset, East Anglia and NW England.

Common Frog *Rana temporaria* Length to 10cm
Our commonest amphibian. Found in damp coastal habitats. **ADULT** has smooth skin,
usually olive-yellow, marbled and blotched with brown. Eye has yellow iris, and note dark
mask through eye. **STATUS** Widespread but local on mainland coasts and some islands.

Marsh Frog *Pelophylax ridibundus* Length to 13cm
Large frog, found in coastal marsh drainage ditches where water may be brackish. **ADULT**
is strikingly green, sometimes with dark spots. Male has a loud croaking song, *whoa-aa-
aa-aa*, when grey vocal sacs are visible. **STATUS** Introduced and locally established,
mainly in SE England.

Common Frog

Marsh Frog

INTRODUCING BIRDS

The coast is a great place for birds, and there is more avian diversity on the sea, and on coastal land, than in any other closely allied collection of British habitats. It's little wonder then that birdwatchers also flock to the coast on a regular basis, where they are guaranteed a good day out.

COASTAL HABITATS FOR BIRDS

The coast offers different things to different bird species, and the way its resources are exploited often vary throughout the year. But in essence, coastal habitats provide places for birds to nest and to feed.

CLIFFS

These days, disturbance by man is an important factor affecting the success or otherwise of coastal breeding birds. Cliffs have the great advantage of being virtually inaccessible. Depending on the geology, some offer an array of alternative nesting places and hence support mixed seabird colonies. Auks perhaps show the greatest range of adaptations to cliff living: Puffins dig burrow nests on the top slopes; Guillemots nest on bare ledges on sheer rock faces; and Razorbills breed among boulders lower down. Various gull species, Shags and, in a few locations, Gannets add to the diversity.

A mixed seabird colony, where Herring Gulls are an ever-present threat to the eggs and chicks of Guillemots and other species.

ROCKY SHORES

Although rocky shores are by far the best places to explore for marine invertebrates and fish, they are impoverished in terms of birdlife. A few specialist feeders live here – Oystercatchers, Turnstones and Purple Sandpipers, for example – but few other species can make a living. Well above the high-tide line, and in remote and undisturbed locations, birds such as Eiders, terns and Oystercatchers sometimes attempt to nest.

SAND AND SHINGLE

In locations where human disturbance is controlled or prevented, nesting colonies of terns and gulls are sometimes able to thrive. Working on the principle of safety in numbers, they typically breed at high densities. In the south, Black-headed Gulls and Common Terns are the typical species, while Common Gulls and Arctic Terns often predominate in the north.

A feeding Bar-tailed Godwit that has just caught a juicy Lugworm.

ESTUARIES AND MUDFLATS

These are the most important habitats for feeding birds, and come into their own outside the breeding season. Among the waders found here, a range of different bill lengths and shapes allows the various species to exploit alternative foods. Wildfowl are also well represented, most having a vegetarian diet. Cormorants, grebes and fish-eating duck species patrol the creeks and inlets, while gulls are ever-present scavengers.

This flock of gulls and Gannets has discovered a shoal of small fish at the surface.

INSHORE WATERS

These are feeding grounds for specialist birds, especially those that catch fish and invertebrates. Grebes, divers and true marine duck species are well represented.

OPEN SEA

The open sea is the domain of the true seabirds, many of which spend their entire non-breeding lives beyond sight of land. Petrels, shearwaters, auks and skuas are arguably the quintessential seabirds.

COASTAL TERRESTRIAL HABITATS

Many terrestrial bird species congregate near coasts in the winter months, simply because the weather is milder and feeding easier. So, flocks of widespread passerines such as pipits, Skylarks and Linnets are a familiar sight in suitable habitats at this time. A few specialists, such as Twite, Snow Bunting and Lapland Bunting, are seldom seen away from the shoreline in winter. With all this potential food available for predators, birds such as Short-eared Owl and Merlin are also relatively easy to see near coasts in winter.

ADAPTATIONS FOR THE MARINE ENVIRONMENT

The marine environment is a challenging place and the bird species that live here have to be well adapted to its unforgiving nature. Whether they feed on an estuary or catch fish in the open sea, they must tolerate salt in their diet; indeed, many species have special ways of removing excess salt from their bodies. Another obvious requirement is that their feathers should provide waterproofing and a considerable degree of insulation.

Strong winds are a feature of the coast and on occasion seabirds have to cope with severe conditions. All true seabirds are seemingly indifferent to anything short of storm conditions, and petrels, shearwaters and Gannets have even evolved to use the wind to their advantage. Particularly severe gales blow in seabird species not usually seen in the region, and force migrating birds to pass closer to shore than would normally be the case.

On the seashore, and particularly on estuaries and mudflats, feeding birds sometimes find their food by sight, but many waders also have sensitive bills that can detect prey deep in the mud. Finding and catching food on the open ocean is a real challenge. Many species spot food using their eyes, but shearwaters and petrels can actually smell their food. Reaching the prey is a different matter; the Gannet is the master plunge-diver, while others submerge at the surface. Webbed feet are obviously a great aid to swimming both at the surface and when submerged, but shearwaters and auks also use their wings – in effect, 'flying' underwater.

A plunge-diving Gannet.

Black-throated Diver *Gavia arctica* Length 60–70cm

Swims buoyantly with bill held level. Dives frequently. Sexes are similar. **ADULT** in summer has a blue-grey nape and head, and a black throat; sides of neck have black and white lines. Back is dark with white spots; underparts are white. Winter adult has mainly grey-black upperparts and whitish underparts; note white patch on flanks at water level in swimming birds. **JUVENILE** is similar to winter adult but with more obvious pale margins to back feathers. **VOICE** Mostly silent. **STATUS** Scarce; typically seen on coasts in winter, in winter plumage. Rare breeding species on large Scottish lochs.

Red-throated Diver *Gavia stellata* Length 55–65cm

Swims low in water, head and dagger-like bill tilted upwards. Dives frequently. Sexes are similar. **ADULT** in summer has blue-grey on face and sides of neck, a red throat, and black and white lines on back and lower sides of neck. Upperparts are otherwise brownish grey and underparts are whitish. Winter adult has grey upperparts spangled with small white spots; underparts are white. **JUVENILE** is similar to winter adult but grubby-looking.

VOICE Mostly silent. **STATUS** Locally common on coasts in winter, in winter plumage. Scarce breeding species in Scotland; nests beside freshwater pools but feeds in shallow coastal seas.

LEFT: **Red-throated Diver, summer**
BELOW: **Great Northern Diver, summer**

Great Northern Diver *Gavia immer* Length 75–85cm

Buoyant waterbird. Large bill is held level or very slightly elevated. Sexes are similar. **ADULT** in summer has a black neck with 2 rows of white stripes. Upperparts are blackish with white patches on mantle and spots elsewhere. Underparts are gleaming white. Bill is dark. Winter adult has dark grey upperparts and whitish underparts with a dark half-collar on neck. Bill is greyish. **JUVENILE** is similar to winter adult but pale margins to back feathers are obvious. **VOICE** Silent in our region. **STATUS** Winter visitor to coastal seas; occasionally, birds in breeding plumage are seen.

Little Grebe *Tachybaptus ruficollis* Length 25–29cm

Dumpy, buoyant waterbird with a powderpuff of feathers at rear end. Dives frequently. Wings are rounded and uniform grey-brown. Sexes are similar. **ADULT** in summer is mainly brownish but neck and cheeks are chestnut. Pale-tipped dark bill has a lime-green spot at base. Winter adult has mainly brown upperparts and buffish underparts. **JUVENILE** recalls winter adult but with a pale throat and black stripes on face. **VOICE** Whinnying trill. **STATUS** Local winter visitor to coasts (lagoons, estuaries and sheltered seas). Breeds on freshwater ponds and rivers inland.

Black-throated Diver, 1st winter

Red-throated Diver, winter adult

Great Northern Diver, juvenile

Little Grebe, summer adult

Little Grebe, winter

Great Crested Grebe
Podiceps cristatus Length 46–51cm
Graceful waterbird with a slender neck and dagger-like
bill. White wing panels are revealed in flight. Dives
frequently. Sexes are similar. ADULT in summer has
grey-brown upperparts and mainly whitish underparts;
head has a black cap and crest, and an orange-buff
ruff bordering paler cheeks. Bill is pink and eye is red.
In winter, has drab grey-brown and white plumage.
JUVENILE recalls winter adult but has dark stripes
on cheeks. VOICE Utters wails and croaks in
breeding season. STATUS Locally common on
coasts in winter, although more usually seen
on freshwater lakes, where it also breeds.

Great Crested Grebe, winter

Red-necked Grebe
Podiceps grisegena Length 40–45cm
Smaller and stockier than the Great Crested Grebe
(above), with striking breeding plumage. Note
diagnostic yellow-based bill. White wing panels
are seen in flight. Sexes are similar. ADULT in

Red-necked Grebe, winter

summer has a red neck and upper breast; head has
white-bordered pale grey cheeks and a black cap. Upperparts are otherwise grey-brown
and underparts whitish with grey streaks on flanks. Winter adult loses neck colours but
often retains hint of a reddish collar. Cheek pattern is less well defined and ear coverts
are grubby. JUVENILE recalls winter adult but with more extensive red on neck. VOICE
Mostly silent. STATUS Scarce winter visitor to sheltered inshore seas and estuaries.

Slavonian Grebe, summer

Slavonian Grebe
Podiceps auritus Length 31–38cm
Buoyant little waterbird with a beady red eye.
Flattish crown and white-tipped, even-shaped bill
(both mandibles are curved) allow separation from
Black-necked Grebe (below). White patches on
both leading and trailing edges of wings are seen
in flight. Sexes are similar. ADULT has a reddish-
orange neck and flanks. Back is black and black
head has golden-yellow plumes. Winter adult has
black upperparts and white underparts, with a
clear demarcation between black cap and white
cheeks. JUVENILE is similar to winter adult. VOICE Mostly silent. STATUS Local winter
visitor to sheltered coastal waters. Rare breeding bird in Scotland, on shallow lochs.

Black-necked Grebe *Podiceps nigricollis* Length 28–34cm
Buoyant waterbird with an uptilted bill, steep forehead and beady red eye. White
patch on trailing edge of wing is seen in flight. Sexes are similar. ADULT in summer

Black-necked Grebe, summer

has a blackish head, neck and back,
with golden-yellow tufts on face.
Flanks are chestnut. Winter adult has
mainly blackish upperparts and white
underparts; told from similar Slavonian
Grebe (above) by head shape and greater
extent of black on cheeks. JUVENILE
is similar to winter adult but grubby-
looking. VOICE Mostly silent. STATUS
Known mainly as a scarce winter visitor
to sheltered coasts. A few pairs nest on
shallow, well-vegetated lakes.

Great Crested Grebe, summer

Red-necked Grebe, summer

Slavonian Grebe, winter

Black-necked Grebe, winter

Gannet *Morus bassanus* Wingspan 165–180cm
Our largest seabird. Has deep, powerful wingbeats and glides on stiffly held wings. Bill is large and dagger-like. Dives from a height to catch fish. Sexes are similar. ADULT has mainly white plumage with black wingtips; head has a buffish wash. JUVENILE has dark brown plumage speckled with white dots in 1st year; adult plumage acquired over next 4 years. VOICE Usually silent, but feeding groups are vocal at sea; nesting birds utter grating calls. STATUS Very locally common. Nests colonially and 75% of world population breeds here; visit Bempton Cliffs in Yorkshire or Bass Rock in Scotland for spectacular views. Otherwise, strictly marine and best seen from headlands and boat crossings.

Gannet, immature

Cormorant *Phalacrocorax carbo* Length 80–100cm
Dark waterbird with a heavy, hook-tipped bill. Swims low in water, propelled by large webbed feet. Wings often held outstretched when perched. Sexes are similar. ADULT in summer is mainly dark with an oily sheen and black-bordered brownish feathers on wings, and white on thigh and head. Eye is green; skin at base of bill is yellowish. In winter, white feathering is absent. JUVENILE has brown upperparts and whitish underparts. VOICE Silent except at nest. STATUS Common, favouring sheltered seas and estuaries.

Cormorant, winter

Shag *Phalacrocorax aristotelis* Length 65–80cm
Smaller than Cormorant (above), with a more slender bill. Leaps in order to submerge. Often perches with wings held outstretched. Sexes are similar. ADULT is all-dark but with an oily green sheen. Has a yellow patch at base of bill and a distinct crest. In winter, loses crest; colours at base of bill are subdued. JUVENILE has dark brown upperparts, buffish underparts and a pale throat. Crown peaks on forehead (peaks on rear of crown in juvenile Cormorant). VOICE Silent except at nest. STATUS Locally common on rocky coasts. Nests colonially on sea cliffs.

Shag, winter

Fulmar *Fulmarus glacialis* Wingspan 105–110cm
Gull-like but recognised by tube nostrils, and by stiffly held wings and effortless gliding flight. Swims buoyantly; gathers in groups where feeding is good. Sexes are similar. ADULT typically has blue-grey upperwings and back. Head, underparts and tail are white. Has a dark smudge around eye. Dark-phase (from Arctic) is blue-grey and seen occasionally. JUVENILE is similar to adult. VOICE Gurgling cackles and grunts. STATUS Locally common. Nests colonially on sea-cliff ledges. Otherwise, seen gliding over sea.

Fulmar

Gannet

Shag, juvenile

Cormorant, summer

Shag, summer

Fulmar

European Storm-petrel *Hydrobates pelagicus*
Length 14–16cm

Our smallest seabird. Flutters low over water with dangling feet when feeding. Note square-ended tail. Feet do not project beyond tail in flight. Sexes are similar. **ADULT** is dark sooty brown except for white rump and white bar on underwing. **JUVENILE** is similar but with a subtle, pale wingbar on upperwing. **VOICE** Silent at sea; gurgling, purring calls uttered when breeding. **STATUS** Very locally common breeder. Nests in burrows on remote islands that are visited after dark. Otherwise, comes close to land in daylight only in severe gales. Easy to see from pelagic boat trips from SW England in summer, and from ferry crossings to N Scottish islands.

European Storm-petrel

Wilson's Storm-petrel *Oceanites oceanicus*
Length 16–18cm

Small seabird, marginally larger and broader-winged than European Storm-petrel (above). Best distinguished by differences in structure, markings and flight pattern. Capable of fast direct flight, but also sustained glides and a hovering feeding action, when feet are pattered on the water. Sexes are similar. **ADULT** is dark sooty brown with a distinct pale panel on inner upperwings, and uniformly dark underwings. Has a broad white rump and square-ended tail. Legs project beyond tail in direct flight. Webs of feet are yellow. **JUVENILE** is similar to adult. **VOICE** Silent at sea. **STATUS** Rare summer visitor from breeding grounds in the southern hemisphere. Keenly sought by pelagic boat tours from Isles of Scilly and elsewhere in the SW. Double figures are usually seen each year. Hardly ever seen from land.

Leach's Storm-petrel *Oceanodroma leucorhoa* Length 16–18cm

More robust and longer-winged than European Storm-petrel (above); flight is ever-changing, with powerful wingbeats and glides. Sexes are similar. **ADULT** is dark sooty grey except for a pale panel on upperwing coverts. Fork in tail and grey central line on rump can be hard to see. Underwings are all dark. **JUVENILE** is similar to adult. **VOICE** Silent at sea; weird gurgling rattles are heard when nesting. **STATUS** Truly oceanic. Very locally common but hard to see. Willingly comes close to land only after dark, at breeding colonies. Otherwise, seen from land only during severe gales.

Manx Shearwater, at nest burrow entrance

Manx Shearwater
Puffinus puffinus Wingspan 70–85cm

Skims low over sea on stiffly held wings. Contrasting dark upperparts and mainly white underparts are seen as bird banks and glides. Gregarious when feeding is good. Sexes are similar. **ADULT** has blackish upperparts and mainly white underparts with dark wing margins. **JUVENILE** is similar to adult. **VOICE** Silent at sea; strangled coughing calls are uttered after dark by nesting birds. **STATUS** Fairly common summer visitor. Seen mostly at sea; visits land only to breed, after dark. Nests in burrows on remote islands. Visit Skomer or Bardsey in Wales for close-up views. (See also photograph on following page.)

Wilson's Storm-petrel

Leach's Storm-petrel

European Storm-petrels

Manx Shearwater

Balearic Shearwater *Puffinus mauretanicus* Wingspan 80–88cm

Structurally rather similar to Manx Shearwater (p. 298) but marginally bulkier and more pot-bellied, and with subtly different plumage. Feet project slightly beyond tip of tail in flight. Sexes are similar. ADULT has sooty-brown upperparts. Underparts are overall grubby white but with a brownish suffusion on face and chest, and brown undertail coverts (white in Manx). Underwings have a broader dark margin than in Manx. JUVENILE is similar to adult. VOICE Silent at sea. STATUS Breeds on Balearic Islands in early spring and moves N in summer. Reaches seas off SW Britain in summer, where it is generally rather scarce. Seen from headlands and on pelagic boat trips, probably most easily from Dorset to Cornwall.

Sooty Shearwater *Puffinus griseus* Wingspan 95–110cm

Consummate seabird, capable of a seemingly effortless, gliding flight. Wings are relatively long and narrow, and held straight in gliding flight, but slightly angled when banking in strong winds. Sexes are similar. ADULT can look almost uniformly black in harsh light. Good views reveal mostly a dark sooty-brown plumage, relieved only by a striking silvery panel on underwings. JUVENILE is similar to adult. VOICE Silent at sea. STATUS Common summer visitor to the N Atlantic from breeding grounds in the southern hemisphere. Fairly common in British waters (Jul–Oct), seen from headlands and on pelagic boat trips.

Great Shearwater
Puffinus gravis
Wingspan 105–120cm

ABOVE: **Great Shearwater**
RIGHT: **Great Shearwater,
'flying' underwater in
pursuit of fish**

Impressive shearwater with distinctive markings. Flight is powerful, often involving a seemingly effortless gliding action. Sexes are similar. ADULT has mostly dark brown upperparts with pale margins to feathers on back and innerwing; note dark cap and white collar, and white rump and dark tail. Underparts are mostly white with a dark shoulder patch, innerwing markings and wing margins. JUVENILE is similar to adult. VOICE Silent at sea. STATUS Common summer visitor to the N Atlantic from breeding grounds in the southern hemisphere. Fairly common in British waters (Jul–Oct), seen from headlands and on pelagic boat trips.

Cory's Shearwater *Calonectris diomedea* Wingspan 115–125cm

Similar to Great Shearwater (above) but marginally larger and more thickset, and with more uniform upperparts. Flight is powerful; capable of sustained gliding in strong winds. Sexes are similar. ADULT has mostly brown upperparts, with no noticeable contrast between body and head, and only minimal white on rump. Underparts are mostly white except for dark margin to wings. At close range, note the dark-tipped, pale bill. JUVENILE is similar to adult. VOICE Silent at sea. STATUS Breeds on islands of the E Atlantic and Mediterranean, visiting British waters in summer (mainly Jul–Oct). Favours offshore waters and is seen on pelagic boat trips; also observed from headlands in the SW during periods of onshore winds.

Cory's Shearwater

Great Shearwater

Manx Shearwater

Sooty Shearwater

Balearic Shearwater

Black-headed Gull
Chroicocephalus ridibundus Length 35–38cm
Our most numerous medium-sized gull. Plumage varies
with age and season, but white leading edge to outerwings
is consistent. Sexes are similar. ADULT in summer has a grey
back and upperwings, white underparts and a chocolate-
brown hood. Legs and bill are red. In flight, trailing edge of
outerwing is black. In winter, loses dark hood; white head
has dark smudges above and behind eye. JUVENILE has an
orange-brown flush to upperparts, dark feathers on back, dark
smudges on head, and dark tip to tail. First-winter bird retains
some juvenile characters but loses orange-brown flush. Adult
plumage is acquired through successive
moults over next 2 years. VOICE Raucous calls
include a nasal *kaurrr*. STATUS Widespread and
numerous. Nests colonially and seen in flocks
outside the breeding season.

Black-headed Gull, summer

Black-headed Gull, 1st winter

Mediterranean Gull
Larus melanocephalus Length 36–38cm
Similar to Black-headed Gull (above)
but has a stouter bill and uniformly
pale wings in adult. Sexes are similar. ADULT in
summer has a pale grey back and wing coverts,
and white flight feathers. Note black hood and
white 'eyelids'; bill is mainly red, with a yellow
tip and black sub-terminal band. Legs are deep
red. In winter, loses dark hood; whitish head
has a menacing look created by dark smudges.
JUVENILE has grey-brown upperparts with pale
margins to back feathers. Note darkish flush
on breast. Bill and legs are dark; tail has a dark
terminal band. Adult plumage is acquired by
successive moults over next 2 years. VOICE
Cow-cow-cow call. STATUS Very locally common,
usually among Black-headed Gull flocks. Small
numbers nest in S England. More widespread
outside the breeding season.

ABOVE: **Mediterranean Gull, summer**
BELOW: **Mediterranean Gull, 1st winter**

BELOW: **Little Gull, summer**

Little Gull
Hydrocoloeus minutus Length 25–28cm
Our smallest gull. Has a buoyant, tern-like
flight. Sexes are similar. ADULT in summer has
pale grey upperwings with white wingtips, a
dark hood, dark bill and short reddish legs. In
flight, upperwings have a white trailing edge
and rounded white wingtips; underwings are dark with a white trailing edge. In winter,
similar but loses dark hood; otherwise white head has dark smudges on crown and ear
coverts. JUVENILE has a striking black bar (forming letter 'W') on upperwings and back.
Note dark markings on mantle, nape and ear coverts, and dark tail band; plumage is
otherwise white. Adult plumage is acquired over next 2 years. VOICE Sharp *kyeck* call.
STATUS Regular but scarce passage migrant and winter visitor; mainly coastal.

Black-headed Gull, summer

Black-headed Gull, winter

Mediterranean Gull, winter

Mediterranean Gull, summer

Little Gull, 1st winter

Little Gull, 1st winter

Common Gull, summer

Common Gull, 1st winter

Kittiwake, summer

Common Gull
Larus canus Length 40–42cm
Medium-sized gull. Slimmer-bodied and smaller-billed than larger Herring Gull (p. 306). Sexes are similar. ADULT in summer has a grey back and upperwings with a white trailing margin; black wingtips have white spots. Plumage is otherwise white. Bill is yellowish and legs are yellowish green. In winter, similar but with dark streaks on head and neck; bill is duller with a dark sub-terminal band. JUVENILE has pale-margined brown back feathers and upperwings. Head and underparts are pale with dark streaks, while neck and breast look grubby. Adult plumage is acquired over 2 years. First winter is similar to juvenile but has a grey back; bill is pink with a dark tip. Second winter is similar to adult but with more black on outerwing and broader band on bill. VOICE Mewing *keeow*. STATUS Locally common. Nests close to water, often inland. Outside the breeding season is common on coasts, least so in the S.

Kittiwake
Rissa tridactyla Length 38–42cm
A true seagull: its non-breeding life is spent entirely at sea. Sexes are similar. ADULT has a blue-grey back and upperwings with black wingtips; plumage is otherwise white. Bill is yellow; eye and legs are dark. In flight, wingtips look dipped in black ink. In winter, similar but head has grubby patches behind eye. JUVENILE has black 'V' markings on upperwing; back and upperwing coverts are grey, and note triangle of white on flight feathers, dark tip to tail, black half-collar and dark markings on head; bill is dark. First winter is similar to juvenile but gradually loses dark half-collar and black tail tip. VOICE Diagnostic *kittee-wake* when nesting. STATUS Nests colonially on coastal cliff ledges but also on dockside factories etc. Non-breeding period is spent far out to sea.

Sabine's Gull *Xema sabini* Length 30–35cm
Distinctive seabird. Can be confused with a juvenile Kittiwake (above), but upperwing patterns are separable with care. Sexes are similar. ADULT in summer has a blue-grey back and upperwings, a dark hood, dark wingtips with white spots and a dark bill with a yellow tip. In flight, upperwing pattern is diagnostic: triangular patches of black, white and grey. Tail is forked. In winter, similar but dark smudges on nape replace dark hood. JUVENILE upperwing pattern is similar to adult but triangle of grey is replaced by scaly grey-brown. Forked tail is dark-tipped. VOICE Silent. STATUS Nests in high Arctic and winters at sea in S oceans. Seen here mainly as a southbound offshore passage migrant: pelagic boat trips from Cornwall often encounter adults in late summer; in autumn, mostly juveniles are seen during W gales from W coast headlands.

Kittiwake, adults

Sabine's Gull, adults

Sabine's Gull, juvenile

Kittiwake, juvenile

Common Gull, winter

Common Gull, winter

Common Gull, 1st winter

Lesser Black-backed Gull *Larus fuscus* Length 53–56cm

Recalls Herring (below) and Yellow-legged (p. 308) gulls, but adult's combination of a dark grey back and upperwings and bright yellow legs aids identification. Sexes are similar. **ADULT** in summer has a dark grey back and upperwings. Black wingtips are darker than rest of upperwing except for white trailing edge; plumage is otherwise white. Bill is yellow with an orange spot. Iris is yellow and orbital ring is red. In winter, similar but with streaks on head and neck, and duller leg and bill colours. **JUVENILE** and 1st winter have streaked and mottled grey-brown plumage, palest on head. Upperwings are dark brown and whitish tail is dark-tipped. Eye and bill are dark. Adult plumage is acquired over 3 years. **VOICE** Distinctive *kyaoo* and anxious *ga-ka-ka*. **STATUS** Locally common in summer, nesting colonially on sea cliffs and islands. Most migrate S to Mediterranean outside the breeding season; small numbers remain.

Great Black-backed Gull

Larus marinus Length 64–79cm

Our largest gull species. Bulkier than Lesser Black-backed (above), and adult has a darker back, massive bill and pink legs. Sexes are similar. **ADULT** has almost uniformly dark back and upperwings; wingtips are only marginally darker than rest of wings. Note white patch at tip of wings and broad white trailing edge. Plumage is otherwise white. Bill is yellow with an orange spot. **JUVENILE** and 1st winter are mottled and streaked grey-brown. In flight, brown upperwings have pale panels and inner primaries. Bill is dark, legs are dull pink and whitish tail is dark-tipped. Adult plumage is acquired over 3 years. **VOICE** Deep *kaa-ga-ga* call. **STATUS** Local and coastal in the breeding season. Often

Great Black-backed Gull, 2nd winter

nests in vicinity of mixed seabird colonies and pairs are territorial. Outside the breeding season, is more widespread and numbers are boosted by migrants from N Europe.

Herring Gull *Larus argentatus* Length 56–62cm

Familiar noisy bird and our most numerous large gull species. Often follows boats. Bold when fed regularly. Sexes are similar. **ADULT** in summer has a blue-grey back and

upperwings, with white-spotted black wingtips; plumage is otherwise white. Legs are pink, bill is yellow with an orange spot, and eye is yellow with an orange-yellow ring. In winter, similar but with dark streaks on head and nape. **JUVENILE** and 1st winter are mottled grey-brown with streaked underparts. Legs are dull pink, bill is dark, and spotted, pale tail has a dark tip. Adult plumage is acquired over 3 years. **VOICE** Distinctive *kyaoo* and anxious *ga-ka-ka*. **STATUS** Common, nesting on sea cliffs and in seaside towns; widespread on coasts in winter.

Herring Gull, 1st winter

Lesser Black-backed Gull, winter

Lesser Black-backed Gull, summer

Great Black-backed Gull, summer

Herring Gull, winter

Herring Gull, summer

Yellow-legged Gull *Larus michahellis* Length 52–60cm

Similar plumage to Herring Gull (p. 306) but adult has yellow legs. Associates with other large gull species. Sexes are similar. ADULT in summer has a grey back and upperwings (darker than Herring Gull), with more black and less white in wingtips. In winter, similar but sometimes with small, dark streaks on head. JUVENILE and 1st winter have a grey-brown back and wing coverts, and otherwise dark wings. Head, neck and underparts are streaked, and are paler than similar-age Herring Gull. Adult plumage is acquired over 3 years. VOICE Similar to that of Herring Gull. STATUS S European counterpart of Herring; scarce non-breeding visitor to Britain and Ireland, most frequent in winter.

Glaucous Gull *Larus hyperboreus* Length 62–68cm

Bulky, pale-looking gull. Similar in size to Great Black-backed (p. 306) but closer to Herring (p. 306) in plumage terms. Note adult's white wingtips; bill is massive and legs are pinkish at all times. Sexes are similar. ADULT in winter has a pale grey back and upperwings with white wingtips and trailing margin. Plumage is otherwise mainly white with variable dark streaking on head and neck. Eye has a pale iris and orbital ring is yellow. In breeding plumage (sometimes seen in late winter), is similar but without dark streaks. JUVENILE and 1st winter are mainly pale buffish grey but with very pale primaries. Pink bill is dark-tipped. Adult plumage is acquired over 3 years. Sub-adult plumages are very pale. VOICE *Kyaoo* call and anxious *ga-ka-ka*. STATUS Scarce non-breeding visitor, commonest on N coasts in late winter.

Glaucous Gull, 1st winter   Iceland Gull, 2nd winter

Iceland Gull *Larus glaucoides* Length 52–60cm

Similar to Glaucous Gull (above) but smaller, less bulky and longer-winged. Has a rounded head and rather small bill. Legs are pink at all times. Sexes are similar. ADULT in winter has a pale grey back and upperwings with white primaries and a white trailing edge to wings. Plumage is otherwise mainly white with dark streaks on head and neck.

Bill is yellowish with an orange spot. Eye is yellowish with red orbital ring. In summer, similar but without streaks. JUVENILE and 1st winter are pale grey-buff with white primaries. Bill is dark with a dull pink base. Adult plumage is acquired over 3 years. Sub-adult plumages are very pale. VOICE *Kyaoo* call and anxious *ga-ka-ka*. STATUS Very scarce non-breeding visitor, mainly to coasts in late winter; W Ireland is a hotspot.

Iceland Gull, 1st winter

Yellow-legged Gull, summer

Glaucous Gull, winter

Glaucous Gull, summer

Iceland Gull, winter

Great Skua
Stercorarius skua
Length 48–52cm
Bulky seabird. Gull-like but note dark plumage, large head, and dark legs and dark bill. In flight, shows a striking white wing patch. Part scavenger, part predator and food parasite of Gannet (p. 296). Sexes are similar. **ADULT** is brown with buff and golden-brown streaks. **JUVENILE**

Great Skua, adults

is uniformly dark brown and rufous. **VOICE** Mostly silent. **STATUS** Locally common summer visitor and passage migrant. Nests near seabird colonies in Scotland; Orkney and Shetland are strongholds. Passage birds are invariably seen at sea.

Arctic Skua, pale phase

Arctic Skua
Stercorarius parasiticus
Length 46cm
Aerobatic, graceful seabird with deep wingbeats and narrow, pointed wings. Food parasite of Arctic Tern (p. 314) and Kittiwake (p. 304). Sexes are similar but adults occur in 2 morphs. **ADULT** has a wedge-shaped tail and pointed streamers. Pale morph has a white neck, breast and belly, dark cap and otherwise grey-brown plumage. Note faint yellowish flush

on cheeks. Dark morph is uniformly dark grey-brown. **JUVENILE** is dark rufous brown. **VOICE** Nasal calls near nest. **STATUS** Local summer visitor to Scottish coasts; coastal passage migrant elsewhere.

Pomarine Skua *Stercorarius pomarinus* Length 42–50cm
Shares some plumage features with Arctic Skua (above) but is appreciably larger, with deep, powerful wingbeats, and long, spoon-shaped tail streamers in adult. Sexes are similar. Two adult morphs occur. **ADULT** dark morph (uniformly dark) is seldom seen. Pale morph is more regular, with white neck and belly, dark grey-brown upperparts, yellow-flushed cheeks and a dark breast band. **JUVENILE** is variably barred dark grey-brown. **VOICE** Silent in our region. **STATUS** Scarce passage migrant; Outer Hebrides, NW Ireland and N Norfolk are hotspots.

Long-tailed Skua *Stercorarius longicaudus* Length 36–42cm
Recalls Arctic Skua (above) but is slimmer and with much longer tail streamers in adult; long, pointed wings lack Arctic's white patch. Sexes are similar. **ADULT** has mainly grey-brown upperparts, a dark cap, and a whitish neck and underparts; note faint yellow flush on cheeks. **JUVENILE** is variably barred grey-brown, palest on nape and chest. **VOICE** Silent in our region. **STATUS** Scarce passage migrant; hotspots are Outer Hebrides in spring, and Cornish and N Norfolk coasts in autumn.

Great Skua, adults harassing
Lesser Black-backed Gull

Arctic Skua, pale phase

Arctic Skua, juvenile

Pomarine
Skua

Arctic Skua,
dark phase

Pomarine
Skua, juvenile

Long-tailed
Skua, juvenile

Long-tailed
Skua

Sandwich Tern courtship

Sandwich Tern *Sterna sandvicensis* Length 41cm

Striking seabird with a buoyant flight and distinctive call. Sexes are similar. **ADULT** in summer has a pale grey back and upperwings; note the dark, crested cap and otherwise white plumage. Legs are black, and long black bill is yellow-tipped. Looks very white in flight. Non-breeding plumage (seen from late summer onwards) is similar but forehead is white. **JUVENILE** is similar to non-breeding adult but back is barred and scaly. **VOICE** Harsh *chee-urrick* call. **STATUS** Locally common summer visitor and an early-returning migrant (often here by late Mar). Almost entirely coastal, nesting on shingle beaches and islands.

Little Tern

Little Tern *Sternula albifrons* Length 24cm

Tiny, pale tern that hovers before plunge-diving after fish and shrimps. Sexes are similar. **ADULT** in summer has a grey back and upperwings, a mainly black cap and otherwise white plumage. Note black-tipped yellow bill and yellow-orange legs. In flight, wingtips are dark. Non-breeding plumage (acquired from late summer onwards) is similar, but forehead becomes white and leg and bill colours darken. **JUVENILE** is similar to non-breeding adult but back looks scaly. **VOICE** Raucous *cree-ick* call. **STATUS** Local summer visitor, with scattered coastal colonies on shingle and sandy islands and beaches. Easy to see on coasts of the Solent and N Norfolk in late spring.

Black Tern *Chlidonias niger* Length 24cm

Rather small but distinctive tern with a buoyant flight. Catches insects in flight and picks insects and small fish from surface waters. Sexes are similar. **ADULT** in breeding plumage (May–Jun) is mainly grey and black, with a white undertail. From Jul onwards, plumage appears increasingly mottled as mainly grey and white non-breeding plumage is acquired. **JUVENILE** is similar to a winter adult but back is brownish grey and scaly. **VOICE** Silent in our region. **STATUS** Has bred here on occasions but is really a scarce passage migrant, sometimes seen on coasts and coastal pools.

Sandwich Tern, juvenile

Sandwich Tern

Sandwich Tern

Little Tern

Black Tern

Black Tern, juvenile

Black Tern

Little Tern

Arctic Tern

Arctic Tern
Sterna paradisaea Length 35cm
Graceful seabird with buoyant flight. Plunge-dives for fish. Sexes are similar. ADULT in breeding plumage (the only one seen in our region) has grey upperparts, a black cap and pale underparts, palest on cheeks, darkest on belly. Has a uniformly red bill, short red legs and long tail streamers. In flight from below, flight feathers look translucent, with a narrow, dark trailing edge to primaries. JUVENILE has white underparts, an incomplete dark cap and scaly grey upperparts. In flight from above, has a dark leading edge and white trailing edge to innerwing. Legs and bill are dull. VOICE Harsh *krt-krt-krt* call near nest. STATUS Locally common summer visitor and passage migrant. Colonial nester, always near coasts; commonest in the N.

Common Tern

Common Tern
Sterna hirundo Length 35cm
Similar to Arctic Tern (above) but separable with care. Sexes are similar. ADULT in breeding plumage has grey upperparts, a black cap and whitish underparts. Compared to Arctic, note black-tipped orange-red bill, longer red legs and paler underparts. In flight from below, only inner primaries look translucent and wings have a diffuse dark tip. Non-breeding plumage (sometimes seen in late summer) is similar but has white on forehead and a dark shoulder bar; bill and legs are dark. JUVENILE has white underparts, an incomplete dark cap and scaly grey upperparts; in flight from above, leading and trailing edges of innerwing are dark. VOICE Harsh *kreeear* call. STATUS Widespread summer visitor, commonest on coasts; also a widespread coastal passage migrant.

Roseate Tern

Roseate Tern *Sterna dougallii* Length 38cm
Our rarest breeding tern. Separable from Common and Arctic terns (above) with care. Sexes are similar. ADULT in summer is pale grey above, with a dark cap and whitish underparts faintly flushed pink. Has a red-based dark bill, red legs and long tail streamers. In flight, looks very pale. In non-breeding plumage (sometimes seen in late summer), has white on forehead and loses tail streamers. JUVENILE has white underparts, a partial dark cap and scaly upperparts; upperwings are uniform except for dark leading edge to innerwing. VOICE Disyllabic *chew-vik* call. STATUS Rare summer visitor; most pairs nest near Irish coasts. Scarce coastal passage migrant elsewhere.

Common Tern

Arctic Tern

Common Tern

Arctic Tern

Roseate Tern

Grey Heron

Grey Heron
Ardea cinerea Length 90–98cm
Familiar wetland bird. Stands motionless for long periods. Flies on broad wings with slow, deep wingbeats; neck is held hunched. Sexes are similar. ADULT has a whitish-grey head, neck and underparts, with dark streaks on front of neck and breast; note white forecrown and black sides to crown leading to black nape feathers. Back and upperwings are blue-grey; flight feathers are black. Dagger-like bill is yellowish. JUVENILE is similar but crown and forehead are dark grey. VOICE Harsh *krrarnk* in flight.
STATUS Common resident. Favours freshwater wetlands but also common on coasts, especially estuaries, where it is most numerous in winter.

Little Egret *Egretta garzetta* Length 55–65cm
Unmistakable pure white heron-like bird. Its long black legs have bright yellow toes. Feeds actively in water, often chasing small fish. Has a hunched posture when resting. In flight, neck is held in an 'S' shape and legs are trailing. Sexes are similar. ADULT has pure white plumage. Note yellow eye. Nape plumes are seen in breeding plumage. JUVENILE is similar to adult. VOICE Mostly silent. STATUS Relatively recent British colonist, now locally common on coasts, particularly in the S. Commonest on S England estuaries.

Mute Swan *Cygnus olor* Length 150–160cm
Distinctive large waterbird that is a familiar sight. Swimming birds hold their long neck in an elegant curve. Typically tolerant of people. In flight, shallow, powerful wingbeats produce a characteristic throbbing whine. Sexes are similar but basal knob of bill is largest in males. ADULT has white plumage, although crown may have an orange-buff suffusion. Bill is orange-red with a black base. JUVENILE has grubby grey-brown plumage and a dull pinkish-grey bill. VOICE Mostly silent. STATUS Typically nests beside freshwater habitats, including coastal lagoons. In winter, widespread on sheltered coasts and, particularly, on estuaries.

Shelduck
Tadorna tadorna Length 55–65cm
Goose-sized duck with bold markings. In flight, note contrast between white wing coverts and black flight feathers. Sifts mud for small invertebrates. Nests in burrows. Sexes are separable with care. ADULT male is mainly white but with a dark green head and upper neck (looks black in poor light), chestnut breast band, black belly stripe and flush of orange-buff under tail. Legs are pink and bill is bright red with a knob at

Shelduck, juvenile

base. Adult female is similar but basal knob of bill is much smaller. JUVENILE has mainly buffish-grey upperparts and white underparts. VOICE Courting male whistles; female's call is a cackling *gagaga…* STATUS Common on most estuaries and mudflats. Migrates to favoured sites like Bridgwater Bay in Somerset for summer moult.

Grey Heron

Little Egret

Little Egret

Mute Swan, male

Mute Swan, male

Shelduck, male

Shelduck

Dark-bellied Brent

Brent Goose *Branta bernicla* Length 56–61cm

Our smallest goose and a similar size to Shelduck (p. 316). Subtle plumage patterns allow separation of 2 subspecies that winter here: **Pale-bellied Brent** *B. b. hrota* (breeds on Svalbard and Greenland) and **Dark-bellied Brent** *B. b. bernicla* (breeds in Russia). Seen in sizeable and noisy flocks. In flight, looks dark except for white rear end. All birds have a black bill and black legs. Sexes are similar. **ADULT** Pale-bellied has a blackish head, neck and breast; side of neck has a narrow band of white feathers. Note neat division between dark breast and pale grey-buff belly. Back is uniform dark brownish grey. Adult dark-bellied is similar but belly is darker and flanks are paler. **JUVENILES** are similar to respective adults but note pale feather margins on back and absence of white markings on side of neck; white on neck is acquired in mid-winter. **VOICE** Very vocal, uttering a nasal *krrrut*. **STATUS** Winter visitor to coasts. Pale-bellied Brents occur mainly in Northern Ireland and NE England; dark-bellied Brents occur mainly in S England.

Barnacle Goose

Barnacle Goose

Branta leucopsis Length 58–69cm

Small, well-marked goose seen in large, noisy flocks. All birds have black legs and bill. Looks strikingly black and white in flight. Sexes are similar. **ADULT** has a mainly white face with a black line from bill to eye; black crown and nape merge with black neck and breast. Belly is whitish grey with faint dark barring on flanks; back is grey with well-defined black and white barring. Stern is white while tail is black. **JUVENILE** is similar to adult but white elements of plumage are often tinged yellow and barring on back is less well defined. **VOICE** Loud, barking calls. **STATUS** Winter visitor to coastal farmland and saltmarshes. Populations on Solway Firth and Islay are impressive.

Mallard, male

Mallard *Anas platyrhynchos* Length 50–65cm

Our most familiar duck. In flight, both sexes show a white-bordered blue speculum. Sexes are dissimilar. **ADULT** male has a yellow bill and shiny green head and upper neck, separated from chestnut breast by a striking white collar. Underparts are grey-brown except for black stern and white tail. Back is grey-brown, grading to reddish brown. Legs and feet are orange. In eclipse, male resembles adult female, but note yellow bill and well-defined reddish-brown breast. Adult female has an orange-brown bill and mottled brown plumage. Legs and feet are dull orange-yellow. **JUVENILE** is similar to adult female. **VOICE** Male utters whistles and nasal calls; female utters familiar quack. **STATUS** Widespread, commonest on lowland lakes but also found on estuaries and sheltered coasts, mainly in winter.

Pale-bellied Brent

Dark-bellied Brent

Barnacle Goose

Mallard, female

Mallard, male

Wigeon *Anas penelope* Length 45–47cm

Attractive duck. Forms flocks in winter. Sexes are dissimilar. ADULT male has mainly orange-red head with yellow forehead. Breast is pinkish; plumage otherwise finely marked grey except for white belly and black and white stern. In flight, has white patch on wing. Bill is grey, dark-tipped. In eclipse, recalls female but with white wing patch. Adult female is reddish brown, darkest on head and back, with white belly and stern. In flight, lacks male's white wing patch. Bill grey and dark-tipped. JUVENILE resembles adult female. VOICE Male utters *wheeeoo* whistle. STATUS Locally common winter visitor to estuaries.

Wigeon, males and females

Teal *Anas crecca* Length 34–38cm

Small duck. Forms flocks in winter. Often nervous and flighty. In flight, both sexes show white-bordered green speculum. Sexes are otherwise dissimilar. ADULT male has a chestnut-orange head with a yellow-bordered green patch through eye. Plumage is otherwise finely marked grey except for black-bordered yellow stern and white line along flanks. Bill is dark grey. In eclipse, resembles adult female. Adult female has mottled grey-brown plumage. Bill is grey, flushed yellow at base. JUVENILE is similar to adult female but warmer buff. VOICE Male utters a ringing whistle; female makes a soft quack. STATUS Locally common winter visitor to estuaries and mudflats.

Teal, male

Garganey *Anas querquedula* Length 37–41cm

Teal-sized summer visitor. Favours emergent wetland vegetation. In flight, male shows a pale blue-grey forewing and white-bordered greenish speculum; female's speculum is brown. Sexes are dissimilar. ADULT male has a reddish-brown head and broad white stripe above and behind eye. Breast is brown but otherwise plumage is greyish, except for mottled brown stern. In eclipse, resembles adult female but retains wing patterns. Adult female has mottled brown plumage; similar to a female Teal (above) but bill is uniform grey with a pale spot at base. JUVENILE resembles adult female. VOICE Male utters a diagnostic rattle. STATUS Seen mainly on migration, mostly on coastal pools.

Shoveler *Anas clypeata* Length 44–52cm

Unmistakable bill shape. Usually unobtrusive. In flight, male shows a blue forewing panel and white-bordered green speculum; in the female, the blue is replaced by grey. Sexes are dissimilar overall. ADULT male has a shiny green head, white breast, and chestnut on flanks and belly. Stern is black and white, and back is mainly dark. Has a yellow eye and dark bill. In eclipse, resembles adult female although body is more rufous and head greyer. Adult female has mottled buffish-brown plumage and yellowish bill. JUVENILE is similar to adult female. VOICE Male utters a sharp *tuk-tuk*; female makes a soft quack. STATUS Widespread on coasts in winter but seldom numerous.

ABOVE: **Garganey, male**; RIGHT: **Shoveler, males**

Wigeon, female

Wigeon, male

Teal, female

Teal, male

Garganey, female

Garganey, male

Shoveler, female

Shoveler, male

Pintail

Anas acuta Length 51–66cm
Recognised by its elongated
appearance; male is
unmistakable. In flight,
male's grey wings and green
speculum are striking;
female's white trailing edge
on innerwing is obvious.
Sexes are dissimilar in other
regards. ADULT male has
a chocolate-brown head
and nape, with white breast
extending as stripe up side of
head. Plumage is otherwise
grey and finely marked, but
note cream and black stern,
and long, pointed tail, often
held at an angle. In eclipse,
resembles adult female but
retains wing pattern. Adult
female has mottled buffish-

ABOVE: **Pintail, male**; BELOW: **Pintail, female**

brown plumage. JUVENILE is similar to adult
female. VOICE Male utters a whistle; female's
call is grating. STATUS Fairly common in
winter, often on estuaries.

Greater Scaup *Aythya marila* Length 42–51cm

Bulky diving duck. Gregarious outside the
breeding season. In flight, has a striking white
wingbar. Sexes are dissimilar. ADULT male has
a green-glossed head and dark breast (look
black in poor light). Belly and flanks are white,
back is grey and stern is black. Has a yellow eye and dark-tipped grey bill. In eclipse, dark
elements of plumage are buffish brown. Adult female has mainly brown plumage, palest
and greyest on flanks and back; has a white patch at base of bill. JUVENILE is similar to
adult female but white on face is duller. VOICE Mostly silent. STATUS Local winter visitor
to sheltered coasts.

Common Scoter *Melanitta nigra* Length 44–54cm

Male is our only all-black duck. Rather long tail is sometimes raised when swimming.
Gregarious outside the breeding season. In flight, looks mainly dark but paler flight
feathers can sometimes be seen. Sexes are dissimilar. ADULT male has uniformly black
plumage. Head sheen is visible only at close range. Bill is mostly dark but with a yellow
ridge; base is bulbous. First-winter male has browner plumage and an all-dark bill. Adult
female has mainly dark brown plumage with pale buff cheeks. JUVENILE resembles adult
female. VOICE Mostly silent. STATUS Locally fairly common in winter, found on coasts
with sandy and mixed seabeds.

Velvet Scoter *Melanitta fusca* Length 51–58cm

Bulky diving duck. Larger than Common Scoter (above), with which it associates. All
birds have white inner flight feathers, most obvious in flight. Head markings are useful
in identification. Sexes are dissimilar. ADULT male has mainly black plumage, with a
striking white patch below pale eye; white on closed wings is sometimes visible when
swimming. Bill is 2-toned: yellow and blackish. First-winter male lacks white under eye.
Adult female is mainly dark sooty brown, with a pale cheek patch and pale patch at base
of bill; bill is dark. JUVENILE resembles adult female. VOICE Mostly silent. STATUS Scarce
winter visitor to coasts and sandy and mixed seabeds. Commonest in the N.

Pintail, male

Greater Scaup, female

Greater Scaup, male

Common Scoter, female

Common Scoter, male

Velvet Scoter, female

Velvet Scoter, male

Goldeneye *Bucephala clangula* Length 42–50cm
Well-marked diving duck. In flight, all birds show white on innerwings (extent greatest in males). Sexes are dissimilar in other respects. ADULT male is mainly black and white. Rounded, peaked, green-glossed head has a yellow eye and striking white patch at base of bill. In eclipse, resembles an adult female but retains his more striking white wing pattern. Adult female has a mainly grey-brown body, pale neck, dark brown head and yellow eye. JUVENILE is similar to adult female but with dark eye. VOICE Displaying male utters squeaks and rattles. STATUS Locally common in winter, mostly on estuaries.

Goldeneye, male

Long-tailed Duck

Clangula hyemalis Length 40–47cm
Elegant diving duck, at home in the roughest of seas. Dives for bottom-dwelling invertebrates. In flight, has dark wings and mainly white underparts. Sexes are dissimilar. ADULT male in winter and spring looks mainly black, grey and white, with a buffish patch around eye and pink band on bill. In summer and eclipse (both seldom seen here), has mainly brown and black plumage, with white on belly and flanks and pale buff eye patch; bill is dark. Adult female in winter is mainly brown and white; face is white except for dark cheek patch and crown. In summer, similar but face is mainly brown, with pale eye patch. JUVENILE is similar to adult female in summer. VOICE Male utters a nasal *ow-owlee*. STATUS Local winter visitor, commonest in the N. Favours shallow coastal seas.

Long-tailed Duck, winter female

Eider *Somateria mollissima* Length 50–70cm
Bulky seaduck with a distinctive profile: wedge-shaped bill forms a continuous line with slope of forehead. Usually gregarious. In summer, female flocks supervise a 'crèche' of youngsters. Sexes are dissimilar. ADULT male has mainly black underparts and white upperparts, except for a black cap, lime-green nape and pinkish flush on breast. In eclipse, plumage is brown and black, with scattered white feathers. Adult female is brown with darker barring. JUVENILE is similar to adult female but with a pale stripe above eye. VOICE Male utters an endearing, cooing *ah-whooo*. STATUS Nests close to seashore and feeds in inshore waters, diving for prey such as mussels.

Red-breasted Merganser

Mergus serrator Length 52–58cm
Slim duck with a shaggy crest. Dives frequently after fish. In flight, all birds show white on upper surface of innerwing; extent is greatest in male. Sexes are dissimilar in other regards. ADULT male has a narrow red bill, green head, white neck and orange-red breast. Flanks are grey and back is black. In eclipse, similar to adult female but retains extensive white on wing. Adult female has a red bill, dirty orange head and nape, and paler throat; body is otherwise greyish buff. JUVENILE resembles adult female. VOICE Mostly silent. STATUS Common on estuaries and sheltered coasts in winter.

Red-breasted Merganser, male

Goldeneye,
male

Goldeneye,
female

Long-tailed Duck, winter male

Long-tailed Duck, winter female

Eider, male

Eider, female

Red-breasted
Merganser, male

Red-breasted
Merganser, female

Razorbill, adult and egg

Razorbill *Alca torda* Length 41cm

Bulky seabird with a distinctive bill and essentially black and white plumage. Swims well and flies on whirring wingbeats. Sexes are similar. ADULT in summer has a black head, neck and upperparts, and white underparts; note white wingbar. Bill is large and flattened, with vertical ridges and white lines. In winter, similar but throat and cheeks are white and bill is smaller. JUVENILE is similar to winter adult, but smaller and with a proportionately smaller bill. VOICE Mostly silent. STATUS Locally common in seabird colonies on rocky coasts in the W and N. Nests under boulders and in crevices on cliff ledges. Pelagic outside the breeding season; healthy birds are seldom seen close to land. Vulnerable to oil spills.

Guillemot, adult and egg

Guillemot *Uria aalge* Length 42cm

Familiar seabird that nests in densely packed breeding colonies. Swims well and flies on whirring wingbeats. Sexes are similar. ADULT in summer has a chocolate-brown head and upperparts (darkest in N birds), and white underparts. Bill is dark and dagger-like. So-called 'Bridled Guillemot' has a white 'spectacle' around eye. In winter, has white on cheeks and throat, but a black line running back from eye. JUVENILE is similar to winter adult, but smaller and with a proportionately smaller bill. VOICE Growling calls at breeding colonies. STATUS Locally numerous at seabird colonies with precipitous cliff ledges. Moves offshore outside the breeding season. Suffers badly in oil spills.

Puffin, adult at burrow

Puffin *Fratercula arctica* Length 30cm

Endearing seabird. Flies on narrow wings with whirring wingbeats. Swims well and dives frequently for fish. Sexes are similar. ADULT in summer has mainly dark upperparts with a dusky face; underparts are white. Legs are orange-red and bill is huge, flattened and marked with red, blue and yellow. In winter, similar but with a dark grey face and smaller, duller bill. JUVENILE is similar to winter adult but with a small, dark, dull bill. VOICE Groaning calls at nest. STATUS Locally common. Comes ashore only in breeding season. Colonial nester, excavating burrows in grassy cliffs. Only storm-driven, sick or oiled birds are seen near land in winter.

Razorbill, summer

Guillemot, summer

Puffin, summer

Puffin

Razorbill

Guillemot

Little Auk *Alle alle* Length 20cm

Tiny, dumpy auk with a short neck and tiny, stubby bill. Flies on whirring wingbeats and can look almost Starling-like in flight. Swims well and dives frequently. Sexes are similar. ADULT in winter has a black cap, nape and back, and white underparts; at close range, note white lines on wings and tiny white crescent above eye. Not seen in breeding plumage in our region. JUVENILE is similar to winter adult. VOICE Silent at sea. STATUS Winter visitor from Arctic breeding grounds, where it is locally abundant. Numerous in N North Sea in winter, but seldom comes close to land.

ABOVE: **Little Auk, winter adults**
RIGHT: **Black Guillemot, winter**

Black Guillemot *Cepphus grylle* Length 34cm

Charming coastal auk. Dives for Butterfish (p. 280) and other bottom-dwellers. Sexes are similar. ADULT in summer has mainly sooty-brown plumage except for a striking white patch on wing. Has red legs and an orange-red gape. In winter, has scaly grey upperparts and white upperparts; black wings and contrasting white wing patch are retained. First-winter bird is similar to winter adult but white wing patch contains dark markings. JUVENILE is similar to winter adult. VOICE High-pitched whistling calls. STATUS Resident in inshore waters of Ireland and N and W Scotland.

Kingfisher *Alcedo atthis* Length 16–17cm

Dazzling bird with a dagger-like bill. Perches near water and plunge-dives after small fish. Flies low over water on whirring wings. Sexes are separable. ADULT male has orange-red underparts and mainly blue upperparts with an electric-blue back. Legs and feet are red, and bill is all dark. Adult female is similar but base of lower mandible is flushed red. JUVENILE is similar to adult but bill tip is pale. VOICE High-pitched call in flight. STATUS Usually favours fresh waters but moves to coasts in winter, especially in cold weather.

Short-eared Owl

Short-eared Owl *Asio flammeus* Wingspan 95–110cm

Well-marked owl that often hunts in daylight. Flight is leisurely, often with stiffly held wings. Perches on fenceposts. Sexes are similar. ADULT and JUVENILE have buffish-brown plumage, heavily spotted and streaked on upperparts; underparts are streaked but paler. Facial disc is rounded; note yellow eyes and short 'ear' tufts. VOICE Silent away from breeding grounds. STATUS Local winter visitor to coastal grasslands.

Hen Harrier *Circus cyaneus* Wingspan 100–120cm

Graceful broad-winged, long-tailed raptor. Typically seen in gliding flight, hunting low over ground. Sexes are dissimilar. ADULT male has mainly pale grey plumage except for dark wingtips, white rump, and white belly and flanks. Adult female is mostly brown, barred underneath and with a white rump. JUVENILE is similar to adult female. VOICE Silent outside breeding season. STATUS Local winter visitor to coastal grasslands.

Little Auk, winter

Black Guillemot, summer

Kingfisher, female

Hen Harrier, male

Black Guillemot, summer

Short-eared Owl

Hen Harrier, female

Osprey *Pandion haliaetus* Wingspan 145–160cm
Fish-eating raptor. Feeds by hovering, then plunges talons first into water. Sexes are similar. **ADULT** has mainly brown upperparts, except for pale crown; underparts are mainly whitish with a darker chest band. In flight from below, looks pale overall with dark carpal patches. **JUVENILE** is similar to adult but darker markings are less distinct. **VOICE** Various whistling calls. **STATUS** Breeds mainly in N Britain. Passage migrants sometimes linger for a few days on S coast estuaries.

White-tailed Eagle *Haliaeetus albicilla* Wingspan 190–240cm
Immense raptor with parallel-sided wings and a wedge-shaped tail. Catches fish and waterbirds while hunting low over water. Sexes are similar. **ADULT** is mainly brown, palest on head and neck. At rest, tail is often obscured by wings. Bill and legs are yellow. **JUVENILE** is similar to adult but tail is dark. Adult plumage is acquired over successive moults. **VOICE** Whistling calls. **STATUS** Reintroduced to a few Hebridean islands; easy to see on Mull. Usually spotted near coasts.

ABOVE: **White-tailed Eagle, juvenile**

ABOVE: **Kestrel, male**
RIGHT: **Peregrine, adult attacking Lapwing**

Kestrel *Falco tinnunculus* Wingspan 65–80cm
Small falcon that hovers where perches are not available. Feeds on small mammals, ground-dwelling birds and insects. Sexes are dissimilar. **ADULT** male has a spotted orange-brown back, blue-grey head, and blue-grey tail with black terminal band. Underparts are creamy buff with bold black spots. Adult female has barred brown upperparts and pale creamy-buff underparts with dark spots. **JUVENILE** resembles adult female but upperparts are more reddish brown. **VOICE** Shrill *kee-kee-kee*… **STATUS** Common in most coastal districts.

Peregrine *Falco peregrinus* Wingspan 95–115cm
Impressive raptor. Soars on bowed wings but stoops on prey (flying birds) at great speed with wings swept back. Sexes are similar but male is smaller than female. **ADULT** has dark blue-grey upperparts and pale, barred underparts. Note dark mask on face and powerful yellow legs and feet. **JUVENILE** is similar to adult but upperparts are brownish while paler underparts are suffused with buffish orange. **VOICE** Loud *kek-kek-kek*… in alarm. **STATUS** Widespread resident on coasts of N and W Britain and Ireland; increasing elsewhere.

Merlin *Falco columbarius* Wingspan 60–65cm
Our smallest raptor. Flies fast and low after prey such as Meadow Pipit (p. 346). Sexes are dissimilar. **ADULT** male has blue-grey upperparts and streaked and spotted buffish underparts. Adult female has brown upperparts and pale underparts with large brown spots. **JUVENILE** resembles adult female. **VOICE** Mostly silent. **STATUS** Breeds on moors in the N. Seen near coasts in winter.

Merlin, female

Osprey

White-tailed Eagle

Kestrel, female

Merlin, male

Peregrine

Oystercatcher *Haematopus ostralegus* Length 43cm

Distinctive black and white wader with a loud alarm call. Powerful bill is used to hammer molluscs off rocks. Sexes are similar. **ADULT** in summer has black upperparts and white underparts with a clear demarcation between the two. Note red bill, pinkish legs and beady red eye. In winter, similar but has a white half-collar. **JUVENILE** is similar to summer adult but black elements of plumage are brownish and bill and leg colours are subdued. **VOICE** Loud, piping *peep* call. **STATUS** Breeds commonly on coasts where not disturbed. Mainly coastal in winter, favouring estuaries and mudflats.

Avocet *Recurvirostra avosetta* Length 43cm

Elegant wader with distinctive black and white plumage. Feeds by sweeping its diagnostic upcurved bill from side to side through water. Gregarious outside the breeding season. Sexes are similar. **ADULT** has mainly white plumage with black on crown, nape and wings. Legs are blue and bill is black. **JUVENILE** is similar but black elements of plumage are dark brown. **VOICE** Ringing *klueet-klueet...* call. **STATUS** Favours shallow, brackish coastal lagoons in the breeding season. In winter, found on estuaries, mainly in SW England.

Golden Plover *Pluvialis apricaria* Length 28cm

Beautifully marked wader with an evocative call. Gregarious outside the breeding season; often associates with Lapwings (p. 334). In flight, note white underwings. Sexes are sometimes separable in summer. **ADULT** in summer has spangled golden upperparts bordered by a white band. In most males, belly is black, grading to grey on neck and face. Most females have less distinct dark underparts and face is often whitish. Breeders from N Europe (seen on migration) have darker underparts than British birds. In winter, underparts are pale, and head, neck and back are streaked golden. **JUVENILE** is similar to winter adult. **VOICE** *Peeoo* flight call and plaintive *pu-peeoo* in summer. **STATUS** Breeds on N upland moors. Widespread on lowland grassland in winter, particularly near coasts.

Grey Plover *Pluvialis squatarola* Length 28cm

Plump-bodied coastal wader. Best known in winter plumage but breeding plumage is sometimes seen in newly arrived, or soon to depart, migrants. In flight, note black 'armpits' on otherwise white underwings. Typically solitary except at roost. Sexes are similar. **ADULT** in winter is greyish overall, spangled above with black and white, and underparts are whitish. Legs and bill are dark. In summer plumage, has striking black underparts separated from spangled grey upperparts by a broad white band. **JUVENILE** resembles winter adult but has a buff wash to plumage. **VOICE** Diagnostic trisyllabic *pee-oo-ee* call, like a human wolf-whistle. **STATUS** Nests in the high Arctic; non-breeding visitor to British and Irish coasts.

TOP: **Golden Plover, juvenile**
ABOVE: **Golden Plover, summer**
BELOW: **Grey Plover, summer**
BELOW RIGHT: **Grey Plover, winter**

Oystercatcher, winter

Oystercatcher, summer

Avocet

Golden Plover, juvenile

Grey Plover, winter

Ringed Plover *Charadrius hiaticula* Length 17–19cm

Small, dumpy coastal wader. Runs at speed before pausing and picking food items from the ground. Note white wingbar in flight. Sexes are separable. ADULT male in summer has sandy-brown upperparts and white underparts with a black breast band and collar. Has black and white markings on face, and white throat and nape. Legs are orange-yellow and bill is orange with a dark tip. Adult female in summer is similar but black elements of plumage are duller. Winter adult is similar to summer adult but most black elements of plumage are sandy brown, and has a pale supercilium. Leg and bill colours are dull. JUVENILE is similar to winter adult but breast band is often incomplete. VOICE Soft *tuu-eep* call. STATUS Locally common. Nests mainly on sandy or shingle beaches. Coastal outside the breeding season; numbers are boosted by migrants from Europe.

Little Ringed Plover

Charadrius dubius Length 15–17cm
Similar to Ringed Plover (above) but lacks the white wingbar. Sexes are similar. ADULT in summer has sandy-brown upperparts and white underparts, with a black collar and breast band, and black and white markings on head. Has a black bill, yellow legs and yellow eye-ring. Female has duller black elements of head plumage than male. JUVENILE has black elements of plumage replaced by sandy brown. Breast band is usually incomplete, leg and eye-ring colours are dull, and head lacks pale supercilium seen in juvenile Ringed Plover. VOICE *Pee-oo* call. STATUS Nests beside flooded gravel pits but migrants turn up on coasts.

Little Ringed Plover, juvenile

Kentish Plover *Charadrius alexandrinus* Length 15–17cm

Dumpy, pale-looking coastal plover. Note white wingbar in flight. Sexes are dissimilar. ADULT male in summer has sandy-brown upperparts and white underparts. Sandy crown has black at front and rufous at back. Has black through eye and dark patch on side of breast. Legs and bill are black. Summer adult female and winter adult are similar, but black elements of plumage are pale sandy brown (same colour as upperparts) and legs are dull brown. JUVENILE Resembles summer adult female. VOICE Soft *bruip* call. STATUS Scarce passage migrant, found on sandy estuaries.

Lapwing *Vanellus vanellus* Length 30cm

Pied-looking wader with a spiky crest. Has rounded black and white wings in flight. Sexes are separable in summer. ADULT male in summer has green- and purple-sheened dark upperparts; underparts are white except for orange vent, black foreneck, and black and white markings on throat. Adult female in summer has less distinct black neck markings and a shorter crest. Winter adult is similar to summer female but throat and foreneck are white, and back feathers have buffish fringes. JUVENILE is similar to winter adult but crest is short and back looks scaly. VOICE Choked *pee-wit* call. STATUS Nests on grassland; flocks gather near coasts in winter.

Lapwing

Ringed Plover, summer male

Ringed Plover, juvenile

Little Ringed Plover

Kentish Plover, male

Lapwing

Dunlin, winter flock

Dunlin

Calidris alpina Length 17–21cm
Our commonest small wader.
Forms large flocks in winter.
Sexes are similar. ADULT in
summer (seen on coasts in
spring and autumn) has a
reddish-brown back and cap,
and whitish underparts with a
bold black belly. Adult in winter
has uniform grey upperparts
and white underparts. JUVENILE
has reddish-brown and black
feathers on back; pale feather margins align to form 'V' patterns. Underparts are whitish
but with streak-like black spots on flanks and breast. VOICE *Preeit* call. STATUS Local
breeding species in N Britain. Locally abundant on estuaries and muddy shores outside
the breeding season thanks to migrants from the Arctic.

Curlew Sandpiper, juvenile

Curlew Sandpiper

Calidris ferruginea Length 19–21cm
Similar to Dunlin (above) but has a
long, downcurved bill and white rump.
Sexes are similar. ADULT in summer
has a spangled reddish-brown, black
and white back, and (briefly) brick-red
on face, neck and underparts (looks
mottled in moulting migrants). Winter
adult (seldom seen here) has greyish
upperparts and white underparts.
JUVENILE (commonest plumage
encountered here) has a scaly-looking back, white belly and buffish breast; note pale
supercilium. VOICE Soft *prrrp* call. STATUS Breeds in the high Arctic and seen here as a
scarce passage migrant, usually on estuaries and coastal pools, and often with Dunlins.

Little Stint, juvenile

Little Stint

Calidris minuta Length 13–14cm
Tiny wader that feeds in a frantic
manner. Legs and bill are dark in all
birds. Sexes are similar. ADULT in
summer has white underparts, reddish
brown on back, and a variable suffusion
of rufous on head and neck. Note yellow
'V' on mantle, and pale supercilium.
Winter adult has grey upperparts and
white underparts. JUVENILE has white
underparts. Reddish-brown and black
feathers on back and wings have pale
fringes that align to form white 'V'
markings. Note pale, forked supercilium and pale forecrown. VOICE Shrill *stip* call.
STATUS Regular passage migrant, most numerous in autumn.

Temminck's Stint *Calidris temminckii* Length 14–15cm

Tiny, slim-bodied wader with a deliberate feeding action. Differs from Little Stint
(above) in having short yellow legs, and a longer tail and wings. Sexes are similar. ADULT
in summer has grey-brown upperparts, and a streaked grey head, neck and breast;
many back feathers have dark centres. Adult winter (not seen here) has uniform grey-
brown upperparts and white underparts. JUVENILE has white underparts and brownish
upperparts with a scaly-looking back. VOICE Trilling call. STATUS Scarce passage migrant,
usually seen on margins of coastal lagoons.

Dunlin, summer

Dunlin, winter

Curlew Sandpiper, summer

Little Stint, summer

Temminck's Stint

Knot, summer

Sanderling, winter

Wood Sandpiper

Green Sandpiper

Common Sandpiper

Knot *Calidris canutus* Length 25cm

Dumpy wader with a white wingbar. Forms large flocks in winter. Sexes are similar. ADULT in winter has uniform grey upperparts and white underparts. Bill is dark and legs are dull yellowish green. Adult in summer plumage (seen in spring or autumn) has an orange-red face, neck and underparts; back is marked with black, red and grey. Legs and bill are dark. JUVENILE resembles winter adult but has a scaly-looking back and peachy flush to breast. VOICE Sharp *kwet* call. STATUS Non-breeding visitor. Locally common in winter on estuaries and mudflats.

Sanderling *Calidris alba* Length 20cm

Small wader. Runs at speed beside breaking waves. Has a white wingbar and black legs and bill. Sexes are similar. ADULT in winter has grey upperparts and white underparts. In summer plumage (sometimes seen in spring or autumn), head and neck are flushed red and back has dark-centred feathers; underparts are white. JUVENILE is similar to winter adult but many back feathers have dark centres. VOICE Sharp *plit* call. STATUS Locally common non-breeding visitor, mainly to sandy beaches.

Wood Sandpiper *Tringa glareola* Length 19–21cm

Elegantly proportioned wader. Legs are yellowish and relatively long. In flight, note white rump and barred tail. Sexes are similar. ADULT has spangled brownish upperparts. Head and neck are streaked, and otherwise pale underparts have faint streaks and spots. JUVENILE is similar but upperparts are browner and marked with pale buff spots. VOICE *Chiff-chiff-chiff* flight call. STATUS Widespread and fairly common passage migrant, usually seen on coastal freshwater pools.

Green Sandpiper *Tringa ochropus* Length 21–23cm

Plump-bodied wader with a bobbing gait. Has a white rump and tail marked with a few broad, dark bands. Sexes are similar. ADULT has dark brown upperparts with small pale spots. Head and neck are streaked. Underparts are white. Legs are greenish yellow. JUVENILE is similar but pale spotting on upperparts is more noticeable. VOICE Trisyllabic *chlueet-wit-wit* flight call. STATUS Widespread passage migrant that winters in small numbers. Found on coastal pools but commoner inland.

Common Sandpiper

Actitis hypoleucos Length 18–20cm

Active wader with a bobbing gait and elongated tail end. Flies low over water on bowed, fluttering wings. Has a white wingbar and dark rump. Sexes are similar. ADULT has warm brown upperparts with faint dark centres and barring on feathers of back and wings. Head and neck are grey-brown. Underparts are white, colour extending up sides of breast. JUVENILE is similar but wing coverts are barred. VOICE Whistling *tswee-wee-wee* call. STATUS Widespread and fairly common passage migrant to coasts. Breeds beside upland streams.

Knot,
juvenile

Knot, winter

Sanderling,
summer

Sanderling, winter

Wood Sandpiper

Green Sandpiper

Common
Sandpiper

Purple Sandpiper *Calidris maritima* Length 21cm

Plump-bodied wader. Unobtrusive and confiding. Legs are yellow in all birds and bill has a yellowish base. Sexes are similar. **ADULT** in winter is uniform blue-grey on head, breast and upperparts, darkest on back; belly is white and flanks are streaked. In summer plumage (sometimes seen in late spring), has reddish-brown and black feathers on back, and dark ear coverts on otherwise streaked grey-brown face. **JUVENILE** recalls winter adult but feathers on back have pale margins, creating a scaly look. **VOICE** Sharp *kwit* call in flight. **STATUS** Local non-breeding visitor to rocky shores and headlands. A few pairs nest in Scotland.

Redshank *Tringa totanus* Length 28cm

Redshank, winter

Medium-sized wader with a shrill alarm call. In flight, note white trailing edge to wings, white back and rump, and red legs. Sexes are similar. **ADULT** in summer is mainly grey-brown above and pale below, but back is marked with dark spots and neck, breast and flanks are streaked. Has a pale supercilium and eye-ring; base of bill is reddish. In winter, has uniform grey-brown upperparts, head, neck and breast, with paler, mottled underparts. Bill and leg colours are dull. **JUVENILE** recalls winter adult but plumage is browner overall, back feathers have pale marginal spots, and legs and base of bill are dull yellow. **VOICE** Yelping *tiu-uu* alarm call. **STATUS** Common on coasts in winter. Some breed near coasts.

Spotted Redshank *Tringa erythropus* Length 30cm

Has longer legs and bill than Redshank (above), and in flight wings lack white trailing edge. Flight call is distinctive. Sexes are similar. **ADULT** in breeding plumage (seen in late spring and summer) is mainly black with a white eye-ring and dotted white fringes to back feathers; incomplete breeding plumage is more usually observed. In winter, has pale grey upperparts and clean whitish underparts. Legs are reddish, and note pale supercilium. **JUVENILE** recalls winter adult but plumage is darker overall and underparts are barred; legs are orange-yellow. **VOICE** Diagnostic *tchewit* call. **STATUS** Scarce passage migrant and winter resident on estuaries, mainly in the S.

LEFT: **Spotted Redshank, summer;** RIGHT: **Greenshank, winter**

Greenshank *Tringa nebularia* Length 30–31cm

Elegant wader. Beautifully patterned but looks very white at a distance. Has yellowish-green legs and a slightly upturned, grey-based bill. Sexes are similar. **ADULT** in summer has grey-brown upperparts with black centres to many back feathers. Head, neck and breast are streaked but underparts are white. In winter, upperparts are pale grey above and underparts are white. **JUVENILE** recalls winter adult but upperparts are darker and browner. **VOICE** Distinctive *tchu-tchu-tchu* call. **STATUS** Scarce breeding species but fairly common passage migrant and winter resident on estuaries.

Purple Sandpiper, winter

Redshank, winter

Spotted Redshank, winter

Greenshank, juvenile

Whimbrel *Numenius phaeopus* Length 40–45cm

Smaller cousin to Curlew (above), with a shorter bill, diagnostic head markings and a distinctive call. Sexes are similar. ADULT has grey-brown to buffish-brown plumage with fine, dark streaking on neck and breast. Head pattern comprises 2 broad, dark lateral stripes on an otherwise pale crown, and a pale supercilium. JUVENILE is similar but plumage is warmer buff overall. VOICE Distinctive bubbling call comprises 7 notes that descend slightly in pitch from start to finish. STATUS Fairly common passage migrant, seen on estuaries; overwinters in the S in very small numbers. Rare breeding species on N moors.

Curlew *Numenius arquata* Length 53–58cm

Large wader with a long, downcurved bill. Call is evocative of coasts in winter. Sexes are similar, although male has a shorter bill than female. ADULT has mainly grey-brown plumage, streaked and spotted on neck and underparts; belly is rather pale. JUVENILE is similar but more buffish brown overall, with fine streaks on neck and breast, and an appreciably shorter bill. VOICE Characteristic *curlew* call. STATUS Widespread and common on estuaries and mudflats in winter. Locally common breeding species on N and upland habitats.

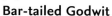

TOP: **Whimbrel**; ABOVE: **Curlew**

Black-tailed Godwit

Limosa limosa Length 38–42cm

Long-legged wader with a long, straight bill. In flight, has a black tail, white rump and white wingbars on upperwing. Sexes are dissimilar in summer. ADULT male in summer has a reddish-orange face, neck and breast. Greyish back is spangled with reddish brown and belly is whitish with barring on flanks. Adult female in summer is similar but reddish elements of plumage are less intense. Winter adult is grey-brown, palest on belly; undertail is white. JUVENILE recalls winter adult but has an orange suffusion on neck and breast, and pale fringes and dark spotting on back feathers. VOICE *Kwe-we-we* call in flight. STATUS Locally common non-breeding visitor to muddy estuaries. Small British breeding population is boosted by migrants from Iceland.

Bar-tailed Godwit

Limosa lapponica Length 35–40cm

Large wader with a long, slightly upturned bill. Looks shorter-legged than Black-tailed. In flight, note absence of wingbar on upperwing; white rump extends to lower back and tail is barred. Sexes are dissimilar in summer. ADULT male in summer has a reddish-orange head, neck and underparts. Back is spangled grey, black and pale buff. Adult female in summer has a buffish-orange wash on head, neck and breast, pale belly and greyish back. Winter adult has grey-brown upperparts and pale underparts. JUVENILE recalls winter adult but has a buffish wash to head, neck and upperparts. VOICE Sharp *kve-wee* call in flight. STATUS Locally common non-breeding visitor to estuaries and sand flats. Breeds in the Arctic.

TOP: **Black-tailed Godwit, juvenile**
ABOVE: **Black-tailed Godwit, breeding male**
BELOW: **Bar-tailed Godwit, summer**

Whimbrel

Curlew

Black-tailed Godwit, winter

Bar-tailed Godwit, winter

Turnstone

Arenaria interpres Length 23cm

Pugnacious wader. Turns stones and seaweed in search of food. Sexes are similar. **ADULT** in winter has grey and brown upperparts. Breast is marked with a blackish band; underparts are white. In summer, has chestnut on back and more distinct head markings. **JUVENILE** is similar to winter adult but paler. **VOICE** *Tuk-ut-ut* call in flight. **STATUS** Common non-breeding visitor.

ABOVE: **Turnstones, summer;** BELOW LEFT: **Ruff, juvenile;** BELOW RIGHT: **Ruff, female**

Ruff *Philomachus pugnax* Length 23–29cm

Variable wader with a small head and orange-yellow legs. Male is larger than female, but size is variable so not particularly useful for separating the sexes. **ADULT** male in summer has brownish upperparts, many feathers with black tips and bars. Variably coloured ruff and crest feathers are seen only on breeding grounds. Adult female in summer has grey-brown upperparts, many feathers with dark tips and bars; underparts are pale. Winter adult has uniform grey-brown upperparts and pale underparts. **JUVENILE** recalls winter adult but has a buff suffusion and scaly-looking back. **VOICE** Mostly silent. **STATUS** Fairly common passage migrant on coastal pools; scarce in winter. Rare breeding species in Britain.

Grey Phalarope *Phalaropus fulicarius* Length 20–21cm

Habitually swims. Spends its non-breeding life at sea. Bill has a yellow base. Sexes are dissimilar in summer. **ADULT** in winter has grey upperparts, white underparts, a dark cap and nape, and a black mark through eye. Adult female in summer (seen rarely) has an orange-red neck and underparts, dark crown, white face patch, and buff-fringed dark back feathers. Adult male in summer is similar but duller. **JUVENILE** recalls winter adult but has a buff tinge and back feathers have buff fringes. **VOICE** Sharp *pit* flight call. **STATUS** Scarce passage migrant. Seen near land during gales; sometimes on coastal lagoons.

Red-necked Phalarope *Phalaropus lobatus* Length 18cm

Habitually swims. Non-breeding life is spent at sea. Bill is needle-like. Sexes are dissimilar in summer. **ADULT** female in summer has brown and buff upperparts, white throat, dark cap and orange-red neck; grey breast and mottled flanks grade to white underparts. Adult male in summer is similar but duller. Winter adult has grey upperparts, nape and hindcrown, black eye patch and white underparts. **JUVENILE** recalls winter adult but grey elements of plumage are mainly brownish. **VOICE** Sharp *kip* call. **STATUS** Scarce passage migrant, seen mostly in severe gales. Breeds mainly in the Arctic; a few pairs nest in N Britain.

Common Snipe *Gallinago gallinago* Length 25–28cm

Long-billed wader. Sexes and ages are similar. **ADULT** and **JUVENILE** have beautifully marked brown, buff and black upperparts; underparts are pale with scaly markings on breast and flanks. Note striking head pattern and yellow legs. **VOICE** Utters a sneeze-like *kreech* as it takes off. **STATUS** Common on coastal marshes in winter.

Turnstone, winter

Turnstone, summer

Ruff, summer female

Ruff, male

Grey Phalarope, winter

Grey Phalarope, summer female

Red-necked Phalarope, summer female

Common Snipe

Red-necked Phalarope, juvenile

Meadow Pipit *Anthus pratensis* Length 14–15cm
Nondescript bird. Forms flocks in winter. Sexes are similar. ADULT has streaked brown upperparts and pale underparts with dark streaks; buffish flush to flanks is most noticeable in autumn. Legs are pinkish and outer-tail feathers are white. JUVENILE is similar but with subdued streaking. VOICE *Pseet-pseet-pseet* call. STATUS Common and widespread resident. Favours rough grassy habitats; common near coasts in winter.

Rock Pipit *Anthus petrosus* Length 16–17cm
Bulky coastal pipit. Sexes and ages are similar. ADULT and JUVENILE have streaked dark grey-brown upperparts and grubby yellowish underparts, streaked on breast and flanks. Legs and bill are dark and outer-tail feathers are grey. VOICE Single *pseet* call. Song, delivered in flight, starts and ends on a rocky outcrop. STATUS Locally common in the N and W. Found on rocky coasts and cliffs in summer; also on beaches in winter.

Water Pipit, summer

Water Pipit
Anthus spinoletta Length 16–17cm
Similar to Rock Pipit (above) but with subtle plumage differences. Sexes are similar. ADULT in winter has streaked dark buffish-brown upperparts and pale underparts, streaked and flushed buffish brown on breast and flanks; throat is white and pale supercilium contrasts with dark eye-stripe. Adult in summer (seen here in early spring) has unmarked underparts, flushed pinkish on breast, brown back, and grey head and neck. JUVENILE is similar to winter adult. VOICE Single *pseet* call. STATUS. Scarce winter visitor to coastal wetlands and beaches.

Pied Wagtail *Motacilla alba yarrellii* Length 18cm
Distinctive bird that pumps its long tail up and down. Sexes are dissimilar. ADULT male in summer has white underparts, with a black throat, breast and upperparts. In winter, similar but throat is white and black on breast is reduced. Adult female recalls adult male in each season but back is dark grey. JUVENILE recalls winter adult female but

Skylark

with greyish upperparts and a yellow wash to face. VOICE Loud *chissick* call. STATUS Common near coasts, especially in winter. NOTE **White Wagtail** *M. a. alba* (length 18cm) is the European counterpart of Pied Wagtail. All birds have a grey, not black, rump. Adult male has a grey (not black) back. Other aspects of plumage and behaviour are identical to Pied. Fairly common passage migrant on coasts.

Skylark *Alauda arvensis* Length 18cm
Renowned for its incessant song, delivered in flight. Sexes are similar. ADULT has streaked sandy-brown upperparts and paler underparts. In flight, wings show a pale trailing edge; outer-tail feathers are white. JUVENILE is similar but with a scaly-looking back. VOICE Rapid song includes trills, whistles and mimicry. Call is a rolling *chrrrp*. STATUS Favours grassy habitats. Commonest near coasts in winter and seen in flocks.

Shorelark *Eremophila alpestris* Length 16–17cm
Unobtrusive bird. Female is duller than male but otherwise similar. ADULT in spring has sandy upperparts. Underparts are whitish with a black breast band and buff flank streaks. Head is yellow with a black mask; black forecrown extends to 2 'horns'. Winter adult and 1st winter are duller and lack 'horns'. VOICE Thin *see-seer* call. STATUS Scarce non-breeding visitor to saltmarshes.

Wren *Troglodytes troglodytes* Length 9–10cm
Tiny bird that cocks its tail upright. Sexes and ages are similar. ADULT and JUVENILE have reddish-brown upperparts with barring on wings and tail. Underparts are greyish white with a buff wash to flanks; has a pale supercilium. Bill is needle-like and legs are reddish. VOICE Loud, rattling alarm call; warbling song ends in a trill. STATUS Widespread resident of coastal scrub.

Black Redstart *Phoenicurus ochruros* Length 14cm
All birds quiver striking red tail when perched. Sexes are dissimilar. ADULT male has slate-grey body plumage, darkest on face and breast. Adult female has grey-brown body plumage. JUVENILE resembles adult female. VOICE Song includes crackling, static-like phrases. STATUS Fairly common passage migrant and scarce winter visitor, mainly to S coasts.

Stonechat, female

Stonechat *Saxicola torquata* Length 12–13cm
Flicks its short, dark tail when perched. Sexes are dissimilar. ADULT male has a dark head, white sides to neck, and dark back. Breast is orange-red, grading into pale underparts. In autumn, head feathers have pale fringes. Adult female is similar but colours are muted. JUVENILE and 1st winter are similar to adult female but with more buffish-orange underparts. VOICE Harsh *tchak* call. Song is a rapid warble. STATUS Locally common on gorse-covered slopes. More widespread in winter.

Wheatear
Oenanthe oenanthe Length 14–16cm
All birds have a white rump and black and white tail. Sexes are otherwise dissimilar. ADULT male has a blue-grey crown and back, black mask and wings, and pale underparts flushed orange-buff on breast. Adult female has grey-brown upperparts, darkest on wings; face, throat and breast are orange-buff, and underparts are otherwise whitish. First-winter birds are buffish, darker above than below. JUVENILE recalls adult female but plumage appears scaly. VOICE *Chak* alarm call. Song is fast and warbling. STATUS Locally common summer visitor. Nests on coastal cliffs and islands; commonest as a passage migrant.

Wheatear, male

Whitethroat *Sylvia communis* Length 13–15cm
Males perch openly. Sexes are dissimilar. ADULT male has a blue-grey hood, grey-brown back and rufous wing panel; has a white throat and pale underparts, suffused pinkish buff on breast. Adult female is similar but hood is brownish. JUVENILE resembles adult female. VOICE Harsh *tcheck* alarm call. Song is a scratchy warble. STATUS Common summer visitor to coastal scrub.

Shorelark, winter

Wren

Black Redstart, juvenile

Black Redstart, male

Wheatear, male

Stonechat, male

Whitethroat, male

Wheatear, juvenile

Whitethroat, juvenile

Carrion Crow

Carrion Crow *Corvus corone* Length 43–50cm

Familiar all-dark corvid. Very wary of man. Sexes and ages are similar. ADULT and JUVENILE have glossy black plumage, and black legs and bill. VOICE Harsh *creeaa-creeaa-creeaa* call. STATUS Common on coasts of England and Wales; in Scotland it is largely confined to S and E of the Clyde–Dornoch line.

Hooded Crow

Hooded Crow

Corvus cornix Length 43–50cm

N and W counterpart of Carrion Crow (above). Sexes and ages are similar. ADULT and JUVENILE have grubby grey body plumage with black wings and tail, and a black head, throat and upper breast. VOICE Harsh *creeaa-creeaa-creeaa* call. STATUS In Scotland, found N and W of the Clyde–Dornoch line; occurs throughout Ireland and on the Isle of Man.

Rook

Rook *Corvus frugilegus* Length 43–48cm

Familiar farmland bird. Feeds in flocks (mainly on soil invertebrates). Sexes are similar. ADULT has black plumage with a reddish-purple sheen. Bill is long, narrow and rather pointed; note bare patch of whitish skin at base. JUVENILE is similar but skin at base of bill is feathered. VOICE Grating *craah-craah-craah…* call. STATUS Locally common, mainly on farmland in breeding season and in coastal grassland in winter.

Raven

Raven *Corvus corax* Length 55–65cm

Our largest passerine. Appreciably bigger than Carrion Crow (above), with a massive bill and shaggy throat. In aerobatic flight, note thick neck and wedge-shaped tail. Sexes and ages are similar. ADULT and JUVENILE have black plumage with an oily sheen. VOICE Loud, deep *cronk* call. STATUS Fairly common resident of rugged coasts. Commonest in W and N Britain.

Jackdaw

Jackdaw

Corvus monedula Length 31–34cm

Familiar small corvid. Has a swaggering walk and aerobatic flight. Often seen in flocks. Sexes are similar. ADULT has smoky-grey plumage, darkest on wings and crown, pale blue-grey eye and grey nape. JUVENILE is similar but plumage is tinged brownish and eye is duller. VOICE Harsh *chack* call. STATUS Widespread and common on cliffs and coastal grassland.

Chough

Chough *Pyrrhocorax pyrrhocorax* Length 38–40cm

Jackdaw-sized corvid with a downcurved red bill, used to probe ground for invertebrates. Forms sociable, noisy flocks. Superb aeronaut with broad, 'fingered' wingtips. Sexes are similar. ADULT has glossy black plumage and reddish-pink legs. JUVENILE has duller legs and a dull yellow bill. VOICE Distinctive *chyah* call. STATUS Local resident of coastal sea cliffs. S and W Ireland, W Wales, Isle of Man and Islay are strongholds. Has recently recolonised the Lizard in Cornwall.

Carrion Crow

Hooded Crow

Rook

Jackdaw

Raven

Chough

Starling *Sturnus vulgaris* Length 20–22cm

Has a swaggering walk. Sexes are separable in summer. **ADULTS** in summer have dark plumage with an oily sheen; female has a few pale spots on underparts. Legs are reddish and bill is yellow, but male has blue base to lower mandible. Winter adult and 1st winter have numerous white spots adorning dark plumage, and dark bill. **JUVENILE** is grey-brown, palest on throat; bill is dark. **VOICE** Repertoire of clicks, whistles and mimicry. **STATUS** Widespread; large flocks form in winter.

Starling, winter

Linnet *Carduelis cannabina* Length 13–14cm

Breeding male is striking. Sexes are dissimilar. **ADULT** male in summer has a grey head, rosy forecrown and chestnut back. Pale underparts have a rosy-pink flush on breast. Note pale panel on wings and streaked throat. In winter, rosy elements of plumage are dull or absent. Adult female has a brown back, grey-brown head and streaked, pale underparts. Note pale panel on wings. **JUVENILE** is similar to adult female but more streaked. **VOICE** *Tetter-tett* call. Song is a twittering warble. **STATUS** Common in coastal scrub in summer, and on coastal fields in winter.

ABOVE: **Linnet, juvenile**
BELOW: **Twite, juvenile**

Twite *Carduelis flavirostris* Length 13–14cm

Upland counterpart of Linnet (above). Bill is grey in spring and summer, and yellow at other times (always grey in Linnet). Throat is unstreaked (streaked in Linnet). Sexes are similar. **ADULT** has streaked brown upperparts, and white margins to flight and tail feathers. Pale underparts are heavily streaked. Rump is pinkish in male, brown in female. **JUVENILE** resembles adult female. **VOICE** Sharp *tveeht* call. Song is a series of trills. **STATUS** Local breeder in the N. In winter, favours saltmarshes and fields, mainly on the E coast.

Snow Bunting *Plectrophenax nivalis* Length 16–17cm

Confiding bunting with white on innerwing, rump and tail. Sexes are dissimilar. **ADULT** male in summer is mostly white with a blackish back, wings, bill and legs. Adult female in summer is similar but black elements of plumage are brownish and has buff streaking. Winter adult has mainly streaked brown upperparts and white underparts; male shows most white. Bill is yellowish. **VOICE** Tinkling flight call. Song is twittering. **STATUS** Mainly a non-breeding visitor to beaches and saltmarshes; commonest on the E coast.

Snow Bunting, 1st winter

Lapland Bunting *Calcarius lapponicus* Length 14–16cm

Unobtrusive bird. Seldom seen here in summer plumage. Sexes are dissimilar. **ADULT** in winter and summer adult female have a brown face with a dark line around ear coverts; note dark crown, streaked brown back, reddish wing panel and pale wingbars. Pale underparts have streaks on flanks. Adult male in summer has a bold black, white and chestnut head pattern. **JUVENILE** resembles winter adult. **VOICE** Rattling flight call. **STATUS** Scarce passage migrant and winter visitor, mainly to E coast fields and saltmarshes.

Starling

Linnet, male

Twite, summer male

Snow Bunting, winter male

Lapland Bunting, winter

Pectoral Sandpiper *Calidris melanotos* Length 19–22cm

Deep-bodied wader. **JUVENILE** (plumage seen here) is brown, grey and black on back, the feathers with pale margins. Has a strongly streaked breast, clearly demarcated from otherwise white underparts. Bill is black, legs are yellow. **VOICE** Mostly silent. **STATUS** Regular autumn visitor from North America to coastal pools.

Buff-breasted Sandpiper *Tryngites subruficollis* Length 18–20cm

Recalls a juvenile Ruff (p. 344). **JUVENILE** (plumage seen here) is buffish overall with a scaly-looking back and yellow legs. **VOICE** Usually silent. **STATUS** Rare but annual visitor from North America; usually on short coastal grassland.

Ring-billed Gull *Larus delawarensis* Length 42–48cm

Regular North American visitor to Britain. **ADULT** Recalls Common Gull (p. 304) but is larger, with yellow legs and a yellow bill with a black subterminal band. **IMMATURES** are similar to Common Gull counterparts but larger, and with a stouter bill. **VOICE** Mewing calls. **STATUS** Around 50 recorded each year, mostly in winter.

Wryneck *Jynx torquilla* Length 16–17cm

Well-marked bird. Feeds mainly on ants. **ADULT** has intricate brown, grey and black markings on upperparts, and barred underparts. **JUVENILE** is similar but has faint crown stripe. **VOICE** Migrants are silent. **STATUS** Scarce on S and E coasts.

Swift *Apus apus* Length 16–17cm

Recognised by anchor-shaped outline in flight. Catches insects on the wing. **ADULT** is blackish brown with a pale throat. **JUVENILE** is darker but with a paler throat and forehead. **VOICE** Migrants are silent. **STATUS** Migrants feed over coastal pools and grassland.

Swallow *Hirundo rustica* Length 19cm

Has long tail streamers. **ADULT** has blue-black upperparts and white underparts, with a dark chest band and red throat and forecrown. **JUVENILE** has shorter tail streamers. **VOICE** Sharp *vit* call. **STATUS** Common; migrants linger on coasts.

House Martin *Delichon urbica* Length 12–13cm

Distinctive insect-eating migrant. **ADULT** has blue-black upperparts with a white rump; underparts are white. **JUVENILE** is similar but plumage is duller. **VOICE** *Prrrt* call in flight. **STATUS** Common; migrants often linger near coasts.

Sand Martin *Riparia riparia* Length 12cm

Hunts insects over water. **ADULT** has sandy-brown upperparts and white underparts with a brown breast band. Short tail is forked. **JUVENILE** has pale margins on back feathers. **VOICE** Rasping twitters. **STATUS** Common; migrants linger on coasts.

Blackcap *Sylvia atricapilla*
Length 14–15cm

Distinctive warbler. **ADULT** male is grey above, pale grey below, palest on throat, and with black cap. Adult female is similar but with a chestnut cap. **JUVENILE** resembles adult female. **VOICE** *Tchek* alarm call. Song is a musical warble. **STATUS** Common.

Blackcap, male

Pectoral Sandpiper

Buff-breasted Sandpiper

Ring-billed Gull

Wryneck

Swift

Swallow, male

House Martin

Sand Martin

Blackcap, female

Sedge Warbler *Acrocephalus schoenobaenus* Length 12–13cm

Well-marked warbler. ADULT has streaked sandy upperparts and pale underparts, flushed buff on breast and flanks. Note dark-streaked crown and eye-stripe, and pale supercilium. JUVENILE has faint streaking on breast. VOICE *Chek* alarm call. Song comprises rasping phrases, trills and whistles. STATUS Common.

Chiffchaff *Phylloscopus collybita* Length 11cm

Tiny warbler. ADULT and JUVENILE have grey-brown upperparts, and pale underparts suffused with yellow-buff on throat and breast. Bill is thin and legs are black. VOICE Soft *hueet* call. Song is a repeated *chiff-chaff.* STATUS Common.

Willow Warbler *Phylloscopus trochilus*
Length 11cm

Has brighter plumage than Chiffchaff (above), longer primaries and pink legs. ADULT has greenish upperparts, a yellow throat and pale underparts. JUVENILE is yellower. VOICE *Hueet* call. Song is tinkling and descending. STATUS Common. SIMILAR SPECIES **Wood Warbler** *P. sibilatrix* is brighter overall with yellow on wings and face, and clean-looking underparts. Song is a warble followed by a silvery trill. Fairly common on migration.

Wood Warbler

Yellow-browed Warbler *Phylloscopus inornatus* Length 9–10cm

Active, well-marked warbler. ADULT and JUVENILE have bright olive-green upperparts and whitish underparts. Note narrow, dark eye-stripe, yellow supercilium, and 2 pale yellow wingbars. Legs are pinkish. VOICE Disyllabic *tsu-eet* call. STATUS Scarce in autumn.

Pallas's Warbler *Phylloscopus proregulus* Length 9–10cm

Energetic warbler. FIRST WINTER (plumage seen in Britain) has olive-green upperparts and pale underparts. On head, note dark eye-stripe, yellowish supercilium and pale median stripe. Has 2 pale wingbars and a pale rump. VOICE Soft *tchuee* call. STATUS Rare but regular in autumn.

Firecrest *Regulus ignicapillus* Length 9–10cm

Tiny bird. ADULT has green upperparts with 2 pale wingbars. Underparts are buffish white, flushed golden on sides of neck. Has striking head markings; crown stripe is orange in male, yellow in female. JUVENILE lacks crown stripe. VOICE Thin *tsuu-tsee-tsee* call. STATUS Scarce, in coastal scrub.

Goldcrest *Regulus regulus* Length 9cm

Our smallest bird. ADULT has greenish upperparts with 2 pale wingbars, and yellow-buff underparts. Has black-bordered crown stripe. JUVENILE lacks crown stripe. VOICE Thin, high-pitched *tsee-tsee-tsee.* STATUS Common in coastal scrub.

Spotted Flycatcher *Muscicapa striata* Length 14cm

Perches upright and catches insects in flight. ADULT is grey-brown above, streaked on crown, and pale below, streaked on breast. JUVENILE has pale spots on back and dark spots on throat and breast. VOICE Thin *tsee* call. STATUS Fairly common.

Red-breasted Flycatcher *Ficedula parva* Length 11–12cm

White sides to black tail are seen in all birds. ADULT male has a brown back, blue-grey face, orange-red throat and upper breast, and whitish underparts. Adult female has a white throat and breast. FIRST WINTER has a buff throat and breast, and a pale wingbar. VOICE Rattling call. STATUS Mainly autumn; scarce.

Sedge Warbler

Chiffchaff

Willow Warbler

Yellow-browed Warbler

Pallas's Warbler

Firecrest, male

Goldcrest, male

Spotted Flycatcher

Red-breasted Flycatcher

INTRODUCING MAMMALS

Coastal habitats are home to a small but select band of mammals. Several terrestrial species forage on the fringes of the ocean and a couple of species have amphibious feeding habits. Seals are mainly aquatic but can venture onto land, albeit awkwardly, whereas whales and dolphins are exclusively marine and would soon die on land.

MAMMAL LIVES
Along with birds, mammals can generate body heat and maintain a more or less constant internal temperature. This is obviously important for terrestrial species, but even more significant for marine mammals that live in permanently chilly surroundings. A thick layer of blubber acts as a superb insulator. All mammals, including the most marine of all – whales and dolphins – are air-breathers and must return to the surface of the sea periodically to replenish their oxygen supplies.

Grey Seal pups are born on isolated beaches in the autumn. Like other mammals, they rely on their mother's milk for the first few weeks of life.

MAMMAL REPRODUCTION
In all mammals, fertilisation is internal and the embryo and developing infant is nourished via a placenta, in which it is implanted at an early stage. Young placental mammals are born with varying degrees of independence and maturity depending on the species involved. In seals, young are born on land, but with whales and dolphins birth occurs at sea and their young must be able to swim from the moment they are born.

TERRESTRIAL AND AMPHIBIOUS MAMMALS
Although widespread inland, a few terrestrial mammals such as Rabbits thrive near the coast. And, surprisingly, Hedgehogs are also common in a few places on the seashore. Amphibious by nature, Otters have adapted to a life on the seashore in parts of Britain.

SEALS

Seals give birth on land and their terrestrial gait is awkward and shuffling. In water, however, they are graceful and speedy, powered by flippers. They have well-developed eyes and prominent whiskers, and our two native species feed mainly on fish.

Cumbersome on land, Grey Seals are in their element in water.

Streamlined and fast, the Minke Whale is the most likely whale species to be seen in British seas.

WHALES AND DOLPHINS

Whales and dolphins live aquatic lives although, of course, they still retain the need to breathe air at the surface. Movement is powered by a broad tail fluke, and fins and flippers assist directional control. Known collectively as cetaceans, their diet includes marine fish and plankton, depending on the species.

Hedgehog *Erinaceus europaeus* Length 23–27cm
Spiny, nocturnal animal. Usually feeds on invertebrates. Hibernates Oct–Apr. **ADULT** has spines (modified hairs) on back; erectile and an effective deterrent when animal rolls into a defensive ball. **VOICE** Pig-like squeal in distress. **STATUS** Foolishly, has been released onto many offshore islands. Feeds along strandline but also eats birds' eggs and young. Eradication programmes operate in some areas.

Lesser White-toothed Shrew *Crocidura suaveolens* Length 8–12cm
Invertebrate-eating mammal that often forages on strandline. **ADULT** has grey-brown fur and white-tipped teeth. **VOICE** Inaudible to human ears. **STATUS** Introduced long ago to the Isles of Scilly, and Jersey and Sark in the Channel Islands. **SIMILAR SPECIES Greater White-toothed Shrew** *C. russula* (length 8–13cm) occurs only on Guernsey, Alderney and Sark in the Channel Islands. **Pygmy Shrew** *Sorex minutus* has red-tipped teeth; widespread but range does not overlap with previous two species.

American Mink *Neovison vison* Length 45–65cm
Unwelcome introduction from North America. Active predator of aquatic life and seabird colonies. Swims well. **ADULT** has a slender body and bushy tail. Fur is silky and usually dark brown. Male is larger than female. **VOICE** High-pitched calls when alarmed. **STATUS** Originated from fur farms ('liberated' animals and escapees) and now widespread.

Otter *Lutra lutra* Length 95–135cm
Sinuous swimmer with a bounding gait on land. Feeds mainly on fish. **ADULT** has a long, cylindrical body, with short legs and a long, thickset tail. Webbed toes aid swimming. Coat is mainly brown but chin, throat and belly are whitish. Fur has water-repellent properties: sleek in water but 'spiky' when dry. **VOICE** Mostly silent. **STATUS** Following past persecution, now recovering and recolonising former haunts. Fairly common on undisturbed coasts in N and W Scotland and Ireland.

Otter

Rabbit *Oryctolagus cuniculus* Length 40–55cm
Long-eared, social, burrowing mammal. Lives in tunnel complexes called warrens. Mainly nocturnal or crepuscular; diet is vegetarian. **ADULT** has mainly greyish-brown fur with a rufous nape and pale greyish underparts. Long ears have brown tips, and tail is dark above and white below. Black forms are sometimes seen, especially on islands. **VOICE** Squeals loudly in alarm. **STATUS** Introduced; now widespread and common. Often abundant on coastal cliffs and grassland.

Rabbit, black form

Goat *Capra hircus* Height 60–90cm
Domesticated animal with several feral populations. **ADULT** has a long, shaggy coat, often piebald or whitish. Male is larger and bulkier than female and has recurved, ringed horns. **JUVENILE** lacks horns. **VOICE** Warning whistle. Females summon their kids by bleating. **STATUS** Feral populations exist in several rugged coastal sites.

Hedgehog

American Mink

Otter

Lesser White-toothed Shrew

Rabbit

Goat

Minke Whale

Balaenoptera acutorostrata Length 8–10m

(Pronounced 'minky'.) Smallest baleen whale but still large and impressive. Tail is not revealed when animal dives. Feeds on shoaling fish. **ADULT** is streamlined, with a narrow, pointed snout. Upperparts are dark grey; underparts are whitish, and broad bands of paler coloration extend up flanks, these sometimes visible on

animals at surface. Curved dorsal fin is set far back on body. Single ridge runs from nostrils to tip of rostrum. Has a diagnostic broad white spot or band on upper surface of flipper; easily seen in swimming animals. **STATUS** Favours relatively shallow waters of the continental shelf and regularly seen from land; Mull and W Ireland are hotspots.

Fin Whale *Balaenoptera physalus* Length 18–22m

Second only in terms of size to Blue Whale *B. musculus*. Uniquely, has asymmetrical markings on head. Fast swimmer, catching shoaling fish. **ADULT** has a slender body with a narrow, pointed head. Body is mainly dark grey, palest on underparts and throat. Right side of lower jaw is whitish (as are front half of right side of baleen plates and tongue), whereas left side is same colour as rest of body. Single median ridge extends from nostril to tip of rostrum. Flippers are relatively long. Dorsal fin is curved, rather large and set a long way back. Tailstock is thick and tail fin is large. **STATUS** Mainly oceanic but sometimes seen in relatively shallow inshore waters. W coast of Ireland is a hotspot.

Humpback Whale *Megaptera novaeangliae* Length 12–15m

Large cetacean that is often active at the surface; breaches and engages in flipper- and tail-slapping on water surface. Feeds on shoaling fish and krill. **ADULT** has a bulky yet streamlined body; broad head is covered in lumpy tubercles. Pectoral fins are long and mainly white; dorsal fin is short and stubby. Tail is typically dark above and white with black markings below. Before a deep dive, arches its back strongly and tailstock and fluke come clear of water. **STATUS** Tolerates comparatively shallow seas if feeding is good, and hence is sometimes seen from land. Regular off W Ireland, mainly in winter.

ABOVE LEFT: **Fin Whale**
ABOVE: **Humpback Whale**
BELOW: **Long-finned Pilot Whale 'spy-hopping'**

Long-finned Pilot Whale

Globicephala melas Length 4–6m

Medium-sized cetacean with distinctive head and dorsal fin shapes. Lives in sizeable groups (pods) and feeds mainly on squid. Head, back and dorsal fin are visible at the same time when cruising at surface. **ADULT** is mainly blackish with a greyish saddle-shaped

mark behind dorsal fin. Has a thighbone-shaped white mark from throat to vent, seen only when breaching. Head is blunt-ended, forehead is domed, and flippers are long and sickle-shaped. Dorsal fin is broad-based and curved. **STATUS** Widespread in NE Atlantic and occurs regularly in British and Irish waters; sometimes seen from land.

Minke Whale

Fin Whale

Humpback Whale

Long-finned Pilot Whale

Risso's Dolphin *Grampus griseus* Length 3–3.5m

Large, blunt-nosed dolphin. Lives in pods of 3–15 animals. ADULT is greyish brown overall, darkest on dorsal fin, flippers and tail, and palest on face, throat and belly. Older animals become very pale and marked with criss-crossed white scars. Head is blunt and forehead is split down middle by a deep crease. Dorsal fin is tall, pointed and slightly recurved. Flippers are long and narrow, and tail fin is broad. STATUS Regular in coastal waters, mainly off W Britain.

Killer Whale *Orcinus orca* Length 4–9m

Distinctive and well marked. The largest dolphin. Lives in pods of 5–20 animals. Feeds on fish, seals and other cetaceans. ADULT male has blackish upperparts with a saddle-like grey patch behind dorsal fin. Underparts are white and band of white extends onto flanks. Also has a white patch behind eye. Dorsal fin is up to 1.8m tall. Flippers are paddle-shaped. Adult female is smaller, with shorter dorsal fin. STATUS Occasional in British waters. Seen close to land if feeding is good.

Killer Whale, mother and calf

Short-beaked Common Dolphin *Delphinus delphis* Length 1.8–2.3m

Our most regularly encountered dolphin. Lives in schools of 10s or 100s. ADULT is overall dark grey above and whitish below, with a broad, tapering yellow band on flanks from eye and mouth to just behind dorsal fin; grey band continues along flanks towards tail. Overall, yellow and grey patches resemble an hourglass. Flippers are narrow and black, with a black line running forward from base to throat. Dorsal fin is broadly triangular and slightly curved. STATUS Mostly oceanic; typically seen from boats, but sometimes from headlands in the W.

Bottlenose Dolphin *Tursiops truncatus* Length 2.5–4m

Bulky dolphin. Lives in schools of 3–4 animals. Diet includes fish and crabs. Playful at the surface. ADULT is greyish brown overall, darkest above and palest on throat and belly; mid-grey band is sometimes seen on flanks. Beak is rather short and blunt, with lower jaw extending beyond upper one. Flippers are rather long and pointed, and dorsal fin is tall, curved backwards and almost shark-like. STATUS Some individuals are pelagic, while other groups favour coastal waters. Moray Firth in Scotland and the Shannon Estuary in Ireland are hotspots.

Bottlenose Dolphin

Risso's Dolphin

Killer Whale, male

Short-beaked Common Dolphin

Bottlenose Dolphin

Harbour Porpoise *Phocoena phocoena* Length 1.4–1.9m

Our smallest cetacean. Lives in groups of 3–15 animals. Playful at the surface. **ADULT** has a stout, streamlined body, blunt head and no beak. Flippers are small and oval, and dorsal fin is triangular. Tail fin is broad. Upperparts are mainly dark grey, while underparts are whitish. **STATUS** Favours inshore waters, including estuaries, river mouths and sheltered coastal bays. Moray Firth and the Inner Hebrides are hotspots.

Common Seal *Phoca vitulina* Length 1.2–1.9m

Has a 'friendly'-looking face. Hauled-out seals are easy to observe. **ADULT** is greyish brown but variably mottled with darker spots. Underside is paler than upperside. Dry coat looks shiny if dusted in sand. Bridge of nose has a concave outline (convex in Grey Seal, below) and muzzle is blunt, creating a dog-like appearance. Seen from front, nostrils are close together at base and splayed in a V-shaped fashion (separated from, and more parallel to, one another in Grey Seal). Front flippers have claws and powerful hind flippers effect propulsion when swimming. Males are larger and heavier than females. **JUVENILE** (pup) is born with a marbled grey-brown coat. **VOICE** Mostly silent. **STATUS** Favours sheltered seas. Widespread on E coast of England and around Scotland and Ireland generally. Easiest to see on N Norfolk coast, especially at Blakeney Point.

Common Seal, male

Grey Seal *Halichoerus grypus* Length 2.2–3.2m

Bulky seal with a proportionately large head. Inquisitive in the water. Hauls out for long periods. **ADULT** is greyish overall with dark, blotchy spots; has fewer, larger spots than Common Seal (above). Males are larger and darker than females. In profile, looks 'Roman-nosed': bridge of nose is convex, more pronounced in males than females. From the front, nostrils are distinctly separated and more or less parallel to one another, not V-shaped. Fore flippers have sharp claws and hind flippers propel the animal through water. **JUVENILE** (pup) is born with white fur; moulted after a few weeks. **VOICE** Low, moaning calls. **STATUS** Often found on rocky shores; tolerates rough seas and heavy waves. Widespread on W coasts and locally in the North Sea. Spectacular views can be had of the breeding colony at Donna Nook in Lincolnshire.

LEFT: **Grey Seal, bulls fighting**
ABOVE: **Grey Seal, female**

Harbour Porpoise

Common Seal, female

Common Seal, pup

Grey Seal, female

Grey Seal, pup

INTRODUCING THE STRANDLINE

A beach marks the zone where land meets sea. It is also where detached and floating matter is washed up and deposited by the tides, typically in well-defined lines. During periods of spring tides, debris is pushed to the top of the shore. But with approaching neap tides, tidal extremes diminish and the high-tide mark drops; the result is a series of different strandlines on the shore. The strandline is a great place for the marine naturalist to explore and find unexpected delights washed up from the depths. But it is also home to a range of specialised animals that exploit the rich supply of organic matter created by decomposing seaweeds and marine creatures.

FISH EGG CASES

Some species of sharks, skates and rays reproduce by laying tough egg cases, or mermaid's purses, each containing a single embryo. Tendrils, or sometimes 'horns', at the capsule corners attach them to the seabed, where they may take many months to hatch; once the juvenile has emerged, the empty egg case will often wash up on the shore. The egg case of each species is different enough in terms of size and shape to allow certain identification of strandline finds. Soak the capsules in water for 24 hours in order to restore them to full size before measuring.

ABOVE: Cuttlebones are often found on the strandline.
BELOW: BLONDE RAY *Raja brachyura* – capsule longer than broad, with 1 flat and 1 convex side. Has 1 pair of horns almost as long as capsule, and 1 pair much shorter and curved; these are often damaged. (For adult, *see* p. 260.)

all capsules are lifesize unless stated

BELOW: **SPOTTED RAY** *Raja montagui* – capsule long and slender; has 4 horns of similar length, 1 pair curled in at tip, the other curled upwards. (For adult, *see* p. 260.)

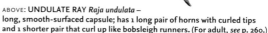

ABOVE: **UNDULATE RAY** *Raja undulata* – long, smooth-surfaced capsule; has 1 long pair of horns with curled tips and 1 shorter pair that curl up like bobsleigh runners. (For adult, *see* p. 260.)

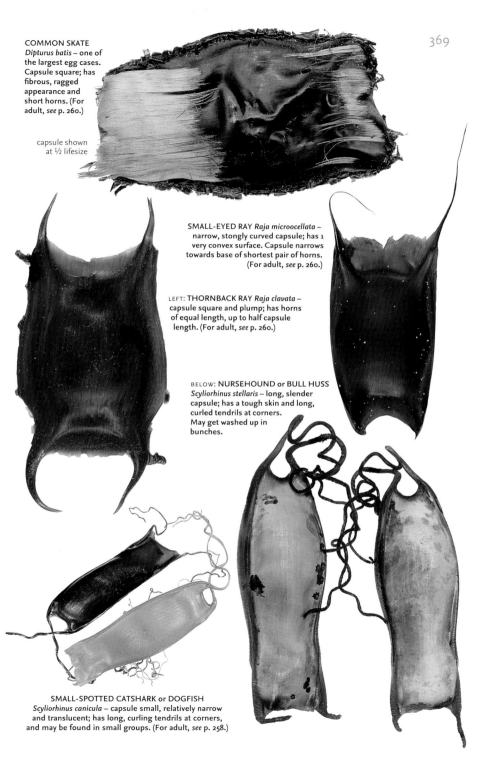

COMMON SKATE
Dipturus batis – one of
the largest egg cases.
Capsule square; has
fibrous, ragged
appearance and
short horns. (For
adult, *see* p. 260.)

capsule shown
at ½ lifesize

SMALL-EYED RAY *Raja microocellata* –
narrow, stongly curved capsule; has 1
very convex surface. Capsule narrows
towards base of shortest pair of horns.
(For adult, *see* p. 260.)

LEFT: THORNBACK RAY *Raja clavata* –
capsule square and plump; has horns
of equal length, up to half capsule
length. (For adult, *see* p. 260.)

BELOW: NURSEHOUND or BULL HUSS
Scyliorhinus stellaris – long, slender
capsule; has a tough skin and long,
curled tendrils at corners.
May get washed up in
bunches.

SMALL-SPOTTED CATSHARK or DOGFISH
Scyliorhinus canicula – capsule small, relatively narrow
and translucent; has long, curling tendrils at corners,
and may be found in small groups. (For adult, *see* p. 258.)

Fossil ammonite on Dorset's Jurassic Coast.

INTRODUCING SEASHORE FOSSILS

In parts of Britain, the seashore is a rewarding place to search for fossils. Constant erosion and deposition, cliff falls and storm damage ensure a regular supply of fossils to some beaches. These may range from magnificent ammonites, present in the seas 100 million years ago, to sharks' teeth, or the footprints left behind by long-extinct species. As well as many animal remains, some plant material may also be fossilised, such as hard seed cases, woody tree trunks, or even delicate fern fronds trapped in layers of silt. Some fossils are embedded in rock and cannot be removed, but others may lie exposed in sand or mud at low tide. Sieving the sand or shingle can sometimes reveal small fossils such as sharks' teeth, fish vertebrae or fragments of mollusc shells.

AMBER – a form of fossilised tree resin, with a rich, translucent golden-orange appearance and smooth texture. Sometimes insects are trapped inside globules of amber and remain perfectly preserved. The S North Sea coast of Britain may yield fragments of amber.

FOSSILISED SHARKS' TEETH – these are usually the only parts of the shark's body to remain, being the hardest part (the skeleton is cartilaginous). Teeth from many species can be found; they are all usually black and very shiny, and often very sharp.

RAY DENTAL PLATES – these fish have crushing teeth arranged in plates, rather than sharp, pointed teeth; fragments are common in areas where other shark species occur.

NUMMULITES – disc-like fossils, the size of small coins, which are the remains of small planktonic organisms that had delicate calcified shells.

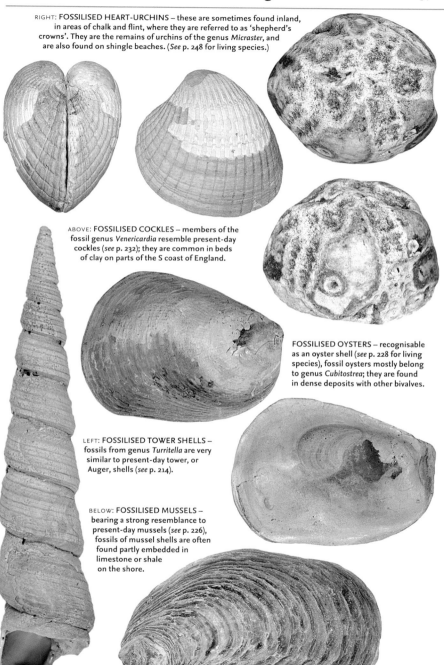

RIGHT: **FOSSILISED HEART-URCHINS** – these are sometimes found inland, in areas of chalk and flint, where they are referred to as 'shepherd's crowns'. They are the remains of urchins of the genus *Micraster*, and are also found on shingle beaches. (*See* p. 248 for living species.)

ABOVE: **FOSSILISED COCKLES** – members of the fossil genus *Venericardia* resemble present-day cockles (*see* p. 232); they are common in beds of clay on parts of the S coast of England.

FOSSILISED OYSTERS – recognisable as an oyster shell (*see* p. 228 for living species), fossil oysters mostly belong to genus *Cubitostrea*; they are found in dense deposits with other bivalves.

LEFT: **FOSSILISED TOWER SHELLS** – fossils from genus *Turritella* are very similar to present-day tower, or Auger, shells (*see* p. 214).

BELOW: **FOSSILISED MUSSELS** – bearing a strong resemblance to present-day mussels (*see* p. 226), fossils of mussel shells are often found partly embedded in limestone or shale on the shore.

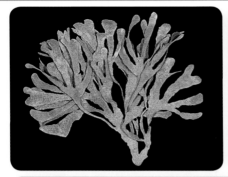

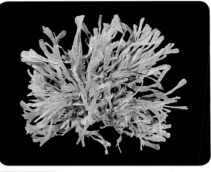

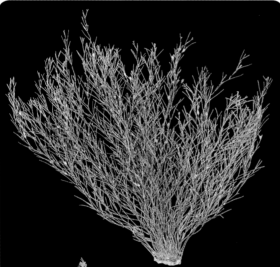

ABOVE LEFT: HORNWRACK *Flustra foliacea* (length to 20cm) – bryozoan, commonly washed up on strandline, sometimes in huge quantities after storms. Looking rather like coarse seaweed, it is actually a colonial animal that lives just offshore attached to shells and stones. Live specimens (p. 254) have a faint scent of lemon.

ABOVE RIGHT: *SECURIFLUSTRA SECURIFRONS* (length to 10cm) – slender bryozoan, less common than Hornwrack (above) but still occasionally found in large quantities. Fronds are strap-like with short branches; there is a small basal holdfast.

LEFT: WHITE WEED *Sertularia cupressina* (length to 50cm) – colonial hydroid that grows attached to stones and shells in shallow water; often found washed ashore. Colonies consist of a main stem, attached at base by a small holdfast, with numerous short feathery side-branches.

LEFT: BOTTLEBRUSH HYDROID *Thuiaria thuja* (length to 25cm) – cylindrical, brush-shaped hydroid with numerous short stems arising from a stiff central stem. A N species that grows on shells and stones in shallow water; often washed up after storms.

RIGHT: SEA BEARD *Nemertesia antennina* (length to 25cm) – colonial hydroid made up of clumps of up to 50 stiff, branchless stems; these are attached at bottom by a tangled mass of tough, fibrous rootlets. Colonies grow in shallow water attached to shells and stones, and are common on most coasts.

ABOVE: *ABIETINARIA ABIETINA* (length to 25cm) – branching hydroid with thick, wavy central stems arising from a root-like holdfast that is often fixed to shells. Short side-branches grow alternately. Common on all coasts and regularly washed ashore.

RIGHT: MERMAID'S GLOVE *Haliclona oculata* (length to 30cm) – much-branched, antler-like sponge that grows on seabed well below the low-tide level (p. 114). Tough remains, with a brittle texture when dry, may be found on the shore after storms.

LEFT: SEA BEAN *Entada gigas* (length to 3.5cm) – drift seeds of many species originate a great distance from our shores; this species will have drifted across the Atlantic from the Caribbean or Central America. The seeds form in a pod on a climbing plant in the pea family, and drop into the sea; their buoyancy and resistance to salt water enables them to survive long periods afloat. Occasional, in the W.

RIGHT: HORSE-EYE SEA BEANS *Ormosia* sp. (length to 3.5cm) – originate in Central America and the Caribbean; the seeds of climbing plants in the pea family that is common on the shore and in low-lying areas. Occasionally found on beaches in SW England, S Wales and Ireland.

ABOVE: KELP HOLDFASTS – fronds, stipes and rootlets of most of large kelps rot away fairly quickly once washed ashore, but the tough base and lowest stipe section are tougher and last much longer, especially when dry. The most striking holdfasts are those of Furbelows (p. 31); found on most coasts.

RIGHT: SEA CHERVIL *Alcyonidium diaphanum* (length to 25cm) – fleshy, non-calcified bryozoan that grows below low-tide level attached to shells and stones. Colonies are very variable in shape and size, but all have the same knobbly appearance and slightly rubbery texture. Handling it may cause skin irritation in some people. Found on most coasts.

RIGHT: SEA WASH BALL (length to 15cm) – spongy mass of smaller capsules, buff-yellow in colour: egg mass of Common Whelk (p. 216) or Red Whelk (p. 216). Usually only one whelk emerges from the mass, after having eaten most of the other eggs. Found on most coasts.

Skulls and bones

The remains of fish, birds and mammals may all be found among strandline debris, and most can be identified with some degree of certainty. Birds can generally be recognised by the shape and structure of the bill. Fish bones are rather delicate by comparison, but sometimes a whole fish skeleton may remain intact. Often, however, it is only the individual vertebrae that are found. Mammal remains are more obvious, and large vertebrae of whales and dolphins are an occasional find on exposed beaches. In areas near seal colonies, seal skulls and vertebrae may also be found. Dolphin skulls have a curious beak-like rostrum, with sockets for the peg-like teeth, but seal skulls have a more recognisable mammal outline, with powerful incisor, canine and molar teeth.

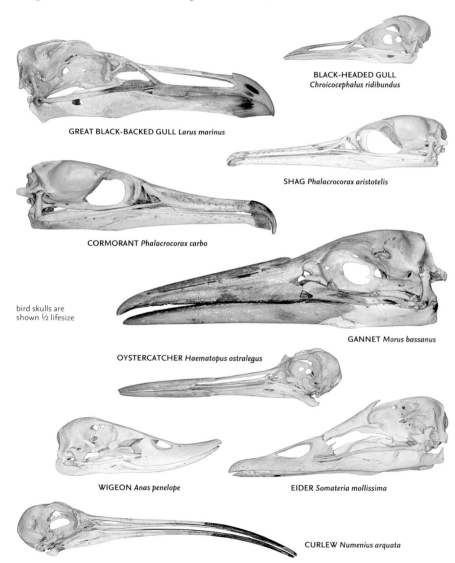

BLACK-HEADED GULL
Chroicocephalus ridibundus

GREAT BLACK-BACKED GULL *Larus marinus*

SHAG *Phalacrocorax aristotelis*

CORMORANT *Phalacrocorax carbo*

bird skulls are
shown ½ lifesize

GANNET *Morus bassanus*

OYSTERCATCHER *Haematopus ostralegus*

WIGEON *Anas penelope*

EIDER *Somateria mollissima*

CURLEW *Numenius arquata*

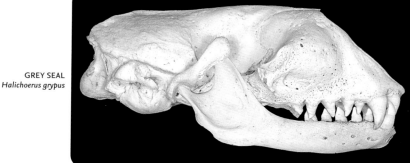

GREY SEAL
Halichoerus grypus

mammal skulls are
shown ¼ lifesize

HARBOUR PORPOISE
Phocoena phocoena

A MINKE WHALE
vertebra is a real
prize find for any
beachcomber.

FURTHER READING

Bunker, F., Brodie, J., Maggs, C. and Bunker, A. (2010). *Seasearch Guide to Seaweeds of Britain and Ireland*. Marine Conservation Society.

Chinery, M. (2005). *Complete British Insects*. HarperCollins.

Fish, J.D. and Fish, S. (1996). *A Student's Guide to the Seashore*. Cambridge University Press.

Hayward, P. (2004). *New Naturalist Seashore*. HarperCollins.

Hayward, P.J., Nelson-Smith, T. and Shields, C. (1996). *Collins Pocket Guide to Seashore of Britain and Europe*. HarperCollins.

Hayward, P.J. and Ryland, J.S. (2009). *Handbook of the Marine Fauna of North-west Europe*. Oxford University Press.

Kay, P. and Dipper, F. (2009). *Marine Fishes of Wales and Adjacent Waters*. Marine Wildlife.

Moen, F.E. and Svenson, E. (2004). *Marine Fish and Invertebrates of Northern Europe*. KOM.

Naylor, P. (2005). *Great British Marine Animals*. 2nd edition. Paul Naylor.

Sterry, P.R. (2004). *Complete British Birds*. HarperCollins.

Sterry, P.R. (2005). *Complete British Animals*. HarperCollins.

Sterry, P.R. (2006). *Complete British Wild Flowers*. HarperCollins.

Wood, C. (2005). *Seasearch Guide to Sea Anemones and Corals of Britain and Ireland*. Marine Conservation Society.

USEFUL WEBSITES

British Trust for Ornithology (BTO) – www.bto.org
Encyclopaedia of Marine Life of Britain and Ireland – www.habitas.org/marinelife
First Nature – www.first-nature.com
Island Sea Safaris (Isles of Scilly) – www.islandseasafaris.co.uk
Marine Conservation Society – www.mcsuk.org
Marine Life Information Network – www.marlin.ac.uk
Marine Life Study Society – www.glaucus.org.uk
National Biodiversity Network Gateway – www.nbn.org.uk
Royal Society for the Protection of Birds (RSPB) – www.rspb.org.uk
Shark Trust – www.sharktrust.org
Wildlife Trusts – www.wildlifetrusts.org.uk
World Register of Marine Species – www.marinespecies.org

PICTURE CREDITS

All the photographs used in this book were taken by Paul Sterry and Andrew Cleave, with the exception of those listed below; these can be identified using a combination of page number and subject. The images were supplied by **Nature Photographers Ltd**.

Mark Bolton: 314 Roseate Tern, 315 Roseate Tern, 321 Peregrine; Andy Callow: 201 Azure damselfly; Laurie Campbell: 361 American Mink, 365 Bottle-nosed Dolphin; Hugh Clark: 367 Common Seal (female); Graeme Cresswell: 364 Killer Whales, 365 Risso's Dolphin, 365 Harbour Porpoise; Michael Foord: 9 Land's End, 360 black Rabbit; Phil Green: 35 Bladder Wrack; Mark Groves: 125 Elegant Anemone, 127 Jewel Anemone, 145 *Bispira volutacornis*, 259 Basking Shark, 265 Angler Fish, 359 Grey Seal; Ernie Janes: 5 Norfolk saltmarsh, 8 Knot (flock), 13 beach groynes, 13 Swyre Head, 338 Sanderling; Hugh Miles: 311 Otter; Lee Morgan: 119 Lion's-mane Jellyfish, 119 Blue Jellyfish, 270 Short-snouted Seahorse, 271 Short-snouted Seahorse, 273 Tub Gurnard, 277 Cuckoo Wrasse (male), 277 Goldsinny, 283 Black Goby (dark form), 295 Black-necked Grebe, 311 Pomarine Skua (adult), 359 Minke Whale; Philip Newman: 329 Hen Harrier (male and female); Pat O'Reilly (First Nature): 265 Sea Trout; David Osborn: 61 Curled Dock, 97 Ribwort Plantain, 321 Osprey, 321 Merlin, 339 Knot (winter); Joe Pender: 311 Pomarine Skua (juvenile), 311 Arctic Skua (pale phase adult), 311 Long-tailed Skua (juvenile); Richard Revels: 189 Small Skipper, 189 Essex Skipper, 197 Sand Wasp, 198 Yellow-winged Darter, 199 Migrant Hawker, 199 Common Darter, 201 Common Blue Damselfly, 201 Blue-tailed Damselfly, 201 Large Red Damselfly, 307 Great Black-backed Gull (standing), 312 Sandwich Tern, 327 Guillemot (in flight), 327 Puffin (in flight), 331 White-tailed Eagle; Don Smith: 127 Dead Man's Fingers; Graham Soden: 198 Red-veined Darter; Roger Tidman: 301 Cory's Shearwater, 311 Arctic Skua (dark phase), 311 Long-tailed Skua (adult), 313 Black Tern (juvenile), 320 Teal, 320 Garganey, 322 Pintail, 324 Goldeneye, 330 Kestrel, 331 Little Ringed Plover, 342 Bar-tailed Godwit, 351 Raven, 355 Sand Martin, 367 Common Seal (pup); Derek Washington: 314 Common Tern.